Inherited Wealth

Inherited Wealth

Jens Beckert

Translated by Thomas Dunlap

PRINCETON UNIVERSITY PRESS

PRINCETON AND OXFORD

First published in Germany by Campus Verlag under the title *Unverdientes Vermögen*
copyright © 2004 by Campus Verlag GmbH, Frankfurt/Main
English edition copyright © 2008 by Princeton University Press
Published by Princeton University Press, 41 William Street, Princeton,
New Jersey 08540
In the United Kingdom: Princeton University Press, 3 Market Place,
Woodstock, Oxfordshire OX20 1SY

Library of Congress Cataloging-in-Publication Data

Beckert, Jens, 1967–
[Unverdientes Vermögen. English]
Inherited wealth / Jens Beckert ; translated by Thomas Dunlap.
p. cm.
Includes bibliographical references and index.
ISBN 978-0-691-12497-1 (clothbound : alk. paper)—ISBN 978-0-691-13451-2
(pbk. : alk. paper) 1. Inheritance and succession—Germany. 2. Inheritance and
succession—France. 3. Inheritance and succession—United States. I. Title.
HB715.B43513 2008
346.05′2—dc22 2007015398

British Library Cataloging-in-Publication Data is available

Printed on acid-free paper.

press.princeton.edu

Printed in the United States of America

1 3 5 7 9 10 8 6 4 2

CONTENTS

ACKNOWLEDGMENTS

The transfer of property by bequest has become the subject of contentious debate in the United States. Attempts to abolish the federal estate tax—or "death tax," as it is called by its opponents—have put the issue of bequeathing private wealth to the next generation on the political agenda. This debate affects not only the economic interests of wealthy property owners, but also the moral fabric of society. How can the inheritance of wealth be reconciled with the principle that property should be acquired through individual effort? How does the bequest of property square with the principle of equal opportunity? What obligations do the wealthy have to society?

Debates on how the transfer of property *mortis causa* should be regulated are not new, nor are they limited to the United States. The controversies are of great social and political interest. Since they concern the institutional organization of social relations, they are also a topic for sociological scholarship. Nevertheless, the sociology of inheritance is only in its infancy.[1] The present book seeks to contribute to this field of study by examining *one* significant part of the topic from a historical and comparative perspective. How have the rules of inheritance law in the United States, France, and Germany changed over the last two hundred years? How can we explain these changes, and what do they teach us about the evolution of the normative structures of modern societies, especially about the relationships among the individual, the family, and society?

I started thinking about writing a book on the sociology of inheritance many years ago. Two fellowships made it possible for me to realize my ideas. From 1999 to 2001 I received a habilitation fellowship from the German Research Foundation (DFG) to work at the John F. Kennedy Institute at the Freie Universität Berlin. During the academic year 2001–2, I was a John F. Kennedy Memorial Fellow at the Minda de Gunzburg Center for European Studies at Harvard University. In both places, I enjoyed an excellent working environment. I would like to thank the German Research Foundation, the Freie Universität Berlin, and Harvard University for making this book possible through their financial and institutional support. I would also like to thank the German-American Center for Visiting Scholars in Washington for hosting me in January and February 2000 so that I could do research in the Library of Congress.

My work on this book was supported by research assistants who helped find archival material and coded parliamentary debates for the quantitative content analysis. I would especially like to thank Dunya Bouchi and Sibylle Kalupner, but also Hauke Rolf, Matthias Schlossberger, Ursula Weppler-Brahm, and Jens Wurtzbacher. Invaluable help was also provided by the staff of the libraries at the Freie Universität Berlin, Harvard University, the Staatsbibliothek Berlin, and the Library of Congress in Washington, who enabled me to work with material that seemed all but inaccessible. I would like to thank Regina Wenzel for her support in many organizational matters.

Most importantly, I would like to thank Hans Joas, who supervised my habilitation (postdoctoral) thesis, for his many invaluable suggestions and the confidence he had in me. Heiner Ganssmann's close reading of earlier versions of the text was very helpful. Ongoing conversations with colleagues helped to clarify many of the issues that puzzled me at various stages of my research. I received very helpful comments from Chris Allen, Andreas Daum, Julian Dierkes, Paul DiMaggio, Frank Dobbin, Oliver Gerstenberg, Peter Hall, Rainer-Maria Kiesow, Wolfgang Knöbl, Martin Kohli, Ulrich Krotz, Michèle Lamont, Kurt Lüscher, Katja Mertin, Hans-Peter Müller, Sighard Neckel, Claus Offe, Jörg Rössel, Philippe Steiner, Willibald Steinmetz, Judith Surkis, Richard Swedberg, Wolfgang Vortkamp, Harald Wenzel, Welf Werner, Viviana Zelizer, and Kathrin Zippel. Workshops and colloquia at the Freie Universität Berlin, Humboldt University in Berlin, the International University Bremen, and the Center for European Studies at Harvard provided excellent opportunities to discuss the results of my research.

The book was first published in German in 2004. The English translation is virtually unchanged, except for some minor corrections and updates on important developments during the last three years. Thomas Dunlap has done a fantastic job of translating the book. I want to thank him for his outstanding work and the spirit of collaboration he brought to the English edition. The translations of chapters 1 and 6 are based on a previous translation by Barbara Harshav. My thanks extend also to Cynthia Lehmann from the Max Planck Institute for the Study of Societies in Cologne, who helped organize the translation and prepared the manuscript for submission.

I dedicate the book to my wife, Farzaneh Alizadeh. Her affection and support give me the necessary strength and confidence to believe in a project's progress even during those difficult phases when things seem to fall apart rather than come together.

Inherited Wealth

Chapter 1

INTRODUCTION

The regulation of inheritance law on the basis of the
essential personal or social conditions always appears to
be a reflection of the various opinions of an age, which
are shaped by national character, its cultural level, and
economic considerations.

Heinrich Ahrens (1871, 249)

1.1. INHERITANCE AND MODERN SOCIETY

EVERYONE who dies leaves something behind. Everyone who owns property leaves it behind. But to whom does this property belong? All societies that recognize individual property rights need rules to reallocate property upon the owner's death. In modern societies, a codified inheritance law defines the rights of the testator to dispose of his or her property by will, the rights of the deceased's family members, and the rights of the state to appropriate all or part of the property. But societies regulate these issues in different ways. *How* to regulate them became a major topic of intense political, legal, economic, sociological, and philosophical debate in the nineteenth and twentieth centuries. For Alexis de Tocqueville the question of inheritance was so important to a society's development that when "the legislator has once regulated the law of inheritance, he may rest from his labor" (1980 [1835], 1:48). John Stuart Mill (1968 [1848], 202–3) saw inheritance law as the most critical area of law, equaled in significance only by contract law and the status of laborers.

The present book explores the development of inheritance law in Germany, France, and the United States since the late eighteenth century. By examining four central controversies over inheritance law during these three centuries, I try to explain how inheritance law developed and why differences exist to this day between the legal systems of these three countries. The four areas of conflict are (1) the degree of testamentary freedom; (2) the legal rights of the testator's relatives, especially his or her spouse and children; (3) entails; and (4) inheritance taxation. Why is the testator allowed only minimal testamentary freedom in France, while that freedom is almost unlimited in the United States? Why did the principle of real partitioning come to prevail in France? Why do family interests play a much more important role in German inheritance law than in American inheritance law? Why, in all three countries, was inheritance taxation introduced or fundamentally reformed in the early twentieth century? Why were much higher estate taxes introduced in the United States than in Germany? Why were entails banned in Germany only in 1919, 140 years later than in the United States and 70 years later than in France?

Inheritance Law and Social Solidarity

These questions lie at the heart of the present study. At the same time, its analysis is embedded in a comprehensive theoretical framework that owes much to Émile Durkheim's sociology of law (1984, 1992).[1] Durkheim analyzed the development of legal institutions as an aspect of the macrosocial evolution of society. He regarded the development of the relationship between individuality and the normative structures of society as a major topic for the sociological analysis of the process of modernization.[2] According to Durkheim, the development of the law is an indicator for the relationship "of the individual to social solidarity" (1984 [1893], xxx).

As early as *The Division of Labor in Society*, but especially in the lectures *Professional Ethics and Civic Morals*, Durkheim applied his view of the law to property rights. According to Durkheim (1992 [1957], 146), the right of property expresses a direct moral bond between the thing owned and the owner. The moral position of the individual is reflected in the legal rights of the owner. The violation of property rights is punished because society recognizes it as a violation of the owner himself. According to Durkheim, the moral status of the individual in relation to the family, to intermediary institutions, and to the state is admitted into the rights and duties of the disposition of property because of the link between property rights and the person. These law-based normative structures of modern society become visible through an examination of the historical genesis of property law.

Durkheim touched on inheritance law in the fragmentary book of lectures *Professional Ethics and Civic Morals,* but his analysis concentrated on contract law. Yet it is the study of the development of inheritance law that allows us to trace most clearly the structures of the relationship of individuality and its social embeddedness. In conflicts over inheritance law, questions about the relationship between individual freedom in the disposition over property, the claims of the family and the state to this property, as well as the role of ascription and individual achievement take center stage and provide a concise indicator of the normative structures that carry out the social integration of the individual. The close link of inheritance law to this question of social integration can also be seen in the fact that inheritance as a social problem emerges only when property rights are individualized and a purely family-based understanding of private property is transcended.

The development of modern inheritance law is linked to the dissolution of the economic unit of the household, in which there was no right of inheritance in the modern sense, because the unit itself was considered immortal (Weber 1978 [1922], 1:359). Upon death, a member ceased to be the bearer of an idealized "share" of the property, but that did not amount to a real transfer of property. According to Max Weber, it was only the processes of differentiation through individualized forms of acquisition, the separation of household and workplace, the growing significance of capital in relation to land as a factor of production, and the institution of dowry that led to increasingly calculated internal family relations and to the individualization of property rights. This, in turn, contributed to the dissolution of the household and created the social problem of assigning property *mortis causa*. Thus, the development of inheritance law is intimately linked with processes of social differentiation. However, as I want to show, this is *not* a process of individualization, understood as an increasing separation of the individual from society, but rather, in the Durkheimian sense, a *transformation* of social solidarity. *How* individual disposition over property *mortis causa* is embedded in conceptions of social solidarity in the three societies investigated is the subject of the present book.

Discourse on Inheritance Law and Legal Development

Although this book follows Durkheim in connecting the examination of the evolution of law with the understanding of modernization, my approach is different from Durkheim's: in *The Division of Labor in Society*, Durkheim suggested that we consider social reactions to violations of the law as an indicator of the development of individuality and social solidarity. For Durkheim, the declining importance of criminal law reflected the diminishing relevance of "solidarity through likeness" and the increasing crystallization of the individual as the moral subject of modern society. The decline of the repressive sanctions of criminal law, through which traditional societies assure their social cohesion, can be read as a sign of the waning significance of collective consciousness. This indicator of moral development, however, is unsuitable for inheritance law. From the outset, inheritance law concerns mostly questions of civil law—although criminal law plays an indirect role with regard to crimes like tax evasion, forgery, or fraud. Moreover, Durkheim's emphasis on the changing reactions to the violation of legal provisions leads him to focus on the actual development of the law. However, Durkheim's focus on the examination of the evolution of legal rules is limited because it obscures most information about the collective representations concerning the transmission of wealth that exist in society. Much of that information can only be found through an analysis of the political discourses surrounding the reform of inheritance law.

As a result, this study is focused largely on the legal and political *debates* on questions of inheritance law. To be sure, some aspects of the relationship between the testator's individual rights of disposal and obligations toward his or her family and society can be seen in the development of the law itself. Yet the goals of the actors and the arguments for or against certain provisions become clear only if one looks at the legal and political discourse conducted within the legislative process, and sometimes outside of it. The structure of these debates provides insights into the perception of causal relationships, the values held by the actors involved, and the structures of political power and the changes they undergo. The discourses reveal *different* positions along with the fundamentally contentious nature of the legal provisions ultimately adopted. I thus follow Durkheim's insight that the development of law can be used as an indicator of macrosocial processes of change. At the same time, the inclusion of legal and political discourses allows for an expanded study that makes the significance of discursive structures accessible for the purpose of studying the development of the law. Among other things, including this level of analysis may allow different collective representations in the three countries to become apparent, representations that might otherwise be hidden behind similar legal developments.

The acceptance of legal regulations, as Durkheim noted, depends on a moral core from which they derive their legitimacy. The emphasis on linguistic processes of communication points to something else in addition, namely the role that a value-oriented formation of political objectives plays in the social integration of modern societies. The political sphere is the "forum" in which—on the basis of the ideas of social justice and causal relationships implicit in a political culture—the legitimacy of rules of law is created or contested, a legitimacy that is usually the precondition for the political enforceability of these rules, and in every case the basis for their practical acceptance. Thus, the examination of legal and political conflicts over the institutionalization of inheritance law takes on a double meaning: the arguments advanced for or against legal reforms are an indicator of the development of ideas about "social solidarity"; at the same time, the moral constitution of society is created and reproduced precisely in these discursive processes.

It is therefore not a question of simply replacing one indicator with another, but of advancing Durkheim's approach on a theoretical level.[3] Durkheim believed that norms derive their validity from religious symbols that in turn, derive their significance from collective experiences during religious rituals. Jürgen Habermas, in particular, objected that Durkheim's explanation did not adequately recognize the "trend toward the linguistification of the sacred" (Habermas 1987, 2:46) and thus the important role that linguistically mediated, norm-guided interaction plays in the integration of modern societies. Social solidarity is created precisely out of linguistic processes of communication (*Verständigung*) in which actors are forced to justify their claims about what constitutes appropriate actions within the normative context of roles and institutions (1987, 2:56). Habermas thus refers to the production of morally binding forces in discourse and rejects the idea of a simple imprinting of norms and values in the process of socialization.

While I share Habermas's assessment of the importance of the role of discourse to the normative development of society, the way in which I incorporate it into my analysis differs from Habermas. Unlike Habermas, I am not concerned with the development of a procedural ethics and with the orientation of processes of communication toward claims of universal validity and the concepts of secularization that go along with this. The role of discourses can also be understood in a very different way.

In his critique of Durkheim's sociology of religion, Hans Joas (2000, 67ff.) pointed out that Durkheim linked processes of institutionalization too directly to experiences of collective excitation. What Durkheim's theory of institutions obscures, Joas argued, is that "the individuals who participate in the collective experience having developed differing interpretations of this experience, . . . only then refine into a collective interpretation through a process of discussion and argument (a process that is pervaded with power)" (2000, 67–68). It is only out of the dynamic of this contingent process of dealing with collective experiences—that is, the interpretation of causes, reasons, results, and possibilities—that institutions emerge, change, and solidify.

Against this background, I regard discourses on inheritance law as processes that generate socially recognized viewpoints and thus lay the foundation for the process by which inheritance law becomes institutionalized. They are not analyzed as ways of generating universally recognized norms of behavior, or as symbolic reflections of the infusion of power into social relations. Instead, the goal of my approach is to examine the intersubjective and conflictual creation of ideas of justice as well as the conceptions of causal relationships and their significance for explaining the development of inheritance law.

Orders of Justification in Inheritance Law

By explaining the development of inheritance law and how it has differed in France, Germany, and the United States, on the one hand, and by examining the development of the relationship of the individual to society, on the other, I am pursuing two goals in this study. These goals are linked by the thesis that the development of inheritance law itself cannot be explained independent of the discursive structures in each of the three countries. The explanation of the development of inheritance law that I am striving for is based on a multidimensional heuristic that incorporates economic interests, demands by the state, and the role of social institutions (especially the family and the legal system), as well as culturally based values that are expressed in the discourse on inheritance law. All of these dimensions are significant for each of the four areas of conflict examined here, although different elements of explanation are paramount in each area. What emerges, therefore, is a complex picture of the development of institutions of inheritance law, which depicts this development as dependent on economic, governmental, social, and cultural influences. This multidimensional explanation of the development of inheritance law stands close to Max Weber, whose theory of institutions was based precisely on the presumed link between ideas and interests.[4]

The three countries included in this comparative study, Germany, France, and the United States, can be seen as part of modern Western capitalism as defined by Max Weber. From the late eighteenth to the early twentieth centuries, all three countries were undergoing a process of profound social, political, and economic transformation. While this development took place against the background of different initial conditions, its thrust was essentially the same in all three countries, as a result of which they confronted fairly similar functional problems. The selection of Germany, France, and the United States is based on this relative similarity, which suggests that inheritance law might have developed in parallel ways.

At the same time, however, the three countries differ in many of the values expressed in the debates over how the law should deal with "inherited wealth." The discourses on inheritance law reflect different ways in which the moral and political problems posed by inheritance were articulated, as well as differences in the consequences the actors ascribed to specific rules of inheritance law. I will show that different "guiding problems" (Kaufmann 2001) exist in each of the three countries for the regulation of inheritance law. These problems form a "discursive field," which is expressed in the justifications offered by actors for their acceptance or rejection of proposed institutional reforms. The term *discursive field* is meant to express that while there is no homogeneous point of view of inheritance law in each of the three countries, the contending parties defend their clashing views with certain dominant patterns of argumentation that are stable over the long term. Discursive fields establish boundaries of discussion and define a spectrum of problems that can be addressed (Wuthnow 1989, 13). Discursive fields thus give expression to socially available systems of meaning, which can provide a basis of legitimizing support for, or opposition to, efforts to change inheritance law. Here one can also speak of "orders of justification" (Boltanski and Thévenot 1991).[5] Discursive fields have a binary structure. The stark juxtaposition of binary alternatives is a mechanism for simplifying complex contexts, and this simplification makes it possible to articulate guidelines for decision making.[6] This book will examine how these orders of justification differ between Germany, France, and the United States, and how—along with economic and political aspects—they influence the development of inheritance law.

Starting from this multidimensional explanatory approach, my thesis is not that the orders of justification expressed in the discursive fields can explain the development of inheritance law, but rather that orders of justification influence legal development *along with* other aspects. The specific lines of conflict in legal discourse are a cultural element of the public sphere that represent *one* factor of explanation for the evolution of law, alongside material interests and functional demands. What makes the discourses relevant to actors is that worldviews are articulated and shaped in them; as cultural background, these views then feed into the interpretations of a given situation. Moreover, they shape the perceptions of causal relationships, thereby contributing to the legitimation or delegitimation of particular positions and thus influencing their political chances of being implemented (Beckert 2002, 106). One reason such a context can be posited is that the successful political implementation of legal reforms is always dependent on legitimation, at least when dictatorial coercion is not available. Legal reforms that can be legitimated with reference to deep-seated cultural understandings thus have an "evolutionary advantage," an advantage that should manifest itself in a link between the structure of the discursive field and the development of the law.

The influence of evaluative schemata that are culturally anchored arises also from the constitutive, a priori understanding of the actors (Beckert 2003; Biernacki 1995; Dobbin 1994). The predominant evaluative standards are related not only to the goals that are considered legitimate, but also to the strategies that guide the rational, intentional choice of means to achieve the desired ends. The deeper underlying reason is this: because complexity and novelty render causal relationships uncertain, a rational choice of strategy as defined by economic theory is ruled out and actors must resort to the "substitute rationalities" they find in their social environment (Beckert 1996, 2002). This critical perspective on economic institutionalism emphasizes the importance that the causal relationships *as asserted* by the actors have for the development of institutions. What I contend is that the choice of the causal relationships regarded as valid from among all the *possible* relationships between the specific rules of inheritance law and their desired or rejected effects is also derived from the orders of justification. The intent here is not to deny the existence of objective causal relations, but to shift attention to the *perceptions* of these relationships, which themselves exert an effect on the political process. In this sense, as I try to show in this book, "ideas" play a role in the development of inheritance law.

Notions of Property and the Structure of Discourses on Inheritance Law

The lines of conflict over inheritance law in the three countries are structured around the question of what kind of intervention in the private disposal over property is legitimate. The unlimited power of disposal by testators over their wealth encounters opposition in all three countries. Yet actors who plead for intervention in this right resort to *specific* arguments that differ *between* the three countries, but exhibit a great long-term continuity *within* the countries. The phrase "notions of property" refers to the primary, *specific* justifications for restrictions on the unchecked individual disposal over private property that appear in the discourses on inheritance law in a given country. By the late eighteenth and early nineteenth centuries—in some cases even earlier—these understandings had shaped and structured the discourses in the subsequent key phases of the development of inheritance law examined in the present study. Some of the argumentative patterns that were relevant during the French and American revolutions as well as in the political debates on inheritance law conducted at about the same time in Germany are still found today. What these arguments consist of and how they differ will be described in the main chapters of the book. Let me offer a brief characterization of the respective notions of property.

In the United States, two fears were dominant: first, that a dynastic concentration of wealth would destroy the social bases of the republican order, and, second, that inheritances would undermine the equality of opportunity, a "sacred" principle behind the justification of social inequality. These fears were countered by arguments that defended the right to unimpeded testamentary disposal over wealth as an integral part of private property, and by economic arguments that rejected intervention in inheritance law as economically detrimental.

Germany saw the emergence of very different structures of justification. In the nineteenth century, unlimited testamentary freedom was frequently seen as a possible cause behind an unbridled individualism (which was rejected on normative grounds) and thus as destructive to social relations within the family and society. There has been a strong tendency to regard property as family property, which makes the legal owner appear as the trustee for the estate of the clan; the owner's death does not lead to a real transmission of property. Moreover, in Germany, government interference in the individual disposal over private property was legitimated with the goal of social justice. This can be traced back to the debates over private property in the first part of the nineteenth century, and it still found its way into the Basic Law of the Federal Republic as the principle of the social obligation of property. One side of the discursive field argued that the testamentary freedom of the testator must be limited to protect the family and—through inheritance taxation—to generate the funds for a social policy aimed at redistributive balance. The point of reference is not equality of opportunity, but rather the result-oriented principle of social justice. In other words: while the American order of justification takes the individual and his or her freedom more strongly as a normative point of reference, in Germany the individual is tied more clearly into a familial and social context. At the same time, the discursive field in Germany also contains liberal economic voices that advocate unrestricted property rights and point to the negative economic consequences of interference in the right of inheritance. Against the background of a stronger individualistic perception of social integration, they infer a right of inheritance unrestricted by state and family.

In France, one side of the debate has maintained that the state has an obligation to the general welfare while maintaining strict neutrality with regard to private interests. This is expressed primarily in a dominant reference to the principle of equality in intestacy law, but also in resistance to the progressive taxation of inheritances, and in the attempt to use inheritance laws for the goals of population policy. Ever since the debates on inheritance law in the Constituent Assembly, this has been opposed by a position that objects to the implementation of the principle of equality by the state and instead emphasizes the individual rights of inheritance of the testator, which are considered to strengthen the family and avoid the economically deleterious consequences of institutionalizing the principle of equality—especially the fragmentation of landed property. In contrast to the German debates, a significant current of the French discourse has argued that the family is endangered precisely by governmental restriction on the rights of the testator. In contrast to the United States and Germany, in France equality and social justice do not play much of a role with respect to individual opportunities or goals of social policy; rather, their main reference is to the problematic relationship between the state and civil society.

For the sake of brevity and greater emphasis, I speak of the individualist-meritocratic understanding of property in the United States, the family-social understanding of property in Germany, and the egalitarian/family-based understanding of property in France. My intent is not to claim that there is a homogeneous perception of property in the respective societies, but to characterize the dominant tensions within which inheritance law reforms take place. The discursive field is structured cognitively and normatively by the respective perceptions of property. In the discourses on inheritance law, the justifications for interventions in the individual disposal over property can be read as cognitive and evaluative differences between actors in the three countries.

At the same time, the ambiguity of the orders of justification when it comes to institutional implementation and the selective reference by actors to specific positions within the discursive field produce a potential for conflict, since opposing views can find *simultaneous* legitimizing support. The discursive field provides no script for determining concrete rules of inheritance law; it merely represents a frame of reference in which actors position themselves by using specific justifications for positions in the debates. Nor can the orders of justification simply be attributed to a right-left schema. Instead, the examination of the legal discourse on inheritance law and parliamentary debates reveals that actors with different material interests justify their political goals sometimes by invoking the same available social patterns of interpretation. In Germany, reference to the principle of family is used both to justify limiting testamentary freedom and introducing escheat as an instrument of social policy, and to reject inheritance taxation as an illegitimate intervention in family wealth. In France, reference to the principle of equality is used both to legitimate restrictions on testamentary freedom aimed at more equal property relations and to reject a progressive inheritance tax. In Germany, testamentary freedom is seen largely as advancing an individualism that is hostile to the family, while in France it is considered by many as providing protection for the family.

Outline of the Book

The core of the book is subdivided into four chapters, each devoted to a central area of conflict in inheritance law. The four areas represent the crucial legal and political debates on inheritance law since the late eighteenth century. Because the significance of the areas of conflict varies in the three countries, the subchapters differ in length. Aspects concerned primarily with technical legal questions are not examined. This includes issues having to do with the specific form of wills or with international cases of inheritance. All chapters, except for chapter 3, focus on examining the debates on these four areas of inheritance law. The analysis centers on legal-theoretical as well as economic and sociological writings on inheritance law during the last two centuries. This provides insight into the structure of the discursive field and how it has changed in each of the three countries. The hermeneutic interpretation of this empirical material is supplemented by the quantitative analysis of parliamentary debates. It is this analysis that offers the best prospect of identifying the dominant lines of conflict in dealing with "unearned wealth." The parliamentary debates are evaluated—as far as possible[7]—in a quantitative content analysis, which helps support the hermeneutic interpretation. More detailed references to the methodology can be found in the appendix.

The actual development of the law is considered along with the discourses on inheritance law. The analysis will identify to what extent the observed changes and the persistent legal differences between the three countries can be explained by changing economic and political conditions, new social contexts, and the different orders of justification.

Chapter 2 examines controversies about testamentary freedom. Testamentary freedom is the fundamental legal institution dealing with the testator's right to individual disposal over property. The question of testamentary freedom and its limitation in the form of an obligatory share for members of the testator's family was an especially controversial area of inheritance law in France and Germany. To what extent do interventions in testamentary rights represent illegitimate limitations on the private disposal of property? What sort of rights do family members have to the testator's property? The starting conditions in the late eighteenth century varied considerably in the three countries. In the United States, which largely took over English inheritance law, testamentary freedom was almost unlimited; by contrast, in France shortly after the Revolution, testamentary freedom was briefly abolished completely along with the compulsory equal division of an estate among the legitimate children of the deceased. During the nineteenth century, testamentary freedom in the United States was somewhat curtailed, primarily through an expansion of the rights of the surviving spouse; in France it was not until the twentieth century that some of the restrictions enshrined in the Code Civil after 1804 were loosened. In Germany, testamentary freedom was debated in the deliberations surrounding the creation of the Civil Code (Bürgerliches Gesetzbuch, BGB) in the last quarter of the nineteenth century, and it ran into a widespread mistrust of the last will in legal philosophy and politics, for many saw it as an institution hostile to the family. Chapter 3 examines conflicts about the rights of inheritance of family members. Intestacy law, which regulates the distribution of property in the absence of a valid will, can be understood as a system of kinship classification whose development reflects changing claims of solidarity within the family system. Who is considered a family member to begin with, and in what position does he or she stand to other relatives within the kinship arrangement? The chapter examines the development of inheritance rights of sons and daughters, first and later-born children, the surviving spouse, and illegitimate children. The rights of inheritance of adopted children and same-sex life partners are also touched on. The development of the legal right of inheritance will be used to show how notions of claims of solidarity within family systems have changed, and which general lines of development can be seen in them.

Paradoxically, individual testamentary disposal over property is linked with restrictions on individual decision-making. In entails, the subject of chapter 4, the testator not only determines the heir, but also decides to whom the (landed) wealth must be bequeathed after the death of the heir. Thus, the testamentary freedom of the heir is in fact abolished. These provisions were intended to prevent the sale or overindebtedness of noble estates and to guarantee the dynastic transmission of wealth by controlling the options of the heir. Entails are connected most closely with aristocracies, which they support by creating a structural dependence between king and nobility. In the eighteenth century, contemporary observers, including Adam Smith, were already pointing to the dysfunctional consequences of entails for capitalism. While the institution did contribute to the stability of the nobility's economic and political power over the long term, it simultaneously impeded economic development. One of the central debates on inheritance law in France and Germany revolved around the abolition of entails and related legal institutions for perpetuating wealth. In France, these conflicts were finally settled at the beginning of the Second Republic; in Germany, only with the November Revolution in 1918. In the United States, entails were forbidden after the Revolution, but multigenerational strategies of bequest could also be pursued by establishing a trust.

Chapter 5 looks at the role of the state as heir. The state is involved in inheritance through taxation, and possibly also through escheat, the right of the state to inherit. This right stipulates that in intestate inheritances, the state enters as an heir if the nearest relatives lack a certain degree of kinship to the testator.[8] Far more significant, however, is the actual taxation of inheritances with which the state appropriates a part of the inherited wealth. In the nineteenth century, moderate forms of inheritance tax existed in all three countries. In the late nineteenth century, in the context of the expansion of state expenses and rising military expenditures, the inheritance or estate tax became a contested political issue in Germany, France, and the United States.

The debates about the inheritance tax revolved, on the one hand, around the growing financial needs of the state, and, on the other, around the question of fiscal justice and the distribution of wealth. Thus, the relationship between individual disposal over private property and the claims of society (the state) to a part of the wealth is also at the heart of this debate. In France, moreover, inheritance taxation was linked with the goal of boosting the birthrate. In the early twentieth century, preferential treatment for families with many children when it came to inheritance taxation was supposed to boost the number of births. What is controversial about the inheritance tax is not only the question of how high it should be and who should be taxed, but also which goals may legitimately be pursued with it. Should inheritance taxes serve as an instrument to redistribute wealth in society, to create greater tax equity, or only to cover state expenses in situations of national emergency?

The political and scholarly controversies regarding inheritance law extend over the entire period in question. Nonetheless, some periods of heightened activity can be readily identified. The debates were most intense and virulent in France and the United States during the revolutionary period and in all three countries between about 1880 and 1930. Debates on testamentary freedom and entail were concentrated in the first half of the nineteenth century, but their ramifications extended far into the twentieth century. Debates about the equality of women and the improvement of the status of adopted and illegitimate children in inheritance law began in the middle of the nineteenth and continued until the end of the twentieth century. Discussions of inheritance taxation were concentrated between 1880 and 1935, but keep flaring up later in the individual countries at various times. Since the 1970s, the estate tax has become once again an important subject of political controversy, especially in the United States. Therefore, the arrangement of chapters also follows a chronological order.

1.2. Social Dimensions of Inheritance Law

The transmission of property derives its social relevance from the influence that inheritances exert on social structures and social relationships. We can

TABLE 1.1
Social Dimensions of Inheritance Law

The economy	The state and the political order
System of values	Social and family structure

distinguish four levels: the normative level, on which the acquisition of property is justified in societies guided by the principle of meritocracy; the economic level, which deals with the economic consequences of inheritance law; the level of social and family structures; and the level dealing with the relationship between individual property and the state.

Inheritance and the Principle of Meritocracy

On the first level, the inheritance of property touches upon central values of bourgeois society: the conception of individual freedom, the meaning of obligations of solidarity, the principle of equality, and the role of the principle of meritocracy. The emancipation of the individual from traditional communal relationships as a result of the economic and cultural developments of modernization led to an understanding of property that had a much more pronounced individualistic imprint (Weber 1978 [1922], 1:375ff.). That, in turn, gave rise to two contradictory consequences for the institutionalization of inheritance law. First, it seems only consistent that the owner can freely determine into whose hands property should pass after his or her death. By means of the testament, the "last will," the testator specifies who will become the owner of the property and what conditions attach to this transfer. The disposition *mortis causa* is an individual's last act of will. However, it creates the problem of how this individual right to testamentary freedom can be reconciled with the interest that the family and society have in the transfer of property. The testator might be interested—by means of his final disposition—in exercising the greatest possible control over the affairs of subsequent generations, and thus curtailing their possibilities of deciding how the property should be used. The living, meanwhile, are interested in restricting the arbitrariness of the last will, thus making possible, simultaneously, the individual freedom of disposition on the part of the heirs. As Thomas Jefferson's famous dictum put it: "The earth belongs in usufruct to the living."

However, the institution of inheritance finds itself in a problematic relationship also with the emerging, individual conception of property, because it contradicts the meritocratic self-conception of modern societies (Beckert 1999a). Inherited property has come to the heir "effortlessly" through the death of another person; it was not earned by personal effort. The institution of inheritance thus runs counter to the justification of unequal distribution of wealth based on individual merit and achievement. In one central respect, inheritance perpetuates social privileges independent of achievement, even though bourgeois society defined itself precisely in opposition to this practice. How can the "unearned" acquisition of wealth be justified within the context of a social order that legitimizes social inequalities as the product of different contributions its members make through personal achievement? Once legal privileges derived from birth and the heritability of offices were abolished, the inheritance of property was and is the central institution of social privilege in modern societies that is based not on effort, but on birth.[9] Critics reject the inheritance of wealth as an alien normative practice in societies that are oriented towards the principles of individualism and achievement. This break with the individualistic justification of the distribution of wealth also violates the principle of equality of opportunity, which asserts that the starting conditions should be as equal as possible for all, so that differences in wealth can reflect the actual accomplishments of individuals.

Inheritance and Inequality of Wealth

Every time one generation succeeds another, the private wealth that exists within a society is allocated to new owners through inheritance or gifts. Given the large amount of private wealth, enormous sums are bequeathed every year. In Germany, the wealth that is currently passed on every year is estimated at between €150 and €200 billion; in the United States the figure is between $600 and $900 billion (Havens and Schervish 1999; Sieweck 2000; Szydlik 1999, 81). However, it is not the size of the wealth transfer by inheritance as such that turns it into a socially important institution. Rather, the issue is how inheritances affect a society's social inequality, the efficient operation of the economy, and the motivation that drives the behavior of economic subjects.

Figure 1.1 shows the current distribution of wealth in the three countries that are the subject of this study. This data should be taken with a grain of salt, because it is the product of different methods of collection and because the numbers on which it is based are not entirely reliable. Still, one can detect a general picture, which shows that a small elite owns large shares of the available private wealth, while large segments of the population have virtually no private wealth at all. In all three countries, the distribution of wealth is far more unequal than the distribution of income.[10] In 2000, for example, the Gini coefficient for the distribution of wealth in the United States was 0.80, compared with 0.36 for income distribution. In Germany, the Gini coefficient for the distribution of wealth was 0.67, compared with 0.27 for income distribution. For France the respective figures were 0.73 for the distribution of wealth and 0.28 for income distribution (Davies et al. 2006, 50; OECD Factbook 2006).[11]

How important are inheritances to the unequal distribution of wealth? It is clear that wealth is acquired not only through individual effort, but also through inheritance. However, the question of what share of private wealth

Share of private
wealth in %

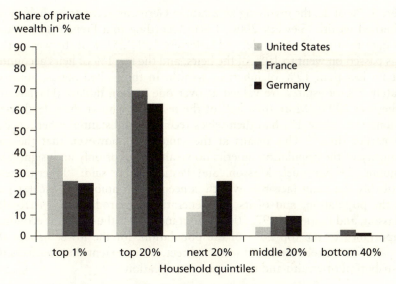

Figure 1.1 The distribution of private property
Note: The data for the United States refers to 1995, for France to 1986, for Germany to 1998.
Sources: Keister 2000; Wolff 2002; Hauser and Stein 2001.

is derived from inheritances is hotly debated by scholars. In the case of the United States, Kotlikoff (1988), using model calculations, concluded that 80% of wealth was based on inheritance, while Modigliani (1988) posited a share of only 20%. This broad divergence is explained by different definitions of what an inheritance is, and what present-day effects on wealth come from an inheritance in the past. Kotlikoff includes all wealth transfers to children after they reach the age of eighteen, along with the accumulated interest after the wealth transfer. Modigliani, by contrast, counts only actual bequests and large gifts and uses only the real value of the wealth transfer in his calculations. Kessler and Masson (1988) use a different approach, asking by what percentage private wealth would be reduced if inheritances were confiscated. In a simulation model, their calculations for the United States and France show that inheritances account for between 35 and 40% of private wealth.

In spite of this broad range of economic calculations, it is clear that inheritances account for a substantial share of private wealth. What makes this finding sociologically relevant, however, is the effect that inheritances have on the distribution of wealth. Here it is evident that inheritances contribute substantially to the inequality of wealth within a society. In France and the United States, about 60% of the deceased leave behind an inheritance (Arrondel, Masson, and Pestieau 1997, 101); in Germany about 55% of the population inherits something (Szydlik 1999, 93). But a mere 16% of deaths involving an estate in Germany account for half of the inherited wealth (Sieweck 2000, 174). According to a French study based on data from 1987 (Arrondel and Laferrère 1994), 51% of the wealth that was passed on went to 10% of the heirs, and the top 1% of heirs accounted for no less than 19% of inherited wealth. In the United States, approximately 2% of estates are valued at over one million dollars (Havens and Schervish 2003). More than half of the testators who at their death were among the richest 1% had themselves received a substantial inheritance at an earlier time.[12] This means at the same time, however, that the vast majority of the population inherits no wealth at all or only an insignificant amount. As Arrondel, Masson, and Pestieau have said: "Inheritance is probably the main factor of wealth concentration among the richest part of the population, and of its intergenerational reproduction" (Arrondel, Masson, and Pestieau 1997, 104). Inheritance law is thus of great economic importance to the top 20% of the population; for the lower half of the population, its relevance is at most indirect, to the extent that it affects the distribution of wealth and thus social stratification.

The Economic Dimension

Like all codifications dealing with property, the rules of inheritance law have a bearing on economic efficiency. Too great a concentration of wealth can be just as dysfunctional economically as the dissolution of wealth after each generation or the removal of landed property from the market through restrictions placed on its sale by inheritance law. Extreme concentrations of wealth prevent competition and economic innovation. Real partitioning of land, or legal provisions for the equal division of an inheritance, such as existed traditionally in various parts of Europe and were introduced in France after the Revolution, limit intergenerationally effective strategies for the accumulation of wealth. The institutions of real partitioning, of the right of succession to an undivided farm estate, of entails, and of primogeniture have shaped agricultural structures in very different ways and exerted a lasting influence on the development of wealth in various regions (Alston and Schapiro 1984; Klippel 1987, 275). In the early phase of industrialization, at a time, that is, when joint-stock companies played a minor role, the long-term cohesion of capital-intensive manufacturing or trading companies also depended on the rules of inheritance law. But the preservation of wealth through inheritance can have negative consequences when unsuitable heirs acquire the capital and run a company into the ground. Inheritances undercut the allocation function of the market, because capital is being removed from competition (see Hoover 1927). An inefficient allocation also takes place through feudal inheritance institutions like family entails, which prevent landed property from being allocated through the market. If land can be neither sold nor borrowed against, it cannot be offered as collateral for loans and thus cannot be used to create investment capital.

This economic importance of inheritance law became the subject of controversy and debate in the nineteenth century, especially through the incorporation of landed property into the market process with the abolition of feudal institutions of inheritance law and the real partitioning of agricultural holdings. The relevance of agricultural landed property declines with the growth of industrial labor markets, which open up alternative sources of income. The inheritance of a farm plays a reduced economic role on both an individual and a macroeconomic level. Still, inherited landed property, especially in the case of France, can initially remain an important protection against impoverishment in the face of frequently interrupted industrial employment. The spread of joint-stock corporations whose shares are widely held, a setup that separates the functions of management and ownership, makes the running of a company largely independent of the ownership structure. It is not important who owns the joint-stock corporation, nor does it matter much that company property is divided among a multitude of anonymous owners. The continuous decline of employment in the agricultural sector, combined with the spread of wage labor, and the increasing shift of national wealth from landed property to more liquid industrial capital cause the economic importance of the rules pertaining to the partitioning of an inheritance to recede into the background. The economic interest of inheritances is increasingly focused on economic groups like the owners of family businesses and the remaining farmers, as well as the private interests of those individuals who, as heirs, benefit from the transfer of wealth *mortis causa*. The transfer of the business to the next generation poses a major problem especially for closely held enterprises (Bös and Kayser 1996; Breuer 2000).

Additionally, there is a link between inheritance and economic efficiency on the level of the motives that spur individuals to action: the possibility of the private bequest of wealth helps to diffuse and maintain the capitalistic spirit of acquisitiveness, in that inheritance can provide an important incentive to hard work and thrift.[13] However, inheritances can also have exactly the opposite effect, in that the inherited property destroys the acquisitive drive among the heirs who move into a comfortable, ready-made position in life.[14] These negative motivational effects of inheritances were invoked especially by liberal commentators, John Stuart Mill and Andrew Carnegie being the best-known examples. One American multimillionaire was quoted in the magazine *Fortune* (29 September 1986) as saying: "How the hell do we keep our money from destroying our kids?"[15] According to a U.S. study (Holtz-Eakin, Joulfaian, and Rosen 1993), the likelihood that someone will abandon the labor market is four times as great for heirs with an inheritance of at least $150,000 as for heirs who receive less than $25,000.[16]

Inheritance and Family

It would be short-sighted to see only the economic consequences and the value-oriented aspects of inheritance laws. The social policy debates over inheritance law were never limited to these dimensions; instead, they also addressed the rights of members of the testator's family to portions of the estate, and the conditions under which these rights could be lost. Inheritance law regulates fundamental aspects of familial solidarity, which makes it relevant to the long-term stability of social structures (Clignet 1992, 1995; Kohli 1994). Bequests constitute a material foundation for family continuity and thereby contribute to the intergenerational stability of social structures (Sussman, Cates, and Smith 1970).

Transfers of wealth independent of individual achievement allow for the intergenerational continuity of social positions, they stabilize spheres of affiliation and thus the social structure of society, and they counteract the vagaries of success in the marketplace. Precisely because wealth disconnects social position from achievement, at least in part, it represents a protective mechanism of social belonging (Clignet 1992; Lüscher 2002; Simmel 1992 [1908], 579ff.). In nineteenth-century Germany this connection is evident in the struggle of the nobility against the abolition of entails, which were a legal institution that restricted the mechanisms of the market. In the United States, Nelson Aldrich (1996) has also emphasized the negative link between wealth and market in families of the upper class: *old money* describes a dynastic elite of a few families that are able, by means of inherited wealth, to reproduce their social status independent of their success in the marketplace, and who for the most part protect their assets from profligate spending through trusts.[17] The elitist justification for this privileged position points to contributions to society that are made possible only by this kind of material independence. Yet even for the middle class, transfers of wealth provide at least a partial buffer against the vagaries of the marketplace, which allows a better education, a higher risk tolerance, and improved living conditions. On a social level, inheritances help to make possible generation-spanning continuities in the sociostructural position of families (Levy 1983, 551).

On an individual level, inheritances—as a form of provisioning—can stabilize the material situation of the testator's family. However, the expectation of an inheritance can also be used by the testator to enforce cross-generational support within the family. The expectation of inheritance—just like gifts made during a person's lifetime (transfers inter vivos)—can promote bonds of solidarity between the generations, though it can also cause conflicts. In this way, inheritance law intervenes in the foundations of family relationships. It should be noted, though, that as a result of rising life expectancy, inheritances from parents, the most important source for heirs, generally come to children only when they are in their forties and fifties.[18]

Rules of inheritance lose importance as ways to provide for one's family especially in the twentieth century, because the spread of labor markets and the creation of state-run social security systems increasingly take on these functions at the death of a family's provider (Schröder 1987).

The institutionalization of social security and the creation of life insurance in the nineteenth and twentieth centuries have made individuals less dependent on familial support systems, while labor markets tend to make individuals independent from familial wealth as the capital basis for their own employment. In the process, the macrosociological importance of inheritances shifts to their function as factors that stabilize sociostructural continuity or social inequality by allowing for the unequal distribution of wealth in society through bequests. From a microsociological perspective, the function of the institution for the individual heir lies in a material benefit that is acquired independent of individual achievement. However, as transfers inter vivos, wealth transfers can also provide important material impulses for stabilizing the socioeconomic position of children, and thus indirectly for strengthening the intergenerational solidarity of the family (Attias-Donfut 1995, 2000; Kohli 1997, 1999; Szydlik 2000). This functional aspect of the transfer of wealth has attracted the attention of sociologists only in the last few years, and it modifies the thesis that modernization weakens the bonds of solidarity in generational relationships outside the nuclear family.

Moreover, inheritances can play a symbolic, identity-creating role in the material representation of family descent and continuity (Carrier 1991; Langbein 2003). Succession to wealth acquired by one's ancestors, as well as the inheriting of individual objects or real estate classified as valuable in the family's memory, can be experienced by heirs as an obligation toward their family background and thus influence the life decisions they make.

Inheritance and the State

In addition, inheritance law also determines, primarily through the estate tax, the contribution that estates must make to funding the state's expenditures. The flip side to the creation of social safety nets and to the relative loss of importance suffered by familial safety systems lies in the state's heightened need for revenue. The taxation of estates and the introduction of escheat contribute to the state's fiscal income. The private right of inheritance is restricted through the compulsory transfer of part of a deceased person's wealth to the state. Beginning in the early nineteenth century, we see a debate about the possible use of inheritances to finance especially social and educational policies. The initial notion was that relatively low inheritance taxes would already be sufficient to finance these policies and thus make it possible to put an end to pauperism. Although the expansion of inheritance taxes at the beginning of the twentieth century took place, in the final analysis, within the context of financing the costs of a military buildup, the idea that inheritance taxes could make a substantial contribution to a socially just financing of public expenditures remained intact until the 1930s.[19]

The imposition of inheritance taxes can serve the goal of bringing about an egalitarian distribution of income, or it can be seen as a contribution to tax equity. However, inheritances can also be simply drawn upon pragmatically as a source of revenues to finance the tasks assumed by the state. Moreover, inheritance taxes affect the support for foundations and other charitable organizations through testamentary bequests (Joulfaian 2000). Instead of passing substantial portions of their wealth to the state in the form of taxes, testators can retain influence over the use of their estates by setting up foundations or making gifts to existing ones. Inheritance law thus acquires relevance for regulatory policy, and gives rise to controversies over fundamental questions concerning the relationship between state power, institutions of civil society, and individual disposal over private property.

The contested discussion about the private transmission of wealth through inheritance reveals important aspects of the development of the normative structures of modern societies. At the same time, the regulations of inheritance are important to the social and economic development of societies. Beginning with the bourgeois revolutions at the end of the eighteenth century, the unearned acquisition of wealth through inheritance stood in a tense relationship with the central values and functional demands of the emerging social order. That is the reason why the inheritance of wealth could become an institution that is contested to this day, as is reflected in the political and scholarly controversies over private law during the last two hundred years. These controversies lay open for the sociologist a fascinating field of research that has hitherto received little attention.

Chapter 2

THE RIGHT TO BEQUEATH: TESTAMENTARY
FREEDOM AND THE INDIVIDUALITY OF PROPERTY

SOCIOLOGICAL RESEARCH often describes the process of modernization as one of increasing individualization. Max Weber's account of inheritance law (1978 [1922], 1:370ff.) also follows this pattern: as economic forms with a stronger orientation toward the individual begin to take shape, there is a tendency for the embeddedness of property within the social relationships of the household to dissolve. Inheritance law, according to Weber, follows this development by strengthening the decision-making power of the testator. Weber was not alone in making this argument. His contemporary August von Miaskowski (1882b, 224), for example, saw the rise of the modern economy as the cause behind the growing need for greater testamentary freedom on the part of the testator. And more than a hundred years later, Dieter Leipold (1997, 13), in the Munich commentary to the German Civil Code, explained the expansion of the rights of the testator by pointing to the emergence of an understanding of individual autonomy, on the basis of which the individual increasingly "emphasized his own accomplishments as opposed to being embedded in the succession of generations."[1] To what extent does this latter theory of increasing individualization provide an adequate explanation for the development of inheritance law?

This chapter looks at the debates and controversies surrounding the principle of testamentary freedom and the limits placed on it by the law of a reserved legal share. Testamentary freedom is the most important individual right in the transfer of property *mortis causa*. Only the possibility of freely determining the heirs allows the property owner to regulate what will happen to his or her property beyond death. In liberal social theory and jurisprudence, this right is regarded as an integral component of private autonomy, and thus as an individual right of freedom. With unlimited testamentary freedom there are no constraints on the testator's freedom, either in choosing the heirs or in laying down the conditions under which they may enter into the inheritance. The surviving spouse and children have no legal claim to a share of the decedent's property. The individual right of the testator is paramount.[2]

Strikingly different rules on testamentary freedom exist in the three countries I am examining. The rights of the testator to control the transfer of property by means of a last will are most strongly constrained in France. By contrast, American law knows virtually no restrictions on testamentary freedom—with the exception of those on behalf of the spouse.

In particular, in the United States it is possible to disinherit one's own children. In Germany, the barriers to testamentary freedom are halfway between those in France and those in the United States. In all three countries, the rules on testamentary freedom and its limitations by means of the obligatory legal share have a long continuity, which in some cases goes back further even than the 200-year time frame of the present study. In spite of fundamental political and economic processes of change during this period, the rules governing this aspect of inheritance law have remained stable over the long term.

Whether to expand or limit testamentary freedom was a central area of conflict within inheritance law, especially in the late eighteenth and throughout the nineteenth century. The present chapter examines the debates over the question of testamentary freedom that were carried on in the three countries in connection with the introduction of the French Code Civil, the German Civil Code (Bürgerliches Gesetzbuch, BGB), and during the late eighteenth century in the United States. In each country this proved to be a key phase when the essential foundations of testamentary freedom were laid down. To a very large degree, the patterns of arguments developed during this period shaped later debates on inheritance law in other areas, as well.

The—at times bitter—clashes revolved around the tension between the testator's individual freedom, on the one hand, and the principles of equality and social justice and the claims of spouses and relatives of the deceased, on the other. Time and again, commentators addressed the effects of testamentary freedom on the family, on society, and on economic development. Does testamentary freedom strengthen the family by reinforcing paternal authority, or does it sanction an institution that promotes a kind of individualism that is a threat to the family? Does testamentary freedom make possible the sort of flexible distribution of goods that is necessary for economic development? Or does it in fact impede that development by creating and sustaining the unproductive structures of large-scale landholding and capital concentration? Does testamentary freedom pose a threat to a distribution of wealth that is not excessively imbalanced and as such the foundation of democratic political structures?

This chapter will show how the debates over testamentary freedom in these three countries gave voice to specific evaluative approaches to dealing with private property, approaches that addressed the questions about the limits to the individual disposition over property transmitted by inheritance. The comparative study, in particular, will reveal that the handling of the transfer of property should not be seen simply as a process of individualization. Rather, we are dealing with a process involving controversial debates on how to balance the relationship between the testator's individual rights and the claims of family and society. The limits on testamentary freedom that existed at the beginning of the period in question have hardly changed. Moreover, individual rights are not justified primarily with reference to individual advantage, but also with reference to positive familial, social, and economic effects they are expected to have. That being the case, the development of testamentary freedom *cannot* be interpreted as the loss of influence on the part of family and state vis-á-vis the individual. The connection between individual, familial, and social elements that is reflected in the discourses on inheritance law is more aptly interpreted as "embedded individuality."

2.1. FRANCE: EQUALITY VERSUS THE FREEDOM OF PRIVATE DISPOSITION OVER PROPERTY

Inheritance law played a prominent role in French politics between 1789 and 1804, the year the Code Civil was enacted. Inheritance laws were passed in rapid succession by the constitutional National Assembly and the Convention. Restrictions on testamentary freedom—indeed, for a while its very abolition—were especially important in these laws. They were intended to realize the principle of the equality of citizens also in inheritance law. Republican forces argued that the break with the ancien régime's system of privileges and the implementation of the republican social order demanded that the unequal testamentary treatment of heirs be stopped. Testamentary freedom thus became an area of the law the regulation of which would help determine the further development of French society.

When it came to reforming inheritance law, changes to the family and society were seen as closely connected. The reform of inheritance law during the Revolution was aimed at altering family structures by establishing equality among the children, abolishing the father's arbitrary license in making decisions relating to inheritance, and preventing the dynastic continuity of noble families. Different from Germany, though, where the family and its protection were often seen as the ultimate purpose of inheritance law, in France the change in family structures brought about by changes in inheritance law was also a *means* for creating the social conditions for new political structures. Family relationships based on greater equality were the foundation stones on which the social structures of the new political community were to be erected. In a constantly recurring metaphor, the family was described as the cell of the nation, whose structure would have a decisive influence on the nature of the political order. Family affairs were thus an *affaire d'état*.

This program of using inheritance law to promote social reform based on the principle of equality ran into political opposition. This opposition derived its justification from the liberal notion of private property and countered the demand for state enforcement of the equality principle with the right of free disposition over property. In the process, the demand for unlimited rights of testamentary disposition was justified by invoking the individual's embeddedness within the long-term structure of the family and the expected negative economic consequences from a partitioning of the estate.

The forced equality of children through restrictions on testamentary freedom was denounced as destructive of family relationships, and the division of landed property was rejected as economically deleterious. During the revolutionary phase, the advocates of this position lost. But their arguments on testamentary freedom were picked up again later, especially in the second half of the nineteenth century.

Inheritance Law and the Equality Principle in the Constituent Assembly

The principle of equality served consistently as the most important normative point of reference in all reforms of inheritance law during the revolutionary period.[3] When Merlin presented a bill to the National Assembly in November 1790 that would establish equality in intestacy law,[4] he justified the proposal with the goal of overcoming the legal fragmentation in France,[5] but especially with the establishment of equality as the preeminent goal of the constitution. The principle of the equality of heirs in statutory inheritance law, he argued, was derived from the natural equality of man, which was enshrined in the constitution of 1789, in the first article concerning the rights of man and the citizen. Merlin believed that the existing inheritance law violated this principle, a violation that, far beyond questions of property law, touched on basic principles of the Revolution:

> Established on the principle of the equality of all citizens, this government is a free government, and the consent of such a government to aristocratic rights of primogeniture or to the rights of male offspring thus stands in contradiction to this spirit and undermines all fundamental principles. (Merlin, Assemblée Nationale, 17 November 1790, 601).[6,7]

Pre-Revolution Inheritance Law

Inequality between heirs existed in the prerevolutionary period especially in the inheritance law governing noble estates. On the basis of the 'droit d'aînesse,' the oldest son inherited two-thirds or more of the family property. This legal provision institutionalized the largely undivided, intergenerational cohesion of property within noble families (Aron 1901, 449ff. Giesey 1977, 276).

Less clear, however, is the unequal treatment of heirs in general inheritance law. That law was split between the 'pays du droit écrit' in the South and the pays du droit coutumier in the North.[8] The written law of the South was derived from Roman law and thus knew the institution of testamentary freedom. However, this freedom was limited by the légitime, an obligatory portion to which relatives in the direct line of the testator (descendants and ascendants) were entitled.[9] By contrast, inheritance law in the regions of customary law—northern and central France—was oriented towards ancient German legal traditions. Here, a distinction was drawn

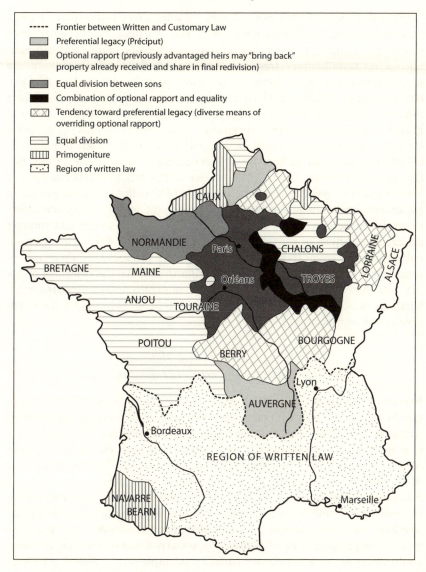

Figure 2.1 Areas of customary law and of written law in the ancien régime
Source: Desan 1997, 604.

between inherited landed property (*propres*) and individually acquired land (*acquêts*).[10] Acquired land could be freely disposed of in a testament, while the disposition over inherited landed property was limited. Four-fifths of the latter had to be passed on within the family as *réserve héréditaire*, with equal division among the children usually stipulated.[11] If there was no heir in the direct line, property was passed on in the family via a lateral line.[12]

What this means is that both systems of inheritance law that were practiced before the Revolution were—with the exception of the inheritance law of the nobility—oriented toward the principle of equality and had limitations on testamentary freedom. To be sure, the legal equality of the heirs under the ancien régime for the most part did not lead to de facto equal division. Rather, various strategies were employed in inheritance practices—gifts, a redefinition of types of property, the refusal of reserved portions, and testamentary dispositions—in an effort to pass on property largely undivided and thus in an unequal fashion. The legal foundations could be used so as to keep wealth concentrated within one family line (Desan 1997; Giesey 1977, 275ff.). Despite the fact that inheritance law was formally oriented toward the principle of equality, it was employed in the inheritance strategies of families to pursue the long-term concentration of wealth, which meant the unequal treatment of the firstborn and younger children, as well as of sons and daughters (Aron 1901, 456). The discrimination against younger siblings and daughters produced by these inheritance practices was the decisive motivation that drove the delegates of the National Assembly—many of whom were younger sons—to support further legal restrictions on testamentary freedom that would compel the equal division of an inheritance.

The Background in Legal Philosophy:
The Conception of Property and Inheritance Law

In the final analysis, the granting of the legal right to dispose of one's property by way of a testament constitutes—like the limitations on testamentary freedom—a regulation pertaining to the right of property. The controversy over testamentary freedom in France saw a clash between two conceptions of property, each of which had different consequences for the question of limits on freedom of testation. On the one side was the defense of private property grounded in natural law, on the basis of which state restrictions on individual right of disposition, including limitations on testamentary freedom, were rejected. On the other side was a conception that regarded private property as a right granted by society, a right in which the state could intervene in a regulatory capacity to implement political principles that were in the interest of the common good (Botsch 1992, 39; Haupt 1989, 33ff.). Proponents of this conception of property elevated the equality of heirs into the most important criterion in creating an inheritance law by which the state gave weight to the common good (see Dainow 1940, 675).

The two camps were in broad agreement when it came to defending the principle of equality before the law. On the basis of this principle, the abolition of the *droit d'aînesse* and the introduction of equal inheritance rights for all descendants in the direct line were largely uncontroversial in the Constituent Assembly. But the two conceptions of property clashed head-on over restrictions on testamentary freedom. There was intense disagreement on the question to what extent the state was permitted—beyond enshrining the principle of legal equality—to intervene in property laws in a way that would promote social equality. Such interventions were advocated, for example, by Mirabeau and Robespierre, who were among the most influential opponents of testamentary freedom. Both men did recognize private property in principle.[13] However, they did not see property as a right that preceded society and therefore merely had to be protected by the state. Rather, it was positive laws that made property possible in the first place:

> Property is only possible on the basis of a social way of life, and, like all the other benefits that society decides upon, it is therefore subject to laws and conditions. Moreover, we see that property law is everywhere subject to certain regulations and, in keeping with the specific circumstances, constrained by more or less narrow boundaries. (Mirabeau, 2 April 1791, in Lettke 2003, 13)

Contrary to the thesis of growing individualization, this interpretation of the law—which became increasingly important in all three countries in question—can be seen as the expression of a growing influence of society on the individual. Individual rights emanate from society. This is also in line with Durkheim's notion of the development of the law and his notion of "moral individualism" (see Durkheim 1992[1957]).

This interpretation of property as an institution of society has, in a second step, immediate relevance for the way inheritance law is seen. Since property laws are themselves based on positive law, it is not possible to legitimate the transfer of property *mortis causa* by invoking natural law; instead, it, too, is anchored in positive law. And when it comes to giving concrete shape to the latter, the good of society is decisive.[14]

This interpretation of inheritance law played a central role in the legal-political controversies about testamentary freedom in all three countries in question. The conception of inheritance law as a positive law established itself in the course of the eighteenth and nineteenth centuries also in Germany and the United States and provided a legal-philosophical justification for the restrictions placed on private inheritance law.[15] In France, this development predates the Revolution and is already found in the middle of the eighteenth century, especially in those legal theorists and political philosophers who were later highly influential for the Revolution. This is particularly true of Montesquieu and Rousseau. In his major work, *The Spirit of the Laws* [1748], Montesquieu highlighted the positive legal status of inheritance law:

> The law of nature ordains that fathers shall provide for their children; but it does not oblige them to make them their heirs. The division of property, the laws of this division, and the succession after the death of the person who has had this division can be regulated only by the community, and consequently by political or civil laws. (1899, 2:62)

Rousseau (1978 [1762]) went even further in his theory of property and derived private property as such from society. Property rights arose only with the social contract, which meant that they always emanated from society. Thus property rights existed only under the conditions laid down by the *volonté générale*. On the basis of this theory of property, Rousseau likewise saw inheritance law as positive law; as a consequence, the property owner could not make any dispositions on the basis of natural law that would take effect only after his death. Once more going beyond Montesquieu, Rousseau maintained that the legislator not only had the right to regulate the transmission of property through positive law, but that the state was obligated to divide estates in such a way that the social inequality within society was ameliorated. He thus combined his theory of property with egalitarian goals.

With the work of Rousseau, the understanding of inheritance law as positive law was joined in political theory by a conception of equality that went beyond the notion of legal equality. This conception influenced the inheritance law reforms in France and is behind the characteristic differences from the discourse on inheritance law that was carried on in Germany and the United States.

Already in seventeenth-century natural law, the notion of natural equality had emerged within political theory as the starting point for the social contract. It was only as equals that members of society could enter into a contract. This did not mean that humans were equal in an anthropological sense; rather, equality before the law was the foundation of the social order established by the social contract (Dann 1975, 1010ff.). In both Locke and Pufendorf, this understanding of equality was combined with the concept of freedom in such a way that equality before the law did not provide any justification for more far-reaching demands for equality. In fact, freedom and the protection of property rights demanded the rejection of a principle of equality that went beyond legal equality in an effort to secure social equality.

By contrast, in prerevolutionary France, especially in the writings of Rousseau, a conception of equality was developed that went far beyond equality before the law, in that social equality was understood precisely as the precondition for political freedom. Rousseau described the history of society as the development of the natural equality of humans in a condition of continually increasing social inequality, which constituted the central political problem. Yet, building on Montesquieu's ideas about the sovereignty of lawmaking, Rousseau saw the constitution of the *volonté générale* as the basis from which the citizens' demands for equality could make themselves heard once again—and to that end, they would have to enact appropriate laws.[16] Parallel to this, Rousseau introduced a notion of freedom that conceives of it as independence from the whims and dominion of others, and with social equality as its precondition. To put it in a nutshell: social inequality establishes power relationships and thus endangers freedom.

That is why freedom and equality always appear in tandem in Rousseau's political thought (Dann 1975, 1016). And that connection was expressed once again in the revolutionary slogan *liberté, égalité, fraternité*.

Ideas about social equality that drew on Rousseau also entered into the debates over inheritance law during the Revolution. Those legal justifications that regarded the principle of equality as the limit to individual disposition over property, and thus legitimated the state's intervention in how property was transmitted upon death, were pursuing not only the goal of equal treatment within the family. Rather, some of the reformers, by restricting testamentary freedom, were also seeking to achieve a socially balanced distribution of wealth.[17]

In its various meanings, the principle of equality became in France a quasi-sacred normative point of reference in the shaping of inheritance law and remained influential in political discourse into the twentieth century. The demand that the state implement the equal treatment of legal subjects who differ by ascriptive characteristics—sons and daughters, the firstborn and younger siblings, noblemen and commoners—can be interpreted, using Durkheim, as the expression of a moral individualism, through which the "sacrality of the person" (Joas 2004) moves into the center of the normative justification of inheritance law. The individual is front and center in the arguments justifying the regulations of inheritance law and displaces ascriptive patterns of legitimation that supported dynastic family continuity, gender-based unequal treatment, and particularistic political structures. This development is therefore the expression of a normative context of reference, and not of a demoralized individualism.

Of course, the theories of property articulated by Rousseau and Montesquieu did not form the *generally* accepted basis in the conflicts over the reform of inheritance law. They were merely one side, which was particularly influential in the political discourse during the Revolution and was repeatedly an important point of reference also in later clashes over inheritance law in France. On the other side of the debates stood a conception of property that accorded absolute primacy to private property, and whose concept of equality did not go beyond equality before the law. This conception aimed merely at the abolition of the prerogatives and privileges of the nobility and the church, and it was broadly uncontroversial within the bourgeoisie. It was especially the freedom of the testator in deciding on the transmission of wealth that was defined here as the core of subjective rights.

The Debate over Inheritance Law in April 1791

During the Revolution, limits on testamentary freedom were first discussed in parliament in April 1791. The discussion, which may well be the most brilliant debate about inheritance law in parliamentary history, centered on enshrining the principle of equality in statutory inheritance law and restricting testamentary freedom.[18] For Mirabeau, the spokesman of those advocating the reform of inheritance law, the fundamental problem of reform lay in the actual *implementation* of the principle of equality through restrictions on testamentary freedom:[19]

> Thus the fundamental question arises: should our law permit the free disposition over goods in the direct line? That is to say, should a father or a mother, an ancestor or ancestress have the right to dispose over their property at will by contract or testament, and thus promote inequality in the ownership of domestic goods? (Mirabeau, 2 April 1791, in Lettke 2003, 11–12)[20]

Mirabeau grounded his rejection of testamentary freedom in his conception of inheritance law as positive law. Property was limited to a lifetime, which is why it reverted back to society upon a person's death. Consequently, wills could not be legitimized by natural law since they made provisions for a time when the right of property had already ceased to exist. Thus, property should rightly revert back to society.[21] Mirabeau, however, circumvented the abolition of private property implicit in this argumentation, at least insofar as it can be passed on, by offering two arguments to justify transmission by inheritance in accordance with intestacy law. First, society had no real interest in keeping this property—it would be too complicated and would also paralyze the entrepreneurial spirit; second, the family of the owner had already acquired a kind of joint ownership right. Inheritance law is here recognized as part of property law, yet the actual form it takes is left to the legislative body, which, in creating that law, had to proceed from the principles of the constitution and especially from the common good.

To Mirabeau, a constitution whose first principle lay in the equality of all citizens could not be reconciled with an inheritance law that violated "the sacred principle of the natural equality" among children and thus exacerbated the inequalities that already existed as a result of differing talents. The call for restrictions on testamentary freedom thus became a constitutional question:

> I do not know, gentlemen, how it should be possible to reconcile the new French constitution, in which everything is traced back to the great and admirable principle of political equality, with a law that allows a father, a mother to forget these sacred principles of natural equality when it comes to their children, with a law that favors differences that are universally condemned, and thus further increases the disparities brought forth in society by differences in talent and industry, instead of correcting them through the equal division of domestic goods. (Mirabeau, 2 April 1791, in Lettke 2003, 24)

The delegate Pétion de Villeneuve supplemented these considerations based on the principle of equality with an argument that is reminiscent of Rousseau, and which justifies the limitations on testamentary freedom as a "protective barrier" against restorationist tendencies: testamentary freedom created a great inequality of wealth within society, and it was only a small step from inequality of wealth to inequality of rights (Pétion, Assemblée Nationale, 6 April 1791, 614).[22]

Alongside arguments about equality, which were central for those who advocated limitations on testamentary freedom (table 2.1), opponents also highlighted especially the effects that the unequal division of inheritance had on family relationships. Where succession followed the rule of primogeniture, the relationship between firstborn sons and younger siblings was often strained, and this had given rise to countless legal proceedings. Moreover, testamentary freedom established a despotic regime on the part of the father, who could threaten his children at any time with disinheriting them. These arguments for building family relationships on the principle of equality were themselves intended as political arguments for building a social order:

> For as you know, gentlemen, the happiness of society consists for the most part of private affections; the feelings and habits that are crucial to public happiness arise at the domestic hearth. (Mirabeau, 2 April 1791, in Lettke 2003, 28)

Compared to later debates over inheritance law, economic arguments played only a secondary role in 1791. This points to the great importance that attached to the implementation of *political* principles in the reform of inheritance law. However, already in 1791 we see a tendency that is later consistently evident: the economic consequences of inheritance law are far more important to those who favor unrestricted inheritance rights than they are to those who oppose them. But in 1791 even the opponents of testamentary freedom introduced a few economic arguments. Mirabeau expected that limiting testamentary freedom would lead to a rise in the number of marriages, a growth in population, and an increase in the number of property owners (Lettle 2003, 514). Pétion expected that a reduction in large-scale landownership with the help of inheritance law would lead to a more balanced distribution of land and thus to an improvement in the miserable economic situation of small farmers and rural laborers, many of whom lived in great poverty (Pétion, Assemblée Nationale, 6 April 1791, 614). Restrictions on testamentary freedom were thus supposed to give rise to greater economic equality.

Supporters of testamentary freedom countered these arguments, first, by pointing to the free disposition over private property: the right of a freely determined succession was the consequence of a right of property that existed *as natural law* and could therefore not be abolished by positive law. For example, Mougins de Roquefort, an ecclesiastical delegate, argued thus: "A man's testamentary freedom, this quality as legislator of the family, is inherent in the right of property, it is the guarantee and support of the same" (Assemblée Nationale, 6 April 1791, 617). Apart from this legal-philosophical justification of testamentary freedom, its supporters introduced above all economic arguments, but also justifications aimed at the practical, de facto acceptance of the law (instead of attempts to circumvent it), as well as family-related arguments that decried chiefly the undermining of paternal authority through the abolition of testamentary freedom (table 2.1). Cazalès and a number of other delegates derived testamentary freedom from the role of paternal authority as a pillar of the social order, an argument that would once again receive considerable attention in the middle of the nineteenth century:

> It is only with testamentary freedom that fathers rule their families; thanks to it they are accorded honor and respect by their children into old age, in a way that virtue would not be able to accomplish. (Cazalès, Assemblée Nationale, 5 April 1791, 575)

Delegate Lambert de Frondeville, a native of Normandy, defended the unequal division of inheritance on the grounds that its repeal would lead to the breakup of landholdings, which would result in the decline of agriculture and thus the destruction of the alimentary foundation of the people and the public welfare. In addition, Frondeville saw in the existing inheritance law an important pillar of support of order and morality in society (Assemblée nationale, 12 March 1791, 48ff.).

In the debate in April 1791, opponents and proponents of testamentary freedom argued on the basis of divergent conceptions of property law. The principle of equality and the value of liberty stood in irreconcilable opposition (Eckert 1992, 174).[23] But there were also different notions about the economic and social consequences of abolishing testamentary freedom, along with divergent ideas about the goals that inheritance law reform was supposed to accomplish: while Mirabeau saw limits on testamentary freedom as an instrument to prevent paternal despotism in family relationships,[24] it was precisely this possible consequence that proponents of testamentary freedom rejected as a threat to social order. Whereas opponents of testamentary freedom pointed to the positive effects from a division of landed property, proponents saw in this division a fragmentation of the land that impeded economic development.

The substantive analysis of the arguments put forth in the debate (table 2.1) shows that opponents of testamentary freedom staked their position more strongly on the value of equality, the deliberate alteration of existing family structures, and society's moral values. Proponents, meanwhile, argued on behalf of preserving existing family structures. Among supporters of an equal division of inheritance, arguments about equality carried great weight, as one would expect, while arguments about liberty did not. One thing that both camps shared is revealed by the frequent mention of arguments aimed at the importance of inheritance law to the integration of society: it is the assessment that inheritance law has profound social and political relevance.

No participant in the debate in April 1791 called for the complete abolition of testamentary freedom; the issue at stake was imposing consistent limitations on it. Even though there were signs that a majority was emerging in support of such a move, in the end no decision was made in the law

TABLE 2.1

The Debate over Testamentary Freedom in the Constituent Assembly, 1790–91:
Reasons Offered by Speakers for Their Positions on Testamentary Freedom and on
the Principle of Equality in Statutory Inheritance Law

	For Testamentary Freedom and against Equality in Intestacy Law	Against Testamentary Freedom and for Equality in Intestacy Law
Reasons inherent in the law	17.6	13.1
Preservation of the legal tradition	4.8	1.3
Standardization of the legal system	0.8	4.6
De facto acceptance of the law	6.4	0.7
Other justifications inherent in the law	5.6	6.5
Political reasons	32.4	55.9
Consequences for the common good	9.6	8.5
Society's moral ideas	4.0	9.9
Principle of meritocracy	4.0	
Principle of equality		19.7
Principle of justice	5.6	7.9
Free disposition over property	9.2	4.6
Promotion of democratic structures		5.3
Economic reasons	27.3	7.9
Consequences for economic development	16.9	5.3
Greater equality in the distribution of wealth and land	0.8	2.6
Preservation of existing economic structures	4.8	
Breakup of landholdings, excessive indebtedness	4.8	
Familial reasons	24.1	22.7
Authority of the father	15.3	6.5
Providing for family members	1.6	0.7
Family cohesion	7.2	15.5
	N = 124	N = 153

Note: Figures are percentages. The contributions to the debate date from the period of 6
November 1790 to 6 April 1791; a total of twelve speakers participated.

promulgated on 8 April 1791. Instead, the question of testamentary freedom as well as the abolition of substitutions was indefinitely postponed, especially because of opposition from the southern provinces, where testamentary freedom existed.[25] The National Assembly merely decided in April 1791 to introduce equal division in intestacy law, which abolished primogenitures in intestacy law and made sons and daughters equal.[26]

Given the far-reaching reform proposals in the proposed laws and the controversial debate, which elevated the limitation on testamentary freedom into a core issue of the Revolution, this change to the existing inheritance law was surprisingly minor. After all, equal division was already stipulated in intestacy law in the southern regions of the country, and the coutumes, as well, for the most part contained rules about equal division. It was actual inheritance practices that were used to pursue de facto divergent inheritance strategies. Consequently, the principle of equality in intestacy law could only lead to an improvement in the actual equality between heirs if testamentary freedom were restricted as well. However, even by the law of April 1791, the provisions of intestacy law could be circumvented by way of a testament.

This development can be interpreted as the bourgeoisie shying away from implementing the principle of equality fully and consistently in inheritance law. After all, the preferential treatment of the oldest and of sons was practiced not only among the nobility to preserve power, but also among the bourgeoisie and peasant families to keep wealth intact and preserve strongly hierarchical family structures. Limiting testamentary freedom would have interfered with these inheritance practices. Moreover, testamentary freedom was an important basis for the concentration of landed wealth in the hands of the church. This ambivalent position on the part of the bourgeoisie was not yet directly apparent in the debate in April 1791, however, because the primary issue at that time was still overturning the legal structures of the ancien régime, as is evident from the clear lines of opposition between delegates of the bourgeoisie and those of the nobility. All delegates sent to the assembly from the estate of the bourgeoisie spoke in favor of limiting testamentary freedom, while delegates from the nobility, without exception, supported testamentary freedom. No delegate of the nobility called for equal division of inheritance, which was demanded in the majority of the arguments put forth by delegates of the bourgeoisie.[27]

The only church delegate who participated in the debate, Roquefort, took a mediating stance by coming out in favor of limitations on testamentary freedom while at the same time rejecting any effort to enforce compulsory equal division.[28] The dilemma of the bourgeoisie, however, was this: while the abolition of the privileges of the nobility in the *droit d'aînesse* could be applauded, restricting testamentary freedom would have endangered also their own intergenerational wealth strategies. After the fall of the Jacobins in the National Convention, resistance would grow among the bourgeoisie to those changes to inheritance law that interfered with the private autonomy of the property owner (Desan 1999). In 1791, the true radicalization of the political situation was still to come. However, the fact that the limitation on testamentary freedom was not enacted by the more moderate Constituent Assembly reveals that the notion of equality could find its political realization most likely in the principle of legal equality. The new class of property owners that was emerging in the Revolution would demand precisely the defense of the system of unencumbered property in order to set itself apart from the have-nots (Botsch 1992, 226). In the conflict between the two conceptions of property, the bourgeois-liberal notion thus kept the upper hand, but it was interspersed with elements of a statist egalitarianism. However, this compromise between the principles of liberty and equality was reached only in the inheritance law of the Code Civil (1804).

The Radicalization of Inheritance Law Reform in the National Assembly

While the treatment of inheritance law in the Constituent Assembly still displayed a rather moderate approach to the matter of the law, the inheritance law reforms during the rule of the Jacobins reflect the radicalization of the political situation. The law of 1791 was merely a first step in the revolutionary legislation. With the takeover of power by the Jacobins, the balance of power shifted in favor of actors like Robespierre and Pétion de Villeneuve, who had already in 1791 voted vehemently for limiting testamentary freedom. Now it was possible to push through what had still been blocked in 1791: on 7 March 1793, following a brief debate (which reflected the authoritarian political situation), the National Assembly passed a law that abolished testamentary freedom entirely.[29]

Now a testator could no longer deviate from intestacy law by means of testamentary disposition; freely determined succession was thus abolished. This law was further tightened half a year later when the Law of 5 Brumaire an II (26 October 1793) decreed that the abolition of testamentary freedom was retroactive to 14 July 1789. This measure reopened legally completed devolutions, and property titles believed by heirs to be secure could be challenged by disadvantaged heirs. At the same time, the law already loosened the prohibition of testamentary freedom a little by making provisions for a *quotité disponible* over which the testator could dispose in his last will, one-tenth of the estate if there were descendants in the direct line, otherwise one-sixth. However, in order to preserve equality among the children, the freely disposable share could not be left to one child, only to non–family members. These stipulations on testamentary freedom were confirmed a few months later, on 17 and 21 Nivôse an II (6 and 10 January 1794), in a comprehensive bill that constituted the high point of the revolutionary legislation on inheritance law (Aron 1901, 446).

The laws passed by the National Assembly in 1793 and 1794 represented drastic reforms of inheritance law. Neither in the United States nor in Germany was inheritance law ever used in a comparable way as an instrument of social reform. For proponents of reform the implementation of equality between heirs was paramount, which would give due recognition to the idea of equality enshrined in the constitution. The backdrop to this was the idea—anchored in Enlightenment thinking—of legal equality in the state of nature, the experience with a concentration of wealth in the ancien régime that was felt to be a threat to liberty, the goal of exerting influence on family relationships regarded as despotic, and the positive notion that social relationships that were built upon the principle of equality promoted the general good.[30]

This drastic curtailment of testamentary freedom was such a profound intervention in existing inheritance practices within French society that it triggered considerable discontent within the population. A multitude of petitions decried the familial effects of the radical reforms of family law, including the introduction of equal division of inheritance (Desan 1999). The repeal of some of the reforms after 1795 also reflected this political protest. The attempt by the revolutionaries to push through their ideas about society (which were based on the principle of equality) through radical reforms of inheritance law aimed at altering existing family structures would have no lasting success. Put in general terms, on the one hand this confirms the finding of legal sociology that legal reforms tend to follow familial developments rather than cause them (Limbach 1988); on the other hand, the reversal points to the power of family structures, a power that puts limits on the political instrumentalization of the family for social reforms.

The Legislation of the Code Civil

The restrictions on testamentary freedom that were enacted in the law of 1794 did not last. The fall of the Jacobins in the National Assembly led to the return of more moderate forces of the Republicans, who revised the inheritance law once again. This process continued right up to the adoption of the Code Civil in 1804. A first relaxation of the law came in 1795, when the retroactivity of the law of 1794 was revoked. Five years later, in the Law about Freedom of Disposition of 4 Germinal an VIII (25 March 1800), the *quotité disponible* was increased, provided there was at least one direct descendant, to a maximum of one-fourth[31] (Hedemann 1910, 22), and this freely disposable portion of the estate could also be bequeathed to one of the children, which meant that they could once again be treated unequally in a will. However, if there were more than four children, the disposable share was reduced further, which means that testamentary freedom remained tightly constrained. The background to this legal reform was the change in the balance of political power, but also the opposition of the property-owning classes to the restrictive inheritance laws, expressed in inheritance practices and public protests. Those laws were often circumvented by "fictitious purchases and sales, sham debts, and similar means" (Schoelkens 1900, 42).

Still, inheritance law was the subject of heated clashes in the Tribunate,[32] which centered once again on the idea of equality. For those who opposed expanding testamentary freedom feared that the preferential treatment of one child made possible by the reform of the law would revive the inequalities the Revolution had fought against. The tribune Duveyrier countered that the inequality under the ancien régime had arisen, not from the lack of a sense of justice on the part of fathers, but from the *droit d'aînesse*, which had been abolished. The de facto suppression of testamentary freedom in the law of 1794, however, had restricted the freedom of the testator in a disrespectful way. Yet even in the debate in the Tribunate, the number of arguments in favor of limiting testamentary freedom predominated. Only a quarter of the arguments called for complete testamentary freedom, while 40% supported restrictions. The principle of equality continued to stand out in France as the normative starting point in shaping inheritance law.

While it is true that the law passed in March 1800 loosened the restrictions on testamentary freedom, it is far more significant that the principle of equality was retained as the dominant criterion. With some qualifications, that is also true of the Code Civil adopted in 1804, which finally made civil law in France uniform.[33] In the area of inheritance law, the Code Civil repealed the law of 1794, and the stipulations it enacted, while building on the legislation of the National Assembly, strengthened the principle of freedom vis-à-vis the principle of equality. Of special relevance to the question of testamentary freedom was the distinction between a *quotité disponible* and the *réserve*. The latter referred to the share of the estate that was not disposable by last will and had to be bequeathed on the basis of intestacy law. Although the principle of testamentary freedom was thus preserved, at least when it came to the *réserve*, intestacy law took precedence over the last will (Aron 1901, 449).[34] To put it differently: for one portion of the estate, the principle of equality takes precedence over the principle of testamentary freedom.

In the debate over the section of the Code Civil dealing with inheritance law, the limitation on testamentary freedom was not controversial; the discussion revolved merely around the question of how extensive this limitation should be and whether it should also apply to collateral relatives (Dainow 1940, 679ff.). From a political point of view, the expansion of testamentary freedom was supposed to restore paternal authority within the family. It was supposed to form "a counterweight to unlimited individual freedom . . . which could become dangerous to Napoleon's reign" (Eckert 1992, 195). This points to a clear conservative strain in the codification of inheritance law in the Code Civil. At the same time, the preservation of the limitation on testamentary freedom attests to the importance of the idea of equality also in the code of 1804. As in the debate of 1791, the legal-philosophical reasoning was grounded in the rejection of a justification of a private right of inheritance on the basis of natural law, a rejection that legitimized the state's intervention in inheritance decisions.

This position simultaneously reveals that the conception of property had a statist orientation: although private property is protected, it has its limitations in laws and regulations enacted by the state (e.g., Art. 544 and 545 C.C.), which are intended to secure the common good against particularistic interests.[35]

This understanding of the role of the state in inheritance law was also advocated by Jean Marie Étienne Portalis, a deputy and coauthor of the Code Civil. It finds expression in his speech introducing the section on inheritance law in the Code Civil: the rights of the owner end with his death, and intervention by the state in the transfer of property was indispensable, because the interests represented in it surpassed those of the individuals involved. Inheritance law should be used to bring about a republican polity, something that was, in the final analysis, in the interest of the state (see Dainow 1940, 680; Hedemann 1930, 75; Sagnac 1898, 34ff.):

> You cannot love your property, but you can direct the spirit of love at the laws. You will have worked not only for the happiness of individual persons and certain families; you will have created a public spirit (*esprit public*); you will have opened up the true sources of the general welfare, you will have prepared the way for the welfare of all. (Qtd. in Fehrenbach 1974, 25)

In the process, the definition of the common good also involved the interests of power politics. For Napoleon, the limitation on testamentary freedom and real division had the political function of curtailing the power of large estates, which would be divided at every devolution. In the debate over the inheritance law in the Code Civil, Napoleon demanded above all restrictions on testamentary freedom for large landed property, whereas he supported a further expansion of testamentary freedom when it came to small and medium-size property (see Fehrenbach 1974, 25).[36] Max Weber (1978 [1922], 2:692) pointed out that the limitation on testamentary freedom in France was "largely politically determined." What stood behind compulsory division for Napoleon was the intention "of destroying the old aristocracy."

According to the Code Civil (Art. 913), the share of the *quotité disponible* depended on the testator's family circumstances: with one child, the testator could freely dispose over half of his property, with two children over one-third, and with three children over one-fourth. If the testator had no children, but there were living ascendants, the freely disposable share ranged between one-half and three-quarters of the estate (Art. 914 C.C.). Compared to the stipulations of the Law of 1794, the testamentary rights were substantially expanded in the Code Civil, so that one can rightly speak of a shift away from the principle of equality and towards a strengthening of the testator's rights of disposition. However, if one compares the regulations of the Code Civil with American or German law, its much tighter restrictions on testamentary freedom stand out. This reflects the importance of the principle of equality, which has persisted beyond the legislation of the revolutionary period.[37] The individual rights of the owner are restricted in order to implement the political goal of treating the testator's children equally, and to defend the autonomy of the state against the possible agglomeration of power through the dynastic concentration of wealth. In this sense, the legislation on inheritance law during the revolutionary period can also be interpreted as the deliberate weakening of civil society vis-à-vis the state. This points to an interesting difference from the United States. The discourse on inheritance law in the United States was also directed primarily against the concentration of power through dynastic strategies of inheritance. But in contrast to France, the goal was to strengthen the democratic foundations of the republican polity through a balanced distribution of property, not to strengthen the state as a *supraordinated* authority to enforce a common good as defined by the state.

With the continued limitation on testamentary freedom, the goal of preserving property within the family as intact as possible, which had been characteristic of noble law and the inheritance practices of the ancien régime, was given up. In its place, the Code Civil demanded real division (Art. 815). According to Article 815 every co-heir could ask for his real share of the assets of the estate. Until the early twentieth century, French civil law (Art. 832 C.C.) stipulated that every heir should receive equal shares of the real estate and the movable assets. Although the Code Civil also intended that this should not lead to the dismemberment of landed property (Art. 832 C.C. and 833 C.C.), the courts adhered rigidly to the principle of real division (Rieg 1971, 91). If the assets were not partible, they had to be publicly auctioned off. The principle of real division was also meant to secure equality by counteracting, through inheritance law, the feared trend toward a renewed, quasi-feudal concentration of landed wealth. Real division was opposed throughout the nineteenth century. Opponents argued that the limitation on testamentary freedom and the stipulation of real division in the Code Civil led to the fragmentation of the land and destroyed the family. However, it would be more than a hundred years before these objections would bring about a loosening of compulsory real division.

The Politics of Testamentary Freedom in the Nineteenth Century

Except for minor changes, the limitations on testamentary freedom that were laid down in the Code Civil at the beginning of the nineteenth century have remained in force to this day. The period between 1790 and 1804 is therefore the key phase in the development of French inheritance law, a phase in which a path of legal development was set that would have long-term repercussions. The increase in individual freedom of disposition that modernization theory would lead one to expect is not found in the Code. Not only is there no substantial broadening of individual disposition rights vis-à-vis the inheritance law of the ancien régime, compared with the right of the obligatory portion in the regions of the *droit écrit*, the Code actually restricts testamentary freedom even more. A broadening of testamentary freedom occurred only in the case of inherited landed wealth (*propres*) in the *pays du droit coutumier*, which had been almost completely excluded from testamentary disposition in the inheritance law of the ancien régime. The discourses on the reform of inheritance law in the revolutionary period show the tension between the defense of unconstrained rights of testation on the basis of natural law, and the discussion of the consequences of legal reform for the family, the common welfare, and the state. Although the principle of individual freedom of disposition played an important role in the debates on inheritance law, its proponents justified it by referring to the familial and social utility it would produce, not to the strengthening of an abstract individualism.

The question of testamentary freedom became a preeminent topic of political discourse one more time in French history. Sixty years after passage of the Code Civil, the politician, manager, and social researcher Frédéric Le Play published a study entitled *Le réforme sociale en France* (1864), in which he addressed the crises brought about by the transformation of French society in his day. The social consequences of accelerating industrialization, the declining birthrate, and the structural changes to the family this entailed had triggered a growing mood of crisis in France. Le Play had examined these processes of social change in family studies published in 1855 under the title *Les ouvriers européens*, in which he had established a causal connection between French inheritance law and what he diagnosed as the destruction of social cohesion and the family. He argued that the limitation on testamentary freedom in the wake of the French Revolution had led to social atomization, selfishness, alienation, and deracination, and was the primary cause behind the political and social instability of France.

Le Play's essay set off an intense debate in politics and the social sciences on the relationship between testamentary freedom and the development of society.[38] This renewed debate showed that while the political balance of power in the Second Empire had shifted substantially compared to the revolutionary period, the structures of the discursive field had barely changed: the argumentative patterns from the revolutionary period were called upon once again.

In his argumentation, Le Play picked up the conservative critique of the revolutionary reform of inheritance law by establishing a link between the order of the state and familial structures, a link that was based on the natural law defense of individual inheritance rights and demanded the unequal division of an estate.[39] The government was based on paternal authority, he maintained, which in turn was dependent on the possibility of free testamentary disposition over property. Testamentary freedom expressed a right that was inherent in the nature of property. This link between testamentary freedom justified by natural law and the support for paternal authority stands in a direct line of continuity to the arguments of those who opposed the limitation on testamentary freedom in the debate of 1791 (Cazalès and Roquefort).

However, the debate over testamentary freedom in the second half of the nineteenth century shows a shift from the debate during the revolutionary age, in that the controversy was less over value principles *as such* (equality vs. freedom), and more about the *social consequences* of translating these principles into inheritance law. For Le Play, the equal division of inheritance as stipulated since the Revolution had three negative social consequences: (1) it destroyed the family, (2) it led to lower birthrates, and (3) it impeded economic development.

1. As Le Play saw it, stable family relationships, which were said to be the foundation for a stable social order, were based, for one, on paternal authority and respect for tradition, and, for another, on a secure home to which family members could retreat especially during phases of economic instability. Both preconditions, however, were being undermined by equal division: paternal authority, because children could not be disciplined by the threat of being disinherited; tradition and a secure home, because the fragmentation of wealth made it impossible to maintain them. The laws on inheritance in the Code Civil thus gave rise to unstable family structures (*famille instable*), which were the cause behind the social crisis (*désordre*) (Le Play 1864, 2:205). French inheritance law, he maintained, promoted the individualization as well as the social differentiation and mobility of family members. This destroyed the desirable structure of the stem family (*famille souche*) (1864, 2:166ff.). Le Play called the existing inheritance law "anti-social" and demanded the introduction of the greatest possible testamentary freedom. It should be limited only by the obligation to support disinherited family members, so that those costs would not fall on society. Testamentary freedom made possible the undivided transmission of the family property and thus supported the stem family, which in turn contributed to good morals, order, solicitude, and, in the final analysis, the flourishing of society.

Stimulated by Le Play's writings, the topic of testamentary freedom played a significant role in the public political arena of France in the 1860s. It was discussed in the daily press, and in 1867, the Académie des sciences morales et politiques posed a prize question on testamentary freedom (Bruns 1882, 161–62). The two winning submissions by Gustave Boissonade (1873) and Charles Brocher (1868) each addressed the writings of Le Play, but they unanimously rejected his reform proposals to expand testamentary freedom. These two essays attest the continuity of the discursive field of French debates on inheritance law, for their argumentation is based precisely on the orientation toward the postulate of equality that was already used to justify limitations on testamentary freedom during the Revolution. Boissonade (1873, 434) saw in equal division the starting point for the establishment of new families. Sons could take the small piece of land as an economic starting point from which to build their livelihood. This foundation would promote marriages and births. He rejected absolute testamentary freedom because it led to injustice within families (1873, 457–58) and ran counter to social utility. Brocher dismissed the absolute testamentary freedom demanded by Le Play with the argument that while the individual rights of freedom that find expression in testamentary freedom deserve to be protected, the restrictions from the *réserve* did not constitute a limitation on individual rights because the rights of liberty had to subordinate themselves to certain rules of morality:

> These prescriptions about the obligatory portion do not serve the purpose of skimming off the deceased's estate through prohibitions: rather, they are part of what is unforeseeable and of individual rights of liberty; their goal is to ensure that what generally seems just and in accord with the interest of society will be respected up to a certain degree. (Brocher 1868, 33–34)

Brocher questioned the economic consequences invoked by Le Play (1868, 351ff.), arguing that they were controversial even among economists. Moreover, the causal connection between testamentary freedom and family stability established by Le Play was not generally accepted. Already in the 1850s, the jurist Félix Parieu (1852), in an examination of English inheritance laws, had praised the advantages of partible inheritance in France, which would be much better at finding a balance between the rights of the owner and the rights of the family. The differing inheritance laws in France and England were not a causal factor that could explain the divergent economic development of the two countries in the industrialization process. Instead, Parieu saw a close connection between primogeniture and the status of the landed aristocracy, that is, a prebourgeois economic form. In a direct revival of arguments from the revolutionary period, Le Play's opponents also maintained that the limitation on paternal authority in inheritance law had led to greater affection in family relationships, and that the principle of equality was reducing family conflicts produced by the preferential treatment of individual children (Dainow 1940, 688).[40]

The conflict between jurists who rejected testamentary freedom and Le Play mirrors once again the opposing positions of the French discourse on inheritance law. On one side stood the strongly statist-influenced tradition that placed the idea of equality front and center, and which emphasized that the state should enforce the general welfare; and on the other side stood an orientation toward inheritance law that emphasized individual rights of liberty and testamentary freedom.

However, it would be an incomplete characterization, at best, to describe Le Play simply as a conservative family researcher and politician (Worms 1917, 118ff.; Zeldin 1979, 185ff.). Le Play cannot be adequately understood as a conservative opponent of social equality and as a promoter of the power interests of the bourgeoisie,[41] but only within the context of his goals of social reform and his liberal orientation toward strengthening civil society vis-à-vis the state. Le Play's critique of the French Revolution can be seen as liberal in the sense that he opposed especially the coercion emanating from state interventionism, which was threatening "to stifle private life and private initiative to an ever-increasing degree" (Nolte 1965, 42). These liberal elements are apparent in Le Play's admiration for England, his critique of a bureaucracy that was getting out of hand, and in his open-minded attitude toward technological innovations and industrialization, which, alongside his unquestionably conservative picture of the family, made up parts of his social theory. Le Play's position can be characterized— slightly contradictory—as "socially conservative liberalism" and as opposition to government enforcement of a common welfare as defined by the state.

At the same time, the contemporary opposition to Le Play's proposals on inheritance law—none of which were in the end implemented, because of the great political resistance they encountered—reveals the continuing influence of the tradition based on the principle of equality, and the persistence of the limitations on testamentary freedom that were institutionalized by the Revolution. The principle of equality as the core of the Revolution of 1789 prevailed as a quasi-sacred point of reference for inheritance law. The sociologist René Worms was able to write as late as 1917: "The overwhelming majority of our fellow citizens remain faithful to the principles that were formulated in this area in the Code Civil" (1917, 145).

2. Le Play saw a connection not only between testamentary freedom and family structures, but also, and especially, between testamentary freedom and the demographic trend. The potential repercussions of equal division on the birthrate in France was a dominant theme in the inheritance law discourse between 1870 and 1930 (Spengler 1979 [1938]). The argument had already been advanced during the debate on inheritance law in the Constitutional Assembly.[42] Mirabeau had linked equal division with the expectation of rising birthrates. By contrast, the deputy Cazalès, an opponent of the abolition of testamentary freedom, had argued that equal division would lead to a decline in birthrates, because a smaller number of children meant that the fragmentation of property could be at least moderated.[43] In fact, one way to interpret the regulations in Article 913 of the Code Civil is that they were creating an incentive structure for small families. The fewer children there are, the larger the *quotité disponible* and the smaller the division of the estate if the freely disposable part of the inheritance is bequeathed to *one* child. Le Play revived the argumentation already put forth by Cazalès, which once again confirms the potent continuity of the discursive structures in the French debates on inheritance law. In the 1860s, Le Play simultaneously encountered a political climate in which questions about the population trend received much greater public attention than they had seventy years earlier.

Although France's population grew during the nineteenth century, its growth was slower than in other European countries, especially after 1850, as a result of which France was overtaken by Germany, Austria-Hungary, and Great Britain in absolute population numbers (Spengler 1979 [1938], 4). The fear that France would fall behind demographically became a dominant theme in public discourse and led to a discussion of the causes behind this development and possible remedies (see, among others, Worms 1917). The alarmist mood among the French public intensified especially after the lost war against Prussia in 1870–71. It was feared that the more rapid population growth in other European countries would lead to long-term political and military advantage. If France wanted to remain a dominant political power, it must not fall behind in the size of its population.

Le Play (1864, 128ff.) saw the demand for the introduction of testamentary freedom as a solution to the demographic problem. In his eyes, the causal connection between inheritance law and the demographic trend was confirmed by the fact that the birthrate did not decline until after the revolutionary legislation and the introduction of the Code Civil, and that it was highest in those regions of France in which the laws were frequently circumvented because of strong traditions and where landed wealth was passed on undivided; by the fact that a smaller number of children was being used as a strategy to keep wealth together; and by the fact that traditions of French society, including the desire for many children, were being severed by the Code Civil. However, whether this link between inheritance law and the demographic trend did in fact exist was politically hotly debated. Spengler (1979 [1938], 152ff.), who systematically examined the political-demographic debate about Le Play's theory, points to a number of arguments that were put forth against Le Play: for example, the system of small-scale division of landed property already existed prior to the Revolution, and it had had no demographic effects. Moreover, the decline in birthrates did not begin immediately after the Revolution, but only around 1850. Contrary to the assertion of Le Play, the birthrate was declining also in parts of the country where family property was being kept intact in circumvention of the intent of the Code Civil. In addition, it had been shown that the right of bequeathing the freely disposable share to *one* heir was being exercised in only a few areas of France. In general, this portion, too, was divided equally among the heirs to avoid conflicts in the family. Finally, there was no strict link between inheritance law and birthrate because birthrates within France diverged strongly and were also developing differently in countries with comparable inheritance law.[44] One might also ask, counterfactually, whether an unequal division of inheritance would lead to higher birthrates. Although the property did not have to be divided, concern for the economic fate of the other children could lead precisely to the desire for a smaller number of children. In 1917, the sociologist René Worms, in his study on the demographic development of France, summed up the critique of Le Play's theory:

It [the limitation on testamentary freedom] is not the cause of the decline in births in France, just as one cannot presume it to be the cause for the decline in the solidarity of the family or the state. (139)

Nevertheless, in the public discourse in France, the question of the declining birthrate always remained linked with inheritance law until the 1930s. In chapter 5, which examines the development of inheritance tax laws, I will show how inheritance tax law in France would come to be employed to boost the birthrate.

3. The third consequence indicated by Le Play as the result of the limitation on testamentary freedom in the Code Civil was the fragmentation of land. This argument, too, had been advanced during the debate of 1791. In the last third of the nineteenth century, however, it took on special significance in connection with efforts to explain France's slower rate of industrialization. For Le Play, the stipulation about the real division of land was problematic, for one, because the destruction of the family's property contributed to alienation and deracination, and for another, because the fragmentation of the soil prevented economies of scale, and if the division progressed far enough, even the yields necessary to sustain the farmer's family could no longer be produced (Le Play 1864, 110ff.). Of course, preventing the concentration of landed wealth was a declared goal of legislation in the wake of the French Revolution, with which republican ideals were to be pursued. However, breaking up the land would be an obstacle to economic development and a source of pauperism.

It is controversial to what extent the inheritance law regulations in the Code Civil can in fact be held responsible for the small-scale agricultural structures in France as well as for the low agricultural productivity. This agrarian structure had predominated in France before the Revolution, and it was at most reinforced by the revolutionary legislation (Brentano 1899; Schoelkens 1900; Spengler 1979 [1938], 152–53). One cause behind the fragmentation of landed property was the high birthrate in the eighteenth century (Botsch 1992, 29). However, it can be empirically demonstrated that the parcels of land in France increased in the nineteenth century, namely from 10.29 million in 1826 to 14.29 million in 1881. At the same time, the average size of the parcels declined from 4.48 hectares to 3.5 hectares (Zeldin 1973, 146).[45] In the 1890s, however, the share of smaller parcels declined again (Spengler 1979 [1838], 153). With respect to the productivity of this small-scale division of land, it was already argued in the early nineteenth century that it had actually led to an increase in productivity. Large landholdings, so the argument went, were often managed inefficiently because of the widespread lack of interest on the part of noble owners. By contrast, the division of landholding led to the cultivation of previously unused land and to more intensive management, because that was the only way the farmers could secure their livelihood in any lasting way (Botsch 1992, 215; Brentano 1899, 142ff.).[46]

Although a strong current influenced by Le Play emerged within French economics, contemporary liberal economists often did *not* follow Le Play's conclusions. Rather, they maintained that custom and mores had long since confirmed the rightness of the equal division among the children—in so doing they affirmed the republican model of the revolutionary period (Steiner 2004, 12).

The problem with the division of landed property could have lain less in the decline of agricultural productivity or alienation than in the reduced pressure toward mobility. Since every child could expect a least a small piece of land with the inheritance, the pressure to migrate to the cities was reduced, which meant that a correspondingly smaller pool of labor was available for industrial production (Darrow 1989, 12). The small-scale organization of agriculture thus had far-reaching consequences for the process of industrialization in France:

> Right up until the late 1850s, the excess population remained on the land. . . . Bound by small and tiny plots of land, able to survive thanks to a multitude of secondary commercial activities, often also cut off from information about opportunities for work, the majority of the French population in the 1850s lived in villages and hamlets. (Haupt 1989, 83)

The process of urbanization was noticeably slower in France than in Germany, for example. Another factor that contributed to the difficult situation of the rural population was the fact that—independent of inheritance laws—landed wealth enjoyed considerable prestige among French farmers and the bourgeoisie, and a lot of capital flowed into its acquisition. This led to inflationary real estate prices. At the same time, this capital was no longer available for industrial investments (Haupt 1989, 119; Zeldin 1973, 147). Landed property allowed the bourgeoisie to attain the prestigious status of *propriétaires*, and if their landed wealth was great enough, they could even be elevated to the nobility.[47]

Testamentary Freedom and Real Division in the Twentieth Century

Criticism of the limitation on testamentary freedom and of the principle of real division during the Second Empire had direct parliamentary repercussions. In 1865, Baron de Veauce, impressed by Le Play's arguments, introduced a bill into the Corps Législatif that called for the introduction of complete testamentary freedom. However, this bill could not muster majority backing (Boissonade 1873, 525; Gotman 1988, 95; Worms 1917, 173ff.). In the following years (e.g., 1869, 1871, and 1889) proposals to expand testamentary freedom that invoked Le Play were repeatedly submitted to the Senate, though all failed to garner enough support.

The topic remained important in parliament also during the Third Republic, though it did not lead to any changes in the law. In 1899, deputy Henri Coulon, citing Le Play, once again proposed expanding testamentary freedom—without success (Dainow 1940, 690). Between 1919 and 1922, various attempts were made to raise the *quotité disponible*, though once again they failed to effect changes in the law (Spengler 1979 [1938], 150). And so one can conclude: "Paternal authority and the freedom of the owner thus did not return. They did not triumph over the republican principle of equality" (Gotman 1988, 97).

However, by 1938 at least a few changes to the law were adopted that made it possible to pass on small pieces of landed property undivided, thus representing a partial break with the principle of real division. After the attempt in 1904 to abolish compulsory real division had failed (Holthöfer 1982, 997), laws in 1909, 1922, and 1938 introduced the legal institution of *attribution préférentielle*, which was then further expanded in the law of 19 December 1961. It now became possible, upon request, to transfer property to one heir (co-owner) as sole property and to pay out the other heirs. This optional assignment applies especially to farms, family businesses, and the living space inhabited by the petitioner (Rieg 1971, 91ff.). Additional changes were enacted in 1971, 1976, 1980, and 2006: although they retained the principle of equal division, they were also intended to strengthen the cohesion of economic entities. The division of the property that was stipulated in Article 826 and could be demanded by a co-heir at any time was restricted, in that the court could order a postponement of the division, or the community of heirs could postpone the division through a contractual agreement (Ferid and Sonnenberger 1987, 610ff.). Only with the reform in 2006, which took effect in 2007, was the need for unanimous decisions by all heirs in the management of an indivisible property abolished and replaced with the possibility of decisions by a two-thirds majority. This reform aimed at preventing paralysis in decision making. Another stipulation in the 2006 law is the possibility for heirs to renounce their anticipated inheritance in favor of another designated person. Such *pactes successoral* are legally binding contracts between family members that allow unequal divisions of inheritances to help family members with special needs, for instance handicapped children. They can also be used to depart from the succession order to bequeath wealth to stepchildren, thereby accommodating the needs of the increasing number of patchwork families. Another important change is that grandparents are allowed to bequeath wealth directly to their grandchildren if the children renounce their inheritance rights. In terms of the *réserve légale* the new law stipulates some changes: The ascendants do not obtain a forced share anymore and the spouse receives one-fourth of the inheritance if the descendant has no children.

These changes to the law can be interpreted as compromises between the principle of equality and the principle of liberty, compromises that take into account economic consequences—preserving the cohesion of landed and industrial wealth—and in which the idea of equal treatment within the family lives on. In spite of the shift in emphasis by the reforms since the early twentieth century, the orientation toward the principle of equality persists. The limitation on testamentary freedom laid down in the Code Civil in 1804 remains in effect to this day. With the law of 2006, especially, possibilities have been created to circumvent these limitations if affected family members consent. The changes enacted in the twentieth century skirt, as it were, the sacral core of the limitation on testamentary freedom, giving consideration to functional necessities without touching on those parts of the law that are especially highly charged symbolically. We are dealing with an interesting form of institutional change in which the "ritual institution" remains formally unchanged, while its actual meaning, however, is progressively eroded by expanded possibilities for deviation from the rules.

Testamentary Freedom in French Inheritance Law

Testamentary freedom assumed great significance in the legal-political discourse in France on two occasions: during the revolutionary period, and from the middle of the 1860s, following publication of the study *Le réforme sociale en France* by Frédéric Le Play. The limitation on testamentary freedom in the Code Civil expressed the normative understanding of necessary legal restrictions on the private autonomy of the testator in the transfer of wealth *mortis causa*. The testator's individual autonomy of action is curtailed so that the relatives in the direct line will have a legal claim to a portion of the estate. Compared to the rules of inheritance under the ancien régime, no expansion of the individual rights of the testator is discernible in the inheritance law of the Code Civil. The *réserve* introduced by the Code Civil constitutes for the vast majority of property transfers *mortis causa* a stronger restriction on individual freedom of disposition than had existed in prerevolutionary legislation. Two connected reasons stand out in this development: the first is the political goal of preventing an excessive concentration of economic power in individual families or the church, which could create power centers outside of the state's central power. The intent is to prevent the return of the aristocracy and break the power of the church.[48] This reflects the strong statist tradition in France.[49] The second reason is the principle of equality that is linked with the Enlightenment and the Revolution. The limitation on testamentary freedom and compulsory real division were intended to realize the equality between firstborn and later-born children and between sons and daughters, thus contributing to egalitarian family relationships.

These two goals both proceed from a conception of property that is oriented toward the common good, a conception that derives the limits to the owner's private autonomy from society's interest in the consequences of individual dispositionary decisions. The state is mandated to maintain strict neutrality vis-à-vis particularistic interests in society and has an obligation only to the common good. This conception of property is confronted during the Revolution and afterwards by a liberal notion of property, according to which interference in testamentary freedom constitutes an inadmissible curtailment of the testator's rights of liberty. It was against this background that delegates in the revolutionary period and after argued against the limitation on testamentary freedom. The mitigation of the restrictions on testamentary freedom following the fall of the Jacobins reveals the ambivalence of the bourgeoisie about implementing the principle of equality in inheritance law. During the restoration, criticism of equal division served the goal of preventing, through undivided testamentary disposition of property, the very division of property intended by the Code Civil, and thus to protect the basis of the old nobility's power.[50]

But when testamentary freedom was again widely discussed in the 1860s, critics of the Code Civil were out to show precisely that the limitation on testamentary freedom was harmful even to the common good: what consequences, they asked, do the regulations of the Code Civil have for the stability of family relationships, for economic development, and for the demography of France? Le Play, who instigated this debate, combined in his argumentation conservative ideas about family relationships with an interest in institutions of inheritance law that would promote the economic development of France and strengthen civil society vis-á-vis the state. In Le Play's eyes, the necessity for later-born children to leave the family farm and take the economic initiative, and the removal of institutional obstacles to a higher birthrate in France, were instruments of a policy of modernization.[51] The combination of a conservative picture of the family and economic modernization expresses very well the ambiguity of the Second Empire. Among wide segments of the public, however, the proposals were seen as an attack on a central achievement of the Revolution, the implementation of the principle of equality in inheritance law, an achievement that had a quasi-sacral status in public awareness. The legitimation of the limitation on testamentary freedom on the basis of the principle of equality made legal reforms more difficult. Of course, the causal links postulated by Le Play can be challenged. But to understand why the numerous parliamentary initiatives that invoked Le Play all failed politically, one must give weight not only to the rational assessment of the arguments, but also to the influence of the cultural symbolic content of the rules limiting testamentary freedom in the Code Civil. The continuing importance of this symbolism finds confirmation also in the fact that the *successful* legal reforms in the twentieth century to reduce the compulsory nature of real division, and to protect businesses against division arising from claims to the *réserve*, carefully skirted the limitations on testamentary freedom in the Code Civil and did *not* directly challenge it. In this way it was possible to avoid a political sacrilege while at the same time adjusting civil law at least in part to changing requirements. The development of testamentary freedom in France shows that the long-term stability of an institution of civil law is based also on its embeddedness within a cultural symbolism that can be invoked as a legitimizing background in political disagreements, and that in actual fact prevents the flexible adjustment of the law.

2.2. GERMANY: TESTAMENTARY FREEDOM VERSUS FAMILY AND SOCIAL JUSTICE

In Germany, too, the issue of testamentary freedom became an important topic of legal and political controversy. What I want to show in this section, however, is that the discursive context that developed in Germany was different from that in France. Criticism of testamentary freedom was not ignited by a threat to natural equality, but by two other aspects: (1) protection of the family against an excessive individualism that found expression in the legal institution of the will and was perceived as a menace to society's moral foundation in the family; (2) the question of how one could create a basis in legal theory for the use of bequests to pursue the goals of social policy.[52]

Critics of testamentary freedom in Germany rejected the will as an alien element that was contrary to the Germanic legal tradition. Germanic law automatically installed the surviving family members as heirs and did not know individual disposition over property (Wegmann 1969, 4; Lübtow 1982, 1ff.).[53] Reference to the Germanic legal tradition thus led to a justification of inheritance law that was derived from family law. Because of their kinship, family members have a right to the assets left behind by the testator, a right that cannot be circumvented. The moral function of inheritance law lies in strengthening the family as the moral foundation of society against an individualism that was regarded as immoral and on the rise.

Of course, the attitude in Germany toward testamentary freedom was not uniform. Its supporters justified it with the principle of individual disposition over private property, which we already know from the French context, a principle that logically had to extend also to the disposition over property *mortis causa* and thus legitimated testamentary freedom.[54]

The discursive field of the clash over testamentary freedom in Germany ranged from the legitimation of unlimited freedom for the testator, at one end of the spectrum, to a legal position focusing on the rights of the family and of society to property, at the other. The stipulation of testamentary freedom in the Civil Code (Bürgerliches Gesetzbuch, BGB) was preceded by a legal and political quarrel that was carried on throughout the nineteenth century against this backdrop; however, that quarrel was not carried on chiefly in parliamentary bodies, but in a jurisprudential and social-scientific discourse. The conflict between the opposing positions was on display especially in the last third of the nineteenth century. This period saw processes of fundamental social change (the rapid spread of economic relationships that were disconnected from the family and more strongly individualized), the resulting social consequences (discussed under the theme of the "social question"), and the creation of the Civil Code.

In the following section, I will first trace the development of the legal and political debate in Germany, and then discuss the conflicts over inheritance law connected with the creation of the BGB in the last quarter of the nineteenth century. The last section will give an account of the revival of this controversy—nearly forty years after work on the BGB was completed—in the reforms of inheritance law by the National Socialists; in the process, I will also show the long-term effects of the conflict structures that arose in the early nineteenth century. Along the way I will bring out the differences and similarities with the development in France, and discuss what importance the structures of discourse had for the regulation of testamentary freedom and the law of the *Pflichtteil* (obligatory portion) in German inheritance law.

The Legal-Philosophical Justification of Inheritance Law

Contrary to what one might expect against the backdrop of the individualization thesis, we find stronger individualistic legal notions at the *beginning* of the legal-political discourse on testamentary freedom in Germany. Legal philosophers of the seventeenth and eighteenth centuries derived the justification of inheritance law chiefly from the law of property and saw testamentary freedom as part of natural law. They demonstrated the link between property and testamentary freedom by deriving the right to dispose over property even after death from the right of the owner to dispose freely over this property as he saw fit. This justification of testamentary freedom on the basis of the conception of property was propounded in the seventeenth century by Hugo Grotius, for example, and in the eighteenth century by Christian Wolff (see Klippel 1984, 120). Grotius saw the testament as an irrevocable disposal in case of death, in which the usufruct of the property is withheld until death. Kant (1965 [1797], §34), too, proceeded from the individual disposition over the inheritance by the testator by positing "the transfer (*translatio*) of the possessions of a dying person to the survivors through the agreement of the will of both" as the foundation of inheritance law. For Kant, testaments were valid by natural law.

However, as early as the seventeenth century this natural-law grounding of inheritance law and testamentary freedom in the law of property became itself the target of criticism within the natural law tradition. The decisive development in this regard emanated from Samuel Pufendorf.[55] For Pufendorf, the right of ownership expires with the death of the owner, which is why there is in fact no justification for testamentary freedom in natural law. Instead, testamentary freedom had to be anchored in positive law. Pufendorf, like Montesquieu in France, thus provided a legal-philosophical justification for the shaping of inheritance law by positive law. Influenced by Montesquieu and Rousseau, this position was then developed further by Fichte (2000 [1796], 318), who saw neither inheritance nor property as based in natural law, thus laying the legal-philosophical foundation that made it possible for inheritance law to become the object of any arbitrary determination by the state.[56]

In the eighteenth century, however, it was not only testamentary freedom that was largely derived from the will of the owner, but also the inheritance right of the family (Klippel 1984, 121). For both jurists who derived the institution of testamentary freedom from natural law, and those who assigned it to positive law, intestacy law was justified as the *presumed* last will of the testator. What that meant is that in the absence of a testament, one could presume that the individual testamentary disposition of a reasonable person would not diverge substantially from succession under the law. Now the important point is not that the divergent positions on natural law came together in a uniform stance on testamentary freedom—this is precisely something they do *not* do—but that the codification of inheritance law is derived *from the will of the individual* and not from the moral functions of the family or from the common good.

> Even the intestacy law is built upon the presumed will of the individual, and even the rejection of inheritance law is based on the argument that death puts an end to the will and rights of the individual. To the extent that a natural inheritance right (testamentary freedom and/or intestate succession) is affirmed, it too rests on the foundations of the individualism of the Enlightenment. (Klippel 1984, 128)[57]

This *individualistic justification of inheritance law*, which predominated until the late eighteenth century, was displaced in the nineteenth century by a position that emphasized the clan or family, a position that was skeptical toward the institution of the testament. However, in Germany, unlike in France, it was not the principle of natural equality that was at the forefront of the rejection of testamentary freedom, but the protection of the family as the moral foundation of society.[58] The rejection of testamentary freedom and the justification of inheritance law on the basis of family law was directed against the spread of individual license, which was perceived as a threat; the cohesion of the family was seen as the guarantor against bourgeois individualism. At the same time, the orientation toward family policy was not focused—again in contrast to France—on the order of the state as the supraordinated goal; instead, its ultimate end lay directly in the protection of the family itself, especially vis-à-vis the state. Moreover, the justification of inheritance law on the basis of family law served in the second half of the nineteenth century as a vehicle for the demand that inheritance law be used for social reforms aimed at achieving greater *social justice*.

In the nineteenth century, the justification of inheritance law on the basis of family law acquired "general dominance in all of the more recent legal philosophy" (Bruns 1882, 144). The starting point for the altered justification of inheritance law and for the legal-philosophical critique of testamentary freedom that went hand in hand with it was, in particular, Hegel's philosophy of law. In a reversal of the natural law arguments of Grotius and Wolff, Hegel perceived the foundation of inheritance law no longer in the individual will of the testator, but in the family (Tschäppeler 1983, 60; Wegmann 1969, 10).[59]

The starting point is Hegel's concept of the ethical nature of the family and his conception of property that corresponded to it. The arbitrary moment of abstract property, in which the "mere individual" (*bloß Einzelne*) fulfills his desire and his self-interest by taking possession of or disposing of property, is transcended in the ethical relationship of the family, because acquisition is driven by concern over something that is shared and in common. Family wealth is joint wealth and should be seen under the aspect of the ethical bonds between family members:

> These [family resources] are common property, so that no member of the family has particular property, although each has a right to what is held in common. (Hegel 1991 [1821], §171)

In death a person exits the family group, though no real transfer of property takes place as a result. Instead, the surviving family members enter into the rights of the deceased.

> The natural dissolution of the family through the death of the parents, particularly of the husband, results in *inheritance* of the family's resources. Inheritance is essentially a taking possession by the individual as his own property of what *in themselves* are common resources. (§178)

Although in Hegel's eyes family property emerges as "the abstract moment of *determinate individuality* [*Einzelheit*]" (§159) upon the dissolution of the family, thus becoming individual property, that does not establish an individual right to the disposition over property that stands above the right of the family. To be sure, when the family is dissolved, property must be reallocated, but the reallocation arises from the circumstances of the testator's family and cannot be an arbitrary (i.e., testamentary) one; if it were arbitrary it would be unethical. In this way, the justification of inheritance law from family law leads to the broad rejection of testamentary freedom, which is conceded only in cases in which the testator has no close kin relationships.[60]

> The simple direct arbitrariness of the deceased cannot be made the principle of the *right to make a will*, especially if it is opposed to the substantial right of the family; for the love and veneration of the family for its former member are primarily the only guarantee that his arbitrary will will be respected after his death. Such arbitrariness in itself contains nothing which deserves greater respect than the right of the family itself—on the contrary. (§180)

In Hegel, as in other German legal philosophers of the nineteenth century, the rejection of too much individual freedom of action in inheritance law is set within the context of the repudiation of Roman law, which was branded as individualistic, and in opposition to which stood German or Germanic law.[61] Hegel rejected above all the individualism of Roman law, which was, after all, the source from which the legal institution of the testament was derived in all later legal codifications. For example, in Hegel's interpretation of Roman law, the father ruled over his wife, children, and the family property as he saw fit, though this situation weakened the ethical nature of family circumstances. Here we can leave open the question of whether Hegel's interpretation does justice to Roman law.[62] Be that as it may, Hegel puts forth arguments that would be picked up time and again in the German discussion over inheritance law in the nineteenth and early twentieth centuries, including parliamentary debates. The right of the family to inherit was conceived of as the original German inheritance law, while the institution of the testament—which hailed from Roman law—seemed like an alien body.[63] An important part of the development in legal philosophy in the early nineteenth century thus provides no legitimization for an expansion of individual freedom of testamentary disposition, but calls for its limitation.

Testamentary Freedom and the Conception of Familial Property in the Nineteenth Century

The legal-philosophical position on inheritance law developed by Hegel was highly influential during the nineteenth century. Of course, testamentary freedom continued to have its defenders in Germany, who derived it from the law of property. What I intend to show here, however, is that the *critique* of testamentary freedom was based substantially on the family-oriented arguments put forth by Hegel, thus contributing to the development of a specific way of looking at the issue of testamentary freedom that was different from the French perspective.

The diffusion of Hegel's criticism of testamentary freedom in the nineteenth century can be traced in the legal-theoretical literature.[64] Eduard Gans, Hegel's successor in Berlin, provided a historical underpinning to the precedence of intestacy law over the testament by demonstrating that among all peoples, dispositions by will played merely a subordinated role vis-à-vis the rights of the family.[65] Gans called for a reform of the Allgemeines Landrecht on the basis of the principles of the French Code Civil and the distinction it contained between the *quotité disponible* and the *réserve* that was excluded from testamentary freedom (Schröder 1981, 443; Welker 1982, 70ff.). In the middle of the nineteenth century, the conservative legal scholar Friedrich Julius Stahl, in his *Philosophie des Rechts* (Philosophy of Law, 1845), agreeing with Hegel, also saw inheritance law as grounded in the family, which meant that testaments could only play a secondary role. The testament, he argued, could not have the function of a disposition over property, but at best that of freely mirroring the natural family situation, comparable to adoption. For Stahl, children continued the personality of the parents and were therefore the natural recipients of their property (Stahl 1845, 383).[66]

At times, the rejection of an individualistic foundation of inheritance law is also found in those writers who were willing to accord greater importance to testamentary freedom. The jurist Karl David August Röder (1806–79), in his work on legal philosophy published in 1846, placed intestacy law and testamentary freedom side by side, though he gave clear priority to the family in inheritance law, a priority that imposed limits on individual arbitrariness.[67] Otto von Gierke's critique (1889) of the draft of the section on inheritance law in the Civil Code was also based on the connection between protection for the family and limitations on testamentary freedom:

> In the German conception, inheritance law is based on family law, while the Roman notion grounds all inheritance law in the declared or presumed will of the individual that is effective beyond death. We have absorbed Roman testamentary freedom into our awareness and in part into our customs and cannot break with it. But unless we wish to throw the entire future of this inheritance law into doubt, we must never construct it on the basis of the individual will! ... The incomparably valuable social function and the immortal inner justification of inheritance law lies only in the realization of the succession of generations inherent in the natural structure of the family, in the assumption of the now empty place by those individuals most immediately destined to do so by virtue of the structure of the social body. (Gierke 1948 [1889], 29–30)

By highlighting the importance of the family-oriented justification of inheritance law in Germany, I do not mean to suggest that testamentary freedom had no legal champions in the nineteenth century. There are many examples of such champions,[68] and on the whole it is true to say that most jurists did not favor the *abolition* of testamentary freedom, but differed chiefly in the scope of the restrictions that should be placed on it (Bruns 1882, 187ff.). In contrast to the justifications of inheritance law that were dominant in the eighteenth century, the primary starting point, however, is no longer the individual rights of the testator, but family law. Therein lies an important departure, one that differentiates the German discussion on inheritance law from the discourses in France and the United States,[69] and which has repercussions for how the concrete functional attributions of inheritance law are perceived.

One exception to the argumentative nexus of a family-orientation and limitations on inheritance rights is the work of Wilhelm Heinrich Riehl, a scholar of the family. In his book *Die Familie* (The Family, 1855), Riehl spoke out in support of preserving and promoting familial values, though to achieve that goal he demanded—just as Le Play did in France at the same time—the *expansion* of testamentary freedom. He argued that the welfare of the family had to be placed above the individual interests of the various family members, which required the patriarchal authority of the family father, an authority that was based substantially on the maintenance of family continuity.[70] Riehl, too, was shaped by the high regard for the family that was characteristic of Germany in the Biedermeier period (Nipperdey 1983, 122). His normative background was the ideal of the family structure of the "whole house," by which were meant structures of the extended family in which patriarchal relationships emanating from the father prevailed, though they also represented systems of solidarity for the weaker family members. From these family structures Riehl distinguished the spreading nuclear family, which consists only of two generations and in which children of majority age leave the house right away. These new families lead to loneliness and individualism.

For Riehl, inheritance law played a decisive role in this development. For it was chiefly in regions of Germany in which *Anerbenrecht* still existed—farms were passed on undivided—that the family type of the "whole house" could still be found, whereas the nuclear families were spreading in the regions of real division in the southwest. Riehl thus also placed the family at the center of the justification for inheritance law. But in contrast to the usual nexus of family and limits on testamentary freedom, Riehl demanded unrestricted testamentary freedom, as this would make possible the preservation of farms undivided and promote his preferred family structure. Although this link between family and testamentary freedom is untypical for the discourse on inheritance law in Germany, it, too, reveals the important role that the connection between family and property played in justifying the proposals for reforms to inheritance law. Riehl is an exception only in his perception of the causal relationship between family and testamentary freedom. To that extent, his argumentation corresponds to that of Le Play. At the same time, a significant difference from Le Play is evident. While for Le Play, and within the French discursive context in general, the family was often seen as the germ cell of the *political order*[71] (whether republican or authoritarian), Riehl saw the family as the germ cell of society, that is, as distinct from the state (Schwägler 1970, 35). Protecting the ethical nature of the family itself is the primary goal of legislation, not the consequences for the political order of the state that can be derived from it. The family is supposed to make possible precisely the stability and identity that guarantee independence vis-à-vis the state and the economic sphere, which is seen as alienating.

Testamentary Freedom and Social Policy

The link between testamentary freedom and an unbridled individualism, the juxtaposition of German and Roman law, and the emphasis on the moral nature of the family formed central points of reference for the discourse on inheritance law in Germany. This moved the consequences that the regulation of inheritance law had for the family into the center of the debate. As a rule, this did not lead to the demand for the *abolition* of testamentary freedom, but it did give rise to the claim that the family and intestacy law took precedence.

And yet the family-oriented justification of the limitation on testamentary freedom in Germany is not aimed solely at the family. Rejecting the justification of inheritance law on the basis of the law of individual property also made it possible to legitimize intervention into inherited wealth that was motivated by sociopolitical considerations. If inheritance law could not be derived solely from the rights of the testator, it was only one more step beyond the claims of the family to legitimize also the claims that society could make upon the distribution of the inherited property. At this point, the justification of inheritance law and the conception of property merge with the goals of reformist interventions in the existing social structures.

This connection becomes clear, for example, in Adolf Samter (1879, 253), a banker and member of the Verein für Socialpolitik (Association for Social Policy). He spoke of a "dual principle" of property that found expression in the limitation on testamentary freedom, namely "that the property of a family member *does not belong exclusively to him*, is not exclusively private property, but also has a societal quality about it."[72] This conception of inheritance law, emphasizing that inheritance law is embedded within a social context, is linked to a parallel conception of property. If one compares the evolution of the discourse on the justification of inheritance law with the evolution of the notion of property in Germany, the parallels become obvious, parallels that point to a connection between the family-oriented argumentation of the discourse on inheritance law and ideas about sociopolitical reforms.

In the conception of property, just as in the discourse on inheritance law, one can find in the nineteenth century a general development from a predominantly liberal thinking to an argumentation that moved society front and center. To put it in abbreviated and simplified terms: the liberal theory of property that went back, in Germany, to Grotius, Pufendorf, and Kant enjoyed continued acceptance only in the early nineteenth century, after which time the idea that property had societal obligations moved increasingly into the foreground.

> The critique of the liberal notion of property concerned chiefly the postulated unrestricted nature of property and—connected with it—its inviolability from state measures, which would have made social reform legally impossible. (Schwab 1975, 106)

The developing doctrines of social obligations stemming from private property were based on the principle that property does not already exist in the state of nature, but is created by the state—much as Montesquieu, Rousseau, and the other proponents of a radical limitation of testamentary freedom had argued in the debate of the constitutional assembly in France in 1791. In Germany at the end of the eighteenth century, this position was taken, for example, by Fichte: "It is the state alone that unites an undetermined mass of people into a coherent whole, into a collective (*Allheit*); it is the state alone that can question all those it accepts into its union (*Bund*); and thus it alone established legally valid property" (Fichte 1979 [1800], 15).

In Germany, as in France, situating property law within positive law was an important source for legitimating socio-reformist interventions in individual property rights to promote the common good (Ritter 1996, 47ff; Schwab 1975, 106ff.). The idea that property had an obligation toward the common good gained wide acceptance in Germany especially after 1850, and it is reflected in such diverse manifestations as the theory of association (*Genossenschaft*) (Gierke 1873), social Catholicism (among others, Ketteler 1977 [1872]), and the conception of property held by important representatives of the German Historical School. As Adolph Wagner put it in 1894:

> The question is not what are the individual's "natural" rights of liberty, and what form of property and contract law, as well as of all of property law, is demanded by the individual conceived of as absolute, and only after that, what rights does "society" have toward the individual and his property. The reverse is the case: what are the conditions of social order . . . ? How, therefore, must the individual's sphere of freedom, property law, the rules of property and contracts be regulated in consideration of those conditions—which must be fulfilled above all else—of social and economic order? (Wagner 1894, 12)[73]

In the discussion over property law, as well, critics juxtaposed individualistic Roman law and Germanic law, which would have a social orientation and correspond to the characteristic cultural quality of the Germans.

Beginning in the 1870s, the growing critical view of the liberal conception of property influenced legal changes, some of which affected inheritance law. This included especially the reintroduction of *Anerbenrecht* (right to inherit a farm undivided) in the agricultural sector, and the creation of a form of encumbered property with *Rentengüter* (land held in perpetuity against payment of a fixed rental) (Merk 1934, 38ff).[74] The full extent of this reorientation in property law becomes apparent only when one includes other restrictions that were also put in place at that time: public-law restrictions on property, laws to protect monuments and landscapes, and the revival of *Erbbaurecht* (heritable right to erect and maintain a building on another's person's property) (Merk 1934, 38ff.). These tendencies within property law placed the embeddedness of property owners within a social context at the center of considerations of reform.

The goals of social reform were rarely articulated directly in the discourse on testamentary freedom. However, one can show that the dominant topoi of family cohesiveness—directed against a rampant individualism—and of Germanic versus Roman legal traditions were also "codes" that referred back to the conception of property held by the social reformers. Scholars of Germanic law claimed that the liberal notion of property had an asocial character, and by their criticism they sought to prove the existence of a tradition of property that was not absolute and genuinely German-social (Schwab 1975, 107). The decision to invoke questions of legal tradition rather than argue directly with socio-reformist goals had political reasons. Depicting Germanic law as a socially just law made it possible, in the discussion over the Civil Code, for example, "to criticize the social implications of the draft without having to use arguments from the socialist realm.

Germanic traditions were highly regarded in the Second Empire. Invoking this value was thus entirely above suspicion" (Schröder 1981, 147). Thus the justification of inheritance law on the basis of family law also functioned to legitimize sociopolitically motivated interference in testamentary freedom.

Testamentary Freedom in the Creation of the Civil Code

What actual influence did this general background of legal philosophy and legal policy exert on the codification of testamentary freedom in Germany? Testamentary freedom was enshrined in all civil law codes that were valid in the nineteenth century in the various German states. The strongest restrictions existed in the southwestern parts of the country, where the regulations of the Code Civil remained in force even after the end of French occupation.[75]

After unification in 1871, Germany remained fractured into a multitude of legal spheres. However, two years later, the Bundesrat decided to transfer the lawmaking competency for civil law to the Reich and to have a uniform civil law drawn up for Germany. This process of creating the Civil Code, which stretched from 1874 to 1896, promises to yield the most revealing insights into how the debates over legal philosophy and legal policy entered into the actual codification of testamentary freedom. The redaction of the Civil Code is indeed the key event for the codification of inheritance law in Germany—comparable to the creation of the Code Civil for France one hundred years earlier. The Civil Code regulations on inheritance law have remained valid to this day without significant changes. In contrast to France, however, the creation of the Civil Code has left hardly any traces in parliamentary debates. To be sure, the work of the expert commission of jurists (which lasted a quarter of a century) was eventually approved by the Reichstag in 1896, though without any significant parliamentary discussion. That is why the history of how the law came to be codified cannot be reconstructed from parliamentary debates, but only from the documents of the commission and the legal commentaries on the drafts of the laws.

A commission was charged with drawing up the Civil Code. It was formed in 1874 and had eleven members; one redactor was appointed to oversee the work on each subsection of private law. In the case of inheritance law it was the Bavarian *Ministerialrat* Dr. Gottfried Schmitt, who presented a draft to the commission in 1879 (Mertens 1970, 11). The draft was based on the principles of testamentary freedom, the right to an obligatory portion, the succession of relatives, and the form of testamentary dispositions as laid down by the commission as a whole as early as 1875 (Mertens 1970, 10). Studies that have dealt in detail with the creation of the draft on inheritance law for the Civil Code (Mertens 1970; Schröder 1981) have shown how earnestly the redactor Schmitt tried to depoliticize the work. In keeping with his task,[76] Schmitt was concerned solely with standardizing the existing legal conditions, and he utterly rejected incorporating the use of inheritance law as an instrument of reform, as was being discussed in legal philosophy. However, Schröder (1981), in particular, has shown that this depoliticized self-conception on Schmitt's part accorded only in part with his actual work. The reason was that Schmitt naturally had to proceed from certain foundations in inheritance law, and in choosing them he automatically took certain positions within the discourse on inheritance law.

It is surprising, given the legal-theoretical debate in Germany, that Schmitt—and the commission entrusting him with this task—proceeded from the principle of grounding inheritance law in the will of the testator. By anchoring inheritance law in the free will of the individual, Schmitt and the commission were rejecting the justification of inheritance law on the basis of family law. The very first paragraph of the first commission draft already lays down the precedence of freely determined succession: "Everyone has the right to dispose over this wealth *mortis causa* by means of a unilateral declaration" (§1 TE, quoted in Mertens 1970, 36). However, the grounding of inheritance law in the will of the testator is evident not only from the way testamentary freedom is framed, but also in Schmitt's legal justification of the obligatory portion, by which testamentary freedom was limited. He did *not* derive the obligatory portion from an obligation of parents toward their children, but from the fact that the will of the testator had committed itself by marriage and the begetting of children (Mertens 1970, 84).

And yet even Schmitt, despite the individualistic justification of inheritance law, clearly referred back to the family. This becomes evident in the positive reference to Frédéric Le Play, who sought to preserve traditional family structures and *to that end* called for complete testamentary freedom. At the same time, it reveals just how strong a point of reference for legal justification the family was within the German discourse on inheritance law: even economically liberal jurists had little choice but to derive the legitimacy of the rules of inheritance law from the consequences they would have for the family.

The unambiguous commitment to the individualistic starting point in justifying inheritance law met with opposition from the commission.[77] The controversy was not over whether testamentary freedom should be anchored in the Civil Code, but over the legal-philosophical question of whether the will of the testator could serve as the ideational starting point for all of inheritance law (Mertens 1970, 36). The commission was unable to come to an agreement on this, whereupon it decided, by way of compromise, to leave the draft largely unchanged while at the same time forgoing any legal-philosophical justification of the statutory inheritance law. That, however, did not put an end to the debate. For the question of how to justify inheritance law—from the will of the individual or on the basis of family law—became the central point of attack for legal critics of the draft after it was published. The important response by Otto von Gierke (1889, 505ff.) focused on the structure of the draft, in which the freely determined succession continued to hold priority. Gierke recognized in this a structure that corresponded to the "Roman consciousness," which he rejected as individualistic. He countered it with his own vision of what inheritance law should be, quoting in part an earlier speech by himself:

> Our national perspective, which alone will guarantee a future for inheritance law, is different. "What appears to us as the primeval source of inheritance law is the organic interconnection of the succession of generations, which encompasses individuals and binds them together, and thus above all the family bond, which takes hold of individuals by virtue of the law and is removed from their arbitrary will. That is why we consider as the normal type of succession the entry into the vacated place that is realized in accordance with the fixed order of the given conditions of the law of persons and by virtue of statutory rules, whereas we see the testamentary freedom that is granted to the individual as merely the means for adjusting the rigid rule of the law to the concrete situation." (Gierke 1889, 506–7)

This opinion was shared by most of the other critics of the commission's draft, and there were only a few scattered voices that approved of the individualistic approach to the justification of inheritance law (Mertens 1970, 39).

What is noticeable about the legal critiques of the strong position that testamentary freedom held in the draft of the Civil Code—especially in comparison with the French debates a hundred years earlier—is how strongly they referred to purely legal-philosophical considerations, and how little sociopolitical goals were *directly* addressed. This can be understood as a form of the already mentioned political coding of the discourse as a result of the conservative political atmosphere and structure in the empire. Social scientists were more likely to directly address aspects of the codification of inheritance law that were relevant to considerations of social reform. The economist Hans von Scheel (1877c, 97), for example, saw in the codification of inheritance law "the possibility of having an ameliorating effect on the distribution of property, in the sense of justice and the national economic welfare," which also required limits on individual arbitrariness. Adolph Wagner (1894, 38) criticized testamentary freedom smugly as the exaggeration of the "lovely, pious principle of 'respect for the dead.'" Anton Menger (1927 [1890]) opposed the aristocratizing tendencies that could arise from testamentary freedom. The critics were picking up motifs that had been introduced into the German discourse on inheritance law since the 1840s by writers like Robert Blum, Julius Fröbel, Theodor Hilgard, and Paul Achatius Pfizer.[78] Discernible in the opposition to testamentary freedom justified by goals of social policy, as in the legal-philosophical rejection of the individualistic justification of inheritance law, is a conception of property that has social-reformist goals and is directed against the individualistic-liberal notion of property.

In response to the critique that the structure of the proposed law reflected Roman legal thinking, the second draft had an entirely different structure. It became the basis of the Civil Code's section on inheritance law, which exists largely unchanged to this day. It begins with a general part on "succession," which regulates both intestate succession as well as the principles of freely determined succession. The will is dealt with in the third part, the law of the compulsory portion in the fifth. Unlike the French Code Civil, the law of the compulsory portion does not establish a ratio of the estate that is freely disposable by testament; instead, it lays down a share of the inheritance to which all legitimate heirs are entitled even if they have been testamentarily excluded from the inheritance, or if the share of the assets provided for in the testament is smaller. The compulsory portion is set at half the statutory inheritance portion. Those entitled to the compulsory portion are the surviving spouse, the testator's direct descendants, and, if no descendants exist, the parents. The compulsory portion in a sense mediates between the individual license of testamentary freedom and family law. That the compulsory portions led to a far smaller limitation on testamentary freedom than in France can be demonstrated with the following example: if the testator has three children and no surviving spouse, under French law only 25% of the estate can be passed down in a way that deviates from intestacy law; under German law the share is 50%.

The second commission made no further reflections on the ideational basis of inheritance law and tried to create the impression that the draft "offered no indications for a decision in favor of the will of the testator or in favor of the family's right of inheritance" (Mertens 1970, 40). Since the second draft contained hardly any substantive changes from the first one, this neutrality is more apparent than real: in the first commission, the redactor Schmitt derived the substantive regulations that eventually became law from a justification of inheritance law on the basis of the testator's individual will (Schröder 1981). If one compares this systematic starting point with the codification of inheritance law in the Code Civil, it becomes clear that testamentary freedom—while granted in both legal texts—holds a very different place: whereas the German Civil Code proceeds from testamentary freedom that is then limited by the law of the compulsory portion, in the French Code Civil the compulsory partition of the inheritance is the rule, with free disposition constituting the exception.

The linkage between testamentary freedom (§1937) and the law of the compulsory portion (§§ 2302–38) in the Civil Code was not a legal innovation in Germany. Testamentary freedom, along with limitations in favor of direct family members, was also enshrined in the private law of the constituent states, for example in the Allgemeines Landrecht in Prussia (Welker 1982, 76f.). The legal institution of the testament, adopted from Roman law, had been used in Germany since the Middle Ages. The Constitution of St. Paul's Church from 1848 (§165) also included testamentary freedom (Conrad 1954, 552ff.; Schröder 1981, 220ff.). Compared to the Prussian Allgemeines Landrecht (ALR), the compulsory portion in the Civil Code was higher for the children if there were few siblings (ALR: one-third of the intestate portion by up to two children), and lower if there were at least four siblings (ALR: two-thirds of the intestate share) (Miaskowski 1882a, 230; Zürn 1892, 123). For spouses, the compulsory portion was half of the statutory inheritance portion in both the ALR and the Civil Code. These alterations cannot be interpreted as a fundamental change. We therefore see, in Germany as well, a great continuity of stipulations of inheritance law, which, in spite of processes of fundamental social and economic transformations, remained relatively stable within a path that had already been charted long before the nineteenth century.

At the same time, the juxtaposition of the legal-philosophical debate about testamentary freedom in the nineteenth century with the laws on testamentary freedom in the Civil Code reveals a striking divergence. Given the contemporary discourse on legal policy and legal philosophy, one would have expected the inheritance law in the Civil Code to be structured much more strongly on the basis of family law, without the possibility of (limited) testamentary disposition being ruled out. The commission, however, at least the important first commission, proceeded in its work clearly on the basis of an individual derivation of inheritance law and justified even intestate succession on the basis of the testator's will. Presumably, this divergence can be attributed to the fact that the formulation of laws by the high-ranking civil servants charged with that task was fairly immune to the public legal discourse. But what is the explanation for this phenomenon?

Given the small number of people who were charged with redacting the various areas of the law, a first explanation can be found no doubt in the personality of the redactor of the first commission, Gottfried Schmitt. Schmitt was guided by the liberal justification of inheritance law and saw its grounding in family law as being out of step with the times. A second line of explanation lies in the depoliticized charge to the commission, which could have led it to the alternative justification on the basis of the rights of the individual. After all, it was precisely the family-law justification of inheritance law that was linked to social reforms in the public discussion over inheritance law, because it offered a basis for legitimizing interventions in the transfer of property *mortis causa* to generate the financial means for sociopolitical reforms. As I have already argued, the depoliticized self-conception of the commission's task certainly did not amount to political neutrality. Schmitt was pursuing politically conservative goals at least implicitly by seeking to exclude any use of the inheritance law to carry out social reforms (Mertens 1970, 56). Whatever the reason—whether it was direct political influence[79] or the commission's understanding of its task—when it came to the question of codifying inheritance law in the Civil Code, the conservative forces were able to prevail against the voices of social reform that were loud and clear in the public discourse. To that extent, Anton Menger's critique of the first commission draft (1927 [1890]) as excessively conservative is understandable.

However, this interpretation applies only to the blocking of social reform measures with the help of the codification of inheritance law, not to the development of the law as such. For the justification of testamentary freedom on the basis of the testator's free will can be understood as a more modern codification vis-à-vis the justification derived from family law, one in which the "moral individualism" (Durkheim) of modern society finds expression. From this perspective, the inheritance law of the Civil Code can be seen as a modernizing push against structuring the law on the principle of family property, which was very important in the legal-political discourse.[80]

The section on inheritance law hardly figured in the parliamentary deliberations of the Reichstag on the draft of the Civil Code. The speakers barely mentioned it during the general deliberation of the Civil Code between 3 and 6 February 1896, and in the second and third reading (27 June and 1 July 1896), the only questions that were debated at length concerned the form of testation and the succession of spouses.[81] The question of whether this was a "German-legal draft" was raised only by the delegate Kaufmann and answered in the affirmative (*Stenographische Berichte des Reichstags*, 9. Legislaturperiode, 4. Ses., 731). The minor attention given to inheritance law in the Reichstag debate suggests that the adopted regulations were largely uncontroversial in parliament. Though building on the individual justification of inheritance law, Book 5 of the Civil Code represented a compromise between complete testamentary freedom and its limitation through the compulsory portion, a compromise that was supported by various parties. Testamentary freedom—constrained by the compulsory portion—was thus enshrined in the new civil law. At the same time, however, the criticism of testamentary freedom from the perspective of family property by no means fell silent. These critical arguments appeared in political debates even decades later, especially those concerning the law of inheritance tax.[82] After the introduction of the Civil Code on 1 January 1900, testamentary freedom itself was only once the target of criticism that was significant in terms of legal policy: this criticism came from the side of the National Socialist ideology of community.

Testamentary Freedom under National Socialism

During the Weimar Republic, the stipulations on inheritance law in the Civil Code remained in force and were also constitutionally guaranteed in Article 154 of the Weimar Constitution: "The right of inheritance is guaranteed according to civil law. The state's share in the inheritance is determined by the laws." Controversial discussions about inheritance law continued in the late empire and the Weimar Republic, though they no longer revolved chiefly around the question of testamentary freedom. Instead, the primary focus was on questions of inheritance taxation and the state's right to inherit, which are discussed in detail in chapter 5. It was only under National Socialist rule that testamentary freedom was once again drawn into the sphere of reforms to inheritance law.

The National Socialists aimed at a comprehensive reform of civil law that was supposed to replace the existing Civil Code with a newly developed Volksgesetzbuch (People's Book of Law). Although that book was never enacted,[83] beginning in the summer of 1933, the Academy for German Law newly set up by the Nazis devoted itself to this legal project. A committee was set up to deal with the reform of inheritance law (Wacker 1997, 36). The reports of this commission and the laws that were enacted provide insights into how the National Socialists injected their ideology of community and race into inheritance law. National Socialist critique of the inheritance law in the Civil Code focused on the lopsided preference it gave to testamentary succession, which it regarded as the expression of a basic individualistic and materialistic attitude that was to be rejected (Hütte 1988, 24). Instead, the justification of inheritance law should be derived from the law of the family and the community. We can see in this a reference to strands of argumentation that had already shaped the debate over the Civil Code. The inheritance law committee used some arguments that "Germanists" had already advanced in the nineteenth century. However, it gave them a completely different thrust by blending them with the Nazi ideology of national community and racism. In the eyes of the National Socialist jurists, the function of inheritance law was "primarily the transmission of wealth within the family, the clan, and the national community; the testator, as the conduit between past and present, was merely seen as the trustee of the overarching community" (Hütte 1988, 136). The ideology of the national community justified limiting testamentary freedom. Although testamentary freedom was not to be abolished, the goal was to prevent testaments that ran counter to the interests of the family or the national community (Hütte 1988, 144). The first step toward achieving that goal was to restrict the multitude of testamentary forms by mandating—as a way of exerting more control over the testator—that testaments could be drawn up only publicly and no longer by hand. However, the testament law of 1938 opted for another way to achieve this goal, making it easier to declare testaments null and void:

> A disposition by virtue of death is null and void if it violates, in a way that is grossly contrary to proper Volk feeling (*gesundes Volksempfinden*), the considerations that a responsible testator must demonstrate toward family and national community. (§48 II Testiergesetz, qtd. in Hütte 1988, 186)

By grossly inappropriate dispositions it meant "bequests to a mistress while disadvantaging the family, bequests of family jewelry or family heirlooms to strangers, bequests to organizations hostile to the state, as well as the appointment of a Jew as heir by an Aryan who bypasses close relatives" (186). In this case, Nazi racial ideology found its way into the regulations governing testamentary freedom, something that is also evident in other stipulations regarding inheritance law enacted by the National Socialists. As early as 1937, the "law on restrictions on inheritance law on account of behavior hostile to the community" decreed that expatriates who took part in "anti-German smear campaigns" could not acquire anything from a German by death or as a gift. In 1941 this was extended to all Jews who had emigrated (Hütte 1988, 184). The law of 1937, by which the Nuremberg race laws of 1935 were implemented in inheritance law, also made it possible to revoke the compulsory portion if the person entitled to it was married to a Jew or, without official permission, to a "Jewish *Mischling* [mixed-blood person]" (255).

Paragraph 48 II of the testation law of 1938 was repealed in October 1946 by Allied Control Council Law 37. The rest of the testation law remained valid and was taken over into the Civil Code in 1953 (Schliepkorte 1989, 239ff.). Testamentary freedom is given in the Federal Republic of Germany within the framework of the stipulations of the Civil Code and protected constitutionally (with some restrictions) by Articles 14 and 2 of the Basic Law (Quebe 1993, 42ff.).

Testamentary Freedom and Social Reform

The development of the legal regulations on testamentary freedom and compulsory portions in Germany reveals a remarkable continuity. To be sure, during the last two hundred years, testamentary freedom has been a variously contested institution that has provoked clashes over legal policy, yet the existing rules have remained largely untouched. Neither the conflict between an individualistic and a family-oriented justification of inheritance law, nor the Nazi ideology of the *Volk* community, exerted any lasting influence on the existing law.[84] In essence, regulations of testamentary freedom derived from Roman law, supplemented with the compulsory portion, exist to this day; they spread through the sphere of German law from the early modern period (Landau 1997). Even the economic and social push toward modernization since the middle of the nineteenth century, with its far-reaching processes of transformation, hardly influenced legal developments. The expectation of a broadening of the individual dispositionary rights of the testator—expected by modernization theory—was fulfilled in the actual development of the law only in the sense that demands for an ever stronger restriction on testamentary freedom, apart from a few exceptions especially in farmers' inheritance law, were not implemented. However, a widening of individual dispositionary rights as an accommodation to altered social structures has not occurred during the last two hundred years.

This confirms for Germany what has already emerged in the case of France, namely a long-term continuity in inheritance law, even across fundamental political and economic upheavals. At the same time, this means that the differences between the two legal systems that existed already two hundred years ago—especially the tighter restriction on testamentary freedom in France—did not lessen in a movement of convergence, but remained in place over a long period. A legal harmonization between France and Germany occurred only in the southwestern states that introduced the French Code Civil after the occupation of Napoleon and retained it until the introduction of the German Civil Code. Put in general terms, this points to the opportunities for substantial legal changes from *external legal intervention*.

The analysis of the discourse on testamentary freedom allows us to get a clearer grasp of the developmental processes and how they differed in the two countries. For example, we have seen that the question of testamentary freedom led to clashes over legal policy when the respective systems of private law were codified (Code Civil and Civil Code), which comes as no surprise. In France, however, the conflict erupted again during the Second Empire. Once again, a link was made between the development of society and testamentary freedom, without any fundamental reform of the system of private law providing the impetus behind it this time. This revival of the question of testamentary freedom in France ran parallel to—but largely independent of—the intensification of this debate in Germany, which coincided after 1873 with the codification of the Civil Code. In both countries, the question of testamentary freedom became a topic of social policy when the process of industrialization picked up steam.

The reason behind this simultaneity is presumably that in the second half of the nineteenth century a host of new kinds of social problems became acute in both societies, with no tried-and-tested institutional tools available for dealing with them. The recourse to testamentary freedom reflects the attempt to solve the "social question" by regulating the distribution of the assets available within a family. By preserving a secure home, Le Play and Riehl, after all, wanted to maintain a kind of protective sphere against the vagaries of modern economic life, a sphere in which family members could seek refuge in times of crisis. And in Germany, the demand for a large compulsory portion that dominates the thinking of commentators on testamentary freedom with an interest in social reform can be interpreted, in part, as the attempt to protect families as much as possible against the spreading market relationships, and thereby contribute to the stabilization of society. However, the actors in these two countries differed profoundly when it came to giving concrete shape to the regulations intended to achieve this goal. Presumably, the firmly established evaluative schemes in France and Germany influenced the perception of causal relationships and therefore also the formulation of policy.

The surprising fact is that the divergent discourses on testamentary freedom in France and Germany in the second half of the nineteenth century largely concurred on the goals they were pursuing: in both countries we are dealing with a reaction—in terms of social policy—against the processes of economic and social transformation that were experienced as a threat.[85] This also provides an interesting clue to how the relationship between the individual and society was understood in the modernization processes: the expansion of markets prompts a reaction involving institutional reforms—or attempts at reform—that are meant to contain these very processes. This hardly points to a linear process by which the spheres of individual action were expanded. It produced a much more complex form of institutional development in which the expansion of individual rights of liberty were systematically linked with their social context.

In the twentieth century, testamentary freedom hardly played any role at all (with the exception of the extremely ideologized reform attempts of the National Socialists), one reason presumably being that it became clear that the regulation of testamentary freedom and the compulsory portion could not truly fulfill the socially stabilizing function originally intended for it. As the welfare state evolved, the function of inheritances to provide for the heirs was pushed back in favor of entitlements derived from social security law.[86] Moreover, the inflation of the 1920s and 1940s, as well as the two world wars, destroyed large parts of the assets especially of the middle class, as a result of which inheritances inevitably became less important in providing for the heirs.

The expanding *role of the state* in protecting individuals against the vagaries of market relationships did not mean that questions of inheritance law as such became unimportant. But the debates over inheritance law show how the perception of where the problem lay shifted as early as the end of the nineteenth century from testamentary freedom to the taxation of inheritance. The widening of the state's function in providing for its citizens moved the question of how to finance the costs of social policy into the center of attention—and the taxation of private wealth can make a contribution toward defraying these costs.

Against this backdrop of developments in the twentieth century, it is interesting to note that there are signs that a renewed engagement with the regulations on testamentary freedom and the law on the compulsory portion has reemerged recently in the legal discourse in Germany.[87] In this debate, the right to a compulsory portion is justified, precisely because of the scaling back of the social security benefits, as the private pillar of an "effective provisioning after death" (Fuchs 2002, 797). The other side criticizes the law on the compulsory portion in the Civil Code as too rigid, because it leads to problems in passing on businesses, and because it fails to do justice to the growing diversity of family models (795ff.). In stepfamilies and patchwork families, relationships of solidarity can shift, after all, from the biological to the children actually raised—but the law does not provide for a compulsory portion or a statutory share of the inheritance for these children.[88] Conversely, the right to a compulsory portion exists for those legally entitled to it also when the relationship to the testator was completely broken. The renewed discussions over testamentary freedom and the position of retaining the right to a compulsory portion that is taken by most of those involved reveal the continuing importance of family-oriented argumentation in inheritance law in Germany—adjusted to the changing family structures. The reform proposals reflect the *change* in familial solidarity.

2.3. United States: Equality of Opportunity versus Individual Rights of Disposition

In contrast to France and Germany, the question of testamentary freedom was at no time an important subject of conflicts over legal policy or legal philosophy in the United States.[89] This does not mean that questions over inheritance law had less importance as such in the United States compared to the two European countries. However, the conflicts focused on other aspects of inheritance law: during the Revolution initially on the abolition of primogeniture and entails, in the middle of the nineteenth century on women's right to inheritance, and half a century later on the taxation of estates. Still, the question of testamentary freedom cannot simply be skipped over, since the *reduced* attention that it received compared to Germany and France calls for explanation.

In this section I will examine the regulations on testamentary freedom in American inheritance law and identify the fundamental currents of conflict in the American debates on inheritance law that emerged during the Revolution and the early nineteenth century. The last part will then look at the question of why testamentary freedom played such a minor role in these debates. My thesis is that two factors came together: (1) the widely shared belief that state interference in social and economic relationships was one of the main *causes* of social inequality (Huston 1993, 1102), and (2) an abundance of land up to the end of the nineteenth century.[90]

Testamentary Freedom in the United States

American inheritance law evolved out of English common law, which was adopted in the American colonies. In England, testamentary freedom over real estate that was held in full right of ownership (freehold land) was first stipulated in 1540 in the Statute of Wills. Restrictions existed only for movable property. However, those restrictions were given up in more and more regions in England in the seventeenth and eighteenth centuries, and in 1724, absolute testamentary freedom became the general principle of English law (McMurray 1919, 110). That freedom was limited merely by local customs and especially by family settlements, which—in result similar to entails—made possible the dynastic inheritance of wealth, but which could also regulate the inheritance rights of the wife.

The American colonies adopted English inheritance law, though they began to change it early on.[91] For example, Massachusetts, as early as 1655, abolished the difference between movable and immovable property along with the principle of primogeniture. Other colonies soon followed this example (McMurray 1919, 118). Only minor changes were made to the principle of absolute freedom of testation. Massachusetts, for example, stipulated in 1700 that children born after a testament had been drawn up, and children not mentioned in the testament, were entitled to a statutory portion of the inheritance. The requirement of an *explicit* testamentary disinheritance of children was introduced in nearly half of the states in the course of the nineteenth century; later, however, that number declined again, and in the 1970s, only one-fifth of all states still had this regulation (Shammas, Salmon, and Dahlin 1987, 166). If children are explicitly disinherited, they have no legal claim to portions of the estate, comparable to the *réserve* in France and the compulsory portion in Germany.[92] The possibility of disinheriting children constitutes one of the most important peculiarities of American inheritance law.[93] Beyond claims to support, no statutory guarantee of the transfer of wealth within the line of blood kinship is institutionalized in American law. This demonstrates that in the United States, free disposition over property is the dominant principle in inheritance law.[94]

The only compulsory portion in American inheritance law exists for the spouse. And here common law placed the surviving husband in a better position in property law than the surviving wife.[95] In American law, a widow was protected against disinheritance by the right to a dower (widow's share). In the nineteenth century, it encompassed lifetime interest to one-third of the husband's nonmovable assets, which could not be curtailed by a testament to the contrary. For example, if the children inherited the landed property, they had to hand over one-third of the income drawn from it to their mother in yearly installments. The children, however, were the owners, which meant that in intestate inheritance, land was always passed down within the man's bloodline.

In the eighteenth and early nineteenth centuries, most states or colonies passed laws granting a widow the right to choose, instead of the usufruct right to landed property, a corresponding share of the movable assets.[96] The background to this development was that land was at this time often uncultivated and produced no income that a widow could have used to support herself (Simes 1955, 13ff.).[97] With the growing importance of movable property, the right of choice offered a better protection to the interests of the surviving wife. It was only in the twentieth century that women were granted not only usufruct rights, but full ownership (fee simple) to the portion of the assets to which they were entitled (Shammas, Salmon, and Dahlin 1987, 164–65). In Pennsylvania, for example, that right was granted in 1917 (171).

The surviving husband had the right to "curtesy." It encompassed usufruct rights to the wife's *entire* landed property during his lifetime. After that, the landed property reverted to the wife's children or her closest relatives. As for the wife's movable property, upon marriage it passed into the property of the husband in any case (at least until the middle of the nineteenth century) and remained there also after her death.

In most states, dower rights were protected against the claims of creditors against the property of the deceased husband (Shammas, Salmon, and Dahlin 1987, 72). In the middle of the nineteenth century, so-called homestead provisions were put in place as an added measure of protection for the immediate surviving family members; their goal was to prevent the complete impoverishment of spouses and dependent children.[98] The house, a few essential utensils, and clothing were placed beyond the reach of creditors; they remained in the possession of the family members, even if the deceased was heavily indebted. As a rule, these items were also excluded from testamentary disposition (McMurray 1919, 120; Friedman 1985, 244–45). In addition, courts in the United States enforce moral norms even today by insisting on strict compliance with wills acts. Wills that do not comply with prevailing normative views are often not upheld by the courts, which effectively reduces testamentary freedom (Leslie 1996). Alongside these protective measures against complete disinheritance, there was also always the possibility of concluding marriage contracts in which the partners could agree that the wife would administer the assets she brought into the marriage (Shammas, Salmon, and Dahlin 1987, 75). As American law developed, the common-law institutions of dower and curtesy were replaced in most states by institutions such as "indefeasible share" and "community property," which led to a substantial strengthening of the position of the surviving spouse.[99]

The Conception of Property and Inheritance Law in the Early Years of the United States

In spite of these indirect restrictions on testamentary freedom, the United States is, without question, the country with the broadest degree of testamentary freedom among the three countries I am examining. The question now is why this freedom on the part of the testator did not become the subject of controversy either during the Revolution—when other aspects of inheritance law played a crucial role in the legal-political discourse—or in later phases of American history. The starting point for an answer to this question lies in the inheritance law discourse during the Revolution and in the early nineteenth century.

Initially, the American discourse overlaps substantially with the legal philosophy prevailing in continental Europe. That is especially true for the evolution of the notion of inheritance law as a positive right. This legal position reached the United States chiefly through William Blackstone's epochal work of 1769, *Commentaries on the Law of England*; Blackstone himself had been deeply influenced by Samuel Pufendorf in his theory of natural law. According to Blackstone, English common law was based on natural law. Property was a natural law that preceded all social institutions. For Blackstone, as for John Locke, individual rights of property arose from the human appropriation of nature. While the appropriation theory, in Blackstone's view, allowed for a natural law justification of private property, he did *not* believe—unlike Locke—that this gave rise to a natural law justification of inheritance law. The possibility of appropriating goods ended at death, which meant that property rights ceased to exist and it was therefore not possible to determine how these goods should be disposed: "For, naturally speaking, the instant a man ceases to be, he ceases to have any dominion: else, if he had a right to dispose of his acquisitions one moment beyond his life, he would also have a right to direct their disposal for a million ages after him; which would be highly absurd and inconvenient" (Blackstone 2001 [1771], 2:9). As civil law, inheritance law could be regulated by society in any way it saw fit: "Wills and testaments, rights of inheritance and succession, are all of them creatures of the civil or municipal laws, and accordingly are in all respects regulated by them" (2:10).

Upon the death of the owner, his property became common property and passed into the possession of the person who first appropriated and used it. The function of inheritance law as civil law was to regulate the conflicts that could be expected to arise from this situation. This notion of inheritance law as civil law—which, as we have seen, asserted itself increasingly also in France and Germany in the late eighteenth century—dominated the legal-political discussion and legislation in the United States after the Revolution (Katz 1977, 7ff.; Chester 1982, 35ff.). However, in the late eighteenth and early nineteenth centuries, two clearly divergent positions can be discerned in the United States concerning the legal-political consequences that flow from the definition of inheritance law as positive law. One position is associated especially with Thomas Jefferson, the other with the legal scholar James Kent.

1. Thomas Jefferson initiated the two central reforms of inheritance law in Virginia in the last quarter of the eighteenth century: the abolition of family entails (1776) and of primogenitures (1785).[100] Jefferson's legal-theoretical reflections on the question of the reasoned foundation for the law of private inheritance are highly important for understanding how the handling of "unearned wealth" has evolved in the United States. Nearly all social reformers of the last two hundred years who sought to influence the distribution of property in the United States with the help of inheritance law invoked the arguments advanced by Jefferson. His line of argumentation consolidated one of the strands in the discursive structure of the American debates on inheritance law that exerted a sustained influence over time. It consists of combining the civil law conception of inheritance law with the goal of an egalitarian distribution of property. The influence that is brought to bear on the distribution of property is supposed to preserve the distributory preconditions of the republican polity and ensure equal opportunity for all individuals. Clearly borrowing from Blackstone, Jefferson formulated the right of political intervention in the inheritance of property as follows:

> I suppose to be self evident, "*that the earth belongs in usufruct to the living*": that the dead have neither powers nor rights over it. The portion occupied by an individual ceases to be his when he himself ceases to be, and reverts to the society. If the society has formed no rules for the appro-

priation of it's lands in severality, it will be taken by the first occupants. These will generally be the wife and children of the decedent. If they have formed rules of appropriation, those rules may give it to the wife and children, or to some of them, or to the legatee of the deceased. So they may give it to his creditor. But the child, the legatee, or creditor takes it, not by any *natural right*, but by a law of the society of which they are members, and to which they are subject. Then no man can, by natural right, oblige the lands he occupied, or the persons who succeed him in that occupation, to the paiment of debts contracted by him. For if he could, he might, during his own life, eat up the usufruct of the lands for several generations to come, and then the lands would belong to the dead, and not to the living, which would be the reverse of our principle. (Jefferson, letter to Madison, 6 September 1789, in Smith 1995, 632)

The dictum that the earth belonged to the living arises directly out of Enlightenment thinking. The idea of the social contract requires the dissolution of ties that were not entered into contractually. However, in contrast to Blackstone, Jefferson does not simply state that inheritance law is a positive law, but links this interpretation with normative ideas about the distribution of property within society. This is clear from a letter that Jefferson wrote four years earlier from France, also to James Madison. In it, Jefferson describes the social situation in France and then continues:

I am conscious that an equal division of property is impracticable. But the consequences of this enormous inequality producing so much misery to the bulk of mankind, legislators cannot invent too many devices for subdividing property, only taking care to let their subdivisions go hand in hand with the natural affections of the human mind. The descent of every kind therefore to all children, or to all brothers and sisters, or other relations in equal degree is a political measure, and a practical one. (Jefferson, letter to Madison, 28 October 1785, in Smith 1995, 390)[101]

Although Jefferson was an ardent defender of private rights of property, he believed that the essential natural rights were political rights and personal rights. However, in his view the completely unfettered right of property was not among them, (Chester 1982, 35; Nedelsky 1990, 35). Since private property was a *means* for achieving a democratic society, property rights had to be weighed against other rights. For Jefferson, as for some of the French revolutionaries, the broad diffusion of property was the precondition for the republican social order. Jefferson's conception of society was shaped by the ideal of an agrarian society in which the economic functions were performed chiefly by independent small farmers. Their position as independent producers was to strengthen the virtues by which private interests would be subordinated to the common good, which was the foundation of the ability of the republican social order to function. The republican political engagement had its social precondition in relatively small and homogenous communities (Katz 1976, 481ff.; Schultz 1992, 16–17). Implicit in this is the notion that only an equitable distribution of property would be able to sustain the social foundations of American democracy over the long term. This was the republican background for social reformers since the late eighteenth century who were calling for a limitation on the private inheritance of property. The dynastic concentration of wealth in the hands of a few endangered the political community, because it would lead to corruption and eventually tyranny. The concentration of wealth would give a few actors too much power, which could pose a threat to the democratic government and individual rights of liberty. According to this republican way of thinking, the important thing was to create comparable economic starting positions for the citizens. Without attacking the principle of private property as such, these distributory preconditions of democracy contained for Jefferson and the critics of an unlimited private inheritance law who invoked him a justification to intervene in the intergenerational distribution of property.

2. Of course, Jefferson's notion of property and the right to intervene in private inheritance law derived from it was not uncontroversial. In fact, the American legal historian Stanley Katz (1977, 18) has shown that Jefferson's view of inheritance law was in fact not very common in the legal-political context of the United States in the late eighteenth century. It was confronted in the early nineteenth century by a position in legal theory that called for unlimited property rights and strictly rejected any interference in inheritance law. However, even influential conservative legal scholars propounded the view of inheritance law as positive law. Someone who advocated property rights with the least possible restrictions in the American legal discourse was the leading American legal scholar of the early nineteenth century, James Kent.[102]

Kent held a conservative concept of property. For him, as for Blackstone, the most important source he drew upon, rights of property already existed prior to society, and it was the state's task to protect the individual's natural right to property. While Jefferson advocated a pragmatic adjustment of the right of property to the needs of society, Kent—and with him the school of legal rationalism—rejected any and all interference in property law (Chester 1982, 40). In his *Commentaries on American Law* (1826–30), Kent discussed Blackstone's interpretation of inheritance law as civil law, and his discussion revealed a marked uncertainty whether or not he should follow Blackstone on this issue. In the end, though, his arrived at the following conclusion:

> But the particular distribution among heirs of the blood, and the regulation and extent of the degrees of consanguinity to which the right of succession should be attached, do undoubtedly depend essentially upon positive institution. (Kent 1971 [1827], 2:263–64).

This makes clear that at the beginning of the nineteenth century, conservative legal scholars, as well, advocated the position that inheritance law was positive law, a position that has remained dominant in jurisdiction in the United States to this day. For James Kent, however, this limitation on natural law was no gateway to the redistribution of property with the help of inheritance law; instead, private inheritance law had to be guaranteed without restrictions through positive law:

> [Entailments] have been effectively removed in this country; and the right . . . to devise, and to transmit property by inheritance to one's descendants in regular order and succession, is enjoyed in the fullness and perfection of the absolute right. (1971 [1827], 2:265)

To be sure, a dominant view of inheritance law as positive law took shape in American jurisprudence during the Revolution and in the early nineteenth century. At the same time, though, two completely different attitudes developed on the question of granting or restricting private inheritance law. Agreement existed only when it came to the abolition of feudal restrictions on the alienation of property (entails),[103] but not when it came to the question of whether the institutionalization of inheritance law could and should be used over and above this to realize ideals of equality and to protect the principles of equality in the distribution of property as a precondition of American democracy.

Why Nearly Unlimited Testamentary Freedom?

Why did no legal-political conflict concerning the limitation of testamentary freedom develop in the United States? Jefferson's view that the foundation of democratic development lay in a distribution of property that, on the one hand, did not permit an economic concentration of power, and, on the other hand, guaranteed the economic independence of (agrarian) small producers, could have formed the starting point for the demand to limit testamentary freedom. Tocqueville, who wrote full of admiration about the introduction of the principle of equality in American intestacy law and the abolition of entails, noted that his home country of France was still a step ahead of the United States in legislation on inheritance law:

> It cannot fail to strike the French reader who studies the law of inheritance that on these questions French legislation is infinitely more democratic than even the American. (1980 [1835], 2:350)

In looking at the United States, what stands out, first of all, is a clear parallel to the two European countries: the *longue durée* of the law. Limitations on testamentary freedom already existed in France and Germany before the codification of a uniform law code, limitations that have remained essentially unchanged in spite of the social and political processes of transformation during the last 230 years. In the United States, testamentary freedom was adopted from England in the seventeenth century along with customary law. Here, too, one finds a strong continuity through all changes, which points also in the American case to the path dependency of inheritance law.

Two specific aspects of the political and social structure in the United States seem important in *explaining* why testamentary freedom was accepted in that country largely without conflict: (1) differences in the conception of private property compared to the two European countries; and (2) relevant differences in the economic conditions up to the late nineteenth century.

1. Compared to France, the goal of social redistribution was less important in the American Revolution. That is true in spite of the incorporation of the postulate of equality into the Virginia Bill and the Declaration of Independence in 1776, on which the French Declaration of the Rights of Man and the Citizen drew thirteen years later. In the political clashes in late eighteenth-century America, the call for equality served largely to justify the resistance of the rebels in the colonies. It was aimed primarily against the unequal treatment of the colonists vis-à-vis British citizens, for whom laws and taxes were enacted by their *elected* representatives (Adams 1971, 63ff.). The legal-philosophical point of reference for the American postulate of equality is Locke's contract theory, which, as explained above, sees equality in the state of nature as the foundation for the social contract. Consequently, obligations that are not based on this contractual self-obligation must be rejected. *This* natural law argumentation does not include any rights to social distributory equality.

This is not to say that there were no demands for an egalitarian distribution of property during the Revolution. They are, after all, clearly evident in Jefferson and are part of the republican tradition that was important in the foundation phase of the United States. However, as the basis for the implementation of redistributive goals, also by means of inheritance law, they certainly did not achieve the political influence they attained, for example, through the Jacobins during the French Revolution: "Egalitarianism was not the animus of the American Revolution" (Katz 1977, 28). One important reason is that the demand for a stronger legal restriction on testamentary freedom to implement ideals of equality would have clashed with a conception of the state that granted it, compared to the two European countries, far fewer rights to intervene in civic society. Limiting testamentary freedom with the goal of redistributing wealth assets would have amounted to the exertion of strong state influence, which would have conflicted also with Jefferson's principle of the smallest possible role of the state in maintaining social order. Against the background of experiences in the European countries, the founders of the American republic were intent on creating legal institutions that would protect individual liberty against arbitrary encroachments by the state. As a result, it was much more difficult in the discursive field in the United States than in the European countries to legitimize legal regulations intended to guide the distribution of property by means of inheritance law.

For one, a strong faction rejected goals of redistribution (goals that also existed in Europe); for another, there was a very critical stance in general toward state intervention in economic transactions. This was further reinforced by the fact that at least until the end of the nineteenth century, until the rise of the Progressive movement, there was an overwhelming tendency within the political discourse in America to regard the meddling of the state in social and economic relationships as the *cause* of social inequality (Huston 1993, 1102). As a solution to the republican problem of the distributive preconditions of democratic development, what prevailed in the United States—different from France—was the idea (developed by James Madison) that the undemocratic influence from the concentration of economic power should be neutralized through institutionalized checks and balances and the separation of power within the political system. According to this view, the maintenance of a democratic form of government did not necessarily require a balanced distribution of property (Schultz 1992, 18).

To the extent that the state in America intervened in a regulatory manner in property law in the first half of the nineteenth century, it was done with the goal of mobilizing property economically. Morton Horwitz (1977) has shown that the orientation of American property law changed during the first half of the nineteenth century from a conception of absolute rights to an economic-utilitarian notion, according to which interventions in private property were justified if they led to economic growth. In the evolution of inheritance law this is evident in the abolition of entails and primogeniture in the late eighteenth century, and in the mid–nineteenth century in efforts to alter dower rights in such a way that they no longer impeded the buying and selling of real estate.[104] This general trend can also be read from the easing of formal legal requirements in real estate transactions, and in the abolition of restrictions on the purchase of land by immigrants. In the case of joint ownership titles, the English legal institutions of "joint tenants" was changed into that of "tenants in common," which made the individual disposition over common property easier.[105] Thus, the notion of property in the United States was transformed between 1780 and 1860 "from a static agrarian conception entitling an owner to undisturbed enjoyment, to a dynamic, instrumental, and more abstract view of property that emphasized the newly paramount virtues of productivity, use and development" (Horwitz 1973, 248).

A prohibition or substantial limitation of testamentary freedom—analogous to what happened in France—would have been incompatible with this trend in property law. The concentration of wealth from an unequal division of inheritance did not impede the economic development of the United States in the early nineteenth century. That alone, however, would have provided a relevant legitimation for state intervention in inheritance law to restrict testamentary freedom. As a result, the individual freedom of the testator within property law remained a higher value than the state's implementation of the principle of equality by restricting the freedom of testation.

2. A second difference between the European countries and the United States that was relevant with respect to inheritance law lay in the highly divergent economic conditions. The United States had no feudal past and had, until the end of the nineteenth century, virtually unlimited resources of arable land.

Tocqueville [1835] pointed already in the early nineteenth century to the greater social mobility within American society. The thrust of this argument was not a denial of the considerable differences of wealth in American society at that time (see Pessen 1971), but a greater social mobility compared to European societies and the reduced importance of dynastic concentrations of wealth. Tocqueville commented that "wealth circulates with inconceivable rapidity, and experience shows that it is rare to find two succeeding generations in the full enjoyment of it" (1980 [1835], 1:51). To explain why dynastic motives were less important in the United States, Tocqueville noted the abolition of entails and primogenitures, as well as the equal division of inheritance in intestacy law. In addition, he pointed out that capital was more profitable when it was not permanently tied to real estate, and that immigration and the constantly shifting frontier led to a reduced importance of long-term, intergenerational strategies of status acquisition. To be sure, aristocratic tendencies certainly did exist in the American colonies, especially in the South, but they shaped the legal structures less than they did in France and Germany. While the limitation on testamentary freedom in Revolutionary legislation and the Code Civil in France was motivated by the goal of breaking up the existing concentration of land among the old aristocracy, this problem was comparatively less important in the United States.

One important condition for the greater economic mobility in American society was the nearly unlimited availability of land. As a result of this, inheritances were far less significant socioeconomically than they were in Europe.[106] While inheritance law in Europe decided whether someone even had the option of living as an independent farmer—or had to hire himself out as a rural laborer, remain on the farm in a subordinate position, move to the city, or emigrate, the noninheritance of land in the United States did not by any means have these social consequences. More land was always available. In contrast to Europe, inheritance law and practices in the early years of the United States did not lead to underemployment or the social uprooting of large sections of the population. Initially, the existing differences in wealth were comparatively unproblematic with respect to their *social consequences*. For example, from the perspective of Jefferson, the important thing was to continue distributing land in such a way that society would be composed chiefly of independent small farmers, something that did not require the division of existing large-scale property, but the opening up of additional land. In the United States, there was no need to break open existing property structures through a consistent limitation on testamentary freedom in order to increase the number of landowners. Unlike in the two European countries, in the early nineteenth century, testamentary freedom in the United States could not be interpreted as a cause of social impoverishment or as an impediment to the development of democratic society.

Private Property and Equal Opportunity

These intellectual and material structures in the United States help us to understand why the question of testamentary freedom played only a marginal role in American conflicts over inheritance law and was of virtually no significance in works on the reform of inheritance law.[107] The basic structure of later debates over inheritance law in the United States, which revolved chiefly around the redistribution and taxation of estates, took shape during the revolutionary period without at first provoking conflicts over inheritance law that were comparable in importance to what happened in France.

And yet, at the time of the American Revolution there arose within the political self-conception of the country a tension that would repeatedly push to the surface in later political clashes over inheritance law. For the natural law tradition that is so important to the political constitution of the United States allows two highly contradictory conclusions when it comes to the institutionalization of inheritance law: the unconditional acceptance of private rights of property also in inheritance law, which leads to unlimited testamentary freedom and the prohibition against inheritance taxes, as well as a radical egalitarianism ("all men are created equal"), according to which private inheritance law cannot be justified because of the unequal opportunities to which it gives rise (Katz 1977, 8–9). Even though the postulate of equality was incorporated into the Declaration of Independence merely in the sense of Locke's theory of natural law, in later social conflicts it was repeatedly invoked to justify the demand for greater social justice, and to this day it has established two clashing forms of society's self-conception.[108] The formulation "created equal" pointed, for one, to the equality of all Americans before the law, and, for another, to the element of equal opportunity. The right to pursue one's personal happiness could be interpreted, with respect to the transmission of property by inheritance, as the right to an inheritance law free of familial and governmental influences, as well as a call to establish material starting conditions that were as equal as possible, which could justify drastic interventions in private inheritance law. Henceforth, this tension marked all debates over inheritance law in the United States. One can see it for the first time in the reform movements of the 1830s and 1840s.[109]

At the end of the eighteenth and in the early nineteenth centuries, the full significance of this conflict was not yet apparent. It was merely latent, as is evident in the positions on property law taken by Thomas Jefferson and

James Kent. What prevailed until the 1860s was a compromise that Robert Dahl (1985, 69) has described as the "classic republican solution." Dahl maintained that as long as property is distributed fairly equally among the citizens, the question of whether the rights of private property or the political rights of equality take precedence remains merely latent for social practice. This compromise presupposed the small-scale property structures of American agrarian society in the first half of the nineteenth century and the availability of more land. But with the transformation of the economy in the direction of structures of large-scale industry, with the drying up of endless opportunity along the frontier, and with the resultant increase in the social polarization of American society, the principle of equal opportunity—which expressed the meritocratic self-conception that legitimated differences in wealth—would invariably clash with the advantages that inheritance law made possible for some. This is precisely the situation that arose in the late nineteenth century.[110] It went hand in hand with a change in legislation on property law (Dahl 1985, 63; Horwitz 1992) and laid the foundation for the debates about the redistribution of inherited wealth that have been going on to this day. The great clash over inheritance law in the United States was still to come.

2.4. CONCLUSION

The question of how the rights of the testator to freely determine the transfer of property *mortis causa* should be balanced against the rights of the family and the social consequences of the intergenerational transfer of wealth led to heated legal and political controversies from the late eighteenth century on in France and Germany, but not in the United States. In the process we can see, first of all, a remarkable continuity in the regulations on testamentary freedom in all three countries. Already in the late eighteenth century, France was the country with the most stringent restrictions on testamentary freedom, the United States was the country with the least restrictions, and Germany took a position somewhere in between, though it was closer to the French regulations. In spite of profound economic and political structural changes in the period under examination, the rules on testamentary freedom remained largely unchanged. No meaningful expansion of individual testamentary rights can be observed throughout the period encompassed by this study, contrary to what one might have expected from the theory of individualization. Only if we extend the chronological range much further back in time, namely to the Middle Ages and the early modern period, can one detect such a trend. Testamentary rights, first laid down in Roman law, were initially nearly completely abolished in the Middle Ages, and then gradually reintroduced into European legal practice beginning in the eleventh century, which the church playing a central role in this process.

In addition, one can discern the emergence of specific discursive structures that constitute, in each of the countries, a framework within which debates about testamentary freedom are carried on. In all three countries we find in the debates the position that calls for the most unrestricted testation rights possible, a position that was in each case built upon the argument that the owner has the right to freely dispose of his property. When it comes to the positions that were developed in defense of *limitations* on individual testation rights, however, different structures are apparent in France, Germany, and the United States.

In France, the restriction placed on testamentary rights is legitimized primarily with the argument that children are by nature equal. The guarantee in inheritance law of equal shares for the children realizes a central constitutional principle and is justified in the interest of the commonwealth as defined by the state.

In Germany, testamentary limitations are justified largely against the backdrop of a conception of property as family property that limits the testator's freedom of disposition. Through the limitation on testamentary freedom, inheritance law guarantees the ethical nature of the transfer of property.[111] Moreover, the notion of property as family property developed in Germany in the nineteenth century into the concept of the social embeddedness of private property, on the basis of which interventions in the transfer of wealth *mortis causa* are legitimate if done for purposes of social policy.

In the United States, where the question of testamentary freedom did not provoke any meaningful political debates, a latent tension established itself in the late eighteenth century between the legitimation of property on the basis of natural law and the principle of equality. But in the United States, the principle of equality became significant for the reform discussion over inheritance law chiefly as equality of opportunity ("all men are created equal"). The critical attitude toward the state that dominates the constitutional discourse in the United States explains, together with the special socioeconomic conditions that existed until the end of the nineteenth century, why testamentary freedom did not assume a prominent place in the legal-political debates in the founding years of the republic. However, this period already saw the rise of the discursive context that would subsequently, beginning in the late nineteenth century, structure the clashes over the taxation of inheritance. The discursive fields that took shape in the late eighteenth and early nineteenth centuries in all three countries influenced not only the debates over testamentary freedom, but also the conflict over family entails and especially inheritance taxation. This will be the topic of subsequent chapters.

The conflicts over testamentary freedom and their embeddedness within the discursive structures I have laid out reveal how the debates over inheritance law move within a field of tension between the rights of the testator, of the family, and of society (the state). This is immediately apparent in positions that take a critical stance toward testamentary freedom, and whose structures of justification invoke the rights of family members, an interest in the democratic development of the polity, or general normative principles like the principle of equality. But the proponents of rights of testamentary disposition that are as unrestricted as possible also legitimate their position by pointing to positive consequences for the family or demography, effects of economic well-being, and the value of individual freedom as the condition of a democratic political polity. These arguments should not be interpreted a priori as opportunistic accommodations with the goal of pushing through particularistic, individual interests. If one sees the political controversies carried on in the three societies as indicators of their normative structures, one perceives, not an increasing individualistic orientation, but rather a process of negotiation in which individual rights and the rights of the family or society are weighed against each other with respect to their reciprocal consequences, claims, and obligations. In this sense, it is problematic to speak of individualization. It would be more apt to speak of *embedded individualism*, a phrase that is meant to express that regulations on testamentary freedom balance the freedom of the testator against the claims of the family and the requirements of society.

The *longue durée* of the rules on testamentary freedom in the three countries indicates that the development of inheritance law very much tends to follow the track that has been laid down, and is relatively independent of changing socioeconomic conditions and constellations of political power. What role do the different discursive structures in the three countries play in this process? To say, against the background of this path dependency, that the discursive structures provide an *explanation* of the different rules on testamentary freedom would be an exaggeration. Yet in all three countries there is a correspondence between varying degrees of restriction on testamentary freedom and the structures of the discursive field that find expression in the debates on inheritance law. Although it cannot be demonstrated that the normative structures are, in a causal sense, decisive for the varying regulations of testamentary freedom in the United States, France, and Germany, it is evident that the existing rules were supported by an important orientation of the discourse on inheritance law. This legitimizing support can help explain why the rules in the political clashes over their reform remained so stable and at the same time different from one another.

The relationship between the discourses on inheritance law and political structures in the evolution of inheritance law will be examined in more detail in chapter 4. The topic of the next chapter will be the provisions of statutory inheritance law, that is, the rules that come into effect if the decedent has died intestate. My focus will be on changes in the norms of kin solidarity within the family systems that are revealed by the development of inheritance law.

Chapter 3

EQUALITY AND INCLUSION: THE INHERITANCE RIGHTS OF THE FAMILY

THE TRANSFER OF WEALTH *mortis causa* gives voice to a social relationship between the testator and the heir. To bequeath a legacy can mean fulfilling an obligation, it can be motivated by the desire for a material symbol of immortality, or it can be understood as a gift that expresses the attachment to another person.[1] However, central to a sociology of inheritance is not so much the individual motivations that prompt the decisions of testators, as the social structures revealed by inheritance practices. Although the willing of property is at the discretion of the testator, within the boundaries of testamentary freedom, the sociological analysis proceeds from the contention that inheritance practices cannot be understood as purely individual decisions. Rather, they are regulated by norms that subject the actions of the testator to social expectations and in this way influence his or her decisions.[2] Whether the farm (business) is left to a child, whether this must be the firstborn male child or a son, whether the principle of equality should apply to the offspring, which shares of the assets should pass to the surviving spouse, and which share shall be given to an illegitimate child—all these questions are subjected to a variety of different social regulations.

The norms regulating the transmission of property are reflected in inheritance practices, but they are also evident from the rules that are codified in statutory inheritance law.[3] The regulations of intestacy law are supposed to lead to a transfer of wealth that accords with what the testator presumably would have stipulated, had he or she left a will *and* acted in a reasonable (socially appropriate!) manner. To that extent, intestacy law expresses the prevailing social norms about the transfer of wealth by legacy, and, conversely, it can be taken as an indicator for the structure of normative rules about the bequest of wealth.

A first important stipulation of statutory inheritance law is that in all three countries in question, *family members* of the decedent are installed as heirs, not the state or charitable institutions.[4] This can be seen, at least in a weak sense, as the extension of a conception of property oriented toward the family (see Durkheim 1992, 174)—in a weak sense, because the testator can depart in his or her will from statutory inheritance law, and it is only the limitations on testamentary freedom examined in the previous chapter that secure the claim of family members to the estate. However, the existence of intestacy law and its orientation toward the family clearly points to the fact that the testator is embedded within a regulatory structure that binds him normatively to the family.

In addition, intestacy law contains precise information on a society's normative ideas about the *structure* of kinship relations.[5] For the rules of distribution codified in statutory inheritance law and in inheritance taxation law also represent classificatory systems of kinship. Kin classifications, of the kind ethnology studies especially in traditional societies, are "a system of ideas, norms, and behaviors that serve to establish systems of solidarity" (Müller 1983, 165). An analysis of the development of statutory inheritance law therefore provides insight into changing claims of solidarity, definitions of social belonging, and the primary social purposes that are connected with the transmission of property.

What norms of property transfer by inheritance exist in the intestacy law of these three countries? What structures of social relationships within the family can we infer from them? How have these structures evolved, how do they differ, and how can one explain these developments? These are the questions the present chapter seeks to answer. To that end I will examine three areas of regulation within statutory inheritance law: the introduction of the principle of equality in intestacy law; the rights of the surviving spouse to the estate of the decedent; and the inheritance rights of illegitimate children. My thesis is as follows: the development of these legal areas, the strengthening and weakening, inclusion and exclusion of groups of individuals in statutory inheritance law open a window onto the changes to normative notions of claims of solidarity in the three countries under investigation.

In the present chapter I will show that intestacy law reveals long-term transformations that indicate a development from solidarity within extensive patrilineal kinship systems toward the narrowing of claims of solidarity—including rights of support—to the immediate nuclear family. Over the course of time, the traditional orientation of inheritance law, closely tied to feudalism and aimed at preserving the status of the male bloodline, is increasingly pushed aside. In its place, an inheritance law is institutionalized that is tailored to the nuclear family composed of spouses and children, and that is based essentially on the principles of equality and on an orientation toward affect.

Here, equality refers to the equal standing of the testator's children in inheritance law and the strengthening of the legal position of the surviving spouse, especially the wife. The equality of the children in intestacy law was established already in the late eighteenth century with the abolition of primogeniture. By contrast, the increasing equality of women in inheritance law, which is closely tied to the development of property law, was a protracted process that began around the middle of the nineteenth century and was not finished until the second half of the twentieth. What developed was a system of inheritance law of a "symmetrically multilineal type," one that did not give preferential treatment to either of the two bloodlines, while at the same time leading to a stronger demarcation of the nuclear family vis-à-vis the families of origin of the spouses, thereby weakening the relationships of solidarity to the expanded circle of kin (Parsons 1954, 183ff.).

A growing focus on affect means that claims to legacies were oriented toward the testator's close familial relationships, which were presumed to be especially important emotionally. This development is evident in the strengthening of the inheritance rights of the surviving spouse especially against more distant blood relatives. In fact, the inheritance rights of distant collateral relatives, who had a blood connection to the testator but for the most part not a close social bond, were generally pushed back. The increasing inclusion of adopted children in intestacy law, and recently also of same-sex partners, can also be interpreted as a broadening of this affect orientation with respect to claims of solidarity. Only in the case of illegitimate children whose parents (fathers!) refuse a social relationship with them is the support function of inheritance law enforced independent of a presumed close emotional bond and justified on the grounds of biological parentage. The claims of solidarity expressed in inheritance law are oriented toward a picture of the family that upgrades the marital relationship, is neutral toward gender differences, does not tie familial membership to the parents' marital status, and is focused more on the individual opportunities of the descendants than on status-oriented, dynastic goals of wealth perpetuation within the male kinship system.

This interpretation of the development of an intestacy law tailored to bourgeois society takes its cues from Talcott Parsons's account of the kinship system in America. Parsons (1954, 180) described the American structure of kinship as a system "that is made up *exclusively* of interlocking conjugal families."[6] Claims of solidarity are largely restricted to these entities made up of parents and their minor children.

Although many aspects of the development of statutory inheritance law in the three countries can be understood by applying this model, which makes it a good point of reference, it leaves out two important aspects.

1. Parsons's description of the kinship system was focused on the model of the American family in the middle of the twentieth century, in which illegitimate children and same-sex partners did not appear. However, one important development of intestacy law is found in the institutionalized equality of illegitimate children since then. In the functionalist literature in the mid-twentieth century (Davis 1939), the exclusion of these children from inheritance law was still seen as a necessary protection of the family's function, which was reproduction. However, instead of interpreting the expansion of inheritance rights to illegitimate children as a potential threat to the bourgeois model of the family (Holthöfer 1987, 167), I will argue that this change actually reveals that the orientation toward the model of mutually interlocked conjugal families continues to be dominant. A process of "internal diversification" has responded to the considerable growth in extramarital births in all three countries since the sixties by disconnecting the norms of solidarity in inheritance law from the marital status of the

parents. The new stepfamilies and patchwork families find support in the altered legal structures for the changing demands on the transfer of wealth.

A similar development is taking place with the inclusion of same-sex partners in inheritance law. Here, too, the bourgeois model of the family is pluralized, in that "marriage" is no longer always tied to the partners being of the opposite sex. In fact, adoption rights for same-sex couples disconnect the model of the conjugal family even from the precondition of the reproductive capacity of the parents. These developmental trends within inheritance law during the last fifty years reflect a diversification of family models that Parsons did not foresee, and they adjust the legal foundations of wealth transfer to these altered familial structures.

2. Parson's model is too strongly oriented toward the notion of a *reciprocal isolation* of conjugal families. Parsons (1954, 185) asserts a structural segregation of individual families, which he sees at the same time as a precondition for the increasing affect orientation within marital relationships and for the fulfillment of functional demands arising from the occupational role. Yet the familial units are perhaps far less segregated than Parsons assumed. For one, the pluralization of family models can at the same time entail strong bonds to various conjugal families. For another, the notion of the isolation of conjugal families does not do justice to the phenomenon of inheritance. Bequests or inter vivos transfers (Attias-Donfut 1995; Kohli 1999; Szydlik 1999) are a material (and affective!) bond of *adult* family generations in the descendant line. Although this does not fundamentally challenge the orientation of intestacy law toward the nuclear family that grew stronger in the course of history, it does point to an important form of the solidarity relationship within families that is not encompassed by Parsons's model of the kinship structure.

Parsons neglected legacies (and inter vivos transfers) presumably because of the assumptions he made in his theory of modernization. That theory is focused chiefly on the urban middle-class segment of society (Parsons 1954, 186), which derives its livelihood from gainful employment. This model is not oriented toward the—naturally—much smaller upper class, for which, according to Parsons, legacies, and thus also family continuity and patrilineal structures, continue to play an important role. For modern society, if we follow Parsons's pattern variables, meritocracy and not the ascriptive achievement of status should be the dominant principle behind the social distribution of resources. This model has no room for inheritances as the effortless accrual of wealth. The fact that inheritances continue to be transferred also in the middle class reveals this assumption as a problematic bias of modernization theory. Bequests and inter vivos transfers challenge the preeminence of an achievement-based distribution of property and thus also the model of reciprocally isolated conjugal families. Needless to say, inheritances are not important for all families, but it is precisely this element of social inequality that is neglected as a category in Parsons's theory.

3.1. The Principle of Equality in Intestacy Law

The change in intestacy law that is presumably of the greatest importance to the structure of family relationships occurred in the early nineteenth century, without triggering any significant legal-political controversies: the equal status of sons and daughters in inheritance law.[7] In all three countries, legal rules were (or had already been) established by which the preferential treatment of the firstborn (primogeniture) or the preferential status of sons over their sisters in inheritance law was abolished.[8] While the bourgeois revolutions of the late eighteenth century were a catalyst for this development in France and the United States, the tendency toward increasing equality in statutory inheritance law was evident long before that.

United States. The American colonies, by adopting English common law, initially introduced primogeniture succession. This meant that realty was passed to the oldest son undivided. But while the right of primogeniture persisted in the British motherland until 1925 (!), the American colonies broke with it as early as the seventeenth century.[9] One argument for abolishing the firstborn's right of inheritance pointed to the unfair treatment of younger sons: in many cases they had contributed to improving the value of the land by working on their parents' holding, which is why their lesser standing constituted an injustice (Shammas 1987, 156). Moreover, money was in short supply, which made it difficult to follow the English model and leave younger children a share of the estate in cash. To leave these children a bequest of any kind, the land had to be divided. Against this background, all New England colonies—with the exception of Rhode Island—had abolished primogeniture succession by the beginning of the eighteenth century, replacing it with the rule of an equal right to inheritance, though with the addition that the eldest son was entitled to a double portion.[10]

In New York and in the southern colonies, this tendency toward equality in intestacy law did not exist prior to the Revolution. For the southern colonies the explanation is economic: the plantation economy depended on large estates that could be kept intact through primogeniture. In the wake of the Revolution, however, the same egalitarian division of inheritance that was found in the other colonies was introduced in the South.[11] What we see here is a close connection between the development of the law and the power to implement politically the doctrine of natural equality, which was used to justify equal inheritance rights (Orth 1992, 35–36; Shammas 1987, 155–56).[12]

There were presumably two reasons why equal division in intestacy law was not very controversial: first, given the existing testamentary freedom, formal equality could exert at best a normative pressure, but it did not *compel* the equal treatment of sons and daughters. Still, the normative stipulation of equal inheritance rights for sons and daughters had de facto repercussions for inheritance practices: for example, a study of wills in one county in Pennsylvania in the late eighteenth century still shows clear preferential treatment of sons; one hundred years later, this kind of unequal treatment all but disappeared in the same county (Shammas, Salmon, and Dahlin 1987, 108–9).[13] Second, equal division was uncontroversial because land, given its abundant availability in the United States, was a commodity that quickly changed owners, and legal stipulations that impeded its free exchange were generally considered suspect (Friedman 1999, 47). According to the ideals of agrarian democracy, land should be put to productive use by its owner, which is why large landholdings in private hands were normatively rejected, at least in the North. The abolition of primogeniture succession was intended to promote the goal of an equal distribution of land and to keep landed property within the market process.

France. Tocqueville (1980, 2:350) pointed to a crucial difference between American and French inheritance law in the early nineteenth century. In his eyes, French legislation was "infinitely more democratic" than its American counterpart, because in France, equal division was in fact compelled through the limitation on testamentary freedom. One thing that must be noted about the development of the law in France, as also in the United States, is that while the Revolution certainly did institutionalize an important legal rule by enshrining equal division in the law of 1791, it by no means "invented" this rule. Primogeniture applied in France during the ancien régime only to noble estates subject to the *droit d'aînesse,* whereas the written law of the south, which was based on Roman law, and most *coutumes* already envisaged equal division in intestacy law (Desan 1997, 601–2). Although the law of 1791 standardized the law for all of France and affirmed the abolition of the inheritance law of the nobility, this development was based on already existing legal traditions.

As is evident from the legal development during the revolutionary period described in the previous chapter, in France, as well, the stipulation of equal division in intestacy law was hardly a contentious issue—what was contested was the limitation on testamentary freedom that was introduced a short time later. The pronounced rise in familial conflicts over legacies in the wake of the Revolution, especially between siblings (Desan 1997), was the result of the combination of equal division and a mandatory portion that *had* to be bequeathed in accordance with the rules of egalitarian division.

Germany. On this point, the legal development in the United States and in France does not differ from what transpired in Germany. Although private law in Germany remained diverse in the nineteenth century, all four legal systems that applied in the various parts of the country—the Allgemeines Landrecht, common law, the French law of the Code Civil, and the Saxon law—provided for equal division between the children. Because of the strength of Roman legal traditions within German law, equal division already existed as a rule in intestacy law in the late eighteenth century; no legal reform prompted by a revolution was necessary to establish this principle. One important exception existed, however, in those areas of the country in which the rules of *Anerbenrecht* held sway, which legally stipulated the transmission of an undivided farm and thus gave preferential treatment to one child. Although such rules were not part of the Allgemeines Landrecht or the common law, there did exist in Prussia, for example, certain provincial laws and statutes that overrode the Landrecht and the common law. Even the Civil Code (BGB) that was enacted in 1896 left the state-specific legal regulations pertaining to the special inheritance law for farmers in place (Mertens 1970, 113ff.). In fact, during the nineteenth century one can even detect an expansion of the *Anerbenrecht*, which undoubtedly culminated in the twentieth century in the National Socialist Reich Farm Inheritance Law (Reichserbhofgesetz) of 1933.

The backdrop to the expansion of the special law for farmers in the second half of the nineteenth century was the growing international competition in the agricultural market, which had been triggered by the abolition of grain tariffs at the beginning of the 1850s. One strategy for countering the agricultural crisis of 1875, the result of rapidly declining grain prices, was protective tariffs, but at the same time there was growing economic pressure to achieve a boost in production through economies of scale (Holthöfer 1987, 140; Wehler 1995b, 56ff.). An agrarian inheritance law prohibiting egalitarian division of inheritance was supposed to prevent farm holdings from shrinking in size. Given how important agricultural landed property was in the makeup of private wealth in the nineteenth century, this stipulation de facto excluded considerable portions of property transmitted by inheritance from equal division. On the other hand, over time the *Anerbenrecht* became less relevant to inheritance law, as agricultural landed property made up a decreasing part of inherited private wealth and today plays barely any role in the total amount of wealth transfers *mortis causa*.

The difference from France is interesting. As described in the last chapter, in France, as well, there were strong political movements to abolish compulsory real division; however, they were slow and late in leading to actual changes to inheritance law: "The egalitarian right of family inheritance was [in 1865], and remained also later, so strongly rooted within the legal consciousness of the French that a solution to the problem by way of a shifting of the weight in favor of testamentary succession had no chance of being successful" (Holthöfer 1987, 151).

Although the legal statute of equal division compelled a largely egalitarian transfer of property only in France—because it was linked in that country with a strong restriction on testamentary freedom—it does reveal an important, general development of inheritance law that provided an institutional anchor for the principle of equality. Moreover, the development of testamentary behavior, as briefly described in the case of the United Sates, indicates that, over the long term, the enactment of laws also influenced the actual decisions made by testators. What becomes clear in this development of intestacy law is that dynastic wealth strategies oriented toward the perpetuation of the family line are pushed back as social norms, while the individual is simultaneously elevated vis-à-vis the family as a lasting social unit.

3.2. THE SPOUSE IN INTESTACY LAW

The second important development of intestacy law that takes place in all three countries concerns the inheritance rights of the surviving spouse. The changes show, on the one hand, the decline in the importance of the family principle of blood kinship relative to the importance of the spouse with respect to claims of solidarity in inheritance law, and, on the other hand, the trend toward placing husband and wife on an equal footing in inheritance law.[14] The increasing improvement in the position of the surviving spouse in inheritance law cannot be seen separate from the issue of gender. Given the usually lower age at marriage of women and their higher life expectancy, and the fact that the formation of wealth by way of property law was focused primarily on men into the twentieth century, these changes improved above all the position of women in inheritance law.

Germany. Of the three countries in question, Germany shows once again the strongest continuities in legal development. In the Allgemeines Landrecht of 1794, the surviving spouse already inherited, alongside the testator's legitimate children, a child's portion, but no more than one-quarter of the estate. That share increased if only distant collateral relatives survived the testator. However, the spouse inherited the entire estate only in the unlikely case that no collateral kin of the sixth degree existed. This meant that even the descendant of a great-great-great-grandfather of the testator still had claim to half the estate, and it reveals the profound importance of the family principle based on blood kinship. Only in the situation where there was a community of property (*Gütergemeinschaft*) between the spouses did the surviving partner receive half of the joint assets, but he or she then had no intestacy inheritance rights (Zürn 1892, 116ff.). One peculiarity of Prussian law was that the surviving spouse inherited the share in full ownership instead of acquiring only a lifetime interest. In this respect, the legal position of the spouse was stronger in Prussia than in France and the United States, which can be attributed once again to the strong tradition of Roman law.

This regulation of the Allgemeines Landrecht found its way into the BGB (Civil Code) with only minor changes. For the widow or widower, it fixed the statutory portion at one-quarter of the estate if there were legitimate children. However, the stipulations of the BGB of 1896 reveal a strengthening of the legal position of the surviving spouse against ascendants and collateral relatives, whose inheritance rights were curtailed next to those of the spouse.[15] In the contemporary discussion of the BGB, the rights of widows under intestacy law were variously criticized as inadequate. Marianne Weber (1907, 488) demanded at the beginning of the twentieth century that the surviving wife should have a claim to at least 50% of the gains accrued during the marriage. However, such a profound improvement in the legal position of the surviving partner occurred only in 1958 in the Federal Republic. At that time, the Equal Rights Act (Gleichberechtigungsgesetz) added to the claim to one-quarter of the estate an equal share as an equalization of accrued gains, which thus raised the inheritance share to a total of one-half of the estate. If the spouse was not a co-heir alongside children, the share rose to 75%, and today, if the only living relatives of the testator are more remote than grandparents, the partner inherits the entire estate (Leipold 2000, 55–56).

It was only the Equal Rights Act of 1958 that abolished the unequal treatment of husband and wife in inheritance law. Until then, §1363 of the BGB stipulated that upon marriage the property of the wife became subject to the administration and lifetime interest of the husband; the wife's wealth accrued during marriage also fell under this provision. According to the property law in force since 1958, the property of the spouses remains separate during marriage, and upon dissolution of the marriage, an equalization of accrued gains is undertaken. Although these regulations of property right are not directly within the purview of inheritance law, they are relevant for the transmission of wealth by inheritance: until 1958, the wealth a woman had inherited could not be administrated by her, but passed into the husband's lifetime interest, an arrangement that manifested the patriarchal character of property rights in Germany until the middle of the twentieth century.

Surveying the development of the status of the surviving spouse in intestacy law in Germany over the last two hundred years, it becomes clear that it has strengthened against the inheritance claims of children and especially of collateral relatives. The decisive step occurred only with the Equal Rights Act of 1958. The gradual improvement in the position of the surviving spouse under inheritance law shows the orientation toward the conjugal family. On the one hand, the principle of blood kinship is pushed back; on the other hand, the legal elevation of the relationship between the spouses focuses claims to support much more strongly on the social relationship between marital partners. The retraction of claims of solidarity on the part of the extended family reveals the trend Parsons (1954) highlighted, namely the reciprocal isolation of conjugal families from the elementary components of the kinship system. With the equalization of the position of husband and wife within property law, the patriarchally oriented legal structures simultaneously develop in the direction of the principle of multilineal symmetry.

United States. In American law, as well, there is today a "clear tendency to privilege the surviving spouse over all other persons, especially over offspring" (Rheinstein 1971, 11). The surviving spouse is the only person who, by common law, cannot be disinherited by the testator. While the American legal system expected children to prove themselves in the marketplace independent of any wealth they might acquire through inheritance, the marital partner's claim to support and maintenance was progressively strengthened. In the states of the Southwest, where community property is practiced under the influence of Spanish-Mexican law, the surviving spouse receives half of the wealth that is accrued during the marriage (apart from legacies and gifts); in most states of common law, intestacy law sets the ratio at half of the estate, elsewhere at one-third (Aker 1998; Wypyski 1976).

In the United States, as well, this standing of the widow or widower in intestacy law is the result of a long process of legal change. In the eighteenth century, the legal situation of the surviving spouse initially deteriorated. The dower rights that existed until the end of the seventeenth century, and which granted the widow one-third of the estate and the children two-thirds, were altered in the eighteenth century in such a way that the widow possessed only the *lifetime interest* to one-third of the realty, and was given full rights of ownership merely to the essential household property (Shammas 1987, 158).[16] With respect to real property, full ownership rights went to the testator's closest blood relative—usually children—a situation that illustrates the importance of the paternal bloodline in the transfer of property *mortis causa*. Lifetime interest rights expired with the death of the widow or upon her remarriage, at which point the economic benefit also passed to the husband's relatives. The widow could not use the husband's wealth to establish a family outside of his bloodline. The property inherited with a lifetime interest had the function of providing maintenance, which, after a remarriage, was the obligation of the *new* husband. As late as the 1890s, about 72% of husbands in one county in Pennsylvania did not bequeath their real property to their wives in full ownership (Shammas, Salmon, and Dahlin 1987, 113), a practice that reveals the importance of the desire to preserve family wealth in the bloodline.[17]

The patriarchal character of intestacy law in the United States in the nineteenth century is reflected most essentially in the *unequal* inheritance rights of the spouses. For if the husband survived his wife, the widower had a lifetime estate in the wife's entire real property. The heirs were her children or the closest relatives in the order of succession. Unlike the husband, the wife had no right under common law to bequeath land testamentarily (Shammas 1987, 159).

However, the patriarchal character of intestacy law becomes fully apparent only in connection with the rules of property law. For the latter stipulated (as in Germany and France) that upon marriage, the disposition over the wife's property passed to the husband. The legal status of the wife was fundamentally altered by marriage. While as an unmarried woman she had full individual property rights, which meant she could enjoy the fruits of her property, sell it, bequeath it testamentarily, and enforce her rights in court; these rights passed to the husband upon marriage. The wife's movable property was transferred to the husband, which meant that he also passed it on by will. In the case of real property, while it remained formally in the wife's possession, its economic benefit belonged to the husband, who was also responsible for administrating it. The only restriction was that husbands could not sell real property owned by their wives without their consent (Shammas, Salmon, and Dahlin 1987, 67).

A husband represented his wife in court. Although he was liable for her debts with his property, he was allowed to use the yield of the property she brought into the marriage to cover his own debts. In short, the wife became a *femme covert*. The legal background to this was the principle of the marital unity in common law, which was connected to the complete community of property between husband and wife in marriage. The "executor" of this unity was the husband. "The husband and wife are one person in law," said the dictum of William Blackstone (2001 [1771], 1:339). The legal existence of the wife was incorporated into that of the husband.

The only way a married woman could obtain greater control over her property was by using the institute of the "settlement," which was also derived from English law. Under this arrangement, the rights of disposition over her property could be transferred to a trustee and thus remain shielded from the husband's direct access. However, since this device was legally complicated, it was unsuitable for the mostly small real property in the United Sates and was little used (Friedman 1999, 51).[18] In South Carolina, for example, only 1–2% of married couples around 1800 had regulated their property relationships with settlements (Shammas, Salmon, and Dahlin 1987, 78). Still, this legal institution developed into a vehicle for strengthening the wife's property rights. At the end of the eighteenth century, Pennsylvania introduced the possibility of establishing "simple marriage settlements," under which the property was no longer administrated by a trustee, but by the woman herself. This was essentially a marriage contract in which a separation of property was agreed upon. It could also stipulate the woman's right to dispose over her real property testamentarily. This is the first step toward equal property rights, which then developed further from the middle of the nineteenth century, when women were given the right to hold and devise their own property (Shammas, Salmon, and Dahlin 1987, 76–77).

The reform of property and inheritance rights for married women in the United Sates was brought about essentially by the Married Women's Property acts that were passed in the various states beginning in 1835, though chiefly in the 1840s (Chused 1983, 1261). These acts granted married women the free control over all property they brought into the marriage or acquired during it, including its testamentary bequest. The beginnings of this development can be traced back to the early nineteenth century, when courts, and in part also new laws, began to strengthen these rights (Shammas, Salmon, and Dahlin 1987, 92). One example of this came in 1833, when "legislators voted to allow mothers inheritance rights in their children's estates even when fathers were still living" (92). These trends, however, did not occur in all states at the same time, and even after passage of the Married Women's Property acts they certainly did not lead to the complete equality of women in inheritance law by the end of the nineteenth century. In a few community property states, for example, women were still prohibited from testamentarily passing on their half of the wealth accrued during marriage. Moreover, the laws about women's property that were enacted after 1848 sometimes encountered a judicial system that interpreted them conservatively. The state supreme court of Pennsylvania, for example, decided in 1853 that husbands continued to be entitled to the income of their spouses (Dahlinger 1918, 80–81; Husbands 1878, 95). In the last third of the nineteenth century, the states passed additional laws that strengthened the status of wives in property law and slowly replaced the principle of the legal unity of husband and wife in common law.

In the second half of the nineteenth century, one can also detect a development whereby a growing number of states abolished dower and curtesy rights and introduced intestacy laws that granted widows and widowers equal rights. In the process, rights to a lifetime interest were increasingly replaced with full ownership rights to the inheritance portion. States that retained the dower expanded the rights in favor of women, even though the preferential treatment of the husband through greater claims in intestacy law often remained in place. This direction in the change of intestacy law is especially apparent in those states that became states after 1850, thus formulating their civil law at a time when the altered conception of the woman's legal status had already been clearly articulated politically (Shammas, Salmon, and Dahlin 1987, 85f.). In addition, the rights of widows were strengthened beginning in the late 1830s by so-called homestead provisions, which stipulated that the homestead could not be seized in the interest of creditors who had claims against the deceased husband.

In the United States, the intestacy inheritance rights of women were thus expanded especially from the middle of the nineteenth century on. With equality in property law, the independent administration of the property brought into the marriage by the woman, some American states had a more progressive law at the end of the nineteenth century than did Germany and France. At least two factors can be listed as the reasons for this: First, there was the growing awareness in the nineteenth century that an inheritance law that placed the widow in a worse position than the widower was unjust. The women's movement that emerged in the 1830s helped to gain passage of the Married Women's Property acts.[19] Early activists were Margaret Fuller, Elizabeth Stanton, and Lucretia Mott, for whom the property rights of women played an important role. The women's movement in the United States, which was recruited chiefly from the social middle class, was opposed chiefly to slavery and demanded restrictions on the consumption of alcohol. But from the middle of the nineteenth century, questions of property and inheritance law also became relevant. Only later did the focus shift to the demand for suffrage (Evans 1989, 76, 102–3). Still, the role of the women's movement in bringing about the changes to inheritance and property law beginning in the 1840s should not be exaggerated. Because of the spread of Romantic notions of family relationships, the beginning industrial production, and the growing importance of the education of children, women assumed a more important place within the family structure (Chused 1983, 1361, 1420–21), which was then also reflected in the emerging reform of the law. The reforms were intended more to give women greater dispositionary freedom within the domestic sphere than to pave the way for economic equality.

Second, the legal reforms had social as well as economic causes. Homestead provisions and the separation of the wife's property from the husband's could help to prevent the pauperization of widows in an increasingly dynamic, and therefore more unpredictable, economy if creditors sought to seize the property a wife brought into the marriage to cover her husband's debts. One goal behind the expansion of women's property rights was therefore protection for the family against creditors, and not necessarily greater economic independence for women (Shammas, Salmon, and Dahlin 1987, 97). This expansion was closely connected chronologically with the economic crisis of 1837, which makes it plausible that its purpose was also to protect the family's social status by segregating part of the property and placing it in the hands of the wife (Chused 1983, 1402ff.).

Property also needed to be shielded against irresponsible husbands who could use up the wealth brought into marriage by the wife, thus thwarting the intent of the inheritance, namely to secure the daughter's livelihood, and the transmission of wealth to blood relatives. Daughters were inheriting more also because of the equal inheritance rights of sons and daughters, and parents took an interest in protecting the property they bestowed upon a daughter in marriage from being wasted by the husband (Friedman 1999, 50).[20] Clignet (1992, 18) has identified the rising social mobility of the American population as one reason behind the strengthening of property rights for married women. This mobility made it more difficult to procure reliable information about the family of the son-in-law, thus making it harder to predict the risk to the property the daughter was bringing into the marriage. This development might also explain an observation made by Bernard Farber (1973, 82), that beginning in the nineteenth century the kinship structure broke away from the model of "multiple memberships" in one's own family of origin and in the husband's family of origin, and oriented itself instead toward a pure descendant model. Through the expansion of marriage markets and the destabilization of marriages, families increasingly lost control over family members by marriage, which is why inheritance law focused on investing in one's own offspring. The precondition for this was the demarcation of an autonomous sphere of property rights for the wife.

Economically, the expansion of the inheritance and property rights of married women, especially the transfer of the inheritance portion in full possession, offered the advantage of a more transparent structure to the real estate market. Since the dower rights of a widow were preserved also when a piece of land was sold, a buyer could often not be certain whether or not the land was encumbered with rights to lifetime interest. Moreover, the restrictions on the wife's legal capacity meant that if the husband abandoned her or became legally incapacitated, she had no legal basis to sell her properties, which impeded the real estate market (Friedman 1999, 50). But it was precisely the organization of property rights focused on economic productivity that dominated the United States in the nineteenth century (Horwitz 1973), and the development of the property rights of married women fits into this paradigm of property law.

The evolution of intestacy law in the United States in the twentieth century can be interpreted as a continuation of the changes that began in the middle of the nineteenth century. Shammas, Salmon, and Dahlin (1987, 164ff.) have charted the clear trend toward the expansion of the surviving spouse's rights. Whereas in 1890 nearly 70% of common-law states had lifetime interest rights for the property inherited between spouses, by 1982 that number had dropped to 12%. At the same time, the intestacy portion of widows and widowers if there were children present increased. In 1890, that portion was less than half of the estate in nearly all common-law states; one hundred years later it was true of only 43% of these states. In Pennsylvania, for example, a reform of inheritance law in 1917 raised the portion from one-third to half of the estate if the decedent had only one child. In another reform in 1978, sparked by the Equal Rights Amendment, the portion was set at half of the estate, without exception, and the intestacy inheritance rights of collateral relatives were also restricted. The entire estate passed to the spouse if "(1) neither children nor parents survived or (2) the value of the estate came to twenty thousand dollars (changed to thirty thousand in 1980) or under and there were no children of the decedent from a previous marriage" (Shammas, Salmon, and Dahlin 1987, 171ff.). Under the law that was valid until 1978, the surviving spouse inherited the entire estate only if there were no siblings, nieces and nephews, uncles and aunts, or grandparents (Wypyski 1976, 43). Here, too, the evolution of the law shows a stronger focus on the inheritance rights of the nuclear family composed of spouses and children. In subsequent changes to the codes in Pennsylvania, the tax-exempt share of the spouse was increased further (Aker 1998, 3).[21]

In the community property states, where the surviving spouse was anyhow entitled to half of the accrued gains, the four states that still prohibited widows from passing on their share testamentarily at the end of the nineteenth century abolished this restriction. Here, too, we thus see, alongside the strengthening of the rights of widows vis-à-vis the relatives, a strengthening of the individual inheritance rights of women.

In the 1970s, another feature was found to be discriminatory toward women in common-law states: although spouses could own separate property, because the husband's income was usually higher, his accrued gains were greater during the marriage. In those states that set the intestacy portion for the surviving spouse at below 50%, for widows this led to a share of accrued gains that was less than half (Shammas, Salmon, and Dahlin 1987, 170).

France. The German and American trends toward a gradual expansion of the inheritance rights of the surviving spouse and the simultaneous trimming of the circle of relatives entitled to an inheritance alongside the spouse are also evident in France. However, French inheritance law in the nineteenth century had one surprising peculiarity: the surviving spouse was not an heir. Only the relatives of the testator were heirs, especially the children—in childless marriages it was the closest relatives, in accordance with the structure of the class system.[22] The spouse had merely an extraordinary, subsidiary right of succession in case no relatives entered into the inheritance; he or she inherited merely before the state did. The systematic thinking behind this regulation was that the families of the spouses were connected only by marriage; with the dissolution of the marriage upon death, the surviving spouse also ceased to be connected to the decedent's family and therefore had no share in the estate of the deceased partner (Baumann 1996, 42). Although the inheritance rights of the spouse were expanded through legal reforms beginning in the second half of the nineteenth century, and especially through the law of 9 March 1891, the weak position of the spouse in French law changed only in most recent times.

This characteristic of French inheritance law, too, can be seen as evidence that over the long term, rules of civil law tend to follow the path that has been laid down. The exclusion of the spouse from statutory inheritance law if blood relatives exist was taken over into the Code Civil from the law of the *coutumes* (Ferid and Sonnenberger 1987, 499). It reveals the normative structure of a conception of property in French law that is oriented toward the line of blood relatives. Although similar regulations existed in American common law and in Germany in both the Allgemeines Landrecht and in common law, they did not have the kind of exclusionary quality that characterizes the Code Civil.

At the same time, the exclusion of the spouse from the group of heirs did not mean that widows or widowers had no claims of property rights against the estate. According to French law, the property relationship that existed was one of a community of movables and acquisitions (*communauté légale*). The common property consisted of all movable goods and whatever real estate was acquired during the marriage. It did not include real estate brought into the marriage by the spouses (Weber 1907, 328).[23] Here we encounter again the distinction between *propres* and *acquêts* that is familiar to us from the *droit coutumier*. Until the legal reform of 1965, in France the administration of all property lay exclusively with the husband, including the special property of the wife and her earned income (Weber 1907, 329; Ferid and Sonnenberger 1987, 157). However, in contrast to American common law, this patriarchal structure of property law did not carry over into a formal unequal treatment of husband and wife in statutory inheritance law, where the principle of equality prevailed.

In the case of the death of a spouse, the surviving partner was entitled to one-half of the common property (Rieg 1971, 83). The extent of the spouse's claim to the estate depended on the ratio between the real property the decedent brought into the marriage and the remaining assets of the estate. Marianne Weber (1907, 330) sees in this regulation of the Code Civil legislation that is more progressive than what is found in common law, because French inheritance law grants the spouses equal standing. However, the reason for the regulations, she argues, was not the equality of the wife, but consideration for her family of origin—protection of the wealth. On this point, French inheritance law has a less pronounced patrilineal structure than either its German or American counterpart, while at the same time being more strongly oriented toward the principle of blood kinship.

The literature on legal policy and legal history overwhelmingly asserts that the wife had a particularly disadvantageous legal status in nineteenth-century French inheritance law. Boissonade (1874, 337ff.), for example, who participated in an essay contest on the question of spousal inheritance rights sponsored by the Académie des sciences morales et politiques in 1871, demanded its reform with the goal of improving the legal standing of the widow. The case he cited to illustrate the need for reform concerned a couple who, because of the disparity in assets, had contractually agreed on property relations other than the *communauté légale*. As a consequence, the woman had no claim whatsoever to the estate after her husband's death.

In fact, it would appear that there was wide agreement in France that the legal status of the surviving spouse had to be improved, and a multitude of small reforms from the 1860s to today have been intended to accomplish just that. In the process, the prevailing law was increasingly criticized for failing to do justice to what was presumed to be a strong affective bond between the spouses—even the illegitimate child of the testator was privileged over the spouse in intestacy law!

The reform of spousal inheritance law began in the last third of the nineteenth century and continued gradually throughout the twentieth century.[24] But it was only in 2001 (!) that a law was passed on the basis of which the spouse was granted full rights of ownership to shares of the estate alongside close relatives: next to common children, the spouse now inherits one-quarter of the estate in full ownership or the entire estate with a lifetime interest; alongside the testator's children from a previous marriage, one-quarter in full ownership, alongside parents, one-half (see the law of 3 December 2001).

The evolution of spousal inheritance law in France over the past 140 years reveals, as in Germany and the United Sates, a consistent trend toward the expansion of the rights of surviving marriage partners. However, one peculiarity that set French intestacy law apart until very recently was the refusal to grant full property rights (*pleine propriété*) to the spouse if she or he inherited alongside the testator's children, ascendants, and descendants; this peculiarity points to the strong orientation of French inheritance law to the principle of blood kinship. In the United States, where lifetime interests were also regulated by law in the nineteenth century, there was a much earlier tendency in the evolution of the law to replace them with full rights of ownership to a portion of the estate. The stronger position of the wife in German intestacy law in the nineteenth century was due to the strong influence of Roman law, which granted the surviving spouse full ownership rights. In the United States, the greater transparency of ownership conditions—that is, the greater security in legal transactions—may have been decisive for the early conversion of lifetime interests to full ownership.

Today, the legal situation in the three countries has become nearly the same. In France, politicians advocated this move for more than one hundred years (Holthöfer 1987, 161). The weak status of the spouse ran counter to the declining importance of the emotional bonds within the extended network of relatives and to the fact that claims to maintenance and support were focused increasingly on marriage.[25]

3.3. THE INTEGRATION OF ILLEGITIMATE CHILDREN INTO INHERITANCE LAW

The development of the inheritance rights of illegitimate children can be described as a process of integration. Two hundred years ago, these children were still largely excluded from claims to inheritance rights. Today, they are more or less—in France and Germany even completely—equal to legitimate children and are thus integrated into the family structure with respect to inheritance law. Definitions of the legitimacy or illegitimacy of children give expression to structures of social recognition by which society regulates its system of family membership while at the same time articulating claims to solidarity. What I suggest is that the evolution of these definitions also reflects the declining importance of inheritance strategies centered on blood kinship, and a changing legal-ethical understanding that emphasizes the natural equality of children independent of the marital status of their parents.

In all three countries, the nearly complete exclusion of illegitimate children from family law at the beginning of the nineteenth century was the result of medieval and feudal legal principles that had emerged under pressure from the church (Renaut 1997, 374ff.). The intent was to suppress concubinage, which was widely practiced in the Roman Empire, in favor of the monogamous marital relationship. Under Roman law, the children of a concubinary relationship had at least limited inheritance rights; with the triumph of Christianity, however, these rights became the target of social criticism and were eventually abolished altogether with the ecclesiastical prohibition of concubinage in 1530 (Hauser 1997, 894–95; Krause 1967, 498–99; Robbins and Deak 1930, 314). The family model that established itself in the Middle Ages was oriented in principle toward the male bloodline *and* legitimacy; the discrimination against illegitimate children served to protect this family structure. It solidified the claims to solidarity of the spouse, the legitimate children, and the (male) relatives, claims that were simultaneously protected by excluding illegitimate relatives.[26] The discrimination against the husband's illegitimate children was in the interest of both the husband *and* his wife. The husband was protected against legal claims to property by the child's mother and the child itself. The wife, however, also had an interest in fending off these claims, because they always had to come at the expense of the legitimate family.[27] At the same time, the discrimination against illegitimate children in inheritance law went against the interests of the child's mother, the child itself, as well as the public authorities, since the latter had to pay the costs of supporting them (Hauser 1997, 935; Krause 1967, 499; Weber 1978 [1922], 1:372).

The legal systems of the three countries do not differ in the fact that illegitimate children were discriminated against in inheritance law, but they do differ in the concrete legal form this discrimination took.

The exclusion of illegitimate children was most thorough and consistent in the early nineteenth century in the United States, where common law denied them any legal relationship to the biological parents. This was based on the categorization of the illegitimate child in common law as *filius nullius*:

> The incapacity of a bastard conflicts principally in this, that he cannot be heir to any one, neither can he have heirs, but of his own body; for being nullius filius, he is therefore of kin to nobody, and has no ancestor from whom any inheritable blood can be derived. (Blackstone 2001 [1771], 1:353)

Illegitimate children had no legal inheritance rights in colonial America, and they could not be legitimized through recognition or the subsequent marriage of their parents. Under common law, an illegitimate child did not even have claims for support against its parents and was dependent on the church for maintenance. It was only to relieve the church of the burden of maintenance costs and to "punish" the procreation of illegitimate children that the English Poor Law of 1576 for the first time imposed an obligation to provide support on the parents, a provision that was then taken over into American law (Robbins and Deak 1930, 317).

In France, as well, illegitimate children had no inheritance claims against their parents under the ancien régime. If they were not recognized, these children were regarded as belonging to no family at all, and if they died childless, their estate was inherited by the spouse or the state. Unlike under English common law, however, illegitimate children did have claims to support from their parents. According to French law, the fact of parentage established the child's natural right to maintenance. This legal status of the illegitimate child in the *coutumes* presumably originated in Germanic law, in which mothers had to care for illegitimate children under the supervision of the clan (Robbins and Deak 1930, 315–16).

The legal status of illegitimate children was noticeably better in Germany. Here, too, the strong orientation of German law toward Roman law was

important. On this issue, state law took its cues from Justinian law. According to the Allgemeines Landrecht, illegitimate children had an equal right to
inherit from the mother alongside her other offspring. Conversely, the
mother inherited from her illegitimate child. These children were therefore
integrated into the matrilineal kinship system. This standing of illegitimate children vis-à-vis the mother has its roots in Roman law, in which
all of the mother's children, legitimate or not, are her offspring (cognates)
(Robbins and Deak 1930, 311) and thus have a kinship relationship to her.
Moreover, according to the Landrecht, illegitimate children, under specific
circumstances, inherited one-sixth of the father's estate.[28] This stipulation
of German law was also derived from Justinian Roman law. In contrast to
France and the United Sates, the illegitimate child was, according to the
Landrecht, always related to the family of the mother. And no distinction
was made in this respect between children born out of wedlock and those
born as the result of adultery.

France. In intellectual discourse, the exclusion of illegitimate children
had already drawn intense criticism before the Revolution, for example,
in Rousseau. The process of making illegitimate children legally equal
began in France with the Revolution. For a brief period, revolutionary
legislation profoundly altered the inheritance rights of illegitimate children. The law of 12 Brumaire II (1793) made illegitimate children equal
to legitimate children, only those produced by adultery had a reduced
claim to merely one-third of the statutory inheritance right of a child.
This reform can be interpreted as an expression of the principle of equality of the French Revolution (Renaut 1997, 389). However, this law was
repealed with the introduction of the Code Civil. Equality for illegitimate
children as part of the reform of the family enacted by the Revolution ran
into considerable public and political opposition in the middle of the
1790s. Equal status was rejected, since it would morally destroy the legitimate family as the cell of the nation (Desan 1999, 115). The defenders of
the rights of illegitimate children, who argued on the basis of the natural
equality of all children, were defeated in the political clash. Against this
backdrop, nonrecognized or nonrecognizable children (the product of
adultery or incest) were once again excluded entirely from inheritance law
and had no inheritance claims of any kind throughout the nineteenth century. It was only in 1896 that a first step was taken toward giving these
children equal legal standing, in that they were granted a claim for support
against the estate of the parents.

With the adoption of the Code Civil, recognized illegitimate children
also suffered a setback with regard to their inheritance rights compared to
the provisions of revolutionary legislation. They inherited only by way of
succession irrégulaire (without *saisine*) and they initially inherited only
from their parents, but not from other relatives (Holthöfer 1987, 168).
Their inheritance claim alongside legitimate offspring amounted to one-
third of the statutory portion, alongside more distant relatives to one-half

or three-quarters of this portion. The entire estate passed to them only if the testator was not survived by any relatives entitled to being heirs.[29] It was not permissible to increase the share under intestacy law through gifts or testamentary disposition (Holthöfer 1982, 991).

The exclusion of illegitimate children from inheritance law reveals that membership in the family group is not the product of natural parentage, but the result of socially constructed rules. Illegitimate children were described as "natural children," which expresses the fact that, in contrast to "legal children," they had no legal relationship to the families of their parents. The circumstance of their illegitimate birth placed these children outside of the existing legal order; as a result, they had only natural rights, which can consist in a claim to maintenance, for example. However, both French and German law allowed for the possibility of a later integration of these children in that they were legitimized by the subsequent marriage of the parents (German *Mantelkind,* lit. "cloak child"), were recognized by them as their children,[30] or were adopted by their parents. Through acknowledgment by the parents, the child became a member of the family of the respective parent.

At the same time, all three countries reveal gender-based differences in the legitimation of illegitimate children, which once again highlight the patrilineal character of the kinship structure. Giving the father the option of refusing to acknowledge an illegitimate child was intended to protect the property of the legitimate paternal kin from the claims of illegitimate children. In France, illegitimate children thus had the right, until 1912, to legally compel only acknowledgment by their mother, but not the determination of paternity. In fact, the Code Civil stipulated: "La recherche de la paternité est interdite" (the search for paternity is forbidden) (Art. 340 C.C.).[31] Only the father himself could initiate acknowledgment. In Germany, the illegitimate child was equal to legitimate children in relationship to the mother, but by law was not related to the biological father. As a result, the illegitimate child, unless the father acknowledged the child on his own, had no legal property claims against him.[32] This situation applied until 1969.

The exclusion of illegitimate children from the kinship system was not intended to punish the illegitimate child, but to uphold the institution of the legitimate family, which was to be defended as the foundation for the fulfillment of society's reproductive function (Davis 1939, 223ff.). With respect to property law, the legitimate family is protected against moral transgressions—at the expense of illegitimate children. The reason why the paternal line was shielded more thoroughly was because it had greater importance within the kinship system (and not because the child was biologically more dependent on the mother, for example). Since the illegitimate child represented a violation of the norms that were meant to uphold the family's reproductive function, the "damage" was minimized by excluding the child from the *more important* family line. That explains why in all three countries, illegitimate children were granted inheritance rights from the maternal side of the family much earlier than from the paternal side.

The exclusion of the illegitimate child is an expression of a kinship system organized along patrilineal lines; the increasing equalization, which accords the child a place also in the father's family system, reflects, conversely, the weakening of this organizational principle as inheritance law evolves.

But *why* was there a tendency to expand the rights of illegitimate children? From a legal-theoretical perspective, the decline of natural law meant that unequal legal treatment could no longer be justified on the grounds that illegitimate children violated the natural order. Instead, law was understood as positive law, and in Enlightenment thought it was based on the principle that all citizens are equal before the law. This equality is violated if children are treated unequally as a result of the behavior of their parents, for which they cannot be held accountable. In this way, the principle of equality exerted pressure in the direction of granting illegitimate children equal status (Farber 1973, 65–66). Equality could be achieved only if the marital status of the parents was abolished as a criterion for classifying the rights of children. A conflict therefore emerged between the Enlightenment legal principle of natural equality and the principle of legitimacy as the precondition for, among other things, acquiring inheritance rights.

In France, this pressure toward legal equality for illegitimate children was reflected in Revolutionary legislation and then in various legislative initiatives that were introduced in parliament in the second half of the nineteenth century. However, legal reform did not happen until 1896. A parliamentary group in the Senate backed the motion of the delegate Letellier, who essentially wanted to reintroduce the Revolutionary law. However, it proved impossible to push the legal equality of illegitimate children through parliament. Opponents saw it as an attack on the institution of marriage itself. It was especially the Catholic Church in France that spoke out repeatedly against the equality of illegitimate children in inheritance law, especially of adulterine children, on the grounds that the legal equality of these children would ruin the family (Rieg 1971, 87; Weber 1907, 325). It was thus not only legal principles that clashed in the conflict over the legal status of illegitimate children, but also moral ideas about the family and the limiting of sexual relations to marriage. In the controversy in France during the Third Republic, the two camps were the Republicans, who focused on the principle of equality, on the one side, and the Catholic Church, which highlighted the protection of the family, on the other side. The compromise in the law of 1896 lay in the moderate expansion of the rights of illegitimate children: the statutory inheritance portion was set at one-half the portion of legitimate children and three-quarters of this portion alongside more distant relatives. Illegitimate children continued to have intestate inheritance rights only against the parents, but not against other relatives. However, the law of 1896 permitted testamentary bequests to illegitimate children (Holthöfer 1982, 991ff.; Weber 1907, 324). "Adulterine children" and "incestuous children" remained without inheritance rights against either their father or mother, and any gift or bequest to their benefit was null and void (Weber 1907, 325). Along with the moral and legal-theoretical issues, the question of the duty of providing support was always crucial to the development of the legal status of illegitimate children. It was only in the law of 1955 that these children were granted a claim to support from their father (Renaut 1997, 394ff.). A right to support from the mother already existed.

Germany. As a result of their integration of the mother's kinship line, illegitimate children in Germany had a stronger standing in inheritance law in the nineteenth century compared to France. However, the legal development in this area all but stagnated in Germany until 1969 (!). In fact, in the middle of the nineteenth century, the legal situation worsened. In the original version of the Allgemeines Landrecht the illegitimate child had a claim to alimentation from the father,[33] for which the father's parents were legally liable. This stipulation was presumably motivated by the desire to prevent infanticide by desperate mothers (Weber 1907, 340–41). This obligation was stricken from the Landrecht in 1854, that is, as a result of the reaction to the Revolution of 1848. This move was justified with the positive effect it would have on female morality (Weber 1907, 341).

The codification of private law in the BGB also failed to bring any improvement in the status of illegitimate children. They were still seen as unrelated to the father and had an inheritance right only from the mother's side. A statutory inheritance right against the father was ruled out. Two consistent differences are evident between French and German law: first, French inheritance law discriminated more strongly against illegitimate children as far as the mother's side was concerned. Second, this area of the law was more highly charged with morality in France. A distinction was made between illegitimate children and adulterine children, with the latter possessing no inheritance rights of any kind.

United States. In the nineteenth century, it was especially the inheritance rights of illegitimate children to the mother's estate that were broadened in America. This development began in Virginia, the first state to place illegitimate and legitimate children on an equal footing in their inheritance rights against the mother (1785), thus integrating illegitimate offspring into the matrilineal kinship system (Freund 1919, 19). In Pennsylvania, illegitimate children acquired the right to inherit from their mothers in 1855 (Shammas, Salmon, and Dahlin 1987, 95–96). By 1919, most American states had passed similar laws, though they differed, among other things, in whether the inheritance right existed only directly from the mother, or whether illegitimate children could also represent their mother. This legal development established a kinship relationship of the child to the maternal side of its biological family in the first place; the children were legally given a place within the kinship system. Still, the discrepancy between the paternal and the maternal sides is also evident in the United States. Rights to inherit from the father existed—if at all—only if he had acknowledged the illegitimate child. At the end of the nineteenth century, however, only a minority of 40% of the jurisdictions granted a statutory inheritance right to illegitimate children even under these conditions (Shammas, Salmon, and Dahlin 1987, 85). For example, the 1855 law in Pennsylvania ruled out the illegitimate child's inheritance rights against the father (95).

As late as the 1960s, the inheritance rights of illegitimate children were generally limited in the United States. For the most part, the children inherited from their mother, though not always on an equal footing with legitimate children. In New York, for example, the presence of legitimate children excluded illegitimate children from intestacy law. In many cases, illegitimate children continued to inherit from the father only if he had acknowledged them (Wypyski 1976, 50ff.), and even a successful paternity suit often did not lead to inheritance rights for the child (Krause 1967, 478).[34]

The discrimination against illegitimate children under inheritance law waned in the late 1960s. At that time there was a more or less simultaneous push in legal development in France, Germany, and the United States: in the two European countries it led to complete equality for illegitimate children, in the United States at least to the strong expansion of their inheritance rights.

In France, the statutory inheritance law was reformed in 1972. Under the new law, illegitimate children whose kinship had been ascertained were given equal status with legitimate children with respect to inheritance claims. For adulterine children, however, disabilities continued to exist if they "were potential heirs alongside the spouse of the marriage violated by the adultery or alongside legitimate children from this marriage" (Ferid and Sonnenberger 1987, 510). In the 1990s, this discrimination was challenged before the European Court of Human Rights, which rejected the French law as discriminatory (Le Monde, 13 May 2001). The law of 3 December 2001 brought to conclusion the legal development that had begun during the Revolution by granting adulterine children equal standing in inheritance law.

In Germany, the Nonmarital Children's Act of 1969 abolished the paragraph of the BGB that declared that illegitimate children were not related to the father (§1589, Sec. 2). By virtue of this law, illegitimate children were incorporated also into the father's family line. However, they still lacked equality in terms of inheritance rights: they were entitled only to a substitutional succession claim consisting of a claim of financial compensation equal to the statutory inheritance portion. As an alternative to their statutory inheritance claim, illegitimate children henceforth had the right to premature inheritance compensation. These special inheritance rules were intended to avoid familial conflicts that were expected if and when marital and nonmarital children as well as the testator's wife who was not related to the child found themselves thrown together into a community of heirs (Leipold 2000, 74–75). This special status was abolished by the Inheritance Law Equality Act of 1997. Since then, illegitimate children form a community of heirs with legitimate children (Leipold 2000, 72).

In the United States, the Supreme Court took on the issue of the discrimination against illegitimate children beginning in 1968 and declared the laws of various states to be unconstitutional.[35] The court maintained that it was incompatible with the Constitution to discriminate against a person in inheritance law on the basis of the behavior of the parents. The complaints were based on the equal protection clause of the Fourteenth Amendment.[36] It is thus not permissible to disadvantage extramarital children in statutory inheritance law for moral reasons, that is, with the goal of promoting family values. Children may not be punished for their parents' conduct (Hauser 1997, 926; Zingo and Early 1994, 77). Moreover, a state may not entirely preclude the inheritance rights of an extramarital child if that child has inheritance rights from the mother (Hauser 1997, 907). Still, in spite of a visible trend toward strengthening the inheritance rights of nonmarital children, "it is still quite difficult for the illegitimate child to obtain either support or inheritance rights from the father" (Jones et al. 1985, 679).[37] For a number of decisions up to the mid-1980s continued to recognize the right of states to assign illegitimate children a different status in inheritance law than legitimate children, which was justified with the protection against unfounded claims of paternity[38] and the desire to secure property within the traditional family (Hauser 1997, 892, 920; Krause 1967, 491ff.; Zingo and Early 1994, 74, 81, 83). For example, it is constitutional if a state excludes illegitimate children from intestacy law if the testator has marital children or the father has not acknowledged the children (Hauser 1997, 907). One motivation behind the limits placed on the inheritance rights of illegitimate children if paternity was not established during the testator's lifetime is to provide protection against unfounded inheritance claims. Also permissible are regulations as in Georgia, where a father can inherit from his illegitimate child only if he previously cared for and supported that child (Mixon 2000, 1776).

If one surveys the legal reforms in the American states since the 1970s, one can see also here a clear trend toward the equal treatment of illegitimate children. Since 1978, Pennsylvania, for example, has no longer recognized any distinction between legitimate and illegitimate children in the right to inherit from the father if the father acknowledged his extramarital offspring, took the child into his home, or paternity was determined by a court pursuant to a paternity suit (Aker 1998, 16–17). This development is also evident from changes to the Uniform Probate Code, a sort of list of federal recommendations on how to structure inheritance law, which is intended to standardize inheritance law in the United States. States can adopt this code as their own law in part or in its entirety.[39] If one compares the versions of the Uniform Probate Code from 1969 and 1990, a development toward greater legal equality for illegitimate children in inheritance law is evident: the version of 1969 still tied inheritance rights to the marital status of the parents, with illegitimate children having inheritance rights against the father only if paternity was determined during the father's lifetime.

The version of 1990, however, laid down the principle that legitimate and illegitimate children had equal rights in inheritance (Hauser 1997, 952); here it is therefore biological parentage—not the emotional or other relationship between father and extramarital child—that is treated as the basis for claims to inheritance rights.

How can one explain the simultaneity of the legal reforms in the three countries since the late 1960s? The legal-theoretical conflict over the natural equality of children, which had already erupted during the Enlightenment, could not have been directly responsible, since it had been going on for more than two hundred years without leading to equality for illegitimate children. Rather, three interconnected developments coincided in the postwar period.

1. The demand for the equal treatment of illegitimate children became louder in international law after the war. The UN's Universal Declaration of Human Rights in 1948 called for equal social protection for legitimate and illegitimate children (Art. 25). Similar demands were enshrined in the European Convention on Human Rights (1959) and the American Convention on Human Rights (1969). In 1967, a UN subcommission of the Commission on Human Rights issued a declaration calling for the legal equality of illegitimate children (Hauser 1997, 897ff.). This development can be interpreted as the already mentioned "sacralization of the person" (Joas), which made the punishment of illegitimate children for their parents' conduct appear increasingly problematic. This trend in international law has a clear chronological connection to the legal reform in the three countries in question at the end of the sixties and the beginning of the seventies.

Two other developments within the law were important for the final equality achieved by illegitimate children in inheritance law in Germany and France at the end of the 1990s. In Germany, one important impulse came from reunification. In East Germany, illegitimate children had already achieved legal equality. Since illegitimate children in the territory being incorporated were not to be deprived of this right, while civil law in Germany was to be standardized, there was political pressure to reform this part of inheritance law (Leipold 2000, 75). In France, the legislature in 2001 followed a decision by the European Court for Human Rights. These contexts are important in terms of legal sociology, because they point to the possibility that outside influence can be exerted on the development of national law and that the latter can break out of the development path to which it has been committed.

2. In all three countries in question, the number of out-of-wedlock births has been on the rise since the 1960s. While illegitimate births accounted for 10% of all births in the United States in the mid-sixties, that figure rose to more than 30% by the mid-nineties. An even more dramatic trend is visible in France: up until 1970, well under 10% of children were born to unwed parents, but by the end of the 1990s, that number had risen to over 40%. The number of illegitimate births in Germany is far below these levels. In West Germany the percentage stood around 10% as late as the end of the

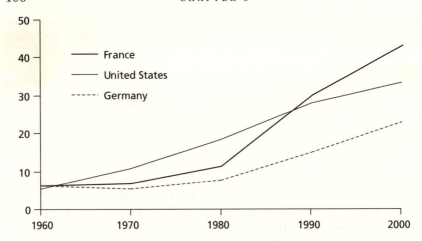

Figure 3.1 The trend in out-of-wedlock births since 1960 (in %)
Sources: Eurostat Jahrbuch 2002; Statistical Abstracts of the United States, various years.

1980s (East and West Germany together, 16% in 1989), by the end of the 1990s it had reached 23% in the unified Germany.

The family has thus changed in all three countries since the 1960s. The rise in the percentage of illegitimate children is presumably related in two ways to the abolition of discrimination against them in inheritance law. First, since the discrimination affects a growing population group, one would expect the political resistance to it would grow.

3. Second, and this is the third aspect, the numbers show—by the conduct of the parents themselves, as it were—a changing notion of legal ethics. The marital status of the parents is no longer regarded as the only normative family model, as nonmarital relationships are meeting with wider social acceptance. That is unquestionably true for the two European countries, where, according to a Gallup poll in 1997, 90% of those asked did not consider it immoral for nonmarried couples to have children. Only in the United States was a more critical attitude found: here, half of the population rejected it as morally wrong for unmarried couples to have children (Gallup 1997). Public opinion might explain why not all the states in the United States, in contrast to France and Germany, have enacted complete legal equality for illegitimate children.[40] Still, on the whole it is true that a significant change in attitude toward extramarital children has taken place in the societies in question during the last thirty-five years, which has certainly worked to effect a change in legal norms:

> In the light of developing concepts of individual freedom and morality, the right of the government to prohibit or discourage any immoral conduct which does no harm to the public interest is being increasingly challenged. (Farber 1973, 71)

As late as the end of the 1930s, Kingsley Davis (1939) had still declared that the discrimination against illegitimate children in inheritance law was the structural precondition for society to fulfill its reproductive function. Even if such children were to achieve legal equality, Davis argued, one had to expect their social stigmatization to continue, because marriage and the family, as the central reproductive institutions, were necessary to the existence of society (1939, 230–31). Davis could not foresee, presumably because the stigmatization of illegitimate children had existed for centuries, that the concrete institutional model within which the reproductive functions were fulfilled could rapidly undergo substantial change.

What consequences, however, did this change have for the kinship structure as laid out by Parsons (1954)? First, one could see in the legal equality of illegitimate children a loss of meaning for or a threat to the bourgeois nuclear family (Clignet 1992, 16–17; Holthöfer 1987, 168), and thus also to the kinship structure of connected conjugal families. However, to the extent that this structure has lost its dominance during the last fifty years, the change is not based—as one might think on the basis of functionalist arguments—on the legal integration of illegitimate children, but rather on the development of sequential marriages and partnerships that are leading to the spread of step and patchwork families. As a result, conjugal families are no longer—as in Parsons's kinship model—linked by only *one* person on each side, who occupies the position of either parent or child. Instead, these families can be linked in multiple ways, which gives rise to ambivalent kinship structure that could possibly throw claims of solidarity into doubt. For example, a loss of solidarity is a threat for children whose parents separate and establish new families. However, a multiplicity of family forms can also establish new claims to solidarity, which can be supported in terms of inheritance law by giving the testator the greatest possible testamentary freedom and disconnecting the inheritance tax from the closeness of the kin relationship.

Ironically enough, the legal equality of illegitimate children can be interpreted as the very attempt to uphold Parsons's kinship model by preserving the solidarity and cohesiveness of conjugal families even if the parents are not married. After all, the internal diversification of the family model produced by the integration of nonmarital partnerships with joint children is oriented toward the structure of the nuclear family. The equal status of children in inheritance law and their integration into the kinship system of the family of origin became—in defiance of the notion that this family model was under threat or becoming meaningless—a factor that stabilized the ordering system of the conjugal family.

3.4. Conclusion

In this chapter I have examined the development of three important regulatory areas within statutory inheritance law. My starting point was the thesis that the changes in intestacy law reveal the change in the normative foundation underlying relationships of solidarity within the family system. The various legal aspects—equality between children, spousal inheritance rights, and inheritance rights of illegitimate children—are not directly connected. However, an analysis of these three areas of statutory inheritance law shows a few overarching trends.

The first trend lies in the declining importance of the principle of dynastic inheritance. Over the course of the last two hundred years, the inheritance rights of distant collateral relatives were curtailed in all three countries. In France and in a few of the American states, the state inherits if the testator is not survived by relatives of the fourth or sixth degree. The trend is also reflected in the expansion of the intestacy inheritance rights of the spouse "at the expense" of the testator's relatives. Conversely related to this is the tendency for the claims to solidarity enshrined in statutory inheritance law to be increasingly focused on the nuclear family. The development of inheritance law reveals the increasing orientation toward individuals to whom the testator is believed to have an especially close emotional bond—the spouse and the children. At the same time, the declining importance of the wider kinship system within the structure of statutory inheritance law indicates that claims to solidarity or support become focused on the nuclear family, with the attendant increasing segregation of the conjugal family from the more distant kinship relationships (Parsons 1954, 184–84).

A second trend becomes visible in the growing assertion of the principle of equality within statutory inheritance law. This applies, first, to the equality between sons and daughters as well as between the firstborn and the later born. Primogeniture succession is given up in all three countries by the late eighteenth century. The privileged position of the firstborn son was most intimately connected to feudal structures in which the ownership of land was tied to public offices and military obligations that could not be divided at will. However, the introduction of egalitarian inheritance is also justified with value beliefs that are based on the natural equality of human beings, thus delegitimizing privileges by virtue of birth.

The orientation toward the principle of equality is also evident in the development of the inheritance rights of the surviving spouse. Here, statutory inheritance law and questions of property law as they relate to family law are tightly interwoven. Only American common law had formally unequal inheritance rights for widows and widowers. Most of them were eliminated in the federal states by the early twentieth century. However, the discrimination against wives when it came to the management and disposition of property they brought into and acquired during the marriage amounted in all three countries to wealth formation and wealth control for the husband, a situation that could entail considerable disadvantages for wives in inheritance law. The equality of wives and husbands in the law of marital property thus had a direct effect on the status of the wife in inheritance law. It is remarkable that in France and Germany this law did not change until the 1950s and 1960s.

Finally, there was a rise in the importance of the principle of equality in the granting of equal inheritance rights to illegitimate children—this, too, was change that occurred substantially only in the second half of the twentieth century. In this area of the law there was a strengthening of inheritance claims based on blood kinship.

A third trend in statutory inheritance law, chiefly in the second half of the twentieth century, is the internal diversification of the model of the conjugal family. What I mean by this is that the legitimation of familial structures begins to disconnect from the requirement of marital status. Statutory inheritance law accommodated itself to this trend by granting illegitimate children equal inheritance rights. The same trend is apparent in the emerging legalization of same-sex partnerships (which I have not discussed here), which is also normatizing claims to inheritance rights. All three countries passed laws during the last decade that allowed same-sex couples to have a contractual relationship modeled after marriage, a relationship that in part also includes inheritance rights (Basedow, Dopffel, and Kötz 2000; Surkis 2002). This development, too, orients claims of solidarity in inheritance law toward the principles of equality and the affective focus. These developments, which still seemed inconceivable to observers like Kingsley Davis (1939), did not mean a turning away from the normative orientation toward the conjugal family, but the attempt to preserve this structural model as much as possible also under conditions of changing ideas of morality and a diversity of partnership forms.

The developments in the areas of statutory inheritance law I have examined all point to profound transformations in the organization of claims to solidarity within the family system. Against the backdrop of a trend pointing generally in the same direction, certain differences are found between France, Germany, and the United States. Looking more closely at the differences, it is noticeable that the fewest reforms were undertaken in Germany between the late eighteenth and the middle of the twentieth century. As a result of the strong influence of Roman law, the equality of sons and daughters in statutory inheritance law was already institutionalized, and the status of the surviving spouse and of illegitimate children had been regulated "more progressively" than in the other two countries. But while France and the United States continued to reform their inheritance law in the second half of the nineteenth century, the BGB introduced virtually no changes in the areas I have looked at. The decisive steps toward strengthening the position of the surviving spouse with respect to inheritance law and granting of equal rights to illegitimate children did not occur until after World War II.

The United States witnessed a push toward reform in the second half of the nineteenth century especially in the development of the law governing marital property and equal rights for women under inheritance law, the kind of reform push that happened in the two European countries only in the 1950s and 1960s. The earlier occurrence could be attributed to a conception of the marital relationship that was based on equality, a conception that was much more pronounced in the United States than in either Germany or France: "[I]n the nineteenth century there was a new sense of impropriety about a husband having that kind of power over his wife's property" (Shammas, Salmon, and Dahlin 1987, 92). That could have something to do with the smaller ratio of women within the American population as a whole and with the fact that the organization of property rights was more strongly oriented toward the needs of free economic relationships (Horwitz 1977). All in all, the legal development points to a more modern family structure in the United States.

In all three countries, the restructuring of statutory inheritance law based on the principle of equality expresses both changing functional demands and changing values. The dynastic, patrilineal principle of primogeniture succession loses importance with the emergence of capitalist economic forms. However, a purely functionalist explanation seems inadequate to explain the introduction of egalitarian inheritance rights. After all, the desire to keep the property (capital!) of the testator together plays an important role under industrial capitalism. Historians have attributed the divergent economic development of France and England (where the right of primo-geniture inheritance existed until 1925) in part to the inheritance laws of the two countries. It is therefore by no means certain that the egalitarian division represents the regulation that is functionally more suitable to a capitalistic order. Rather, the immediate institutionalization of equal inheri-tance rights for sons and daughters in the French and American revolutions cannot be understood independent of values that experienced a potent political articulation at that time. They include, first of all, the political weight of the normative legal conception of natural equality. But in a broader sense, other, specifically bourgeois-liberal values are also reflected in the principle governing the division of inheritance: the independence of the individual becomes more important than the dynastic continuity of the fam-ily embodied in unequal division. Moreover, egalitarian inheritance among siblings reveals a competitive thinking: a material equality of opportunity applies to siblings, not ascriptive unequal treatment. At the same time, division of the estate assuages bourgeois concerns that an inheritance could tempt a sole heir into a life of leisure, while denying siblings the chance to receive a material foundation for their own success in life. Equal inheri-tance portions can be interpreted as startup help toward an independent life, which gives each child the opportunity "to conquer freedom and life" (Brentano 1899, 142) without making possible a "life without effort."[41] This specifically bourgeois orientation is given preference over the dynastic principle and points simultaneously to the deep normative anchoring of a kinship structure of mutually segregated conjugal families (Parsons 1954). The principle of the egalitarian division of inheritance contains bourgeois values such as equality of opportunity, individuality, and meritocracy, and the development of intestacy law cannot be understood without looking at how they spread as normative points of reference.

The growing orientation of inheritance law toward the immediate nuclear family can be interpreted, on the one hand, as reflecting the declining importance of the extended family as an economic unit of production. However, that alone does not explain why the focus of inheritance law placed the relationship of solidarity to the testator's spouse increasingly at the forefront. The notion that inheritance law should be structured by claims to support and not by dynastic interests does not flow from economic functional demands themselves. The introduction of state-funded social security, which also establishes claims by the spouse, reduces the functional pressure toward improving the status of the spouse under inheritance law in order to provide her with support. It would appear, therefore, that it is not primarily economic motives that can explain the expansion of the spouse's inheritance rights. We must add a changing conception of obligations of solidarity with which the stronger segregation of the nuclear family is legitimated.

The incorporation of illegitimate children into inheritance law also corresponds to a functionalist economic logic only to the extent that the question of how to provide for these children had to be resolved in some way. Here, the view prevails that biological parenthood creates obligations and rights of support. At the same time, the increasing integration of illegitimate children since the 1960s follows changing ideas of morality, which are also reflected in the increase in out-of-wedlock births in all three countries in question and their overwhelming acceptance—at least in France and Germany.

When it comes to explaining the development of intestacy law, changing values and changing demands on inheritance law cannot be separated from each other as "independent variables" in a model of causality—they are too closely interconnected. Just as the development of capitalistic structures contributes to the rise of values "that are inwardly related to the lifestyle of capitalism" (Weber 1907, 383), these normative orientations in turn exert influence on the change in legal structures. In this sense, ideas and interests are inextricably intertwined in the evolution of inheritance law.

Chapter 4

POLITICAL STRUCTURE AND INHERITANCE LAW: THE ABOLITION OF ENTAILS

TESTAMENTARY FREEDOM is the central institution for the individual disposition over property in inheritance law. At the same time, testamentary freedom is linked to the paradox that its unlimited application can lead to the elimination of individual control over wealth—namely, if testamentary directives are put in place that limit the heirs' rights of disposition. There are a variety of legal ways of doing this, such as the appointment of subsequent heirs, or, primarily in Anglo-Saxon law, the establishment of family foundations (trusts) that give heirs access only to the capital generated by the assets, but not to the assets themselves.[1]

During the period under examination here, however, family entails[2] were the most important—and most controversial—instrument for placing testamentary restrictions on the heirs' rights of disposition.[3] If real property is entailed, it cannot be sold by the owner of the entail; instead, it is passed on from generation to generation according to the succession determined by the founder.[4] As a rule, the landed property was bequeathed to the eldest son and had to be passed on in all subsequent successions to the eldest son in the next generation. Entails are a legal institution of dynastic bequest through which the testator can control the use of his property across many generations, thereby exerting influence on the property relationships of the succeeding generations. The wealth is directed by the "dead hand" of the person who established the entail.

Entail was a special form of property that was removed from the market process and was not subject to the regulations of statutory inheritance law. This prevented the division of the property through sale or devolution. In Germany, *Fideikommisse* were unlimited in time and were difficult to rescind. In the General Law Code of Prussia, for example, abolition was only possible after 1807 upon the unanimous decision of the family council composed of all living claimants. Other German states established even higher hurdles. In some of the American colonies—Virginia, for example— entails could be abolished before the Revolution only through a decision of the assembly approved by the governor. In France, by contrast, most entailed substitutions had been limited to two degrees since 1560.

Although the law on entails was regulated differently between the three countries and was also not entirely uniform within the countries themselves, the most important features can be characterized in general terms.

The holder of an entail had the ownership, administration, and usufruct of the entailed property. At the same time, he was obligated to leave the entail in an unchanged condition; he was not allowed to mortgage it, alter it, or diminish it (Eckert 1992, 97). The fact that entailed realty could not be encumbered became a topic of heated debates in the nineteenth century, because an entail was virtually undistrainable for creditors. The flip side of this risk for creditors was that the credit basis of entailed estates was reduced, which led to a scarcity of necessary investment capital. Moreover, entails were also seen as an expression of an inappropriate mistrust toward future generations, a mistrust that diminished paternal authority, was unfair toward children excluded from the inheritance, and violated the principle of legal equality.

To see entails primarily as a legal institution by which the testator seeks to control the cohesiveness of wealth in the subsequent generations of his family would be inadequate, however. The present chapter will broaden and supplement this perspective by putting forth the thesis that entails and the timing of their abolition in the three countries in question can be explained only by the close connection with the changes of political structures. This particular legal institution expresses a close connection between private property and the holding of political positions, a connection that was abolished only with the establishment of political systems based on the principle of civic equality. To be sure, entails also came under pressure beginning in the eighteenth century because they represented a way of organizing private property that was economically inefficient for the development of capitalism and ran counter to notions of equality. However, it is the comparative study that demonstrates that economic reasons were, in the final analysis, not critical to the abolition of entailed property, even though the abolition of entails helped capitalistic market principles to triumph.

The Development of the Entailment of Property

The immediate political importance of entails that existed alongside the interest in family status (*splendor familiae*) is readily apparent from the historical roots of this legal institution, which can be found in the conflicts over power between the feudal nobility and the claims to sovereignty advanced by centralized, patrimonial states. The entail developed in the spheres of German and French law beginning in the fifteenth century;[5] it evolved largely out of the Spanish law of *majorat*, which in turn had arisen out of the medieval Islamic legal institution of the *wakf*, a pious foundation (Weber 1978, 2:1096–97).

By establishing a foundation for a godly purpose, the owner relinquished the right to dispose over his property and simultaneously stipulated the purposes for which the income was to be used. For example, property could be donated for mosques, whereby the family of the donor had a right to fixed shares of the income generated by the foundation. The religious foundation itself could not be distrained by the secular power, while the donor's family could be supported with a portion of the income from it. In the face of the growing arbitrariness of patrimonial political power, the donor was seeking sacred protection for his property to keep the secular power from laying hands on it. The Spanish majorat and the right of entail that develops out of it in the various European countries are a "secularized imitation" (Weber 1978 [1922], 2:1097) of this originally Islamic legal institution.[6] In German jurisprudence, it was combined, beginning in the seventeenth century, with the German legal institution of the *Stammgut* (family estate) and with the Roman entail (*Fideikommiss*).[7] Essentially, however, it was a Romanistic transformation of the particular law (Söllner 1976, 661). In France it was also integrated into Roman law and further developed (Brentano 1899, 8ff.; Eckert 1992, 79ff.).

The spread of the legal institution of the entail in Europe in the sixteenth and seventeenth centuries is directly connected to political developments. Since the nobility was always faced with the threat of being put on trial for high treason in its clashes with the crown, the entail was one way to protect property against arbitrary confiscation. In Germany, the nobility saw the legal institution of the entail as an effective protection of property after the Thirty Years' War (Felix 1903, 106). In France, a growing number of entails were established by the feudal nobility in the sixteenth century, that is, at a time of growing conflict with the centralized royal power in the process of forming the French nation (Brentano 1899, 12ff.; Schunck 1994, 19ff.). The French Crown cast a critical eye on this legal instrument intended to strengthen local powers, and in a decree of 1560 it limited the validity of the entails to two generations.

These historical roots reveal the connection between entail and the prevailing political order. Originally, its importance lay not in controlling the actions of the heirs through the "dead hand" of the institutor, but in the desire of the feudal nobility to protect its property. Weber (1978 [1922], 2:1096) explained the emergence of this legal institution out of uncertain property conditions—with the paradoxical phenomenon that economic rationalization is brought about through the expansion of the sphere of sacral bonds.

The function of entails changes, however, with the consolidation of centralized structures of power. While entails had initially been a defensive strategy by the high nobility, after the victory of centralized power structures, the central power itself used them as an instrument to secure its position. Entails now became a device of inheritance law by which the nobility was kept dependent on the crown (Brentano 1899, 13–14). The move to establish the wealth of individual noble families on a lasting foundation and to link the entailment of property with political offices placed in the hands of the nobility an instrument to secure its position of power permanently. Entails immunized property against the risks of economic exchange, and the link between entailed estates and rights of political power—in the

European countries, entails came with seats on parliamentary bodies—made possible for the nobility the structural connection between office and private property.[8] At the same time, the privilege of entailing property was now granted by the ruler and no longer achieved by sacralizing property, which meant that the nobility became dependent on the central power. An additional dependency was created in that it became necessary to provide for family members of the nobility excluded through the entail from the family wealth by securing appropriate positions in the military, the church, and the administration. The assignment of these positions was controlled by the monarchy, and this gave it another means to compel the loyalty of the nobility.[9] The dependency of the nobility as a result of privileges it was accorded in property law could become an instrument to stabilize absolutist rule. Beginning in the late eighteenth century, it was used to fend off the political demands of the bourgeoisie (Heß 1990, 131). In fact, at the beginning of the nineteenth century Napoleon even created a new nobility from the bourgeoisie through the establishment of majorats as a way to secure his power.

Criticism of Entails

Against this backdrop, criticism of entails, which grew more vocal in the eighteenth century and persisted until their abolition, was aimed in two directions simultaneously. First, it opposed the patronizing treatment of future generations by the dead hand of the person who set up the entail. This reveals a development of the notion of property that can be linked to Durkheim's (1992 [1957]) concept of the sacralization of the individual. The religious origins of this legal institution point to what Durkheim highlighted as the sacral roots of property, which was initially given special protection as church property. With the secularization of the legal institute, the family—conceived of as an entity transcending the lifespan of the individual—assumes the position of the "sacralized" owner. The growing criticism of entails expresses the spread of an individual conception of property, in which the restrictions on individual rights of disposition through entail constitute a violation of individual rights.

Second, criticism of entails is aimed at the special privileges for one class of property-owners embodied in this legal institution, and at the political structures that are propped up by these privileges. The preferential treatment of one social class in property law runs counter to the principle of civic equality, which serves as the normative foundation of the bourgeois critique of the entailment of property. Liberal social theory rejected the entail as an instrument for the dynastic perpetuation of the nobility's privileged social status. In contrast to the question of testamentary freedom, the restriction of which was (as shown in chapter 2) highly controversial, the attitude toward entails was unambiguous: they were regarded as a feudal relic. At the same time, this criticism was combined with economic arguments pointing to the negative economic effects from restrictions on the mobility of property.

This characteristic reference to the principle of legal equality *and* the economic repercussions of the entailment of property is especially evident in Adam Smith. In *The Wealth of Nations* (1978 [1776]), Smith described the entail as a legal relic of the feudal era. Its function lay in securing the privileged status of the nobility, and it was simultaneously economically dysfunctional: large-scale landholding led to an unproductive use of the land, because the owners had neither capital for, nor interest in, an efficient use (Smith 1978 [1776], 409–10). In a very similar way, John Stuart Mill (1976 [1848]) denounced entails as an aristocratic institution, the holders of which did not have the capital to invest to boost the productivity of the soil. Mill demanded a free-market solution. Land would be worked efficiently only if it was a freely traded commodity. The importance of bourgeois values is also reflected in the liberal critique. Mill argued that entails promoted an economic culture that ran counter to the acquisitive desire: the "heir of entail, being assured of succeeding to the family property, however undeserving of it, and being aware of this from his earliest years, has much more than the ordinary chance of growing up idle, dissipated, and profligate" (1976, 895).

The conflict over entails is part of the conflict over the political, social, and economic order in the three countries in question. In the liberal worldview, the entail goes against civic equality, individual rights of freedom, the concept of meritocracy, the process of economic modernization, and political democratization. Defenders of this legal institution noted that the nobility was an important pillar of the state, and that it could perform its political functions only on the basis of secure landed wealth. The exclusion of land from the exchange of commodities is depicted as economically advantageous, because it alone made genuine long-term investment possible in the first place. Moreover, entails were seen in Germany as institutions to fend off the individualism of Enlightenment thinking—entailment of property placed the individual as one link in a chain of succession that transcended him. Just as opponents of entails criticized the exclusion of land from the market process as economically inefficient, supporters—at least in Germany—defended precisely this restriction on the market as important for the preservation of the ethical foundations of the economy and society.

Entails and the Development of Inheritance Law

The debate over entails represents another focal point in the controversies over inheritance law in the nineteenth century, and its dynamic extended into the twentieth century. More so than in the question over testamentary freedom, this conflict revolved around the abolition of feudal political and economic structures, that is to say, the development of the political and economic systems of modern societies. For that reason, it is much easier to identify interest groups in the clash over entails: this was a fight between primarily noble holders of large estates and the emerging bourgeoisie, which was demanding that rights attached to particular estates be abolished and that property be made to conform to the market. This clear battle line was blurred by the fact that the motivation of the dynastic formation of wealth, the attainment of power and social prestige, certainly did find favor also in the eyes of the bourgeoisie. In Napoleon's France, loyal bourgeois followers of the emperor were granted primogenitures. In the second half of the nineteenth century in Germany, entails were also set up by bourgeois landowners, who were, first, intent on protecting the wealth they had acquired in trade and industry, and, second, eager to "buy" the social prestige that came with a title of nobility. The United States saw the spread of family trusts and charitable foundations in the nineteenth century. As instruments for a dynastic inheritance of wealth, they were the functional equivalent of entails, though without removing landed property from the market process and without creating political privileges. However, these mimicry strategies on the part of the bourgeoisie were not able to reproduce the estatist, aristocratic character of the entails. The creation of foundations can preserve only a part of the private law dimension of the dynastic transfer of wealth, but not the political functions of entailed estates.

It is my contention that the broad chronological range of 140 years in the abolition of entails in the United States (around 1780), France (1848), and Germany (1919)[10] reflects primarily the differences in political development. In all three countries there is a direct connection between the triumph of republican political structures and the abolition of entailed property.

The account in the present chapter focuses especially on France and Germany, as these two countries witnessed by far the most intensive and protracted conflicts over entails. The contrast to the United States reveals the importance the feudal past and aristocratic political structures had for the legal development in the nineteenth century. The quick abolition of entails in the United States and the lengthy battle to do the same in the two European countries show that the explanation for the entailment of property and its abolition cannot be found chiefly in economic development and in the private motivations of the dynastic perpetuation of wealth, but especially in the functions this legal institution had within the respective *political* systems. Moreover, the varying discourses in the three countries illustrate at the same time the significance of notions of property rights.

4.1. THE DOUBLE ABOLITION OF SUBSTITUTIONS IN FRANCE

The abolition of the entailment of property in France is directly related to the Revolution. The cohesiveness of noble estates and the inequality in the distribution of land was largely based on the right of substitution, which allowed the undivided transmission of realty from generation to generation.

Three years after the Revolution, the law of 14 November 1792 outlawed substitutions and declared that the existing entailments of property were abolished. In the debates over the abolition of entails, the impairment of the freedom of heirs by the "dead hand" of the testator and the removal of *existing* aristocratic social structures were in the foreground of the controversy. Doing away with the entailment of property was aimed at creating equality in inheritance law and realizing the Enlightenment concept of the contract, according to which contracts derived their validity from the autonomous self-commitment of the contracting parties. That, precisely, was not the case in entails, because the will of the ascendant restrained the owner in the use of the property. Moreover, it was expected that the abolition of entailment would lead to the breakup of the nobility's large estates, which would dissolve the economic foundation of the nobility's power. In that sense, the prohibition against substitutions should be seen as forming a unity with the principle of equality in intestacy succession and the limitation on testamentary freedom. It was only the combined action of these instruments that would make it possible to achieve the goal of legal equality and a more egalitarian distribution of land. A more balanced distribution of land was not an end of economic policy for its own sake, but was seen as an essential foundation of political liberty. To that extent, the abolition of entails in France, as in the United States, was aimed at creating or stabilizing a republican state structure. However, compared to the United States it occurred under completely different political conditions—namely, against the backdrop of an absolutist state whose structures had to be dismantled.

It is therefore not surprising that the abolition of the entailment of property in France triggered vehement sociopolitical controversies that lasted into the middle of the nineteenth century. Substitutions were abolished once and for all only in 1849 in the Second Republic, and the last remnants even survived until 1904. Still, in France the process of dissolving entails was completed seventy years earlier than in Germany, which points to the greater political power of the bourgeoisie in France and, conversely, to the delayed modernization of property law in nineteenth-century Germany.

Entails in the French Revolution

When the debates over inheritance law during the revolutionary period dealt with the question of the abolition of entailed substitutions, the delegates were able to draw on critical discussion of this legal institution that had been carried on for decades. Rousseau, Voltaire, Montesquieu, Raynal, d'Argenson, and Le Trosne had wrestled with entails and primogenitures during the eighteenth century, and all had rejected them. As early as the first half of the eighteenth century, entails had also become the subject of a political debate under Louis XV, when the legal provisions of substitutions were to be uniformly regulated, which happened with the Ordonnance concernant les substitutions in 1747.

The important role that the principle of equality played in the discourse on entails is reflected in Montesquieu's contemporaneous critique of this legal institution. According to Montesquieu, laws must fit the respective form of government. While substitutions were suitable for a monarchy, they were not appropriate to the aristocratic state and a democracy. Since monarchy was based on the principle of honor, the nobility had to be protected, and one way to do that was through substitutions and primogenitures. The aristocratic state, however, was based for Montesquieu on the virtue of moderation, and since that virtue was threatened by an excess of inequality, there could be neither a right of primogeniture nor substitutions. Rather, wealth should approximate equality through a continual division of inheritance (Montesquieu 1899 [1748], 1:52ff.). Democracy as a third form of government was based on the love of equality, which ruled out the concentration of wealth through inheritance (1:43ff.).

Alongside the argument of equality, two other arguments were put forth against entails in France in the eighteenth century. First, the unclear regulations pertaining to substitutions gave rise to numerous lawsuits, which could lead to the ruin of the families affected. The ordinance of 1747 was intended to remedy this situation. Second, because substitutions could not be seized, creditors could suffer loan defaults, and the institution was therefore seen as harmful to free commerce. Montesquieu wrote in a famous passage that "substitutions are a restraint to commerce" (1899 [1748], 1:54).

The prevailing attitude toward substitutions in the political discourse in France in the eighteenth century was negative. However, since this issue touched on fundamental interests of the nobility, it is surprising how little controversy the debate over the abolition of entails engendered during the revolutionary period—in contrast to the question of testamentary freedom. In the great debate over inheritance law in 1791, only four speakers expressed an opinion on the matter: all came out in favor of a prohibition of entails, and—with one exception—they did not even bother to justify their position. The rejection of the ancien régime's system of privileges was unanimous in the Constituante. The entailment of property was recognized as the central institution of the nobility's position of economic power; it contradicted the principle of equality in that it established a special inheritance law for the nobility and disadvantaged after-born children; finally, it went against the principle of individual freedom by allowing the deceased testator to restrict the heirs' freedom of action. This particular legal institution thus encompassed precisely those elements of the ancien régime that the Revolution of 1789 had opposed.

Nevertheless, the law of 8 April 1791 did not yet make any provisions regarding substitutions, most likely because they were linked with the contested issue of testamentary freedom. It was not until August 1792 that a bill in the Assemblée Nationale called for a prohibition on the future establishment of substitutions. The introduction to the report to parliament listed the Revolution's principles of liberty and equality and the prevention of familial legal quarrels as the reasons behind the prohibition:

> In view of the fact that the origins of the entails are odious; that they are the most baneful of the scourges in individual fortunes; that they incite hatreds and cast ruin over families, where they are the source of a thousand ruinous suits; that they serve to establish a monstrous inequality of wealth; that their preservation is incompatible with the sacred principles of liberty and equality, and that sound politics demands the most vigorous prohibition, regulations are considered to be urgent. (Arch. Parl. 1st Ser., 49:55, qtd. in Eckert 1992, 183)

The bill was not deliberated, however, and it was only the National Convention that enacted the prohibition of substitutions by the law of 14 November 1792. This law was much more radical than the bill put to the Constituante in the summer, in which only *future* substitutions were to be outlawed. By the law passed in the fall, entails were abolished immediately, giving their respective holders full ownership of the land. A few years later, during the Napoleonic occupation, this law became valid law also for the German territories on the left bank of the Rhine.[11]

That the prohibition against substitutions was not a law that sprang merely from the radical spirit of the National Convention and would later be revised again, as was the case with the abolition and gradual reintroduction of testamentary freedom, is evident from the fact that it was incorporated into the Code Civil: Article 896 upholds the prohibition. As an exception, Articles 897 and 1048–50 allow the substitution of parents in favor of their children, that is, the institution of parents as an heir in tail and with childless testators the testamentary bequest to nieces and nephews, with the institution of their parents as heirs in tail (Lingenthal and Crome 1894–95, 4:377ff.). This regulation, which was highly controversial during the deliberations over the Civil Code because some feared a creeping reintroduction of substitutions, was intended to give the testator the possibility of appointing an heir regarded as wasteful merely as an heir in tail as a way of preserving the estate for grandchildren or nephews. However, the institution of a grandchild as the reversionary heir concerned only the *quotité disponible*, and all children of the heir in tail had to be given equal consideration as reversionary heirs. The controversy around the introduction of this limited interference in the principle of egalitarian division reveals, conversely, the unanimity with which the legal institution of the entail was rejected at this time in the legal-political debate in France. In the discussion over the Code Civil, not one of the courts of appeal that were consulted voted in favor of reintroducing entailed substitutions, and in the State Council "no voice spoke up in favor of reintroducing the old substitutions" (Eckert 1992, 202).

The Introduction of Majorats by Napoleon

Looking only at the period between 1789 and 1804, we find a clear parallel in the legal development in France and the United States. Both countries, within the context of the revolutions of 1789 and 1776, respectively, were quick to pass laws outlawing the perpetuation of wealth through entails, and in both countries it happened without any intense or lasting parliamentary opposition. That is not to say that the holders of entails affected by this—or those in line for them—did not reject the new laws, merely that resistance was hardly present on the political level. The forces of revolution intent on thoroughly abolishing the legal institutions of feudal state structures were predominant.

Nevertheless, the situation in the United States and France was not as congruent as it may appear at first glance. That becomes clear as soon as one traces the subsequent development of entails in both countries after 1804. While legislation on the prohibition of entails in the United States abolished this legal institution once and for all, France experienced—in 1807 and 1826—the reintroduction of the legal basis for the entailment of property. In each case, the social and political groups in France that were behind this were different. In 1807, Napoleon introduced majorats to secure his rule, precisely by exercising his domination over the aristocratic ruling elites of the ancien régime. In 1826, the aristocratic forces defeated in the Revolution prevailed under Charles X and tried to return to the legal institutions of the ancien régime. In both instances, the motivation behind the reinstitutionalization of the entailment of property was to prop up structures of political power. That confirms the thesis put forth in this chapter, namely that the explanation for the history of the entailment of property is to be found largely in the link between entails and political power, and that economic and familial aspects play only a secondary role.

This is especially apparent in Napoleon's stance, who in the discussions over the Code Civil in the State Council had come out clearly against substitutions by invoking the revolutionary principles of freedom and equality (Eckert 1992, 203). Driven by calculations of power politics, Napoleon was aiming at destroying the aristocratic elites of the ancien régime, because the economic foundation of their power—large landholdings—would be progressively diminished by egalitarian division. This particular calculus is also evident from the fact that when the discussions over the Code Civil deal with restrictions on testamentary freedom, Napoleon had especially large landowners in mind. For smaller holdings he would allow a higher *quotité disponible* (Fehrenbach 1974, 25). At the same time, Napoleon was well aware of how important loyal support from a social elite was to the maintenance of power, and of the role that property privileges could play in this.[12]

After his coronation as emperor, Napoleon proceeded in keeping with this calculation. He began to create a new hereditary nobility that was recruited substantially from bourgeois circles and endowed with some of the privileges that had been abolished during the Revolution. This included also the reintroduction of entails, though for reasons of political tactics they were not brought back under the name *substitutions* that was rooted in the French legal tradition, but under the Spanish designation *majorat*, which was largely unknown in France. In this way Napoleon was trying to avoid the impression that he was betraying the central revolutionary principles of legal equality and was trying to undo the redistribution of land that had been carried out after the Revolution. He could not afford to create the appearance that the introduction of the entailment of property meant that the national holdings created from confiscated private and church estates would be placed back into the hands of a nobility, and that the abolition of aristocratic privileges when it came to the awarding of posts in the military and the state administration was coming under attack. The majorat was thus an institution for securing power, one that gave the emperor the direct possibility of creating a loyal social elite.[13]

The care that Napoleon took to avoid the impression that he intended to restore the prerevolutionary system of privileges is also evident from his gradual approach, introducing the majorat law step by step. Finally, in 1807, Article 896 of the Civil Code was altered in such a way as to permit majorats as exceptions to the prohibition against substitutions. Napoleon had thus created a legal institution that made it possible to set up perpetual substitutions for the benefit of firstborn sons. The emperor had the sole power to decide on the establishment of majorats. These estates could not be attached or seized, selling or mortgaging them was impossible, and even the income from majorats could be seized only to a limited extent (Villequez 1863, 200–201). Napoleon made abundant use of the possibility of creating majorats: by 1813 there existed 3,081 majorats with nearly 29 million francs in annual income (Eckert 1992, 217).[14]

The Reintroduction of Substitutions in 1826

The introduction of majorats by Napoleon was ambivalent when it came to stabilizing the changes to property structures implemented by the Revolution: on the one hand, with the entailment of property Napoleon brought back a legal institution that had been abolished in the Revolution; on the other hand, the goal of this step was the creation of a *new* ruling class that was to be recruited largely from the bourgeoisie and replace the old elites of the ancien régime. In this respect the majorats, to the extent that they propped up Napoleon's rule, helped precisely to block the forces of restoration of the ancien régime from seizing power.[15] Regardless of how one assesses Napoleon's intentions in this regard, one thing is clear: after his downfall and the return of the old power elites, the majorat laws were used as the basis for further legal reform that was now clearly aimed at restoration and the rejection of the changes the Revolution had wrought in property law. At least in retrospect, the introduction of majorats thus appears as a first step in the restorationist return of the entailment of property and the revival of the monarchist political system. At the same time, the attempt to bring back entailed substitutions during the restoration period is evidence for the close connection between monarchical political structures and the entailment of property.

This development culminated in 1826 in a bill introduced by Charles X in the Chambre des Pairs that called for the return of the right of primogeniture and substitutions. Right-wing royalists saw these two institutions as the precondition for the preservation of the wealth of the aristocratic class and the foundation for securing its power over the republican forces of the bourgeoisie. The bill of 1826 had been preceded as early as 1817, under Louis XVIII, by a royal decree that stipulated that henceforth a person could become a *pair* of France only if he had previously set up a majorat (Brentano 1899, 49). Once again, political office and property law were linked, and the functional differentiation between economy and politics that had been achieved by the Revolution in this respect was undone. The bill of 1826 was aimed directly at the reestablishment of the *droit d'aînesse* and thus at the heart of the Revolution of 1789. Here, too, the direct political goal of the entailment of property is immediately apparent. Any intended economic consequences were merely a means toward stabilizing the monarchical political system.

The declared aim of the law of 1826 was to prevent the further fracturing of landed property by reintroducing primogeniture succession; however, this was meant not only to secure the economic basis of landowners, but also to stabilize precisely their political influence. According to existing electoral law, the active franchise was tied to a direct tax of 300 francs per year. Although the majority of the estimated 100,000 qualified voters belonged to the group of landowners (Medzeg and Nohlen 1969, 457), the shrinking of landed wealth as a result of egalitarian division reduced the number of landowners eligible to vote—and they were the most important pillar of political support for the monarchy. At the same time, the number of qualified members of the bourgeoisie, whose wealth came from their profits from trade and industry, was rising. There was thus a danger "that the political weight would shift from agriculture to industry and trade" (Brentano 1899, 60).

This immediate political backdrop of providing support for the class of landowners is evident in the bill's stipulation that the introduction of primogeniture rights and substitutions would apply only to realty on which at least three hundred francs of taxes were due. If the property met that criterion, the *quotité disponible* would automatically devolve upon the eldest son if the testator had not left a will containing different arrangements. Article 3 of the bill also stipulated that the *quotité disponible* could be entailed, though only in the direct line and to the second degree. In other words, the son or grandson could be appointed the heir in tail and the great-grandson as the reversionary heir, who would once again acquire the estate as unencumbered property.

The proposed law triggered a long and controversial debate, both in the Chambre des Pairs and in the Chamber of Deputies. The debate in the Chambre des Pairs, which came first, focused on the right of primogeniture; after the Chambre des Pairs rejected the reintroduction of primogeniture succession, the Chamber of Deputies limited its debate to substitutions (Villequez 1863, 202–3). Supporters of the measure in the Chambre des Pairs pointed especially to the fragmentation of landed property through the egalitarian division of the Civil Code, a situation that posed a threat to the monarchy, and presented the controversy as a clash between a republican and a monarchist social order. Baron Montalembert, for example, put it this way: "I am not afraid to proclaim boldly that our laws regarding successions, as they relate to property, were established among us in a spirit of zealousness for the republican system and in a spirit of hatred for the monarchical system" (Arch. Parl., 2nd Ser., 46:519ff., quoted in Eckert 1992, 220). In that sense the clash over the reintroduction of the right of primogeniture and substitutions can be aptly characterized as a battle "between the modern bourgeoisie, which was rooted in movable wealth, and the landed aristocracy that was eager to restore conditions as they had been before the Revolution, between the interests of the bourgeoisie and the ideas of feudalism" (Brentano 1899, 49)—except that the discussion did not revolve primarily around questions of an economically efficient property law, but around political questions of how to organize structures of power.

Connected with this in the debate were also aspects of economic-cultural identity. Proponents of the bill saw the justification of the *droit d'aînesse* and the monarchical order as grounded in the dynastic principle of the family. The family was then held up as the diametrical ethical opposite to the bourgeois individualism rejected as immoral. In short: the functional differentiation of property and family was rejected. Here the moral stature of the family, which was held in high esteem also within the French bourgeoisie, was used to combine this normative attitude with a legal institution that was contrary precisely to the principles of equality and liberty. Therein lies a significant difference from the discourses over the abolition of entails in the United States: although defenders of the dynastic family principle were also found in that country in the late eighteenth and early nineteenth centuries, the dominant attitude was opposition to heritable family dominion, which was seen as the basis of the aristocracy's social and political privileges. If—as in the United States—the dominant justification of property is derived from a Lockean theory of property, that is to say, the fruits of one's own labor are the starting point for the legitimate acquisition of property, this stands in contradiction to a view of the family as an institution that makes possible social privilege independent of merit and achievement. This does not mean that the family was not supposed to be also an important realm of personal protection within American self-understanding; but it played that role with respect to the achievements of the individual, not by virtue of dynastic family luster. The absence of a dynastic notion of family as a normative reference point in American discourses on inheritance law has to do also with the desire to set American society apart from the rejected aristocratic political traditions of Europe.

Supporters of the reintroduction of the right of primogeniture already invoked the link—established later by Le Play and other conservative commentators on inheritance law—between inheritance law and the demographic development. However, around 1830 the causal connection was inverted, and here a reference to the Malthusian population theory is evident: small-scale agricultural structures, it was argued, contributed to *higher birthrates*, which should be rejected because they led to a reduced urbanization in France. Small-scale property led to more marriages and children, since all children, not only the firstborn, could acquire land through inheritance and therefore did not migrate to the cities. Primogenitures and entails thus served to regulate the population.[16]

By way of continuity with the political self-conception of absolutism (as well as of the Revolution), the debate reveals an acceptance of the state's right to interfere in civil society to promote the common good. Thus Justice Minister Villèles countered protests against the reintroduction of the unpopular *droit d'aînesse* by emphasizing that the criterion for intestacy law was not custom and habit, but only what the public weal demanded (Eckert 1992, 220–21).

Opponents of the bill did not argue against the monarchial form of government as such. Rather, they defended the revolutionary principles of liberty and equality. Primogeniture and substitution, they maintained, were an attack on central principles of the Revolution because they violated legal equality. The reintroduction of inequality was a manifesto against the existing social order. Claims about the supposedly negative economic consequences of egalitarian inheritance law were rebuffed with the counterclaim that small-scale agricultural structures were more efficient. And the family-oriented arguments of the supporters of the *droit d'aînesse* were said to be unfounded, since the bill affected only 60,000 families (Brentano 1899, 87). On the other hand, it would promote the proletarization of the rural population if agricultural land would henceforth be passed down only to the eldest son, which would in fact pose a threat to the family.

Given the restorationist thrust of Charles X's policies and the power of the king (as laid down in the Charte constitutionelle of 1814) to fill the nonhereditary seats in the Chambre des Pairs (whose number could also be increased) with his own supporters, the rejection of the introduction of primogeniture in the Chambre des Pairs by 120 to 94 votes must come as a surprise. One explanation lies in contemporary public opinion: "All of France was so opposed to the reintroduction of inequality that it delighted in the vote in the Chambre des Pairs as in a victory" (Brentano 1899, 103). However, the explanation for the defeat of the government must also take into account that primogeniture succession had not existed even during the ancien régime, with the exception of the special law for aristocratic estates. Its general introduction would therefore not only have violated the principle of equality in the Revolution's inheritance law, but constituted a break with the inheritance law that existed before 1789, which meant that it could *not* be justified by invoking French legal tradition. This is another instance of the *longue durée* of inheritance law.

The Law in the Chamber of Deputies

The Pairs approved merely the third article of the law regarding the introduction of substitutions. The government then presented this portion of the law to the Chamber of Deputies in April 1826, where a debate over substitutions ensued. Eighteen speakers participated in this debate between 8 and 11 May 1826. Of the total of 407 arguments introduced about substitutions, 212 were in favor of the bill, 195 opposed.

Table 4.1 shows the distribution of the arguments according to the political leanings of the speaker. It reveals very clearly the political polarization between conservative and leftist political groupings, while those in the middle were divided in their opinion.

The content analysis shows the main focal points in the argumentation of the speakers. The first thing that becomes clear (table 4.2) is that there was a

TABLE 4.1

Supporters and Opponents of Substitutions according to Their Place on the Political Spectrum: Debate of 1826 in the Chamber of Deputies

Political Spectrum	Arguments in Favor of Substitutions	Arguments against Substitutions	Percentage of Total Arguments
Parties of the Right (Droite, Majorité royaliste, La Majorité)	100.0		38.6
Liberal parties (Opposition libérale, Les ministériels, Party Members Benjamin Constant, Républicaine)	29.7	70.3	22.2
Parties of the Left (Gauche)		100.0	22.0
Party membership unknown			17.1
Total	52.3	47.7	100.0
	N = 212	N = 195	N = 409

Note: Figures are percentages.

TABLE 4.2

Entails in France, 1826: Reasons Offered by Speakers in Support of or Opposition to the Reintroduction of Substitutions

	Reasons in Favor of Substitutions	Reasons Opposed to Substitutions
Reasons inherent in the law	8.0	26.1
De facto acceptance of the law		11.8
Legal consistency	2.8	6.1
Preservation of the legal tradition	2.8	1.5
Other reasons inherent in the law	2.4	6.7
Political reasons	49.8	42.4
Strengthening of the monarchical order	21.7	
Strengthening of democratic structures		9.1
Loss of the right to vote	4.2	
Principle of equality	0.9	17.4
Principle of justice	1.4	2.6
Free disposition over property	3.3	2.6
Consequences for the common good	9.4	2.0
Moral ideas of society	8.9	8.7
Economic reasons	23.1	14.8
Fragmentation of land	6.6	
Preservation of the aristocracy's economic power	4.7	1.5
Effects on poverty	3.3	
Consequences for the economy in general	8.5	13.3
Familial reasons	20.0	15.3
Paternal authority	3.3	4.6
Preservation of the family's wealth	2.8	1.0
Family cohesiveness	9.4	8.2
Providing for family members	3.3	1.5
	N = 212	N = 195

Note: Figures are percentages. The debate took place between 8 and 11 May 1826; a total of eighteen speakers participated.

substantial convergence with regard to the argumentative points of reference of all the speakers. Both opponents and supporters invoked primarily the political, economic, and familial consequences of the possible reintroduction of substitutions.

The great importance of arguments relating to the structure of the political system confirms the thesis that it was this aspect, especially, that stood at the center of the clashes over entails. Needless to say, opponents and supporters of the reintroduction of the entailment of property had very different political goals in mind. Supporters of entails welcomed substitutions as an instrument to strengthen the monarchy. That goal becomes clear in arguments that substitutions would preserve the economic basis of the aristocracy's power and that the division of property could result in the loss of the franchise. Nearly one-third of all the arguments advanced by supporters are thus directly related to the goal of consolidating the monarchical order.

Opponents, meanwhile, invoked the values of the Revolution, as indicated by the reference to the principle of equality, the link they made between their position and the strengthening of democratic structures, and the argument that entails lacked legal acceptance. At the same time, both groups invoked existing social notions of morality, but they differed in how they characterized them and what kind of conclusions they drew from them.

The other two large blocks of arguments that were advanced represent economic and familial justifications of the positions taken by the opposing sides. However, compared with later clashes over inheritance law, economic arguments were still relatively minor in significance. The one argument that stands out concerns the possible fragmentation of land through real division, which was to be stopped by substitutions. The great number of familial arguments reveals the great importance that attached to the family as a crucial normative point of reference in the debates over inheritance law in France. It is very interesting in this regard that the attribution of the consequences of the reintroduction or rejection of substitutions for the family was not clear-cut by any means. Both groups invoked the role of paternal authority and of family cohesiveness as positive values and linked their respective political position with positive effects on the desired familial structures. This points to the wide interpretive leeway that existed when it came to identifying the functional consequences of regulations of inheritance law, a situation that allowed conflicting political positions to employ them as arguments.

The Definitive Abolition of Majorats and Substitutions

The Chamber of Deputies approved the reintroduction of substitutions in May 1826 with 261 to 76 votes. This amounted to the substantial restoration of the system of substitutions that had existed between the royal decree in 1747 and its abolition in 1792. However, the right of primogeniture had not been brought back, and the restrictions on testamentary freedom prevented the concentration of wealth, which meant that the social significance of the law was, in any case, minor.

The subsequent course of legal development shows that this restoration was merely an interlude. Although the republican forces of the bourgeoisie in France—unlike in the United States—were confronted with strong restorationist forces at the beginning of the nineteenth century, the latter were not able to make any lasting headway against the liberal principles of legal equality and the free disposition over property. During the restoration phase as well, as revealed by the structure of the arguments in the debate of 1826, the principle of civic equality remained a central normative point of reference in the French conflicts over inheritance law. After the fall of Charles X in the July Revolution of 1830, a first step was taken in 1835 when the establishment of new majorats was outlawed. A majority of the Chambre des Pairs opposed the abolition of substitutions. But after the February revolution of 1848, the law of 1826 was repealed in the Second Republic and the law returned to the original prohibition against substitutions in accordance with Article 896 of the Civil Code. Once again, the close link between republican state structures and the abolition of entails becomes clear.

By the law of 7 May 1849, majorats that had been set up at the initiative of the institutor (*majorats sur demande*) were converted immediately into free property if the second succession of a reversionary heir had already occurred. Otherwise, once again the transfer to reversionary heirs already born or conceived on the day of the publication of the law was permitted. About 400 such majorats existed in France in 1847, with a total capital of around 100 million francs (Eckert 1992, 222). Majorats that had been established with endowments from the sovereign (*majorats de propre mouvement*) were not mentioned in the law of 1848 and continued in existence. However, they automatically reverted to the state if there were no more male heirs in the family. Since they could no longer be established after the law of 1835, the number of these estates declined steadily. The last remaining 39 majorats were dissolved in 1904 when the French state bought them back at a price that was far below market value (Eckert 1999, 222).

4.2. The Delayed Abolition of *Fideikommisse* in Germany

Compared to the United States and France, Germany lagged behind when it came to the abolition of entailed property. The entire process was far more protracted. It was only in 1919 that the abolition of *Fideikommisse* was stipulated in the Weimar Reich Constitution, and the actual dismantling of the existing entails was not concluded until after 1945. Between 1848 and the November Revolution of 1918, *Fideikommisse* were among the most contentious issues in inheritance legislation. The conflict was fought out largely between the aristocratic owners of large estates fighting for privileges and positions of political power, on the one side, and bourgeois liberals and Social Democrats, on the other.

The controversies surrounding *Fideikommisse* reflect a discrepancy between the rapid pace of economic development and the lagging modernization of property law. This is one example of what Hans-Ulrich Wehler has called the "partial modernization" of Germany (1980, 17–18), which led to growing clashes between the middle class pushing for political equality and participation and the industrial proletariat, in one camp, and the monarchical state and the aristocratic landowners, in the other camp. Fighting a defensive battle, the landowners were trying to protect their traditional privileges. By blocking legal reforms, they resisted change to the social conditions and the structures of political power. To that extent the controversy over *Fideikommisse* was part of a larger sociopolitical conflict that was *also* waged through this institution of inheritance law; primarily, though, it revolved around the position of power of the landowners relative to industrial and commercial capital, around the estate-structured society and democratization.[17] The development in Germany differs from that in France not in the varying interests pursued by the participating political groups, but in the ability of the landowning aristocracy to successfully defend the legal institution of entails all the way into the twentieth century.

The differences between the two countries are far less pronounced in the first half of the nineteenth century. Although Germany did not witness the complete reshaping of civil law, comparable to the establishment of the Code Civil, French occupation and the economic crisis triggered by defeat at the hands of Napoleon did lead in Prussia to cautious reforms, including the law of *Fideikommisse*. (Moreover, substitutions were reintroduced in France by Napoleon and during the restoration period after 1815.) However, in contrast to France, the failure of the Revolution of 1848 in Germany, and the power of aristocratic landowners that remained unbroken until the end of the empire, had the result that *Fideikommisse* were maintained for a long time even within a highly industrialized economy. In fact, during the second half of the nineteenth century the number of such estates continued to grow, and even a loosening of existing legal restrictions on the establishment of new *Fideikommisse* was on the political agenda until 1917.

Fideikommisse in the First Half of the Nineteenth Century

Liberal bourgeoisie criticism of entails goes back further than the *Vormärz* period (1815–48): as early as the eighteenth century, and then increasingly after the laws passed by the French Revolution, it became a topic of controversy also in Germany. At that time, the arguments were frequently still linked with a critique of the feudal system. Opponents rejected both institutions chiefly with the liberal arguments of property rights and the negative economic effects of entailed property. Legal scholars like Justus Claproth (1773), Friedrich Anton von Heynitz (1785), and Johann August Schlettwein (1779) emphasized that it was unnatural to subject the will of the descendant to that of the testator, as this ran counter to property law. They pointed to the uncertainty of credit and noted that it was desirable to reduce the size of large landholdings as a way of boosting economic productivity and prosperity (Eckert 1992, 233ff.).

Beginning in the 1790s, the conflict over *Fideikommisse* was then fought out against the backdrop of the reception of the legislation of the French Revolution. Wilhelm von Humboldt dealt with testamentary freedom in his tract *Ideen zu einem Versuch, die Gränzen der Wirksamkeit des Staats zu bestimmen* (Ideas for an Essay to Determine the Limits of the Efficacy of the State) (1993 [1792], 124ff.), and he called for the prohibition on stipulations that prescribed to the heir how the estate must be used, since this interfered with his freedom. Carl Gottlieb Svarez (1960 [1790–91], 336–37) opposed *Fideikommisse* directly, on the grounds that they limited personal freedom in the use of property. *Fideikommisse* led to the concentration of wealth, impeded economic exchange, disadvantaged younger brothers, and caused many undesirable lawsuits within the family.

However, these liberal approaches in the political discourses did not lead invariably to the demand that *Fideikommisse* be abolished. Rather, in the legal thinking of the day, the critique of the entailment of property merged with the assessment that it formed the precondition for the absolutist state with respect to property law, hence it was indispensable and had to be retained. Svarez, for example, who was one of the chief authors of the General Law Code of Prussia (Allgemeines Landrecht) (ALR) that came into force in 1794, argued that the detrimental economic consequences of this legal institution, and the fact that it seemed dubious from the perspectives of justice and equality, had to be set against its function within the monarchical system. In the existing estate-based society, he maintained, *Fideikommisse* stabilized the nobility:

> For it is in the interest of a state to continually preserve its nobility in such a way that, on the one hand, it does not, on the whole, lack sufficient wealth to support its duties as the first estate of the state, and, on the other hand, that the greater part of its members are left with enough motivation to make up for the lack of inherited wealth through diligence and skill in the state's service. *Fideikommisse* are very helpful for achieving this. (Svarez 1960 [1790–91], 338)

Reference to the nobility's function as the pillar of the state reveals that the clash over entailed property was a conflict between different visions of the political order; and while arguments about economic efficiency and social justice were marshaled against *Fideikommisse*, their abolition was simultaneously seen as incompatible with the existing order based on estates. Even authors who otherwise rejected the entailment of property on the grounds of familial justice and economics, defended this practice to the extent that they wished to retain this political order. We find this line of argumentation in the early nineteenth century in Hegel and the jurist Zachariä von Lingenthal, for example.

In the section on private law in his *Elements of the Philosophy of Right*, Hegel opposed *Fideikommisse* (1991 [1821], §180) because they violated the principle of the freedom of property and because the unequal inheritance of wealth within the family was unethical. However, this clear rejection of this legal institution is followed in the section on the law of the state, to which Hegel had already referred in §180, by a justification of *Fideikommisse* for reasons of state. Here, Hegel regards the first estate's possession of secure property that it cannot dispose of a prerequisite for its independent ability to fulfill its political tasks:

> The justification of primogeniture lies in the fact that the state should be able to count on a disposition [to political service] not just as a possibility, but as necessarily present. Now it is true that such a disposition is not tied to the possession of resources; but the relatively necessary connection between the two consists in the fact that someone of independent means is not limited by external circumstances, and is accordingly able to play his part without encumbrance, and to act in the interests of the state. (1991 [1821], §306)[18]

The mutually exclusive positions in private and state law can be interpreted as a point of confusion in Hegel's thinking (Bayer 1999, 294–95). However, it is more useful to see this "confusion" as an expression of the sociopolitical situation in Prussia in the early nineteenth century—namely, the situation of a bourgeoisie that was not yet able to emancipate itself from the monarchical state system. The same argumentative ambivalence characterizes other contemporary commentators on *Fideikommisse*. One example is the legal scholar Zachariä von Lingenthal (1835), who was also an opponent of *Fideikommisse* but wanted to retain the monarchy at the same time. He argued that the political system of democracy required a different inheritance law than a monarchy, from which he concluded that the abolition of *Fideikommisse* was contrary to the constitution:

> Let us then compare the spirit of these constitutions [of the states that were German in origin] with the principles according to which landed property is and should be an unrestricted and unrestrictable right. This principle, taken to its logical conclusion, is the immediate death sentence of such a constitution. (Lingenthal 1835, 9)

In the late eighteenth and the early nineteenth centuries, there was no political force in Prussia that could have pushed through a republican state system. Given the weakness of the bourgeoisie, political modernization emanated from enlightened absolutism and its officials. Although the connection between the entailment of property and the state order was understood, the conflict that was inherent in this connection had not yet become a rancorous sociopolitical issue—unlike what happened in France. As long as writers sought to defend the principle of an estate-based society, it was quite possible to denounce the economically dysfunctional and normatively undesirable social consequences of entailment, while arguing that the upshot of this criticism could be at most a reform of this legal institution, not its abolition.

As a result, the *Fideikommiss* continued to be legally authorized in the General Law Code (ALR II 4 §§47–226). The founder of the *Fideikommiss* was given a free hand with respect to the conditions and the manner of succession, and the law provided for no possibility of dissolving *Fideikommisse* once they had been created (Eckert 1992, 236). The predominantly political function of this legal institution is evident from the fact that *Fideikommisse* could be set up only for landed and capital wealth of considerable size,[19] though once they exceeded a certain size, they required special permission from the ruler.[20] The concern was therefore, on the one hand, to protect the wealth of an elite within the nobility, and, on the other hand, to provide the ruler with the possibility of intervening against an excessive concentration of economic power in individual families.

The Influence of the French Revolution

The discussion about *Fideikommisse* in Germany at the beginning of the nineteenth century was carried on against the backdrop of the events of the French Revolution. That holds true in three respects.

1. German legal scholars followed the development of French law attentively, especially the introduction of the Code Civil, always bearing in mind the question of a possible adoption of French law in the German states. Conservatives, like the later Prussian minister of justice von Kampetz, rejected the adoption of the Code Civil and its provisions on inheritance law by pointing to the different social and political situation in France. It was especially the abolition of the privileges of the aristocracy in the Code Civil that conservatives opposed. Opponents of entails, by contrast, saw in the adoption of the regulations of the Code Civil a chance to dissolve entailed property. This was justified chiefly with arguments drawn from economic liberalism—such as the negative consequences for trade and the development of industry—and the freedom of property (Eckert 1992, 246ff.). What is important from a systematic point of view is the fact that the reception of the legal development that was taking place in another country provided impulses for attempts to reform property law.

2. The French Revolution influenced not only the intellectual discourse about entailed property, but also had direct practical legal consequences at the beginning of the nineteenth century. The Code Civil was introduced as valid law in the territories on the left bank of the Rhine that were occupied by France. In keeping with the French law of 1792, *Fideikommisse* were therefore dissolved in these areas. By contrast, in the states of the

Confederation of the Rhine (Rheinbund) that were aligned with France, French law was not adopted in toto, though there were intensive discussions about the question of adopting it in nearly all of the Confederation states (Fehrenbach 1974, 13). And a private law that was oriented toward the Code Civil was in fact introduced after 1806 in Baden, Westphalia, Berg, Frankfurt, Lippe, East Frisia, and the Hanseatic departments.

However, the legal reforms, in spite of their French foundations, had little bearing on existing entailed property in Germany. For one, French law in the German states was usually changed so as to leave the privileges of the nobility untouched. For another, after 1806 Napoleon was trying to support his political power with the help of the nobility in the Confederation states. In contrast to France, no attempt was made in these states to replace the leading stratum of the nobility. Accordingly, there was no real external pressure toward abolishing entails that could have supported the efforts of the reformers from within. On the contrary, Napoleon propped up the ruling nobility in the Confederation states with his policy of majorats. In contrast to France, the bourgeoisie was so weak in the German states, and also so little interested in landed property, that it could not replace the aristocratic elite. As Fehrenbach has said: "What was missing was the social class of the propriétaires and rentiers, and therefore the rentier-bourgeoisie that was so characteristic of French society" (1974, 147). Thus the existing Fideikommisse were not dissolved in the Confederation states, but merely transformed into the legal form of majorats in some states. The states that had abolished the old law of Fideikommisse during the Confederation period included Westphalia, Berg, Arenberg, Württemberg, Bavaria, Frankfurt, and the Hanseatic departments. In these states the old law of Fideikommisse was then reintroduced during the restoration phase after the Wars of Liberation (Eckert 1992, 386ff.).

3. Eventually, even Prussia, which continued as a politically independent state, was influenced. A powerful intellectual influence emanated from the developments in France. Moreover, the military defeat by Napoleon had such a deleterious effect on the economic situation that it gave rise to a strong impulse for the Prussian reform laws after 1807. The French Revolution gave a further boost to the bourgeois ideas of liberty and equality in Prussia and helped to delegitimize the absolutist regime. In addition, after the defeat by France, the country slid into a deep economic crisis that called for economic policy measures to restore prosperity. This pressure toward political and economic modernization led to the Prussian reform legislation after 1807 that was guided by von Stein and Hardenberg, and which also reformed the law on entailment. This reform, whose intellectual roots lay not only in the French Revolution, but also in Adam Smith's conception of a liberal society, aimed at integrating entailed property more strongly into the economic exchange and at dissolving the boundaries between estates.

The October edict of 1807 allowed bourgeois property owners, as well, to set up *Fideikommisse*, while at the same time making possible a stronger integration of *Fideikommisse* into the market by introducing the hereditary leasing of entailed landed property, a simpler encumbrance of entailed estates, and the possibility of dissolving or altering *Fideikommisse* through a family decision. These were cautious steps toward integrating entailed property into the market, though they remained far from an actual abolition of *Fideikommisse*. The state bureaucracy played a crucial role in the reform of the institutional basis of family power that could be passed down through inheritance. It is revealing that in order to achieve legal equality, reformers chose the path of granting the right to establish *Fideikommisse* also to the bourgeoisie, instead of abolishing entailed property altogether. In this instance, the principle of legal equality was given its due, paradoxically enough, by expanding a legal institution that was aristocratic in origin.

In spite of the moderate character of the reforms, there was immediate and fierce political opposition aimed against the economic mobilization of land. The reform was seen as a threat to the economic basis of the nobility. This hostility to the incorporation of entailed landed property was also reflected in the contemporary intellectual discourse. And it was not only noble landowners who opposed the reform of *Fideikommisse*. Supporters of this legal institution also came from within the movement of political romanticism. For example, the leading Catholic political theorist of romanticism (Ritter 1996, 48), Adam Heinrich Müller, defended *Fideikommisse* as a protection of the family against bourgeois individualism in his lectures *Elemente der Staatskunst* (1922 [1809]), delivered in the winter of 1808–09.[21] For Müller, whose writings were a direct attack on Prussian reform legislation (Hanisch 1978, 136), the aristocratic institutions of landed property were the purest form of property, which was not individual but belonged to the invisible community of the family. Represented within the owner were the absent descendants and ancestors, who shared the property simultaneously (Müller 1922 [1809], 172ff.). Müller was an ardent opponent of the individualism of liberal contract theories, which traced social bonds back to the voluntary assumption of obligations by members of society, and this alone makes them compatible with the freedom of the individual. The ideas of the Enlightenment were the foundation for the demand that entailment be abolished, both in the French Revolution and in Thomas Jefferson, for example. By contrast, Müller saw this as an inappropriately ahistorical stance, which did not do justice to the embeddedness of the individual within the generations that came before and after. In his mind, the two most important intergenerational social institutions were the state and the family, neither of which could be understood—in opposition to the Enlightenment's conception—as contractual constructions. Consequently, the notion of property in liberal thought was also flawed, since it proceeded from the right of individual disposition over property and thus failed to do justice to the fact that property was part of an ownership that transcended the individual (1922 [1809], 154ff.). For Müller, as for Jefferson and Mirabeau, the living generation enjoyed merely a lifetime interest in property.

Yet Müller derives from this the opposite conclusion, because he sees this as a justification for limiting the individual's rights of disposition. For him, *Fideikommisse* embodied—as he explained in lecture 9, "Of the Law of the State and the Nobility"—precisely this familial, generation-spanning conception of property, which is why this legal institution had to be protected against the alienability of landed property.

Müller's defense of *Fideikommisse* was, of course, only one—if an influential—position on entailed property; it stood alongside liberal, bourgeois voices calling for further reform or even the abolition of *Fideikommisse*. His discussion, however, reflects a skepticism toward a liberal-economic conception of property that would remain relevant for the debate on inheritance law in Germany into the twentieth century.[22] Later, the Catholic Center Party came out in support of *Fideikommisse* during parliamentary debates—not as an expression of its support for aristocratic privileges, but rather as a way of strengthening the family.

The political opposition against the liberal reform of the law on entails, both from landowners affected by it and from the intellectual discourse, prevented further steps toward reform in this area of the law. Although additional changes to entailed land were contemplated, such as the possibility of changing entailed landholdings into a monetary entail by selling the land, even von Stein wanted to retain the institution in principle. His reasoning also points to the link between the system of property and the political structure: because a wealthy nobility was necessary for the state, it was in the state's interest to safeguard the land in the hands of the nobility (see Eckert 1992, 378). Given these political premises, the reforms were unable to go beyond the changes I have described, and additional laws enacted down to 1841 also expanded the dispositional rights of the holders of entails only marginally. Moreover, a wide variety of laws pertaining to knighthood that were passed up to the Revolution of 1848 also reveal that the first estate was to be protected precisely in its political functions by providing economic safeguards (Koselleck 1989, 521).

The Law of Fideikommisse in the Revolution of 1848

The reception of the development of French law had lasting political repercussions in the German states. The intense discussions around the Code Civil in the states of the Confederation of the Rhine and the Code's more indirect influence in Prussia contributed to legal reform and to the intellectual development of the bourgeoisie, which supported political reform organizations in the *Vormärz* period. It is "no coincidence that the liberal movement of the *Vormärz* arose in the former Confederation states and in the lands of Rhenish law ... The southern German and Rhenish civil servant and 'privy councilor liberalism' in particular, is unthinkable without the mediation of the ideas disseminated by the Code Napoléon" (Fehrenbach 1974, 150–51). However, bourgeois liberalism achieved its breakthrough only in the period of revolutionary upheaval in 1848, which had been triggered in part by the political events of the February revolution in France (Nipperdey 1983, 595).

The year 1848 is a key date in the conflict over the entailment of property in Germany. The constitution-making National Assembly had the twofold goal of creating a German national state as well as a constitutional order for it. The whole point, at least from the liberal and left side, was to make a break with the absolutist structures in Germany and to rebuild state and society on the basis of equality before the law and the guarantee of individual rights of liberty. In terms of property law, *Fideikommisse* symbolized the absolutist, estate-based state against which the Revolution of 1848 was rising up.

In the National Assembly, the question of *Fideikommisse* was initially debated in the Constitutional Committee and in the Committee for Economics, and was then discussed in the plenary session during two readings in October and December 1848. The committee could not arrive at any agreement about a constitutional proposal concerning *Fideikommisse*. While conservative deputies wanted to retain this legal institution, the parties of the center, especially, were racked by disagreement about how far and how quickly the dissolution of the entailment of property in Germany should proceed. In the end, the deputies deliberated on a number of proposals, which ranged from the establishment of complete testamentary freedom, including the new establishment and expansion of *Fideikommisse*, to the stipulation of complete equality in the division of inheritance, combined with the immediate dissolution of all *Fideikommisse* (Eckert 1992, 456). However, in the debate over the proposals, most arguments were aimed at prohibiting the entailment of property, and only a minority demanded the unrestricted retention of *Fideikommisse* (table 4.3).

Compared with the revolutionary situation in France after 1789, when no parliamentary support of any kind for entails can be found in the debates, the situation in Germany in 1848 was much more ambivalent. The entailment of property was politically defended. In the process, a clear correlation is evident between the positions taken by the speakers and the estate to which they belonged. This can be interpreted as another indication that the conflict was primarily one about the basis of heritable family power within property law. The majority of aristocratic delegates (57.5% of the arguments) came out in favor of continuing *Fideikommisse*, while bourgeois delegates were almost unanimously opposed (84.4%). An even clearer correlation exists with respect to party membership.[23] The Right and the Left were polarized.

Arguments in defense of entailed property were put forth only by delegates from conservative groups and the center right. The center right was just as undecided about its position as the liberal groupings were in France in 1826. Membership in a political party is connected with the delegate's estate: all of the aristocratic delegates who participated in the debate belonged to parties

TABLE 4.3
Fideikommisse at the St. Paul's Church Assembly: The Importance of Estate
Membership and Political Orientation in the Arguments of the Delegates

	Arguments Supporting Fideikommisse	Arguments Rejecting Fideikommisse	Percentage of All Arguments
Estate			
Noble	57.5	42.5	26.8
Common	15.6	84.4	73.2
Party membership			
Right (Pariser Hof, Café Milani)	85.2	14.8	18.1
Center right (Right Zentrum, Casino)	26.6	73.4	43.0
Center left (Left Zentrum, Landsberg, Württemberger Hof)		100.0	26.2
Left (Donnersberg, Nürnberger Hof, Vereinigte Linke)		100.0	12.8
Percentage of arguments	73.2	26.8	
	N = 39	N = 102	N = 141

Note: Figures are percentages. The percentages in the first two columns refer to the rows.

of the Right. Noble and common delegates are found together only in the Right Zentrum and in the Casino party group.

In analyzing the argumentative justifications, one can ask about the extent of convergences with the discursive structures of the debate in France in 1826. The close link between the political system and the entailment of property, which I have posited in this chapter, should show itself—as it did in France—in the quantitative weight of relevant arguments. However, given that industrialization had progressed further by 1848, it is to be expected that economic arguments would play a bigger role than they did in the French debate of 1826. Moreover, the divergent understanding of property in the two countries should be reflected in the lesser importance given to arguments of equality and a more frequent marshaling of arguments aimed at social justice.

Table 4.4 lists the distribution of arguments among those who supported and those who opposed the entailment of property. Only two argumentative points of reference played an outstanding role in the debate of 1848: the basic principles of the political system and economic arguments. Compared to France—and contrary to what one would have expected—familial arguments are clearly secondary. Supporters of *Fideikommisse* justified this legal

TABLE 4.4

Fideikommisse in Germany, 1848: Most Frequent Reasons Offered by Speakers in Support of or Opposition to the Abolition of Entails

	Reasons in Support of Fideikommisse	Reasons Opposed to Fideikommisse
Reasons intrinsic to the law	23.1	16.7
De facto acceptance of the law		2.0
Legal coherence	2.6	9.8
Other reasons intrinsic to the law	20.5	4.9
Reasons pertaining to the political order	25.6	50.0
Free disposition over property	12.8	9.8
Principle of meritocracy		8.8
Principle of equality	5.1	5.9
Principle of justice		4.9
Rejection of legal privileges		4.9
Political stability	5.1	5.9
Repercussions for the common good	2.6	9.8
Economic reasons	43.6	26.0
Economic productivity	5.1	13.7
Fragmentation of the soil	15.4	
Promotion of small-scale agricultural holdings	10.3	
Effects on poverty	12.8	12.7
Familial reasons	5.1	4.9
Providing for family members		2.0
Family cohesion	5.1	2.9
	N = 39	N = 102

Note: Figures are percentages. The debate took place in the fall of 1848 in St. Paul's Church; a total of fifteen speakers participated.

institution especially with the argument that the free disposition over property was an integral right of liberty. The preservation of the monarchical system appears less frequently as an argument why entailment should be maintained than was the case in France in 1826, which presumably can be attributed to the different circumstances under which the debates took place: in France it was the time of the restoration, in Germany the time of the bourgeois revolution. A positive invocation of the monarchical order was politically not very opportune in this situation, although the self-understanding of the aristocratic conservatives—according to which existing privileges should not serve particularistic interests but benefit the common good by contributing to the stabilization of desirable social and cultural structures—is evident. Freiherr von Vincke defended *Fideikommisse* by noting that the nobility was a pillar of the state and had a long-term stabilizing effect, thus preserving traditions, and that the individual was embedded within the lasting entity of the family. Thus, so argued Freiherr von Vincke, entails were based "on the feeling that each individual does not live for himself alone but also for his family; on the desire to subordinate the selfish pleasures of the moment to the welfare of the whole; on the perspective that makes one plant oak trees that will bear fruit only in a later generation" (von Vincke, 20 December 1848, in Wigard 1848, 6:4286).[24]

At the forefront of the argumentation, however, stood the frequent reference to the liberal principle of the free disposition over property. In other words, in the political situation of 1848 defenders invoked a liberal value to preserve the aristocracy's privileges in the realm of property law.

It is likely that the great importance that attached to economic arguments in the debate of 1848 can be attributed to the experiences contemporaries had with economic crises and pauperism. Compared to the French discussion twenty years earlier, sociopolitical references to poverty now played a much more prominent role. However, conservatives, unlike the liberal opponents of *Fideikommisse*, defended entailment of property precisely as a guarantor of economic stability and social security. The dissolution of *Fideikommisse*, they argued, led to the fragmentation of land, which destroyed the economically advantageous structures of large-scale landownership. The entailment of property, on the other hand, made property more stable, because it could not be mortgaged or sold, and thus fragmented. That made it possible to prevent the advance of the capitalist focus on money (Bally, 29 September 1848, in Wigard 1848, 3:2546) and to work the soil more competently because of the long-term ownership relationships (von Vincke, 20 December 1848, in Wigard 1848, 6:4285).[25] The fact that this contrary interpretation of the causal connection—which is so characteristic for the debate in St. Paul's Church—was actually reflected upon[26] speaks for my thesis that the debates over inheritance law are also about the *construction* of perceptions of causal connections that cannot be unambiguously determined.

The opponents of entailed property invoked liberal principles and the ideals of social justice in the political order. They saw the abolition of *Fideikommisse* chiefly as the prerequisite for the free disposition over property. Reference to the meritocratic principle and the opposition to the nobility's legal privileges reflected in the entailment of property likewise attest the liberal grounding of the arguments. The leftist delegate Friedrich Löwe, for example, a member of the Nürnberger Hof, maintained that the principle of liberty was violated by *Fideikommisse* because they did away with the freedom of disposition of succeeding generations (Löwe, 11 October 1848, in Wigard 1848, 4:2548). In addition, opponents of *Fideikommisse* denounced unequal inheritance within a family as an injustice and decried the fact that broad segments of the population had no property as detrimental to productivity:

> Gentlemen, the result of the entailment of land, where it exists, is that a rural aristocracy sorely oppresses the mass of the people. The result of the entailment of land is that the oldest or the youngest son inherits everything, while the other children sink down to the status of day laborers. The result of the entailment of land is a deep hatred within the family; the result is the hopelessness of the after-born; the result is that the day laborer has no prospect of working his way up to becoming a farmer, a landowner. (Mohl, 29 September 1848, in Wigard 1848, 4:2328)

The population "could not attain prosperity through hard work; thus it has come about that the entire population is an oppressed one; the nobler, free spirit cannot arise there, for only the free spirit rises" (Mölling, 11 October 1848, in Wigard 1848, 4:2544). *Fideikommisse* were also detrimental to productivity because they destroyed the acquisitive values of the future holders of entails, who were born "to idleness" (Löwe, in Wigard 1848, 4:2549). This ethical argument was linked with an economic one as speakers pointed to the inefficient distribution of land, the result of the fact that landed property was not—as in the system of free competition—worked by the most industrious.

In contrast to France, the principle of equality played a much smaller role in the German debate. Instead, political semantics were oriented more strongly toward the concept of social justice, which points to the connection between inheritance law policy and social policy. Economic arguments played a smaller role for opponents of *Fideikommisse*, though they carried greater weight than they did in France twenty-two years earlier. The reason was presumably the fact that economic development had been accelerating during this period and proved vulnerable to crises. The speakers also referred to the problem of poverty. Broadening the acquisition of landed property within the rural population was supposed to provide the basis for a livelihood to larger segments of the population and thereby reduce day labor as well as emigration (Salzwedel, 29 September 1848, in Wigard 1848, 3:2330; Zimmermann, in Wigard 1848, 3:2334). The reform of inheritance law was thus also seen as a contribution to the solution of the social question. This reflects the experience of the growing pauperization since the 1840s and the awareness that the fourth estate could pose a potential threat to the social order. Opponents of *Fideikommisse* expected that their abolition would promote economic growth and increase the flexibility of capital. Dissolving entailed property, the argument went, would make possible a more efficient working of land, which would increase the national income. *Fideikommisse*, by contrast, led to an inefficient working of the land, because it was impossible to take out the necessary loans (Hermann, in Wigard 1848, 3:2335), while the inalienability of entailed estates and their latifundium character rendered improvements in productivity unnecessary.

The debate on *Fideikommisse* that took place in the National Assembly in the fall of 1848 does reveal the clear emergence of a dividing line between liberal and leftist forces, on the one side, and conservative delegates (often from the high nobility), on the other side. But the conflict was over more than questions of the distribution of property, dynastic ambitions, and private law issues of equity within families. At stake were the principles of the political order itself: whether an aristocracy whose economic basis was politically protected by special property laws was to be preserved, or whether the emergence of liberal legal principles should be supported through the abolition of entailed property, the separation of property privileges and political office. The delegates were fully aware of this dimension of the debate over *Fideikommisse*; it was no coincidence that the question was discussed within the context of the basic rights.

In December 1848, the National Assembly, by a majority vote, approved the abolition of *Fideikommisse* as §36 of the basic law section of the Reich Constitution. However, it was left to the individual states to formulate transition rules, and they were given the option of introducing special regulations concerning the princely houses. The more radical proposal by Moritz Mohl to declare *Fideikommisse* as dissolved was rejected by the delegates. The decision by the National Assembly must therefore be judged as very restrained, but this restraint was very much in agreement with the goal of establishing a constitutional monarchy.

The compromise agreed upon for the constitution never became law because the large German states rejected the constitution drafted in St. Paul's Church. Although the Revolution of 1848—unlike the Revolution in France—failed, and with it also the abolition of *Fideikommisse*, the constitution is relevant because this was the first time that the structures of a democratic German state were debated and agreed upon in a constitutional assembly—including the abolition of the entailment of property. The year 1848 revealed the close connection between the elimination of entailed property and democratization. The democratic spirit was politically smothered again in the restoration phase that followed the revolution, but the outcome of these efforts remained a central orientation point for the political development in the second half of the nineteenth century. The debate and the arguments and positions put forth by the speakers would shape the discussion over entails in Germany until the end of the empire.

A number of individual German states also saw constitutional debates in 1848. They were a response to the March revolution and their goal was the establishment of constitutional monarchies. Although I will not examine these debates in detail (see Eckert 1992), it is relevant to note that in various states, including Prussia, constitutions were approved that called for the abolition of *Fideikommisse*. In Prussia, Article 40 of the constitution that was imposed by sovereign fiat in January 1850 prohibited the establishment of new *Fideikommisse*. A statute was supposed to regulate how existing *Fideikommisse* would be converted into unentailed property. This is remarkable, since this constitution was enacted by the king himself and not by the constitutional assembly. In the final analysis, however, it was tactical political considerations that gave rise to these changes, not a genuine willingness to pursue reform (Nipperdey 1983, 648ff.). Prohibitions against the establishment of *Fideikommisse* were also enshrined in the constitutions of other German states, such as the Grand Duchy of Oldenburg, the principalities of Lippe and Schwarzburg-Sonderhausen, and the duchies of Anhalt-Bernburg and Brunswick (Eckert 1992, 498ff.). These decisions reveal that the abolition of entailed property was a key theme in the revolution.

The success of the opponents of *Fideikommisse* was short-lived. With the failure of the revolution and the resurgence of the forces of restoration, the constitutional articles concerning the abolition of *Fideikommisse* were either not translated into implementing laws or deleted from the constitution.[27] In Prussia, a constitutional change took effect in June 1852 that repealed the provisions regarding *Fideikommisse* in §40 and introduced merely a prohibition against the establishment of fiefs. One important argumentative basis for the conservative supporters of *Fideikommisse* was §65 of the Constitution of 1850, which stipulated that the First Chamber of the Prussian parliament should be composed in part "of the heads of such families upon whom is conferred, by royal decree, the right—hereditary in accordance with primogeniture and lineal succession—to a seat and vote in the Chamber" (Eckert 1992, 516). The conservatives argued that the hereditary seats in the Upper Chamber could not be linked with a specific property if the dissolution of *Fideikommisse* meant that the retention of this property within the family could not be guaranteed. Once again it becomes apparent how closely *Fideikommisse* were connected with estate-based political structures.

The Expansion of Fideikommisse in the Empire

Family *Fideikommisse* continued in existence during the years of restoration and could also be newly established. What is remarkable about the development in Germany after 1850 is that the modernization of economic structures through the spread of market relationships in the industrialization process did not lead to a gradual erosion of *Fideikommisse*, one that would have turned them slowly into an antiquated legal institution. On the contrary: the statistical data on *Fideikommisse* reveals that this legal institution was spreading. For example, of the 1,083 *Fideikommisse* that existed in Prussia in 1900, more than half (567) had been set up after 1850; in fact, the development shows an acceleration during this fifty-year period. In 1912, 7.0% of the land in Prussia was entailed property, and in Silesia and Hohenzollern the figures were no less than 17.3% and 16.5%, respectively. The vast majority of the newly established *Fideikommisse* was found in East Prussia (Heß 1990, 145). Moreover, the average size of the new *Fideikommisse* was smaller, which indicates that this legal institution was being also used by groups that owned little landed property. In the first half of the nineteenth century, the average size of *Fideikommisse* in Prussia was 2,412 hectares, while the *Fideikommisse* created in the second half averaged only 1,580 hectares. Of the *Fideikommisse* that were found in Prussia in 1912 (a total of 1,277), no fewer than one-third were below 500 hectares in size. Among the bourgeois holders of *Fideikommisse*, who accounted for 12% of all holders, more than half held land of less than 200 hectares (see Eckert 1992, 111ff.). In 1912, the land entailed in bourgeois holdings was only 2.2% of all the entailed land in Prussia (Heß 1990, 154). This, too, reveals that it continued to be a property form used primarily by the nobility, in spite of the fact that the bourgeoisie had formal access to this legal institution.

If one bears in mind that this development of *Fideikommisse* went hand in hand with a rapid industrialization (especially after 1871), and thus also with the mobilization of capital and the individualization of economic relationships, we see here a drifting apart of property form and economic development, a situation that was rife with potential conflict and gave reason to expect increasing tensions in political clashes. And yet these two developments can certainly be seen as connected if one regards the establishment of *Fideikommisse* as an attempt at the long-term stabilization of wealth by the landowning nobility, an instrument that was used by the aristocracy as an anchor to secure their wealth status *precisely* because industrial and commercial capital was gaining economic ground. The new *Fideikommisse* are a private reaction—made possible by the law—to uncertainties of the market economy *and* to the individualization promoted by the development of the economy.[28] The stronger the pressure on large aristocratic landownership, the more it looks for a *political* guarantee for its property situation. This puts the nobility in a defensive struggle in which the economic and legal realities drift apart more and more, and which must eventually lead also to the political intensification of the conflict. *Fideikommisse* were increasingly perceived as a legal institution that offered economic protection for aristocratic large landowners, a situation that exposed the nobility as a weakened social group that could no longer cope with the new social conditions. What need is there for special laws if, as representatives of large landowners claimed, large-scale landholdings were the superior economic form (see Heß 1990, 210)?

Fideikommisse in the Political Debates after 1848

Fideikommisse remained a dominant theme for the reform of inheritance law after 1848 and until their abolition in the Weimar Constitution. However, few new arguments were added to those put forth in 1848. The justifying discourse of supporters and opponents of *Fideikommisse* constantly referred to the same fields of themes that had positive connotations within society, a circumstance that reveals the cultural continuity of the discourse.

In the legal-political discussion over *Fideikommisse*, the argument that justified the entailment of property with reference to the family prevailed also after 1848. The legal scholar Carl Friedrich von Gerber, in his *Contributions to the Doctrine of the German Fideikommiss* (1857), tried to refute the argument that *Fideikommisse* were merely an instrument to preserve aristocratic power. In justifying this legal institution, he combined the bourgeois principle of individuality with the idea of family continuity. The establishment of a *Fideikommiss*, he argued, was the "expression of his [the founder's] personality" (1857, 54). With the *Fideikommiss*, the founder expressed his desire "that his voice be heard in its original intent even after centuries" (54).[29] The entailment of property was intended to ensure that landed property "is not dispersed again already two generations later, that individual pieces of it are not soon possessed without any memory of their origin" (54). To that extent the *Fideikommiss* is a manifestation of the testator's freedom under private law. At the same time, Gerber sees the *Fideikommiss* as containing the "much more profound idea of a creation" (59). The act of establishing a *Fideikommiss* "prepares the ground of a family history" (60). Creating an interconnection between the various generations of a family achieves a "moral elevation of the person" (56), and it was this that legitimized the *Fideikommiss* in the first place. The *Fideikommiss* represents the "principle of sociality" between the generations; a reference with which Gerber sets himself apart from the contractual individualism of the Enlightenment. The proximity to the argumentation of Adam Heinrich Müller is evident not only in the emphasis on the role of the family order, but also in the parallel to the state highlighted by Gerber. For Gerber, the fatherland "itself was a kind of large *Fideikommiss*" (56), because it, too, could not be reduced to an individual contract, but transcended individuals.[30]

Even opponents of the legal institution argued on the basis of family property. For example, Ferdinand Lassalle, in his *System der erworbenen Rechte* (System of Acquired Rights) (1880 [1861]), appropriated Hegel's notion of family property.[31] Since the *Fideikommiss* was the property of the family as a lasting entity, if it was dissolved it could not pass to the current holder as his sole property, but had to belong to the entire family. Lassalle combined the Hegelian skepticism toward individual carriers of rights with the Hegelian notion of the state as the means of carrying out a history of reason, and from this he derived the justification for the state's decision to dissolve *Fideikommisse*. In Lassalle, the family-oriented notion of property thus went hand in hand with opposition to the entailment of property.

In the wake of the National Assembly in St. Paul's Church, it was Lorenz von Stein who offered another incisive statement of the liberal argument against *Fideikommisse* (1888 [1870], 217ff.). In his eyes, the *Fideikommiss* was economically disadvantageous and contradicted the principle that only work should be the foundation of property. In addition, it was an expression of the political structure of aristocratic rule in which the nobility's position of social preeminence was maintained by privileges in property law. However, von Stein argued, the basic principle of the *civil society* was the principle of legal equality. Apart from the equality of political entitlement, it also contained the equality under private law. As von Stein saw it, the transformation of the political order in the direction of a civil society led invariably to the dissolution of entails.[32]

After 1848, the discourse on *Fideikommisse* was altered especially by the growing importance of economic arguments. Economists played an increasingly prominent role in the debate. The economists August von Miaskowski (1882a and 1882b), Adolf Wagner (1879), Gustav Schmoller (1882), Hans von Scheel (1877a), and Johannes Conrad (1888) all came out against *Fideikommisse*, pointing to the unproductive use of the land, the absurdity of keeping landed property inalienable, the concentration of wealth and its political consequences, and the exclusion of large segments of the rural population from private real property. Anton Menger (1927 [1890], 214ff.) criticized *Anerbenrecht* in particular as an expansion of aristocratic rights to the legal conditions of lower population groups. In 1904, on the occasion of the Prussian government's publication of the bill to reform the law of entails, Max Weber, who dealt extensively with questions of agrarian sociology in his early writings, also criticized the entailment of property. However, some of the critics, for example, Wagner and Schmoller, aimed at reforming this legal institution, not abolishing it. Economists were also found among the supporters of *Fideikommisse*, two examples being Wilhelm Roscher and Max Sering.[33]

When it came to the *party political* conflicts over family *Fideikommisse*, the front lines had been clearly drawn between Liberals and Conservatives since the clashes in St. Paul's Church. In the second half of the century, this constellation was transformed by the addition of the Social Democratic position. It cannot be simply assigned to the liberal side of the debate. While Social Democrats like Kautsky (1988 [1899], 202) joined Liberals in calling for the abolition of *Fideikommisse* as relics of the feudal past, they simultaneously opposed the liberal demand that large-scale agrarian landholdings be converted into the private property of small free farmers. Kautsky (1988 [1899], 207) regarded *Fideikommisse* as the "highest stage of agriculture attainable within the capitalist mode of production," since it made possible the accumulation of capital. And yet, large-scale entailed landholdings were often not worked efficiently, since the rules of competition did not apply to them. The Social Democrats accepted that the large-scale land structure as a method for working the land was in principle superior to small-scale farm holdings. Entailed large-scale holdings were seen as the transition stage to the goal of nationalized property, as articulated in the declaration of the Stuttgart Congress of the Social Democratic Workers' Party in 1870:

> As a transition stage from the private working of agricultural land to communal (*genossenschaftliche*) working, the Congress demands that one begin with . . . state domains, *Chatullengüter* (estates in a prince's privy purse), *Fideikommisse*, church lands, communal landholdings, mines, and railways, and it therefore declares itself opposed to any conversion of the above-listed state and communal property into private property. (Liebknecht 1876, 183n)

The Debate over a Reform of Fideikommisse in Prussia Up to 1917

The creation of the BGB could have been the legal and political place to decide the fate of *Fideikommisse*. But as I have shown in the chapter on testamentary freedom, the commission was concerned precisely to interfere as little as possible in political clashes with its legal code. Had the commission dealt with the issue in a substantive way, it would have been forced to take a stance within the charged political debate. Instead, it chose to leave regulations regarding *Fideikommisse* to state law and not deal with them in the BGB.[34] On the one hand this decision can be interpreted as a missed opportunity to modernize the law; on the other hand it prevented *Fideikommisse* from appearing in the new civil law at all. In the eyes of Gottfried Schmitt, the redactor of inheritance law, the *Fideikommiss* was an "abnormal" law that went against his own legal thinking, which was strongly shaped by Adam Smith's economic liberalism. Since there is no reason to assume that parliament would have accepted the BGB with an article prohibiting *Fideikommisse*, their exclusion can be interpreted at least as a step toward preventing this legal institution from spreading into other legal realms. Notwithstanding this assessment, it is true that the decision not to deal with *Fideikommisse* in the BGB also meant "a substantial cave-in to particularistic and feudal special interests" (Eckert 1992, 592).

The decision to exclude the legal regulations pertaining to *Fideikommisse* from the BGB meant that the laws regarding this part of the issue of inheritance law remained a matter of the individual states. Between 1895 and 1917, an intensive parliamentary confrontation took place—especially in Prussia—over the standardization and reform of entail law.[35] During this period, the government presented draft bills on *Fideikommisse* to parliament on three occasions (1903, 1913, and 1917), though in each instance debate on the bill was delayed and eventually suspended because of the irreconcilable positions of the political parties and the vacillating positions of the government. These bills would not have abolished *Fideikommisse* but reformed them; it was the government's intent that this reform would ensure the future of this legal institution. The reform was driven by the conservative parties, in part with the intention of expanding *Fideikommisse* further, though in part also with the intention of excluding certain groups—rich members of the bourgeoisie, non-Protestants, Poles—from the possibility of setting up *Fideikommisse*. Moreover, the regulations pertaining to entailed property were to be revised to bring them more in line with the needs of modern economic exchange.

One goal that the conservatives pursued in the conflicts over entail law between 1895 and 1917 was to make it easier to establish *Fideikommisse*. Thus, a central concern was to reduce the stamp tax of 3% assessed when a *Fideikommiss* was set up. This tax was in fact significantly cut in the government's bills through a graded scale based on the size of the estate and the type of land it encompassed. The conservatives justified their efforts to stabilize and expand *Fideikommisse* by pointing to their importance to the politics of the state: the families holding *Fideikommisse* were said to be "active to an eminent degree on behalf of the state and society" (Heß 1990, 120) and produced outstanding statesmen. They maintained that the government, too, proceeded from the premise that the German Reich "cannot exist without old-established large landowners" (124), which is why the *Fideikommiss* was a kind of savior of the nation. Here we can see the continuation of the argument from the early nineteenth century that justified *Fideikommisse* precisely on the basis of the important role the first estate played in fulfilling state functions. The reasoning behind the draft bill of 1903 justifies the *Fideikommiss* consistently as a means for ensuring the lasting preservation of a class of large landowners able to serve the state.[36] This view was also reflected in those who commented on the draft bill, like Max Sering (1904, 66), who said that the "reason for the institution of the *Fideikommisse* lies in the ethical-political value of the aristocratic tradition and mind-set."[37]

The conservatives wished to make it easier to establish small and medium-sized *Fideikommisse*; in particular, the yield of the estate that was necessary to set up a *Fideikommiss* was not to be raised above the existing level. By contrast, critics of the expansion of *Fideikommisse*, like Max Weber (1904, 555), demanded that the required yield be *raised* in order to limit the spread of this form of property. The conservative parties argued that small *Fideikommisse* would strengthen the farming class and achieve the goals of "internal colonization."

The notion of internal colonization referred to the expansion of agricultural productivity through the settling of farmers and the opening up of land to cultivation in the east, as well as the political goal of settling Germans and displacing the Poles in predominantly Polish areas. Would the broadening of *Fideikommisse* to include small holdings achieve the goals of internal colonization or exactly the opposite? Conservative advocates maintained that it would prevent the fragmentation of land and that farmers would acquire economically relevant competence if the land were worked for generations by a single family. Opponents saw the expansion of *Fideikommisse* as a threat to small farmers, for whom less land would be available on the real estate market, and whose land would also be virtually sucked up by the

Fideikommisse. Consequently, in 1899 the Freisinnige Partei demanded in the Prussian Lower House that the settlement of farmers be promoted precisely by abolishing *Fideikommisse*. The goals of internal colonization would be threatened by the expansion of *Fideikommisse*, it maintained, which is why the simultaneous promotion of *Fideikommisse* and internal colonization by the Prussian government was a stark contradiction (Heß 1990, 123).

This link was confirmed by Max Weber in his essay on agrarian sociology (1904, 513–14, 540ff.): although large landholdings did further the goal of raising productivity, at the same time employment and population on a given area of agricultural land declined, seasonal labor increased, and the wage level dropped, all of which should be rejected for reasons of social and ethnic policies. Weber called for restricting *Fideikommisse* to forestland, which would be subjected to a more efficient cultivation through this legal form; at the same time, better-quality land would be easier to acquire for farmers, which would promote their settlement. Weber saw in the attempt to expand *Fideikommisse* in Prussia the very anticapitalist economic culture that chose the life of the rentier over capitalist acquisitiveness (1904, 573). To him, *Fideikommisse* were part of what was on the whole a misguided economic policy that was, at its core, grounded in Bismarck's policy of protective tariffs.

Another concern behind the reform of the law on *Fideikommisse* was standardizing it across the state and introducing regulations for taking on debts, for selling parts of the land, and for allowing the exclusion of "unworthy" holders or candidates, with all of these steps intended to accommodate this form of ownership to the requirements of modern legal transactions. Moreover, the establishment of monetary *Fideikommisse* was to be prohibited. The intent was thus certainly to modernize the existing law, though the goal was the permanent stabilization of this legal institution, not its abolition.

Around 1900, the Prussian government put forth a new argument why *Fideikommisse* should be promoted: they were a suitable instrument for strengthening the presence of ethnic Germans in the east of the state, that is, in the Polish regions. This meant that the legal institution was no longer justified primarily as a protective privilege for the aristocracy, but with nationalistic interests (Eckert 1992, 618). This line of argumentation had practical consequences. For one, in the period after the turn of the century, German authorization offices prohibited the establishment of *Fideikommisse* by Poles almost without exception (Eckert 1992, 634). Conservative parties even suggested linking ownership of a *Fideikommiss* to the Protestant confession (636). For another, the number of newly created *Fideikommisse* showed a dramatic rise, especially in Silesia, as a result of which twice as much land was entailed in this province as was the average in the state. This was promoted in particular by the possibility of reducing the stamp tax that was due upon the establishment of a *Fideikommiss*, thanks to a decree that was in force between 1905 and 1913, and it was eagerly seized upon under the political pretext of promoting Germanness (Heß 1990, 186ff.).[38]

The expansion of the *Fideikommisse*, which was welcomed by the conservatives, also intensified the political conflict over this legal institution. Beginning in around 1910, political attention shifted more strongly toward the spread of entailed property, and the predominant feeling it aroused was one of concern. The Prussian government now also saw the spread of *Fideikommisse* as economically disadvantageous, because it threatened the independent, small-scale farm holdings. This crisis of legitimacy gave rise to a bill introduced in parliament in 1913 that proposed an upper limit of 2,500 hectares per entail and would permit the creation of new *Fideikommisse*—"except under conditions of special public interest"—only if less than 10% of the land in the district was already entailed. Moreover, setting up a *Fideikommiss* would be permissible only for those large landholdings that had been within a family's possession for at least fifty years. This would de facto exclude members of the bourgeoisie who had attained their wealth through industrialization from establishing such estates.[39] During deliberations in the Upper Chamber, the restrictive provisions of the bill were progressively diluted by conservative delegates who were still intent on expanding *Fideikommisse*. In complete contradiction to the general political and economic development, their goal was to consolidate the property law privileges of aristocratic holders of large estates, which made the controversy over *Fideikommisse* increasingly vehement.

The argumentative structure of the parliamentary debate can be seen in table 4.5. In the deliberations over the government's bill of 1913, which took place in the Prussian Chamber of Deputies in June 1914, economic arguments were clearly front and center—unlike what had transpired in St. Paul's Church. The clash of opinions revolved chiefly around the question of the structural consequences that the entailment of property would have for agriculture. Those who opposed *Fideikommisse* were unanimous in wishing to contain large-scale landownership in favor of the settlement of independent farming families. High land prices caused by a shortage of land undermined the goal of internal colonization.

The defenders of entailed property, who hailed almost to a man from the conservative parties and the Zentrum, were faced with an argumentative dilemma. On the one hand, the conservatives defended the *Fideikommiss* as the way to guarantee the preservation of large landholdings, which were supposedly economically superior. At the same time, they sought to deflect the impression that they were representing the purely particularistic interest of a powerful minority: the expansion of *Fideikommisse* to encompass smaller farm holdings was supposed to spread the advantages of entailed property to them. This was also a concern of the Center Party, whose delegates argued chiefly that they were promoting small agricultural holdings and the preservation of the family.

TABLE 4.5
Fideikommisse in the Prussian Chamber of Deputies, 1914: Reasons Offered
by Speakers for Their Position

	In Support of Fideikommisse	Opposed to Fideikommisse
Reasons inherent in the law	22.8	6.4
Legal coherence		3.2
Legal tradition	22.8	
Other reasons inherent in the law		3.2
Political reasons	22.9	38.6
Principle of equality		3.2
Principle of justice	1.3	3.2
Rejection of legal privileges		22.5
Political stability	8.9	
Consequences for the common good	12.7	9.7
Economic reasons	44.5	51.6
Economic productivity	3.8	9.6
Fragmentation of the land	1.3	
Promotion of small-scale agricultural holdings	17.8	37.2
Promotion of large-scale holdings	21.6	4.8
Familial reasons	10.4	3.2
Providing for family members	2.6	
Family cohesion	3.8	3.2
Preserving family wealth	3.8	
	N = 79	N = 62

Note: Figures are percentages. The debate took place on 12 and 13 June 1914; a total of thirteen speakers participated.

The attempt to avoid the impression of pursuing policies on behalf of particularist interests is also evident in other arguments. Proponents pointed to the existing legal tradition, the cohesion of the family, and the common good, all of which would be furthered by the entailment of property. Opponents, by contrast, put an argument pertaining to the political order front and center: the rejection of privileges relating to property law. It is interesting to note that in the debate of 1914, sociopolitical arguments played only an indirect role and referred only to agricultural structures.

The argument of the free disposition over property and reference to the meritocratic principle no longer mattered to opponents of *Fideikommisse*.

The goal of the conservatives was to stabilize and expand *Fideikommisse*, while the Freisinnigen and the Social Democrats saw in them an anachronistic legal institution that had to be abolished to make room—so the Freisinnigen argued—for liberal meritocratic thinking.[40] Thus, the Liberals repeatedly pointed out that the only reason large estates needed special property law protection through the establishment of *Fideikommisse* was because they were evidently economically inefficient and could therefore not exist under free market conditions (Heß 1990, 121). The controversy thus revolved primarily around the question of modernizing existing economic structures to align them with the market, whereas the holders of *Fideikommisse* were eager to erect a legal barrier. "In the face of the strengthening of industrial and commercial capital," the conservatives "now saw in family *Fideikommisse* primarily a dam that was meant to protect the old privileges of the landed aristocracy against the onrushing flood that was pounding the old Prussia and the prevailing legal and social order" (Eckert 1992, 665). This conflict was therefore a clash of different economic cultures. The landowning nobility opposed the mobilization of landed property, which was supposed to remain within the family's possession in perpetuity, and rejected the market-based, individual notion of property. The Prussian minister of finance, Miquel, laid this out to the Upper House as early as 1895 by characterizing the commodification of landed property as contrary to German legal thinking, thus justifying why the reform of entail law should provide a new legal basis for the need to preserve family property (Eckert 1992, 611, Prussia, *St. Ber. Herrenhaus* 1895, 1:340–41). These arguments, which can be traced through the entire second half of the nineteenth century, express the opposition of the holders of *Fideikommisse* to the implementation of capitalist economic principles. In clear contrast to the development of property law in the United States, free market individualism was opposed by a conception of the organization of property that was oriented toward the principle of the family.

The Dissolution of Fideikommisse after 1917

In the final analysis, the conflicts over entails in Prussia during the first two decades of the twentieth century reflect the defensive struggles waged by a noble class of large landowners who saw their economic foundation and political privileges increasingly threatened by the development of the modern economy and the calls for democratization. This class refused to adjust the political and property-law structures to the changed social conditions. At the end of this conflict in 1917, in the midst of World War I, the political camps had become so entrenched in their positions that an agreement on reforming *Fideikommisse* was no longer on the horizon. The policy—running through the entire period of the empire—of privileging what was chiefly an East Prussian, aristocratic class of landowners (Wehler 1980, 54ff.), which continued to be politically and economically propped up despite the erosion of its economic basis, collapsed with the end of World War I. The conflict over *Fideikommisse* shows in exemplary fashion the dysfunctional nature of a political system that represses its own reforming impulses. The provision for the dissolution of *Fideikommisse* in the Weimar Constitution of 1919 appears, at least in historical hindsight, as a legal reform that was long overdue and too late by decades.

The process of breaking up existing *Fideikommisse* began in Germany in 1919, 140 years later than in the United States and 70 years later than in France. Article 155, Section 2, Line 2 of the Weimar Constitution stipulated: "*Fideikommisse* shall be dissolved." It is the very formulation that had already appeared seventy years earlier in the constitution of St. Paul's Church, though at the time it was not implemented politically. In 1919, however, the establishment of new *Fideikommisse* in Germany was finally halted, and it was bindingly declared that existing *Fideikommisse* had to be dissolved. The implementation was the responsibility of state legislation, as provided for by the introductory law to the BGB. The process of dissolution, however, extended into the second half of the twentieth century, because there were transition periods, complicated legal issues had to be resolved, and attempts were made to delay the inevitable.[41]

Right after 1919, the initial concern was over the interests of later-born children, the agnates. *Fideikommisse* were tolerable for male agnates excluded from ownership as long as it was possible, within the existing estate-based state, to obtain privileged positions within the military or the administration that provided them with status and income, and as long as unmarried daughters could be provided for in aristocratic or ecclesiastical convents. The holders of *Fideikommisse* were obligated to support family members financially in their efforts to establish themselves in this way. The disinheriting of the later-born and of daughters was linked with a provisioning system that could no longer exist under democratic conditions, where all citizens had equal access to government positions. This provisioning element alone explains why *Fideikommisse* were supported within aristocratic families and agnates did not insist on egalitarian partition. The dissolution of *Fideikommisse* threatened the interests of agnates, insofar as the conversion of entails into unencumbered property made the holders of *Fideikommisse* sole owners, without providing any compensation to the agnates. This situation gave rise after the war to associations of agnates. Once again, the close connection between entails and the structures of the estate-based state is evident.[42]

I will not examine the particulars of the dissolution of *Fideikommisse* here, since these were questions of legal detail of no sociopolitical consequence. By 1932, about half of the *Fideikommisse* that had existed in Prussia in 1919 and about two-thirds of the 2,314 entails in the Reich had been dissolved (Eckert 1992, 714ff.). However, some of this property was bound up again into other forms of special law, for example, in protected woodlands (*Schutz-forsten*) or forest holdings. During the Weimar Republic there were repeated protests against the slow pace at which *Fideikommisse* were dissolved.

It is surprising that after the takeover of power by the National Socialists, when those representing the interests of holders of *Fideikommisse* hoped once again that the process of dissolution could be halted, it actually accelerated. Although the National Socialists had a strong ideological interest in the entailment of landed property, which found expression above all in the Reich Farm Inheritance Law that was passed as early as 1933, they were suspicious of large-scale aristocratic landholdings. *Fideikommisse* were essentially a legal device open to the nobility, whereas the National Socialists sought to promote the indivisibility of small-scale farms and the rootedness of farmers by means of the *Anerbenrecht*. The antimodern tenor of the entailment of property agreed with Nazi ideology, but the privileging of the nobility did not. A decree on the dissolution of *Fideikommisse* from 1938 transferred legal authority from the *Länder* to the Reich, and with the Law on the Termination of Family *Fideikommisse* and Other Entailed Wealth, the National Socialists ordered the dissolution of all *Fideikommisse* by 1 January 1939. All *Fideikommisse* ceased to exist as of that date. However, what began initially was a restrictive period during which measures to protect and secure the property were to be taken. It was only the issuing of an entail dissolution certificate that converted the property definitively into free property. Since this process was not completed during the war, the unwinding of *Fideikommisse* extended into the period of the Federal Republic. In those areas that fell under the control of Soviet military administration and in Reich territories that were ceded to Poland, large landowners were expropriated, and that settled the question of *Fideikommisse* in these parts of Germany.

4.3. The Abolition of Entails in the American Revolution

Entails were introduced into the American colonies with the adoption of English common law. In the process, a legal institution that had developed within Europe's feudal structures encountered completely different political, social, and economic conditions. The colonies had neither a land shortage nor an aristocratic elite that could attain political privileges through the entailment of real property.

Historians of colonial America disagree on how widespread entails were at the end of the eighteenth century. What is undisputed is that the entailment of property was of no importance in the colonies of New England.[43] The establishment of entails was impeded in Massachusetts and in other New England colonies as early as the seventeenth century, though they were not entirely and consistently prohibited. This circumstance, in conjunction with the replacement of primogeniture succession by a system of equal division among siblings (discussed in the previous chapter), indicates that these colonies were eager to break with feudal structures of inheritance law long before the Revolution.[44] Where entails did exist in New England, they were the exception from the general pattern of the free and equal bequest of landed property (Brewer 1997, 342; Morris 1927). Inheritance practices in New England "were not aimed at intergenerational consolidation and accumulation of family property" (Ditz 1986, 165). Historians also agree that in the years immediately after the Revolution, most states prohibited entails by law[45] or restricted them in such a way that long-term entailment of property was no longer possible.

A point of contention is whether entails were also irrelevant in the southern colonies. Until recently there was a broad consensus in historical scholarship that entails were not very common in these colonies, which is why the abolition of entailment after 1776 had largely symbolic importance. The basis for that assessment was primarily C. Ray Keim's dissertation of 1926 in which he systematically analyzed wills in three countries of Virginia. Keim (1968 [1926], 565) shows that in the vast majority of wills in the counties in question, landed property was passed along unentailed. When property was entailed, it often applied to only part of the land that was being bequeathed, while other portions passed into the hands of the heirs as free property. However, one must bear in mind that once landed property was inherited in entail it no longer appeared in the wills of subsequent generations, because this property was excluded from any freely determined succession. Still, on the basis of the additional examination of land transfer documents, Keim concludes that "much of the land was being held and transferred in fee simple" (574).

Based on this analysis of wills, one could also question whether entails did in fact promote tendencies toward aristocratization in American society in the eighteenth century. Keim (1968 [1926], 561) showed that entails, though more prevalent among large landowners, were not limited to a specific social or economic group. Even some small landholdings were bequeathed in entail, though in wills drawn up by the testators themselves this was in some instances probably the result of an erroneous use of legal terms (568).[46] To this one must add that entailment was also used as an instrument to protect property from unreliable sons-in-law. When land was bequeathed to daughters, the entailment of property could exclude a husband from any control over it and thus secure the property within a certain line of succession (562). In this case, entails functioned to protect property against sons-in-law deemed unreliable and did not serve to perpetuate wealth in a way that was politically dubious. Keim (586) therefore concludes that when "the Revolutionary War era swept away the last vestiges of the old feudal type of tenure, it affected, of course, the small proportion of land still held in entail, but it did not fundamentally alter the land system of Virginia." The importance of the prohibition was thus more symbolic, the legal expression of a clear break with a feudal institution of property and the affirmation of a market-oriented republicanism that did away with feudal legal structures (Katz 1977, 13).

The abolition of entails was thus not a conflict between social groups that were vying for political power or economic interests by means of this legal institution, but rather the formal abolishment of a legal institution that was contrary to the fundamental notions underlying the founding of the American state and expressed the rejection of aristocratic European traditions.

Based on Keim's empirical analysis, this position was long shared by most American historians (Bailyn 1971, 153ff.; Brown and Brown 1964; Hartz 1955; Katz 1977; Tolles 1954). Ten years ago, however, the historian Holly Brewer (1997) published an article in which she reanalyzed Keim's data and put forth the thesis that at the time of the American Revolution, *up to three-quarters* of the landed property in those parts of Virginia that were settled by colonists were held in tail. The crux of her argument is that Keim had underestimated the cumulative effect of entailment. Without addressing Brewer's arguments in detail here—an evaluation would also require yet another examination of the empirical data—I will highlight only the importance that attaches to this finding if it is even approximately true. For it would mean that in eighteenth-century Virginia, and possibly in other southern colonies, as well, a far greater proportion of land was entailed than was the case at any time in France and Germany, countries that were disengaging themselves from a feudal tradition.[47]

If Brewer is right, the questions arise why entails were able to become so pervasive in Virginia, and why, in contrast to the two European countries, they were dissolved after the Revolution of 1776 with such speed and comparatively little conflict. The answer must take into account the divergent legal, political, and economic conditions, as well as the values expressed in the discursive structures of the public political arena in America.

The possibility for entails to spread in the American colonies was aided, first of all, by the low threshold of formal requirements for the entailment of property, which made the establishment of entails easier than in France and Germany: whereas the entailment of property was largely reserved for the aristocracy in the two European countries, in the American colonies any owner could bequeath land of any size—and in some cases also slaves—in entail. In principle this meant that the group of potential founders of entails comprised all property owners; entails were de facto a general legal institution. This is clearly evident in Keim's analysis of wills (1968 [1922]), which shows that even small landholdings were bequeathed in fee tail. Added to this was the fact that in American law, entails could be easily set up with a corresponding formula in the will. In contrast to the European countries (Eckert 1992, 95–96.), it did not require any participation by the state, and no maximum and minimum acreage limits existed for the establishment of entails. Consequently, the property that could potentially be entailed encompassed not only all owners, but also every piece of land.

The low threshold of legal requirements to set up entails had its counterpart in legal stipulations that made it nearly impossible to dissolve existing entailment of property. At the beginning of the eighteenth century, entail law in Virginia was reformed in such a way as to make it more rigid than in the British mother country, where simplified legal possibilities of dissolving entails had existed since the fifteenth century. According to a law passed in Virginia in 1705, the dissolution of entailment was permissible only by a legislative act, which involved considerable expense and effort and was often rejected by the assembly or the governor (Brewer 1997, 323ff.; Orth 1992, 40). Although small parcels of land were exempted from this law in 1734, the large estates, which were important both quantitatively and politically, continued to be very difficult to free from entailment by heirs. The goal of this regulation, which existed from 1705 to 1776, may have been precisely to allow the emergence of a nonexistent aristocratic social structure by promoting the concentration of wealth, and "not the more general libertarian goal of letting people do what they would with their own" (Orth 1992, 40). These legal conditions in Virginia do in fact raise the possibility that considerable portions of landed property in the American colonies were entailed. If that is true, at least Virginia, and possibly other southern colonies, as well, did not have, at the time of the Revolution, property conditions characterized by equality and individualism (Hartz 1955). The abolition of entails in Virginia in 1776 would have been not merely a symbolic act, but a profound break in legal structures that were solidifying unequal conditions of ownership and blocking dynamic market processes.[48]

But how, then, does one explain that entails in the United States were abolished after 1776 without triggering—as was the case in the two European societies—lengthy conflicts? If Keim (1968 [1926]) was right that only a small part of landed property was in fact entailed, the explanation is easy. But how can one explain the swift abolition of this legal institution during the revolutionary period if, as Brewer (1997) claimed, considerable portions of landed property were entailed?

Values, Political Conditions, Economic Conditions

One important element of explanation lies undoubtedly in the situation of revolutionary upheaval itself, in which the implementation of republican and liberal principles of property law found strong ideological and political support. As I have laid out in chapter 2, some of the political elite of the Revolution subscribed to the view that an equitable distribution of property within society was a social precondition for democratic political structures. Many political leaders of the American Revolution believed that precisely the institutions of entailment and primogeniture succession were partly responsible for the social and political conditions in Europe they rejected, which is why they saw their abolition in America as an urgent task. For example, when Benjamin Franklin was in France, he wrote that two attitudes impeded social development in Europe: "one, that useful labor is dishonorable; the other, that families may be perpetuated with estates" (qtd. in Huston 1993, 1090). This partly value-oriented background is also clearly evident in the legal documents on the abolition of entails. Jefferson's preamble to the law of 1776 that abolished entails in Virginia, for instance, listed as the motivation behind the law the implementation of liberal market principles, sociopolitical concerns, family-related goals, and pragmatic political considerations:

> Whereas the perpetuation of property in certain families by means of gifts made to them in fee-tail, is contrary to good policy, tends to deceive their fair traders who give a credit on the visible possession of such estates, discourages the holder thereof from taking care of and improving the same, and sometimes does injury to the morals of youth, by rendering them independent of, and disobedient to, their parents; and whereas the former method of docking such estates tail by special act of assembly formed for every particular case, employed very much of the time of the legislature, was burthensome to the public, and also to the individuals who made application for such acts . . . (Jefferson, in Smith 1995, 560)

The intention of preventing potential tendencies toward aristocratization in American society is expressed more clearly still in the preamble to the law on the abolition of entails passed in North Carolina in 1784: "entails of estates tend only to raise the wealth and importance of particular families and individuals, giving them an unequal and undue influence in a republic" (qtd. in Orth 1992: 41–42). Further evidence for this antiaristocratic motif comes from the autobiography of Thomas Jefferson, where he recalls the abolition of entails in Virginia:

> The transmission of this property from generation to generation, in the same name, raised up a distinct set of families, who, being privileged by law in the perpetuation of their wealth, were thus formed into a Patrician order, distinguished by the splendor and luxury of their establishments. . . . To annul this privilege, and instead of an aristocracy of wealth, of more harm and danger, than benefit, to society, to make an opening for the aristocracy of virtue and talent, which nature has wisely provided for the direction of the interests of society, and scattered with equal hand through all its conditions, was deemed essential to a well ordered republic. (Jefferson 1959 [1829], 50–51)

Entails were judged to be a threat to the republican system, the necessary foundation of which Jefferson believed to be the widest possible diffusion of landownership. A good deal of literature on the abolition of the entailment of property in the United States during the revolutionary period offers the individualistic-meritocratic conception of property as the normative background to the legislation that abolished entails (Ditz 1986; Katz 1977; Orth 1992). To the extent that the family appears in the discourse on entails, it did so in connection with the danger of a potential aristocratization of American society.

Entails were even rejected by conservative legal scholars like James Kent. Presumably against the backdrop of the concentration of land along the

Hudson valley in New York, Kent spoke out against the impediment to the real estate market created by the entailment of property:

> Entailments are recommended in monarchical governments, as a protection to the power and influence of the landed aristocracy; but such a policy has no application to republican establishments, where wealth does not form a permanent distinction, and under which every individual of every family has his equal rights, and is equally invited, by the genius of the institutions, to depend upon his own merit and exertions. (1971 [1827], 2:20)

While these value-driven motivations are undoubtedly *one* aspect behind the swift abolition of entails in the United States, this explanation remains incomplete. If nothing else, it leaves open the question why there was no sustained political opposition. At the very least, social groups interested in the legal institution of the entail could have—as they did in the European countries—put forth arguments defending entails based on economic considerations, political and social values, issues intrinsic to the law, or familial considerations, thus bringing about at least a protracted political confrontation.

In fact, there were voices of opposition, though they are much more poorly documented than in Europe. For example, in the debate on 14 October 1776, Edmund Pendleton opposed the law introduced into the Virginia assembly by Jefferson; he tried to push through an amendment requiring the consent of the current tenant and the next in line before an entail could be dissolved (Brewer 1997, 341). Jefferson's law encountered "the stiffest resistance" (Myers 1969 [1939], 11) and was very nearly defeated by the opposition (Jefferson in Smith 1995, 561). Following passage of the law prohibiting entails in Virginia, Landon Carter, a descendant of Robert ("King") Carter, the richest man in that colony in the early eighteenth century, and himself the holder of large entailed estates, wrote a letter to George Washington, asking the American Senate for help in resisting the abolition of entails (Brewer 1997, 341).[49] Early biographers of Jefferson noted that the bill on the abolition of entails earned the future president the lasting enmity of the planter aristocracy in Virginia: "The day that Mr. Jefferson brought his bill to abolish entails into the House of Delegates, he banded for the first time against himself a numerous and very influential body of enemies" (Randall 1858, 201–2). But even if one takes into consideration that possible opposition to the abolition of entails in the United States is much more poorly documented than in the European countries, it does not seem plausible to assume that comparably intense conflicts over this legal institution ever took place.

Any explanation must also include the different political, legal, and economic structures. In the case of New England, one must bear in mind that entails evidently played hardly a role there as an inheritance strategy before the Revolution. In the case of Virginia, where a considerable part of the land may have been entailed, we must take into account the interests of the holders of entails and their families, which were much more ambivalent than in the two European countries, a situation that has to do with sociopolitical and economic structures that were very different from Europe. For example, we do not find in the United States, even during the colonial period, the *political motives* that were decisive for the entailment of property in the European countries. In Germany and France, entails were connected with political privileges; the political structure of aristocratic rule was also based on this legal institution. In the United States, entails did not have the function of securing the material basis of a nobility that was also invested with political power. At best, the entailment of land could serve the exercise of economic power. As a result, entails lacked the most important precondition in terms of politics and the structure of the state.

The divergent constellation in the United States also had the result that there was no state-organized compensation of any kind for later-born children excluded from inheriting the entailed land. They were not entitled to positions in the military, the church, or the administration, which meant that America lacked the balancing mechanism that made it more or less tolerable for agnates in the German states and under the ancien régime in France to be shut out from inheriting the entailed estate. In America, entails had to lead to a much greater degree of intrafamily conflicts and to the rejection of this legal institution by the later-born children also of the social upper class. This confirms the close connection between entails and an estate-based political order, and thus the thesis that it would be inadequate to interpret entails chiefly as a private instrument by the testator to control wealth across generations. In the United States, where the motivation for the establishment of private entails was invariably limited to the private perpetuation of wealth, they were not able to sustain themselves.

To this we must add that precisely the wide prevalence of entailed land (assuming Brewer is correct) was an economic reason why the holders of entails in Virginia had little interest in perpetuating them. The rigidity of the real estate market produced by entails stood in stark contrast to the dynamism of the geographical expansion and its attendant mobility in the early phases of the history of the United States. One example of how the entailment of property impeded market allocation processes is the failed attempt by Thomas Jefferson to sell a piece of property that his wife had brought into the marriage, which was entailed and at a distance from where the Jeffersons lived. Even though Jefferson offered to entail a piece of land of equal value in the county where he lived, the dissolution of the entail was prohibited by the governor in 1774, which made the land inalienable (Brewer 1997, 327–28).[50]

The economic conditions of an abundance of land, the geographic mobility of the population, and the importance of landed property as the most important object of speculation made forms of property that could be freely disposed over by individuals attractive. The entailment of property was an impediment to mobility, limited the possibility of credit, and obstructed speculative real estate investments. To that extent it was the completely different economic conditions under which the legal institution of the entail—adopted from England—operated in the colonies that created within the social upper class a strong interest in abolishing it (see also Brewer 1997, 341). Against the backdrop of the political and economic structures in America, the republican demand that the entailment of property be abolished could succeed much more easily than was the case in the two European countries. This also points to the social conditions under which the individual-meritocratic conception of property was able to take shape in the United States. Even in the nineteenth century, and especially in comparison with England, commentators repeatedly highlighted how important the abolition of entailment and primogeniture was to preventing the dynastic concentration of wealth.[51] Only in the late nineteenth century was there a growing realization that equal property conditions demanded more extensive intervention than an inheritance law aimed at equality (Huston 1998, 202ff. and 354–55).

The explanation for the rapid and relatively conflict-free dissolution of entails in the United States lies in the interplay of various factors. First and foremost, this particular legal institution was not systematically integrated into the structure of the political system, which was the case in Europe and created an interest in the entailment of property. In addition, republican ideals were deeply rooted in the political elite of the revolutionary period, and there were economic conditions that made the entailment of property appear especially dysfunctional, even to the landowning economic elite. This left only private motives of the dynastic transmission of wealth. However, alternative legal institutions were available that did just that while avoiding some of the most serious disadvantages of entailment. Common law allowed for the establishment of trusts, which made it possible to control the dispersal of the income from the bequeathed wealth up to twenty-one years after the death of the last heir who was alive when the testator died; only then could a trust be dissolved.[52] Under this setup, wealth could be controlled for about 100 years (Friedman 1966, 340; Orth 1992, 39–40). In contrast to entailment, trusts did not remove assets from the market, since the trustee could freely sell them in the interest of the beneficiaries. This circumvents at least one negative effect of entailment.

4.4. Conclusion

The intergenerational binding of property through *Fideikommisse*, substitutions, and entails was one of the main areas of conflict in inheritance law policy of the late eighteenth and the nineteenth centuries in Germany, France, and the United States. The liberals and later the emerging workers' movement fought against the privileged treatment by property law of landed wealth that was for the most part in aristocratic hands, the removal of landed property from market processes, the prevention of the division of land in succession, and the power of the "dead hand" over realty as the structure of a bygone era.

Entails were abolished in all three countries in question, though at times that were widely separated in time: in the United States within the context of the Revolution of 1776, in France first in 1789 and then—following their reintroduction in the restoration period—for good at the beginning of the Second Republic, in Germany not until the revolution in November 1918. This chronological staggering reveals the close interconnection between the entailment of property and monarchical state structures.

In the United States, this legal institution was introduced along with English common law, but in the New World it encountered completely different social, political, and economic realities, which is why entails made little headway in broad sections of the American colonies. The United States had no aristocratic elite that could have secured its political power by means of this legal institution. And because the country lacked a feudal past, the Revolution and the prohibition of entails was not followed by a restorationist countermovement. But the United States differs from the two European countries in another respect: while land was an exceedingly scarce resource in France and Germany and landed property was the most important form of property in these agrarian societies, the availability of land was almost unlimited in the American colonies. In France and Germany, the removal of land through entails and their undivided transmission by inheritance meant that fewer people could acquire landed property and that prices were kept high through scarcity. This increased the pressure on urbanization and emigration. This situation intensified the clashes over entails on both sides: the growing shortage of landed property led to agrarian economic competition from which aristocratic landowners sought to shield themselves; at the same time, it led to greater social pressure for the abolition of entailment from those social groups who felt deprived of the possibility of acquiring landed wealth.

This situation was the same for Germany and France, however. How, then, does one explain the difference of seventy years between the abolition of entails in France and in Germany? Two factors can be singled out: first, the weaker political standing of the liberal bourgeoisie in Germany, which contributed in general to a delay in the modernization of political conditions. A powerful symbolic expression of this was the failed Revolution of 1848. The result in Germany was an increasingly conflict-filled situation where rapidly advancing industrial modernization was accompanied by the expansion of an institution of property law whose function lay precisely in shielding land from the processes of capitalistic utilization. This shows that under the right balance of political power, an institution of inheritance law can persist for long periods even as economic structures develop that render this institution increasingly dysfunctional in economic terms.

Second, different legal-political discourses about entails were carried on within the three countries. In all three countries there were liberal political forces that spoke unanimously in favor of the abolition of entailment by invoking the liberty and equality of the heirs and pointing to this legal institution's negative social, familial, and economic consequences. The arguments that were put forth can be traced back largely to the contractual thinking of the Enlightenment and to economic liberalism, and they also reflect the spread of market conditions. In the second half of the nineteenth century, this group of opponents of entails in Germany was joined by representatives of the workers' movement, who rejected the entail as the remnant of feudal legal structures.

The discourse on inheritance law in the United States in the late eighteenth century was clearly dominated by liberal, enlightenment thinking, and even conservative jurists like James Kent, for example, agreed with liberal republicanism on the question of the abolition of entails. Promoting dynastic forms of property that are removed from the market is not one of the goals of the organization of property laws in the United States. All in all, on the three levels of the economic functionality of entails, the prevailing political structures (including the absence of a feudal past), and discursive attitudes in the legal-political discourse, the situation in the United States was thus the most favorable for a swift abolition of the entailment of property.

In France, the values of freedom and equality attained a dominant position in the legal-political discourse in the Revolution. Therein lies an important difference from the inheritance law discourse in Germany, where the principle of equality—which can be an important argumentative basis in the discussion over entails—did not carry the same weight. However, different from the United States, there existed influential aristocratic elites of the ancien régime who rejected equality and bourgeois individualism. The family as a supraindividual normative point of reference in the shaping of the law and the defense of aristocratic privileges played a substantial role in the legal-political discourse after the Revolution. The antagonism between these positions and the attempt by the old elites to restore the political conditions led to the clashes over the reintroduction of substitutions in the 1820s.

In Germany at that time, even opponents of entails, some of whom rejected them with the liberal arguments I have outlined, were still defending the entailment of property from the perspective of state law and state politics. This is clearly evident in Svarez, von Stein, and also Hegel. Here, the inherent link between entails and structures of aristocratic authority and power was decisive. An influential republican movement took shape in Germany only in the *Vormärz* period and culminated in the Revolution of 1848. In St. Paul's Church, liberal voices—which spoke out in favor of the abolition of entailment—were in the majority. Yet a minority of conservative voices looked askance at the notion of placing land at the disposal of the market; they presented the principle of the family as being clearly superior morally to bourgeois individualism, and rejected the republican form of the state. The familial and the liberal conceptions of property stood side by side in Germany, and this legal-political ambivalence prevented an *unambiguous* delegitimation of the institution of entailment by the political and legal elites, similar to what happened in the United States and to a lesser degree also in France. Entails were not rejected with one voice; they were normatively highly contested in the legal-political discourse.

Political, economic, and legal-political aspects influenced the history of entails in France, Germany, and the United States in different ways. However, the greatest importance for explaining the long time-span that separates the abolition of entailment in the three countries belongs to the development of the political structure. The triumph of republican conditions robbed entails of their political support, and in all three countries that was precisely the situation when they were abolished.

Chapter 5

SOCIAL JUSTICE THROUGH REDISTRIBUTION?
THE TAXATION OF INHERITANCE

WEALTH IS UNEQUALLY DISTRIBUTED.[1] A small elite owns large portions of the private property that is available in any given society.[2] One cause for this inequality, which is far more pronounced than the inequality in income distribution, is inheritances. The majority of wealthy testators were themselves heirs.[3] As property is handed down from generation to generation along the line of descendants, social inequality is reproduced without any effort from the recipients of the wealth. If the distribution of property is supposed to be oriented toward meritocratic criteria, why are inheritances not subject to very high taxes as a way of creating comparable financial starting positions for all and realizing the principle of equality of opportunity? Would it not be possible to achieve the goal of a balanced distribution of wealth precisely by taxing property that has become "masterless" upon the death of its owner?

In fact, the early nineteenth century already saw the emergence of a discourse among liberal and early socialist social reformers in which inheritance taxation was seen as an important instrument for realizing the promise of equality and for solving the "social question." Within the framework of liberal social theory, this taxation appeared an especially suitable tool for achieving equality of opportunity *within* a system based on private property (Beckert 1999a). Since inheritance taxation falls upon property that passes to heirs without any effort of their own, taking part of that wealth through taxation seems a sensible solution in a context in which the legitimation of inequality is guided by individual achievement. In normative terms, inheritance taxation seems far less problematic than an income or consumption tax, for example.

The most influential advocate for restricting the right of private inheritance was probably John Stuart Mill (1976 [1848]), who proposed limiting the wealth a person could inherit to a sum that would allow for a modest standard of living, what he calls a "moderate independence" (889). Mill emphasized the meritocratic principle as the basis for justifying social inequality and was almost hostile in his opposition to inequality generated by inheritances. For him, the "accidents of birth" had no normative place in the liberal social order.[4]

To justify restrictions on inheritance, Mill pointed to the change in the structure of property in bourgeois societies. Speaking of earlier societies, he argued that "[e]xclusive individual property in the modern sense scarcely entered into the ideas of the time." Rather, the family was traditionally the owner of property. For that reason, when a family member died, there was no succession, because one share of the family wealth simply passed to the other members of the family. Death and birth merely changed the identity of those who participated in the common property. Modern society, however, was characterized by a fundamental change in family structures. That change made it meaningful to speak of individual property in the first place, but at the same time it had consequences for the legitimation of inheritance:

> But the feudal family, the last historical form of patriarchal life, has long perished, and the unit of society is not now the family or clan, composed of all the reputed descendants of a common ancestor, but the individual; or at most a pair of individuals with their unemancipated children. (Mill 1976 [1848], 222)

Mill's call for restrictions on inheritances was controversial within liberal theory (Beckert 1999a). The connection between inheritances and unequal material starting positions for individuals does not give rise in liberal thinking to a clear normative commitment to the goal of redistribution. The principle of equality of opportunity as a guiding political notion had to be balanced normatively against the legal, economic, political, and sociostructural consequences of placing restrictions on the bequeathal of property. In the conflict over the taxation of inheritance, arguments derived from the principle of equal opportunity and sociopolitical goals clashed essentially with concerns related to property law and the economy.

In terms of property law, inheritance taxation was criticized as interference in private property that violated the principle of individual disposition over private property, at least if it was motivated by redistributive goals. Even greater weight attached to economic arguments that can be traced back to Adam Smith (1978 [1776], 391). For Smith, inheritance taxes were "more or less unthrifty taxes that increase the revenue of the sovereign, which seldom maintains any but unproductive labourers; at the expence of the capital of the people, which maintains none but productive" (391). Inheritance taxes reduced the stock of capital, which reduced investments and impeded economic development.[5] The opponents of inheritance taxation feared negative effects on the savings rate and the motivation to engage in economic activity, since high inheritance taxes created incentives to increase consumption at the end of life and institutionalized negative incentives for the accumulation of property.[6] But the proponents of inheritance taxation likewise argued on economic grounds: inheritances are an inefficient way of allocating capital, because the distribution of capital through transfers *mortis causa* was removed from the market mechanism and the heirs might lose their acquisitive drive as a result of their secure material condition.

The taxation of inheritances is bound up in a complex, conflicting web of clashing values, sociopolitical considerations, and demands placed on its economic function. In terms of tax theory, the issue concerns primarily the balance between the two principles of tax efficiency and tax equity.[7] However, it is not clear which institutionalization of inheritance taxation is economically optimal, nor is it possible to unambiguously derive fair institutional structures of the tax system from abstract principles of justice, for example those of utilitarianism or Rawls's political philosophy (Stiglitz 2000, 473ff.).[8] The various alternatives of taxation often appear unpredictable in their consequences, dilemmatic, contradictory, and problematic in some of their complex repercussions.[9] Moreover, when it comes to political battles over distribution, the actors involved cannot be made to embrace abstract principles of justice if their implementation can be expected to produce disadvantages for their own situation. Consequently, actors try to use the ambiguous consequences of inheritance law to push through their own interests. The question of who must pay how much in taxes is determined in a conflictual process of social struggle. And normative principles that are expressed in the discursive structures are themselves used as an instrument for defending one's own interests.

But inheritance taxation is also conflictual because it has a new quality compared to the questions of inheritance law examined previously. Inheritance taxes interfere in private rights to transfer property in that *the state* appropriates a part of the property left behind by the deceased. Questions of individual property rights, of equality, of justice, and of the economic and familial consequences of the rules of inheritance law are no longer discussed in reference to the distribution of property *within the family*, but in reference to the distribution *within society*.[10] How, then, is the relationship between the private bequeathal of wealth and the claims of the state perceived in the countries in question?

The conflict over the taxation of inheritance was the most important theme in inheritance law in the twentieth and early twenty-first centuries.[11] In this chapter I will examine how inheritance taxation developed in Germany, France, and the United States, how these societies in the process dealt with the liberal dilemma between individual property rights and the meritocratic principle, and how one can explain the differences in taxation between the three countries. I will develop the thesis that it is only the confluence of normative conflict with the growth of the state's need for revenue and the rise of social-reformist political movements that caused these tensions to become acute on a political level. This happened about the same time in France, Germany, and the United States, at the end of the nineteenth century, when the modern state with its broad range of activities began to take shape, when large companies asserted themselves as new economic structures in the economy, and questions of social inequality moved to the forefront of political clashes as a result of the social consequences of industrialization. In the present chapter, I will show that the more or less synchronous institutionalization of a modern system of inheritance taxation on the level of the nation-state—in France in 1901, in Germany in 1906, and in the United States in 1916—can be explained by the coincidence of financial crisis and the political conflict to establish a system of taxation that was both efficient *and* equitable.

However, differences between the three countries exist when it comes to the concrete manifestation of the tax—its rate, progression, and inclusivity, and I contend that these differences cannot be explained solely from different financial demands and the varying strength of interest groups. Rather, they can be understood only against the background of the prevailing legal traditions and the divergent perspectives on the normative and functional aspects of inheritance taxation that are reflected in the political discourse. The varying conceptions of the meaning of inherited wealth that I have laid out in the previous chapters appear once again in the controversies surrounding inheritance taxation. In each of the three countries there developed, beginning in the early nineteenth century, a specific discursive field within which the taxation of bequests was evaluated in very different ways. One side of the field is characterized in all three countries by misgivings about inheritance taxation based on property law and the economy. On the other side we find arguments specific to each country.

Among supporters of inheritance taxation in the United States, the principle of equality of opportunity and concerns over the antidemocratic consequences of the concentration of wealth are front and center; the great fortunes are always the implicit point of reference of the debate. Opponents, meanwhile, see the tax as a threat to economic efficiency and as unjustified interference in private property. In Germany, the tax is defended chiefly as a means of financing social policies and rejected by opponents as an illegitimate interference in the family. The point of reference in the debate is family wealth, which contributes to providing for surviving family members, and the changing role of the family within the process of modernization. In France, where inheritance taxation received the least political support, the conflict has focused on questions concerning the right to an individual disposition over property, and the compatibility of progressive taxation and the principle of equality. The point of reference here is the abstract entity of "national wealth" as the economic foundation of the French nation. Thus, the issue is less the individual consequences of taxation as its societal repercussions.

I contend that these different perspectives on the normative and functional meaning of the taxation of inherited wealth are relevant aspects for explaining the concrete shape that the tax took in the various countries. This approach is aimed once again at explaining the development of institutions by taking into account the interplay of functional (financial) demands, interests, institutional paths, and the values that find discursive expression.

5.1. EQUALITY OF OPPORTUNITY VERSUS PRIVATE PROPERTY: THE ESTATE TAX IN THE UNITED STATES

When it comes to the taxation of inheritance in the United States, we can distinguish two phases: first, the period between 1890 and 1935, when the estate tax[12] was introduced (1916) and its structure was put in place with progression rates that are very high compared to Germany and France; second, the period from the late 1960s until today, when the estate tax has come under increasing political pressure, resulting in a law that provides for its phaseout in 2010.

This section examines the development of the American estate tax in these two phases.[13] I will argue that the *introduction* of the estate tax can be explained by the confluence of the expansion of the state's need for money and the emergence of social reform movements, though not the *specific form* the tax took. Rather, the latter goes back to the conception of property expressed in the discursive structures concerning the taxation of inheritance. I will first look at the debates over inheritance taxation in the nineteenth century in order to bring out the continuity of the critique of unearned wealth that took shape during the revolutionary period (see chapters 2 and 4). The argumentation of populism and the progressive movement that was critical of inheritance reveals the stability of the discursive field dealing with tax policy. An analysis of the debates in the American Congress over the introduction of the estate tax is intended to provide further insight into the controversy. The second part looks at the development since the late 1960s. The question here is why there was a break with the estate tax system that was established in the early twentieth century. How can one explain the growing opposition to this tax? How does the decision to phase out the tax in 2010 relate to the inheritance-critical discourse that has accompanied the history of the United States since its founding?

Inheritance Taxation and Social Reform

The chapters on testamentary freedom and the abolition of entails laid out the central line of conflict that emerged during the revolutionary period in the American discourse on inheritance law. The defense of the greatest possible freedom to dispose over private property was confronted by a position that took a highly critical view of the bequeathal of wealth. According to this position, the inheritance of property entails the danger of a dynastic concentration of power, which could eventually threaten the foundations of the republican political system; moreover, it violated the principle of equal opportunity. However, the question of taxing inheritances was of little importance during the revolutionary period.[14] This changed in the 1830s when radical-liberal social reformers seized on the topic of inheritance law and highlighted especially the taxation of bequests as a central element in the reform of inheritance law.

In the early nineteenth century, the Transcendentalists around Ralph Waldo Emerson and the communities in Massachusetts organized by Robert Owen decried the strong concentration of economic power as well as the unequal distribution of wealth in American society. Against this background they demanded comprehensive social reforms, which included the redistribution of wealth through inheritance taxation. The authors, most of whom belonged to the liberal political camp, to the extent that they defended private property,[15] saw in the transmission of wealth through inheritance a serious violation of equality of opportunity and the meritocratic principle, both of which they considered among the basic values of American society. It was not private property itself that was criticized—in fact it was vehemently defended—but the creation of dynastic wealth. The concentration of wealth in the hands of only a few, it was argued, would negatively prejudice the chances of all others, damage the spirit of individualism and personal responsibility, and thus endanger democracy.[16] The political point of reference for the reformers was especially Thomas Jefferson's critique of the bequeathal of property. This is evident, for example, in the writings of Thomas Skidmore (1829) and Orestes Brownson (1978a [1840], 1978b [1840]).

Skidmore, a New York social critic and labor leader, published *The Rights of Man to Property* in 1829. His goal was to secure the right of every citizen to property through a plan of radical redistribution. Invoking Thomas Jefferson and Thomas Paine, Skidmore wanted to take the maxim "all men are created equal" seriously by handing over the same amount of property to each person upon the age of majority (Skidmore 1829, 153). This would be made possible by a confiscatory inheritance tax: "When the death happens, of either of any two married persons, the survivor retains one half of the sum of their joint property, their debts being first paid. The other half goes to the State" (143).

Orestes Brownson, who was a member of the radical-liberal movement of Transcendentalism, penned an article entitled "The Laboring Classes," which caused a tremendous stir when it was published in 1840. In it he called for the introduction of confiscatory inheritance taxes, which alone were compatible with the principle of equality of opportunity and individual entrepreneurship that were deeply rooted in American society: "A man shall have all he honestly acquires, as long as he himself belongs to the world in which he acquires it. But his power over his property must cease with his life, and his property must then become the property of the state, to be disposed of by some equitable law for the use of the generation which takes his place" (Brownson 1978a [1840], 24).

Brownson's intent was not to bring about social equality nor to convert private property into communal property, but merely to endow individuals with equal resources at the start of life. To that end, ascriptive material privileges were to be abolished (Brownson 1978b [1840], 60ff.). Invoking Kent, Blackstone, Bentham, Mirabeau, and Jefferson, he argued that property rights terminated upon death and property thus reverted back to society.

The implication, to Brownson, was that there was no natural right to testamentary freedom. Rather, testamentary freedom was a convention, while from the perspective of natural law, the death of the property owner created once again the original situation of unappropriated land (71). Brownson likewise denied that children had any kind of inheritance right that was grounded in natural law. Instead, natural law demanded the redistribution of property after the death of its owner, whereby this distribution had to be guided by the principle of equality. If property became "free," "one man can rightfully appropriate to himself no more than, in an equal division of the whole among all the members of the new generation, would be his share" (75). After the death of the owner, property thus did not revert to society as communal property, but was allocated to the members of society *as private property*. Brownson's goal with his reform proposal was to implement the meritocratic principles of the liberal social model. For him, inequality as a result of varying talent or effort was not a problem as long as everyone always began with equal material opportunities (78–79). At the same time, he sought to use redistribution to counteract the proletarization of growing segments of the population.[17]

The radical-liberal demands of the early nineteenth-century American reform movement for high or even confiscatory taxation of inheritances did not yet cause inheritance taxation to play an eminent role in the sociopolitical discourse in the United States at that time. Back then there was not yet pressure for more active exercise of state functions on the part of the federal government, not were the social reform movements influential enough to place the topic effectively on the legislative agenda. It was only in the late nineteenth century that the conflict (already present at the foundation of the country) between the liberal economic conception of private property, which largely rejected interference in the individual dispositionary rights of owners, and the rejection of a strong concentration of wealth through the unearned acquisition of inherited wealth became virulent. At that time, the normative ideals from the revolutionary period clashed head-on with the tendencies toward social polarization of industrialization and urbanization and the rising revenue needs of the federal state. James Huston (1993, 1080ff.) has brought out just how much the American self-conception was shaped until the 1880s by a republican notion of distribution, which was aimed at an equitable distribution of the wealth available within society. According to Huston, this notion, which was initially shaped during the revolutionary period by the political elite but then diffused into society at large, contained various elements: the idea—going back to Locke and Protestant doctrines—that property had to be acquired through individual effort; the rejection of a strong concentration of wealth and aristocratic inheritance strategies; and the fear that the aimed-for social equality could be maintained only under conditions of relatively low population density. This vague picture of a legitimate distribution of property and its preconditions was undermined in the last two decades of the nineteenth century by the actual development of the economy, and this pushed American society to search frantically for a new understanding (Huston 1993, 1080).

The structural transformation from an agrarian to an industrial society, the agrarian crisis of the 1890s, the growing dominance of large business conglomerates, and the social problems of immigration and urbanization moved questions about the distribution of wealth and opportunity into the center of political attention. The simultaneous closing of the frontier (Turner 1920) also contributed to destroying the picture of an agrarian society of property owners, in the process also challenging the existing notions of the social foundations of American democracy. By making inheritance an issue and calling for the creation of greater equality of opportunity through inheritance taxation, social reformers were taking their cues from the liberal ideas of the revolutionary period. They blamed the concentration of power in the hands of "big business" for the social crises and—by reaching back to the ideas of the Founding Fathers—pursued a reform that was aimed at a redistribution of wealth and equality of opportunity.

INHERITANCE TAXATION AND SOCIAL REFORM IN THE PROGRESSIVE ERA

The last decade of the nineteenth century marked the beginning of the first key phase in the political debate over inheritance taxation in the United States; this phase would last into the 1930s. Before that, inheritances were taxed only moderately by a few individual states, whereby these taxes were often nonprogressive, the tax rates of most states were below 10%, and only the inheritances of collateral relatives were taxed.[18] On the federal level, inheritances were taxed only three times in the nineteenth century; in each instance it was war-related and did not last very long: at the beginning of the century during conflicts with the French navy, during the Civil War, and at the end of the century to finance the war against Spain (Paul 1954; Ratner 1967).[19] With a top rate of 5% for lineal family members, this tax, too, was low and was repealed every time after the end of the conflict. The tax derived its legitimacy from a sense of patriotic solidarity, and this, together with the very moderate tax rates, might explain why it did not lead to pronounced political conflicts.

This close connection between a military emergency and inheritance taxation was loosened at the end of the nineteenth century.[20] The chief reason behind this was the increasingly difficult fiscal situation and the growing strength of the movements of social reform.

Financially, the existing sources for funding the federal budget—chiefly import tariffs, consumption taxes, and revenue from land sales (Holtfrerich 1991, 256–57)—proved inadequate to pay for the costs of the government's activities, which had risen after the Civil War vis-à-vis the individual states.[21] New sources of revenue had to be tapped for the federal budget.

Social reform movements gathered political strength in the 1880s, especially populism and the Progressive movement, which gave voice to important changes in the social and political self-conception of the United States.

The populist movement in the late 1880s and the Progressive movement around 1900 provided a lasting impulse to the political discourse on inheritance taxation. Both movements were especially active in opposing the unequal distribution of wealth and called for political measure to improve the living conditions of the lower social classes—in populism especially the rural population and small producers.

1. The Populists criticized the lavish life style of the upper class in the Gilded Age as a particular provocation—documented, for example, in Thorstein Veblen's *The Theory of the Leisure Class* (1979 [1899])—and demanded that the great fortunes be used to improve the living conditions of the lower classes. Populists saw the industrial tycoons as a parasitical social class that was living at the expense of the productive class and was not bearing its fair share of the tax revenues (Schimmer 1996). Their ideas about economic policy were guided by the ideals of agrarian democracy from the revolutionary period, with their emphasis on an egalitarian distribution of property and independent, small-scale agricultural producers. The emphasis of Populist demands regarding taxation was a reduction of indirect taxes and levies, the introduction of a progressive income tax, and the taxation of corporate profits. The call for fair taxes also led to the demand that inheritances be limited. One example is the proposal by the economist Charles Bellamy (1884), brother of Edward Bellamy, who was close to the Populists: the size of an estate should be limited to assets the income from which would provide a generous living, with the rest of the estate flowing to the state. These state revenues would presumably render other taxes superfluous (Bellamy 1884, 144–45).

By opposing the concentration of wealth in the hands of the few, the Populists helped to legitimize inheritance taxation in the public perception.[22] In the elections of 1892, the Democratic Party made itself into the spokesman for many of the tax demands of the Populists, and the income and succession tax enacted by Congress in 1894—but then overturned by the Supreme Court—can be explained by the political mobilization on the part of the Populists (Steinmo 1993, 70–71).

2. The Progressive movement that emerged around 1900 had its primary base in the professional middle class. This was a heterogeneous movement that drew support from both political parties, and the Republican president Theodore Roosevelt was perhaps its best-known representative. The movement shared the Populists' mistrust of a concentration of power in large corporations, but also in the unions. Politically, the Progressive movement aimed at constraining uncontrolled economic centers of power by strengthening the government, which was to help democratize the political system. The Progressive movement was shaped by the guiding ideas of a restoration of equality of opportunity, constraints on the ideology of laissez-faire, and the possibility of creating a more rational and more just society with the help of science and technology (Heideking 1999, 245–46). The movement's political orientation tended toward "the middle, toward balancing class

antagonisms and reconciling currents that had been running through American history since Jefferson and Hamilton" (246–47).

In its conception of state planning and intervention as instruments for shaping social conditions, the Progressive movement displayed a fundamental reorientation from the reform movements of the early nineteenth century and also a different approach than the Populists, who continued to be strongly oriented toward the normative ideas of an agrarian democracy as the model of society. The notion of a positive role for the state in regulating the market so as to preserve fair competition marks a change in the understanding in the United States of the connection between the concentration of wealth and the state. The conflict between the demand for unconstrained disposition over wealth, and the criticism of dynastic concentration of wealth, was directed at the option of *government* redistribution. The Progressive movement legitimizes the state as an instrument of reform. This made it possible to consider inheritance taxation as a political strategy for limiting the dynastic concentration of wealth. The first of the two phases in inheritance taxation examined here (1890–1935) was characterized by the link between the criticism of inherited wealth *and* of the legitimacy of the state as a regulative institution. The Progressive movement was an important political crystallization point for this development.

A particularly influential voice calling for the introduction of inheritance taxation within the Progressive movement was that of Theodore Roosevelt: during his second term in office (1904–8), he wanted to push through a tax reform with the goal of enacting a progressive income and inheritance tax.[23] Roosevelt expressed his support for the inheritance tax in his 1906 State of the Union speech, which subsequently became a reference point for supporters of the tax. Clearly evident in the speech is the agreement with the inheritance-critical arguments from the revolutionary period, a fact that illustrates once again the strong continuity of the discourse in the United States.

As a reason behind a progressive inheritance tax, Roosevelt mentioned first of all the desire to tap into additional tax revenues, but then went on to discuss chiefly social and political considerations:

> The man of great wealth owes a peculiar obligation to the State, because he derives special advantages from the mere existence of government. Not only should he recognize this obligation in the way he leads his daily life and in the way he earns and spends his money, but it should also be recognized by the way in which he pays for the protection the State gives him. (Roosevelt 1909, 28)

While this argument calls for tax equity, another argument aims at the prevention of an oligarchy of wealth:

> [I]n my judgement the pro rata of the [inheritance] tax should increase very heavily with the increase of the amount left to any one individual after a certain point has been reached. It is most desirable to encourage thrift and ambition,

and a potent source of thrift and ambition is the desire on the part of the bread-winner to leave his children well off. This object can be attained by making the tax very small on moderate amounts of property left; because the prime object should be to put a constantly increasing burden on the inheritance of those swollen fortunes which it is certainly of no benefit to this country to perpetuate. (Roosevelt 1909, 29)

This criticism of the dynastic concentration of wealth was not based on the idea of class warfare aimed at a socialist model of equality, but was a direct expression of the liberal meritocratic tradition from the founding period of the United States. This is an important difference from the argumentative structure used by the advocates of inheritance taxation in the two European countries.

The growing criticism of the dynastic transmission of wealth in the United States in the late nineteenth and early twentieth centuries found expression not only in the social reform movements, but also in two other areas:

1. First, it appears among a segment of those captains of industry who, ironically enough, were the very reason behind the social criticism of the reformers. The best-known example is Andrew Carnegie (1992 [1889]), who came out in favor of a steep tax on inheritance and criticized the transmission of wealth within the family.[24] For Carnegie, the property owner is merely the trustee of the wealth who is obligated to use his assets to achieve a favorable development of the community, which is done through philanthropic engagement. A person of wealth should set up philanthropic institutions *during his lifetime*. The person who bequeathed his wealth to communal purposes in his *testament* was for Carnegie no better than the testator who left his wealth to his children: "The man who dies thus rich dies disgraced" (1992 [1889] 140).

This was Carnegie's solution to the problem of how to justify the accumulation of wealth far beyond what was needed to provide for one's own livelihood, a problem that arose against the backdrop of the meritocratic principle, of the Lockean theory of property, and the Protestant-Christian commandment to earn one's livelihood through work.[25] While wealth is eagerly pursued, it is at the same time morally problematic. Carnegie saw the owner as merely the trustee of the wealth, and society as the moral owner. Wealth was returned to society by transferring it to philanthropic foundations.[26] In contrast to the progressivist demand for the *state* to take control of wealth that is transferred *mortis causa*, Carnegie gives expression to the idea of a quasi-public form of private property.[27] The establishment of foundations, on the one hand, curtails the dynastic acquisition of wealth within the family and makes possible the use of capital to promote the common good; at the same time, though, it allows the name of the founder to be "immortalized," thus pointing, in addition to an interest in the common good, to a radical individualistic orientation.[28] Moreover, Carnegie's thinking reflects—in contrast to the Progressive movement—a strong skepticism toward the state as a regulatory authority.

2. Second, since the 1890s, inheritance taxation has been a topic for social scientists. It became a research topic for economists who can be assigned to the camp of the reform movements. They include the previously mentioned Charles Bellamy, but also a number of others, primarily from the institutional school. These economists opposed the laissez-faire ideology of orthodox economics, assigned the state an important role in regulating the economy, but at the same time rejected socialist ideas about the nationalization of property (Eisenach 1994, 138ff.). They understood the taxation of inheritance as an instrument for a more equitable distribution of private property.

Invoking the critique of the dynastic concentration of wealth that emerged in the revolutionary period and was linked with Jefferson played an outstanding role also among reform economists. In his 1888 book *Taxation in American States and Cities*, Richard T. Ely declared that inheritance taxation was "in accord with the principles of Jeffersonian democracy, and also with the teachings of some of the best modern thinkers on economic and social topics" (1888, 318).[29] The inheritance tax, he argued, gave direct expression to the American Revolution's individual-meritocratic understanding of property:

> One of the principles which controlled the action of Jefferson and other founders of the republic, was the abolition of hereditary distinctions and privileges, and their aim was to force each one to rely on his own exertions for his own fortune, desiring to give all as nearly as practicable an equal start in the race of life. (Ely 1888, 318–19)[30]

The topic of inheritance taxation thus pushed into the political discourse of the United States at the end of the nineteenth century from various social fields: from social movements that emanated from the lower social classes as well as the middle class, from property owners themselves, and from scholarly discourse. In the process, inheritance taxation did not meet with universal approval. However, beginning in the 1890s, there was increasingly a climate of public opinion in which the demand for the (progressive) taxation of inheritance was no longer perceived solely as socialist radicalism, but as a necessary measure of reform to enhance equality of opportunity, as a counterweight to the existing concentration of wealth, and as a contribution to tax equity—and thus as an expression of the realization of American values.[31]

The demand, as part of the debate, for *state* intervention to achieve equality of opportunity goes back to a change in earlier beliefs about the causes of economic inequality. Prior to the end of the nineteenth century, the expansion of state power was seen in the United States precisely as the cause behind political and social privileges. It was only the Progressive movement that helped to establish the notion that the economy produced social inequality that could be rectified by political measures (Huston 1993, 1101ff.). A new understanding of the role of the state in social reform began to articulate itself around the turn of the century, one that would shape large sections of American history in the twentieth century. In the process, the reform movement, like Roosevelt and Carnegie, was aimed—in contrast to the socialistic ideas in the European countries—not at the abolition of private property or its severe limitation, but at the *defense of the liberal social order*. The latter was seen as threatened by dynastic wealth and the concentration of capital.

In their defense of inheritance taxation, almost all commentators referred directly or indirectly to Jefferson's republican conception of equality, still the normative point of reference in the legal-political debates, at a time when social reality strongly contradicted the model of agrarian democracy. While the Populists, following in the footsteps of the early nineteenth-century reform movements, took an ambivalent and in part antimodern stance toward industrial society, the Progressive movement pursued reforms that sought to reconcile the institutional implementation of the democratic ideals of the revolutionary period—among others, equality of opportunity—with the demands of modern industrial society, and to use the state as an instrument of reform to achieve egalitarian goals of distribution. The debate over inheritance taxation was carried on as a democratic reform discussion. During the reform period around the turn of the century and extending into the 1920s, the call for a tax on inheritances resonated within the heterogeneous political mainstream. The individualistic-meritocratic understanding of property created a basis for the justification of inheritance taxes. Of course, there were also vehement opponents of such taxes,[32] but the strong forces of reform provided the political backdrop against which the tax became the topic of parliamentary debates in Congress in the late nineteenth and early twentieth centuries.

The Introduction of the Estate Tax

How did this political background manifest itself in the parliamentary debates in Congress and in the shape that the taxation of inheritance would take? The American tax debates were dominated up to World War I by the question of whether state revenues should continue to be derived chiefly from import tariffs and indirect taxes, or from direct taxes, especially an income tax.[33] The breakdown of interests in this controversy was clear: import tariffs were in the interest of American companies, who were protected from competition and were able to sell their products at a higher price. Indirect taxes that were born by consumers fell more strongly on the lower income groups, because a larger portion of their expenses invariably flowed into consumption. By contrast, income that was saved escaped taxation. Less clear was the party-political breakdown of interests in Congress. The majority in the Democratic Party and the Progressive Party favored the income and the inheritance tax.[34] The majority of Republican representatives and senators, in particular those who held key positions, supported the interests of entrepreneurs and the wealthy. However, within the Republican Party there emerged a progressive wing of the "insurgents," which must be classified as part of the Progressive movement. This enhanced the chances that political majorities could be found in support of a restructuring of American tax policy. The inheritance tax, called for by the Republican President Roosevelt beginning in 1906 and also by his successor, William H. Taft, became a topic of budget debates in Congress.[35]

That the inheritance tax was no longer seen merely as a war tax at the beginning of the twentieth century was already evident in the debate over the repeal of the tax that had been introduced to finance the war against Spain.[36] Thereafter, the introduction of an inheritance tax on the federal level was repeatedly debated in the House of Representatives. During the budget debate of 1909, the inheritance tax finally became a permanent parliamentary topic in the context of the question over equitable taxation and social redistribution.[37] There was hardly a speaker who used the argument that the inheritance tax could be levied by the federal government only in times of crisis (table 5.1). Instead, supporters of the tax mostly put forth arguments of fairness and equity, criticized inheritances as the effortless acquisition of wealth, and pointed to the need to boost revenues for the federal budget. Opponents, meanwhile, largely advanced the defensive argument that the inheritance tax was a source of revenue for the states and should be reserved to their exclusive use.

The political pressure for the introduction of the inheritance tax increased further when the Commission on Industrial Relations, which had been appointed by the Senate, presented its final report (Manly Report) in 1915. The commission had probed into the reasons behind the discontent of American industrial workers. As the main cause it identified the unequal distribution of wealth and income in the United States. The report attacked the existing inheritance laws, which allowed an "industrial feudalism," and proposed using taxation to limit inheritances to one million dollars. The revenue was to be used for education, social services, and infrastructure projects. Once again, reference was made to the connection between the dynastic concentration of wealth and a threat to the democratic polity:

> Effective action by Congress is required . . . to check the growth of an hereditary aristocracy, which is foreign to every conception of American Government and menacing to the welfare of the people and the existence of the nation as a democracy. (Manly 1916, 35)[38]

Economists also continued to press for a taxation of inheritances. Wilford I. King (1915), another student of R. T. Ely, and Scott Nearing (1915) called for the tax as a means of social redistribution and state financing.[39] In part they were motivated by concern over the distribution of wealth in American society. King (1915) examined the income distribution trend between 1860 and 1890 on the basis of the files of probate courts in Massachusetts and Wisconsin. By his calculations, the richest 2% of the population held around 60% of the wealth around the turn of the century,

TABLE 5.1
The Inheritance Tax in the Budget Debate in Congress, 1909: Reasons
Offered by Speakers for Their Position

	Opposed to the Inheritance Tax	In Support of the Inheritance Tax
Reasons inherent in the law	75.7	4.0
Inheritance tax interferes in the tax authority of the states	62.2	
Federal government may levy inheritance tax only in wartime	8.1	
Inheritance tax is unconstitutional	5.4	
Other reasons inherent in the law		4.0
Fiscal reasons	0.0	28.0
Boost in budget revenues		28.0
Political reasons	8.1	56.0
Rejection of privileges from effortless acquisition of wealth		16.0
Tax equity	2.7	28.0
Free disposition over property		4.0
Reference to public opinion	5.4	4.0
Economic reasons	16.2	12.0
Economic consequences	16.2	12.0
Other reasons		4.0
	N = 37	N = 25

Note: Figures are percentages. The debate took place between 23 March and 2 April 1909; a total of ten speakers participated.

while the lower 65% of the population owned merely around 5% (King 1915, 79). When King compared the American data with that in France, Prussia, and England, he found that the distribution of wealth in the two continental European countries was roughly comparable, while the distribution in England was far more unequal, still.[40] King's explanation for England's special position pointed to the differing laws on inheritance: England still had the right of primogeniture succession. King thus established a causal relationship between income distribution and inheritance law. Although he refrained from making a direct recommendation, he noted that the inheritance tax could change the distribution of wealth. The political discourse, in which a strong distrust of the concentration of wealth predominated, was thereby steered once again toward inheritance taxation as a corrective instrument.

The introduction of the estate tax in the budget bill of 1916 must be seen against the backdrop of this reform discussion, as well as the country's possible entry into the war. It is a hypothetical question whether an estate tax would have been introduced in the United States even without World War I. There is no doubt that the budget bill of 1916 was written with the war in Europe in mind. At the same time, however, there was considerable public pressure by the reform movement for the introduction of the tax. Independent of war financing, this movement was demanding a reduction in the concentration of wealth and in the high cost of living, which was partly the result of indirect taxes.

Needless to say, the debate over the introduction of the estate tax continued to be extremely polarized in 1916 (Paul 1954, 108–9; Myers 1969 [1939], 262). Although the Democratic House majority leader, Claude Kitchin, tried to present the inheritance tax as a bipartisan consensus in his speech opening the budget debate in 1916 (Appendix C.R., vol. 53, 1916, 1938), the debate and the vote ran along the already established line between Democrats and progressive Republicans, on the one side, and the great majority of Republicans, on the other.

The draft of the 1916 budget bill included inheritance taxation in the form of an estate tax. This structure for taxing the transfer of wealth *mortis causa* is specific to the United States. Under this scheme, the tax would be imposed on the *transfer of property* and not on the property of the testator or the heirs, which would have been unconstitutional.[41] At the same time, however, structuring the tax as an estate tax made it impossible to graduate the tax rates depending on how closely the heir was related to the testator. The tax was levied on the estate as a whole before it was divided among the heirs. The fact that this structure of the tax—in contrast to France and Germany—did not become a primary point of criticism in the debate also shows that concerns of family policy played at best a subordinate role in the inheritance tax discourses in the United States. When the introduction of an estate tax was on the table in Germany and France (to be discussed in the following two sections), it led to a political storm of protest: the tax, it was said, would destroy families. In the United States, by contrast, not a single speaker in the debates of 1909 and 1916 put forth a family-related argument.

The most detailed substantive justification for the introduction of the estate tax was presented in the debate by Democratic representative Cordell Hull, who had already supported the introduction of this tax back in 1909. For Hull, the taxation of estates was fair because it was the only tax that was levied on unearned wealth to finance the government's tasks. Having established its legitimacy, Hull went on to discuss how this source of taxes could be efficiently and fairly tapped to satisfy the financing needs of the federal budget. The inheritance taxes of the states did not achieve this goal: wealthy citizens could move their residence to another state with a lower or no inheritance taxation, because there were a lot of unclear legal points on the state level when it came to calculating inheritance taxes, and because a number of states (twelve) exempted immediate family members (C.R., 8 July 1916, 10656–57). The introduction of an estate tax on the federal level could circumvent these obstacles to a fair taxation of inheritances and lead to a fivefold increase in the revenue from this tax.[42] In an effort, no doubt, to avoid a potential conflict with the states over inheritances as a source of tax revenue, Hull suggested following the British example and leaving one-third of the revenues to the states. Hull saw the estate tax as part of the country's permanent fiscal income (and not as an emergency tax in times of national crisis) and its introduction as a reaction to the growing assumption by the government in Washington of state tasks that had previously been borne by the states. In this sense, the inheritance tax also expressed the shift in the balance of power in the United States from the states to the federal government.

The importance of these arguments is also evident from the content analysis of the debate (table 5.2). Supporters of the estate tax for the most part invoked the argument of tax fairness (43.9%), while reference to a boost in fiscal revenues accounted for another 15.1% of the arguments.

A second line of argumentation justifying the estate tax picked up the contemporary discourse critical of inheritances by invoking the meritocratic understanding of property. Democrat William Cox from Indiana demanded that dynastic wealth be broken up through the taxation of inheritances: great wealth "breeds up in this country a class of unproductive men and women without energy, without initiative, without knowing any of the hardships or toils of life. . . . It is unjust, un-American, and undemocratic to let such tremendous fortunes . . . be transmitted . . . without an inheritance tax laying its hands upon a part of [the] estate" (C.R., 10 June 1916, 10732).[43] Arguments that were aimed at abolishing privilege derived from the effortless acquisition of wealth, or, with a stronger economic orientation, at greater equality in the distribution of wealth, made up more than one-fifth of the arguments put forth by supporters of the estate tax (table 5.2).

Opponents of the estate tax did not speak out against the intent of the tax, presumably for tactical reasons; instead, as they had already done in the debate in 1909, their chief argument concerned double taxation. Republican representatives Charles F. Curry, Charles H. Sloan, and Walter W. Magee, for example, demanded that this particular source of tax revenue be reserved for the states. Content analysis of the debate in July 1916 reveals that opponents of the estate tax pointed almost exclusively to this legal issue (75% of the arguments). Substantive justifications for their opposition were of only minor importance.

On the whole, the analysis of the debate of 1916 in the American Congress shows a clear continuity with the debate of 1909. It is evident, though, that among supporters of the tax, arguments aimed against the unequal

TABLE 5.2
The Estate Tax in the Budget Debate in Congress in 1916: Reasons
Offered by Speakers for Their Position

	Opposed to the Estate Tax	In Support of the Estate Tax
Reasons inherent in the law	87.6	7.5
The inheritance tax interferes with the tax authority of the states	75.0	1.5
Federal government may impose an inheritance tax only in times of crisis	6.3	
The inheritance tax is unconstitutional	6.3	
Other reasons inherent in the law		6.0
Fiscal reasons		15.1
Tax revenues		15.1
Political reasons	12.6	57.4
Rejection of privileges derived from the effortless acquisition of wealth		10.5
Tax equity		43.9
Free disposition over property	6.3	1.5
Democratic legitimation of the tax		
Reference to public opinion	6.3	1.5
Economic reasons		12.1
Greater equality in distribution of wealth		12.1
Other reasons		7.5
	N = 16	N = 66

Note: Figures are percentages. The debate took place between 6 and 10 July 1916; a total of thirteen speakers participated.

distribution of wealth or emphasizing the privileges bestowed by inheritances independent of personal merit had become even more important.

The tax bill was approved on 10 July 1916 by the Democratic majority in the House, with thirty-nine Republican representatives also voting for it. The Senate passed the bill in September and President Wilson signed it. The rates for the estate tax introduced in 1916 ranged from 1% for a taxable estate of less than $50,000 to 10% for an estate over $5,000,000. The first $50,000 were tax exempt.[44]

The Postwar Period: To Keep or Abolish the Estate Tax?

The estate tax remained in place after the end of the war. In contrast to previous episodes, it was disconnected from war financing (Chester 1982, 68; Hudson 1983, 16).[45]

Social-reformist pressure for a taxation of inheritances also continued. In the summer of 1918, the reform-minded businessman Harlan E. Read published *The Abolition of Inheritance*, in which he called for limiting inheritances—with a few exceptions—to $100,000. Typical for the political mood after the end of the war was also the speech by the president of the American Economic Association, Irving Fisher (1919), who called the unequal distribution of wealth in the United States the most important problem of economic policy in American society and appealed to his colleagues to take a greater interest in this problem. His goal was the redistribution of property. Fisher himself drew his inspiration from a plan for inheritance taxation developed by the Italian Eugenio Rignano (1901, 1904, 1905, 1924). It proposed a tax of one-third on inherited wealth, two-thirds on the same wealth in the next generation, and 100% on what was left in the third generation. The goal was a confiscatory taxation of inheritances, though stretched out over three generations to moderate its impact on those affected.[46] In clear concordance with the American tradition since the revolutionary period, his argumentation was based, first, on the legal classification of inheritance law as positive law, and, second, on the connection between the distribution of wealth and democracy. The existing situation, whereby 2% of the population owned more than half the capital, was "an undemocratic distribution of wealth" (Fisher 1919, 13).[47]

The structure of the cut in the estate tax enacted by Congress in 1919 reveals the regulatory goal of inheritance tax policy, which was essentially in agreement with the reform ideas of the economists I have mentioned: the reduction affected only estates valued at below $1.5 million, which led to a relative increase in the taxation of larger estates. Here we can already see the specifically American way of taxing inheritance, which continued until 1981: in comparison with Germany and France, it is subject to an especially steep progression, whereby at times almost confiscatory tax rates were reached for sufficiently large estates. In addition to generating revenue, the goal of the estate tax is also to reduce the oligarchic concentration of wealth.

The conservatives, however, launched a vigorous attack on the estate tax in the 1920s, which almost led to its abolition. The Democrats had lost the presidency in 1921, and Calvin Coolidge, the Republican who assumed the office after the death of President Warren Harding, was, like his influential secretary of the Treasury Andrew W. Mellon, an ardent proponent of tax cuts and declared opponent of the estate tax (Brownlee 2004, 72ff.). Until 1929, the United States experienced an economic boom period, which improved the fiscal situation and made tax cuts possible. The inheritance tax became a political target.

The majority in Congress continued to back the tax, however. It was chiefly Republican congressmen from the Midwest who saw the estate tax as a fair burden on the wealthy establishment of the Northeast that was regarded with resentment. Because American representatives have a high degree of independence, the result in part of the absence of party discipline, the administration had no way of pushing through its ideas on tax policy (Steinmo 1993, 94). In fact, in 1924 the estate tax was even raised. Rates now ranged from 1% for estates of $50,000 to up to 40% for estates over $10 million. This meant they were higher than they had been during the war. It was also agreed to credit state inheritance taxes up to 25% of the estate tax, which was a concession to pressure from the states and an incentive to standardize the inheritance taxes of the states. Henceforth, not imposing an inheritance tax was no longer an advantage in the tax competition between the states, since the federal tax was levied on estates, in any case. The most obvious loophole in the estate tax was also closed in 1924: until then, there had been no gift tax, which is why no tax was due for gifts if they had been made at least two years before the death of the donor.

Although it appeared in 1924 that the taxation of estates had stabilized institutionally, the most massive attack was in fact about to happen. In October 1925, Treasury secretary Mellon proposed to the House Ways and Means Committee that the estate tax and the gift tax be abolished. Mellon wanted to leave this source of tax revenue to the states, and he saw the estate tax introduced in 1916 as an economically destructive burden on capital. In his view, this tax was justified only in wartime. The continuation of the prewar argumentative structure is evident in his comments. Mellon denied the need to break up large fortunes, since equal division as enshrined in statutory inheritance law already provided for the breakup of inheritances (Mellon 1924, 123).

The estate tax was debated at great length in Congress's deliberations over the 1926 budget bill, with the disagreements taking on an even harsher tone than they had during the debate over its introduction in 1916. The arguments that were put forth had not changed substantially (table 5.3). However, the argument for an equitable taxation of large capital fortunes became even more important, while the aspect of the expected tax revenue receded into the background. The reason behind this was the fact that the economic situation in the United States had stabilized in the midtwenties. Opponents of the estate tax demanded that the revenue from taxes be cut, for example by abolishing this particular tax. Once again, the question about the dual taxation of inheritances at the federal and state levels played an important role, though advocates of the estate tax now put forth the argument that it was in the interest of the states to have an estate tax. The reason was that the introduction in 1924 of a credit for the inheritance tax of the various states had led to a standardization of that tax and was helping to reduce the tax competition between the states.[48] Among opponents of the tax, dual

TABLE 5.3
The Estate Tax in the Budget Debate of 1926: Reasons
Offered by Speakers for Their Position

	Opposed to the Estate Tax	In Support of the Estate Tax
Reasons inherent in the law	53.6	16.2
The inheritance tax interferes with the tax authority of the states	32.1	4.2
Standardization of the tax system	17.9	2.7
Other reasons inherent in the law	3.6	9.3
Fiscal reasons	14.3	9.6
Tax revenues		9.6
Reducing the tax revenues of the federal government	14.3	
Political reasons	21.5	49.5
Rejection of privileges derived from the effortless acquisition of wealth		3.8
Acceptance of social inequality	1.8	
Tax equity	12.5	37.6
Free disposition over property	1.8	
Democratic legitimation of the tax	3.6	8.7
Reference to public opinion	1.8	0.4
Economic reasons	3.6	13.2
Greater equality of distribution of wealth	1.8	10.6
Other economic reasons	1.8	2.6
Other reasons	3.6	3.9
	N = 56	N = 263

Note: Figures are percentages. The debate took place between 11 December 1925 and 3 February 1926; a total of thirty-three speakers participated.

taxation was still the most frequently used argument, though compared to the debate of 1916, it was less important for them.

That the estate tax was not abolished in 1926 despite the pressure from the administration presumably had something to do with the skillful maneuvering on the part of the Democrats. They agreed to a compromise that raised the credit for state inheritance taxes to 80%. This boosted the fiscal interests of the states and their representatives in this tax. The incentive to move one's residence for tax reasons was reduced, and most of the income from the estate tax was left to the states. Moreover, the budget bill of 1926 cut the rates of the estate tax and repealed the gift tax. Specifically, the exempted amount was raised to $100,000, and the top rate for estates over $10 million was scaled back to 20%.[49]

The changes in 1926 meant for the estate tax a clear reduction in the taxation of large fortunes and a decline in the revenues the federal budget received from this tax. Of course, the higher tax credit for inheritance taxes paid to the states contributed to this. At the same time, and this was the most important result for the long term, the basic structure of the tax was retained: in the absence of a military emergency, in a fiscally stable environment, and in spite of a heavy political attack aimed at abolishing it.

The Estate Tax in the Great Depression

The environment of financial policy was dramatically altered by the global economic crisis that began in 1929. The policy of tax cuts in the 1920s was based on a strong economy, interrupted only by minor downturns. However, with the collapse of 1929, the revenues from the income tax declined, and other sources to fund the government had to be found. One was the estate tax: the 1932 Tax Law cut the exempt amount in half and more than doubled the rates, with a top rate of 45%. Moreover, the credit for state inheritance taxes was limited to the rates of 1926, and the gift tax was brought back (Paul 1954, 155–56; Ratner 1967, 467). Gifts were taxed at 75% of the estate tax rate, but charitable gifts were tax exempt.[50] The lower rate was intended to encourage gifts, so that the government would derive revenue earlier from the wealth transfers *mortis causa*. The drastic increases in the tax bill signed by President Hoover on 6 June point clearly to the fiscal emergency in the economic crisis. Even Treasury secretary Mellon, until 1929 a decided opponent of the estate tax, now supported the tax plans.

In the United States, the distrust of dynastic concentrations of wealth can be traced back to the political discourses of the revolutionary period, as can the suggestion to redistribute property through the taxation of inheritances. I have already shown the kind of support that inheritance taxation received at the beginning of the twentieth century from political reform movements, social scientists, and even the wealthy. Within the context of the individualist and meritocratic understanding of property, the dynastic concentration of wealth was criticized as a distribution of wealth unrelated to effort and merit and as a threat to democratic political structures. This political and cultural background is also reflected in the congressional debates I have analyzed. At the same time, the timing of the introduction of the estate tax and of the subsequent changes to the rates between 1898 and 1932 points to the connection between inheritance taxation and the circumstances of fiscal policy. It is only the interplay of the political reform discussion and changes in the fiscal situation that provides an explanation for the institutionalization of the estate tax in the United States.

In the 1930s, however, there was a shift in this relationship. Under President Franklin D. Roosevelt, the motive of wealth redistribution moved to the forefront of inheritance tax policy. Roosevelt favored a stronger engagement of the government in guiding the American economy by means of an active economic, social, and tax policy, which was made possible by the New Deal legislation. Although it is possible to see the line of continuity from the Progressive movement to Roosevelt's policies, the legislation of the mid-1930s clearly went beyond the reforms at the beginning of the century. Thus one can speak of a shift "from a business-dominated society to a government-dominated society [that] was indeed a social revolution of major proportions" (Baltzell 1964, 229). Roosevelt responded to the threat to liberal democracy from the global economic crisis and its political consequences with a far-reaching reform program that met with vehement resistance from the "Protestant establishment" (Aldrich 1996, 229ff.).

The inheritance tax played an important role in Roosevelt's policies for two reasons: first, the redistribution of wealth through the taxation of inheritance could channel purchasing power to the lower social classes, who would spend the additional income on consumption and thus help to jumpstart the economy. Second, Huey Long, a Democratic senator from Louisiana, had called a populist movement into life with his call for a more radical redistribution of wealth, a movement that could become dangerous to Roosevelt. In February 1934, Huey Long organized the Share Our Wealth Society. Its goal was to impose a confiscatory tax on fortunes over one million dollars and income of more than $4 million, using the revenue to provide every family with $5,000, a guaranteed income of $2,000, free university education, and other benefits (Fried 1999, 65ff.). By 1935, the Share Our Wealth movement had grown to 7 million members distributed among 27,000 clubs in all the states, though concentrated chiefly in the South. Roosevelt's speech to Congress in June 1935, in which he proposed the introduction of a new succession and gift tax to exist alongside the estate tax, reflects this political situation with its heightened mistrust of dynastic concentrations of wealth:

The transmission from generation to generation of vast fortunes by will, inheritance, or gift is not consistent with the ideal and sentiments of the American People. The desire to provide security for one's family is natural and wholesome, but it is adequately served by a reasonable inheritance. Great accumulations of wealth can not be justified on the basis of family and personal security. In the last analysis such accumulations amount to the perpetuation of great and undesirable concentration of control in relatively few individuals over the enjoyment and welfare of many, many others. Such inherited economic power is as inconsistent with the ideals of this generation as inherited political power was inconsistent with the ideals of the generation which established our Government. (Roosevelt, C.R., No. 79, 9:9712, 19 June 1935)[51]

Critics saw Roosevelt's inheritance tax plans as "stabs at the very heart of the monied establishment" (Baltzell 1964, 243), but at the same time they took the wind out of the sails of Long's demagogic movement. A look at the argumentative structure in the debate in Congress in August 1935, which revolved around a hike in the estate tax, an increase in its progressivity, and the inclusion of life insurances reveals the changes from previous debates (table 5.4). Moving to the forefront now were economic arguments, which were strongly related to the question of the redistribution of wealth. Speakers blamed the economic crisis on the inequality of wealth. Opponents of the tax, meanwhile, pointed more strongly to the negative economic consequences of steep taxation, and they also argued that such high inheritance taxes were not supported by the people. And for the first time in the American debate over inheritance tax policy, one speaker introduced family-oriented arguments. However, Republican representative Clarence Hancock, invoking the consequences for the family members of the deceased, spoke out specifically against the inclusion of life insurances in inheritance taxation.

However, it is not so much the intensification of the political rhetoric about a redistribution of wealth that makes the period of the mid-1930s into a crucial phase in American inheritance policy, as changes to the tax laws themselves, which increasingly reveal the goal of a real curtailment of large fortunes. As early as 1933, estates over $10 million were taxed at a rate of 60%.[52] These changes are reflected in the strong rise in estate tax revenue beginning in 1934: it went from $34.4 million in 1933 to $212 million in 1935, while also growing substantially as a share of total tax revenue (see figure 5.1).[53] In 1935, Congress, at Roosevelt's suggestion, approved the introduction of an additional inheritance tax with rates between 4% and 75%, but the Senate voted it down with reference to the high administrative costs involved in levying a new tax. The compromise that was reached further raised the progression for the already established estate tax with two new levels at $20 million and $50 million. For estates over $50 million, the tax rate now stood at 70%.

The tax law that came into effect in 1935 for the first time achieved rates that one could in fact see as an attempt to substantially curtail the transfer by inheritance of large fortunes (Cahn 1940, 310; Hudson 1983, 19–20). These rates were introduced at a time when the country had already pulled out of the worst of the depression, which is why they cannot be understood solely as a reaction to the deteriorating budget situation. Moreover, the *structure* of the tax progression in this phase reveals that the goal was not to maximize the absolute tax revenue from the estate tax—that would have required a heavier taxation also of smaller estates—but chiefly to dismantle concentrations of dynastic wealth.[54]

TABLE 5.4
The Succession Tax in the Budget Debate in Congress in 1935: Reasons
Offered by Speakers for Their Position

	Opposed to the Inheritance Tax	In Support of the Inheritance Tax
Reasons inherent in the law	26.3	5.4
De facto acceptance of the law	21.5	2.7
Other reasons inherent in the law	4.8	2.7
Fiscal reasons	11.9	21.7
Raising budget revenues	11.9	21.7
Reducing the tax revenues of the federal government		
Political reasons	12.0	25.9
Privileges from the effortless acquisition of wealth		9.6
Acceptance of social inequality	2.4	
Tax equity	2.4	16.3
Free disposition over property	7.2	
Economic reasons	16.7	35.4
Greater equality in the distribution of wealth		24.3
Other economic reasons	16.7	8.4
Reasons of social policy		2.7
Familial reasons	33.4	
Providing for family members	33.4	
Other reasons		12.3
	N = 42	N = 74

Note: Figures are percentages. The debate took place on 2 and 3 August 1935; a total of seven speakers participated. One speech (Pettengill) had already been given on 13 February 1935.

This was certainly understood by contemporary observers, who, depending on their political position, either spoke of a dangerous socialist experiment or saw the new tax law as an important political step in the direction of more social justice.[55]

The staying power behind the change in tax policy is also evident from the fact that the tax rates were maintained in the second half of the 1930s.

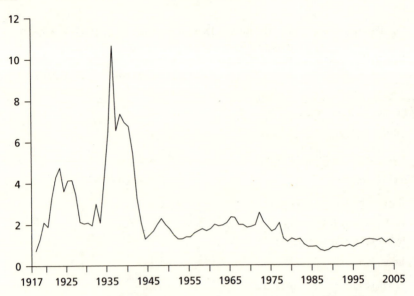

Figure 5.1 Estate and gift tax as share of total tax revenues in the
United States, 1917–2005 (in %)
Source: Internal Revenue Service.

In 1940, already under pressure from the need to finance Allied war costs in World War II, the progression was even raised to a top rate of 70%, which was levied on estates valued at more than $10 million. The estate tax did in fact lead to redistribution effects during this period (Eisenstein 1956; Hudson 1983, 31). The inequality in the distribution of wealth in the United States declined between the end of the 1920s and the 1970s (Wolff 2002, 31ff.). Although that was not the result primarily of the inheritance tax, but also of the depression, the slower growth in wealth, and the high income tax (Piketty and Saez 2001), the estate tax rates do attest to the institutionalization of a tax aimed at preventing the dynastic concentration of wealth.

Had the motivation behind the increase in estate tax rates been merely the heightened financial needs in the wake of the global economic crisis and World War II, they would have been scaled back again in the 1950s, at the latest. In fact, the top rate of 77% was retained until 1976. Apart from institutional inertia, the reason for the continuing high taxation of estates during the economically prosperous postwar period could be seen to lie in the persistent need for the government to pay for war and military expenses, and in the expansion of state programs. On the other hand, because of the prospering economy and the acceptance of Keynesian fiscal policy, the pressure to lower taxes was weak. When it came to tax policy, Congress was largely deadlocked during the postwar period, which is why no fundamental change

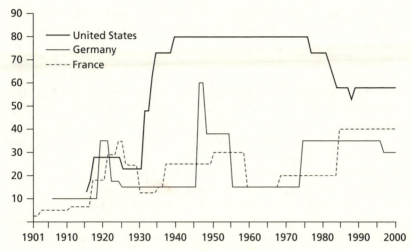

Figure 5.2 Progressive rates for the estate tax for immediate family members, 1901–2000 (in %)

Note: Top rates for the estate tax or the inheritance tax in France, Germany, and the United States (1901–2000). For France and Germany calculated on the basis of the top tax bracket, for France partly on the assumption that the testator is survived by two children.

Source: Tax codes.

in the course of tax policy could be pushed through (Steinmo 1993, 137). As a political topic, inheritance taxation lost importance between 1940 and the late 1960s.[56]

THE ABOLITION OF THE ESTATE TAX?

In June 2001, President George W. Bush signed a law that will phase out the estate tax in the year 2010.[57] This law did not come out of the blue. Rather, it formed the conclusion, for the time being, of a process that began in the late 1960s and saw the estate tax coming under growing political pressure and increasingly losing the political support it had enjoyed during the Progressive Era and the New Deal. In that sense, the period since the end of the 1960s can be described as a second, distinct phase in the conflicts over inheritance taxation in the United States. How can one explain this clear change in course in American tax policy? And how does one explain that in the United States, unlike in the two European countries, inheritance taxation has become once again the topic of considerable political controversy?

The change in inheritance tax policy is part and parcel of an overall transformation of tax policy in the United States, one in which different principles of policy have been brought to bear. We are dealing with an ideological reorientation against the background of changes in economic and fiscal policy. Between the 1940s and the 1960s there was little pressure to lower taxes. Thanks to the strong economic growth and low rate of inflation during the "long boom" that extended into the late sixties, the average real income of broad segments of the population rose steadily. Added to this was the unchallenged supremacy of Keynesian economic and fiscal policy as well as the broadening of the liberal consensus, which helped to sustain the continuation of the social and economic reform begun in the New Deal into the mid-1960s. The social reform movements of the fifties and sixties were focused on the ideal of equality of opportunity and the improvement in the social situation of underprivileged groups through government social policies financed by taxes.

This political and economic situation changed in the late sixties and early seventies. Economically, the growth boom of the postwar came to an end: inflation rose sharply in the seventies, the growth in prosperity slowed, and the rising costs of the war in Vietnam forced the government to raise other taxes, as well. Politically, there was growing resistance to strong state intervention in the economy. A polarization occurred between supporters of additional state reforms to implement equality of opportunity and social justice—especially President Johnson's Great Society program—and those who rejected additional regulatory, bureaucratic interference in society. The understanding of the role of the state that had developed under Progressivism and the New Deal was transformed once again. Strong government interference in the economy and high taxes were increasingly blamed for the country's economic troubles—a development that culminated in the "Reagan Revolution."

In economic policy, the Keynesian consensus disintegrated and was replaced in the late 1970s by a supply-side policy guided by monetarism. Advocates of this approach demanded that the forces of the market be strengthened and government regulation of the economy be scaled back. In fiscal policy, the concept of the Laffer curve became influential and formed the basis for tax cuts to initiate economic growth. Reduced top tax rates were supposed to boost economic activity and thus make growth possible, which would make it possible to keep fiscal revenues steady in spite of a cut in tax rates. Henceforth the dominant paradigm in the discourse over fiscal policy was not redistribution and the threat to democratic structures from the concentration of wealth, but the question of the interconnection between tax policy, economic prosperity, and government regulation. The ideological changes in the seventies and eighties can be seen as the second "great transformation" of the economic system in the twentieth century (see Blyth 2002).

The estate tax with its high progressive rates and an exempt amount that had remained unchanged since the 1940s—and was therefore quite low— was part of a bloated tax system that was heavily criticized and thus came under political pressure. If the tax system is confronted with the dilemma of, on the one hand, being the most important instrument for a redistribution of wealth, and, on the other hand, coming under suspicion of impeding economic growth, an estate tax with a top rate of 77% becomes part of the problem, not part of the solution.

How was it possible for the perception of the problem of estate taxation to change so clearly in so short a period of time? The thesis I will pursue here relates to the *specific* tension between rights of private property and rights of political equality in the United States. The tension between an egalitarian, republican liberalism and an economic liberalism as the two main currents within the American discourse on inheritance taxation finds expression in clashing notions on how to deal with unearned wealth. These notions allow at most for an unstable balance and can easily lead to renewed political controversies. In Germany—which I will examine in detail in the next section—the proponents of high inheritance taxation are guided by goals in social policy. In the context of this result-oriented perspective, inheritance taxation was merely *one* possible means of generating the resources for the state's social policies, resources that could, in principle, come from other sources. This made possible a compromise—in which the Social Democrats were also included—through which inheritance taxation lost its political explosiveness fairly early. In France, also discussed in detail below, the redistribution of private property through inheritance taxation found only moderate political support even from leftist forces of reform, which was the result of the strong property-orientation of French society and the problematic relationship between progressive inheritance taxes and the principle of equality. In the United States, where ideas of justice are based chiefly on the "input-oriented" perspective of equality of opportunity and where restrictions by the state on individual rights of disposition over property are at the same time rejected by a strong, liberal-economic position, the conflict between constraints on "unearned wealth" and the consequences of this kind of redistribution cannot be resolved by resorting to other sources of tax revenue. The point, after all, is to reduce the unequal starting positions in life. It is therefore much easier for the dilemma posed by equality of opportunity and the private accumulation of capital as the prerequisite for economic growth to become politically virulent. This is what happened in the early seventies in light of the impending economic crisis.

Equality and Property Rights in Inheritance Law
Discourse since the 1970s

What path has the political discourse over the estate tax taken in the United States since the seventies? At that time, the inheritance tax was rediscovered as an important political topic by both political groups, egalitarian liberalism and economic liberalism. The structure of the discursive field, the arguments and proposals advanced by those involved, form a clear line of continuity with the Progressive Era and the revolutionary period. The discourse over inheritance taxation is split once again between those positions that sought greater equality in the distribution of wealth and justified this with arguments about equal opportunity and the distributive preconditions of democracy, and those positions that defended the rights of private property against state interference and emphasized the economically dysfunctional consequences of redistributing wealth through steep inheritance taxes. However, unlike what had happened at the beginning of the century, in the seventies the proponents of stronger redistribution through inheritance taxation increasingly lost influence. The supply-oriented position gained more and more ground, and from the midseventies it shaped the discourse as well as the legal reforms of the estate tax.

The call to greater equality of wealth through higher taxes on inheritance culminated symbolically in 1972 in Democrat George McGovern's failed bid for the presidency. During his campaign, McGovern had called for changing the estate tax into a progressive inheritance tax, which would reach 100% for gifts or inheritances above half a million dollars (Weil 1973, 74). This demand was part of McGovern's plan for a policy of income redistribution, the core of which was a guaranteed minimum income. The continuity to similar demands by Orestes Brownson and Huey Long is obvious. McGovern assumed that the vast majority of voters had strong reservations about the existing concentration of wealth in American society and would therefore support his plan. McGovern's politics was based on the reform movements of the fifties and sixties. But the failure of McGovern shows that the political mood in the United States had changed by this time. The presidential candidate was able to win the support mainly of the New Left, yet in contrast to the popularity of similar calls for redistribution through inheritance taxation during the Progressive movement and the New Deal, the broad American middle class now turned its back on such a demand. And so McGovern discovered during the campaign that even workers who would never be personally affected by the tax rejected the idea of a confiscatory inheritance tax as unfair. In response, the plan was changed during the campaign into a tax of "only" 77% (Weil 1973, 77). But McGovern did not win the election and his plans thus failed.

McGovern himself attributed the rejection of the confiscatory inheritance tax to a "lottery effect" (Weil 1973, 77): many people hope that one day they will enjoy the good fortune of a large inheritance, and they do not wish to lose that possibility, as unlikely as it is.[58] Although this may be part of the explanation for the rejection of steep inheritance taxation, the weightier part is presumably found in the growing distrust among American voters of further redistribution by the government. McGovern's proposals for reform were seen as a threat to individual rights of property and not as a necessary and just social reform. A sociological explanation could proceed from the gains in prosperity that large segments of the American population had enjoyed since the 1940s. This development led to a broad orientation toward upward mobility, which meant that a larger share of the population could see itself as potentially affected by the higher inheritance tax, which would threaten cross-generational strategies of social mobility. The growing prosperity of the middle classes made the inheritance tax appear no longer as a burden solely on the rich. But that, precisely, had been the source of its legitimacy in the first half of the twentieth century. The growing inclusion of the middle classes in the tax was evident from the fact that the number of estates subject to the tax kept rising steadily from the 1950s because the exemption ($60,000) was left unchanged, which meant that more and more heirs had to pay the estate tax.[59]

However, the rejectionist stance toward the redistribution of property through inheritance taxation could also reflect a change in the way large fortunes are perceived within American society. Around the turn of the century, the large-scale industrial structures of the American economy were identified with the robber barons as their symbolic figures. The reform movement blamed them for the social and political defects and for the crisis in a society that had an agrarian imprint. During the New Deal, responsibility for the massive economic and social crisis was also looked for in concentrated large industry and the behavior of its wealthy owners and managers. In both cases, the redistribution of wealth through inheritance taxation seemed like a social reform that responded to the causes behind the social upheaval. This experiential context became less and less important in the postwar period. The economy, structured by large-scale industrial organizations, generated sustained gains in prosperity for broad segments of the population in the 1950s and 1960s. Thus, the concentration of wealth could now be seen as a precondition for economic prosperity, and no longer as the cause behind social crises. Because observers could point to the connection between capital accumulation and the development of wealth, it was possible in the seventies—in a reversal of the earlier perspective—to see attempts at disentangling wealth as a potential threat to meritocratic individualism.

Although the failure of McGovern's bid for the presidency clearly showed that a policy of radical redistribution in the United States was no longer politically possible, raising inheritance taxes continued to be discussed in the social sciences in the seventies, primarily by leftist economists. Lester Thurow (1975) and John A. Brittain (1978) called for a redistribution of wealth against the background of the empirical demonstration that there was no correlation between wealth and merit. They were thus invoking once again the liberal political self-perception of the United States, according to which social inequality is justified only if it is the result of divergent performance on the part of individuals.[60]

In the political context of the seventies, however, this position no longer attracted broad support. In the debate at the beginning of the twentieth century, demands for a redistribution of wealth and social justice through inheritance taxation had held a clear preponderance within the political discourse. The demands found broad political and scholarly support, which was also reflected in Congress. In this sense the proponents of reform exercised a discursive hegemony when they were able, in their interpretation of the situation, to invoke a normative and functional view—widely diffused through American society—of the relationship between a democratic political order, the distribution of wealth, and inheritance taxation. Of course, there was opposition to the reforms by the wealthy also in the first half of the century, but they were confronted with the—at least latent—accusation of selfishness and were not able to claim broad social legitimation for their position.

The situation is very different in the discourse on inheritance taxation that has been going on since the early seventies. At the forefront are no longer motives concerning a redistribution of wealth and a greater financial participation by the wealthy in the tasks of the state, but questions about the economic consequences of a high estate tax, about its justice, and about the legitimacy of state interference in the distribution of wealth.

Political influence was exerted by those economists and political philosophers who opposed the redistribution of wealth through inheritance taxation by invoking economic arguments, moving away from the principle of equal opportunity, and defending private property, thereby helping to bring about the political transformation.

1. Among economic arguments the importance of capital accumulation for the capitalist development of prosperity was prominently invoked. Because inheritance taxes provide an incentive to consumption, they displace investments and thus economic growth, and this creates fewer jobs and generates less income. As a proponent of this line of argumentation, Gordon Tullock (1971) explained why the prohibition against the private inheritance of wealth would be inefficient. If wealth were subject to an inheritance tax of 100%, that is, nothing could be passed on, the savings rate and thus the level of investments would drop. Nobody would have any incentive to possess any property at the end of life. The stock of private capital would be either consumed, or, and this amounted to the same thing, paid into a pension fund that paid a monthly income to the depositor until his death. Although the declining rate of investment would lead to a temporary boost in the level of consumption, long term it would impede economic growth, that is, it would result in a loss of prosperity. If this description of the functional economic interaction is correct, nobody—regardless of his or her personal circumstances of wealth—could advocate, on the basis of economic welfare, a confiscatory taxation of inheritance and the equality of material starting conditions to be achieved by it.

However, this argument did not yet assert that there should be no taxation of inheritance at all. Rather, Tullock (1971) and Wagner (1977) showed that the rate of inheritance taxation must not exceed an optimum level. This optimum was determined by the sum of all inheritances and tax revenues. The assumption was that the size of inheritances is an elastic function dependent on the rate of the inheritance tax. The higher the tax, the lower the inherited wealth will be, because the "price" for inheritances rises in relationship to consumption spending. For each dollar that is passed on to the heir, the testator must have saved several times that amount. The shape of the function is based on the assumption of opportunity costs based on given preferences. As long as the reduction in the sum of the inheritance is smaller than the absolute increase in tax revenue, the inheritance tax will have a positive effect on the rate of investment.[61]

2. The second argument from opponents of redistribution was based on the demand that private property must be inviolable. In the process, they resorted to an argument that had been used in the discourse on inheritance since the eighteenth century but had found little echo in the United States given the dominant view of inheritance law as positive law: private property entailed not only the right to dispose freely over it during one's lifetime, but also to determine to whom it should pass after death. A particularly radical assertion of this position came from Robert Nozick in *Anarchy, State, and Utopia* (1974) in that he granted natural law status to testamentary freedom in his entitlement theory. What are the criteria, Nozick asked, by which a person is entitled to goods? The person must have acquired the originally ownerless goods in accordance with either the principles of just initial acquisition, or the principle of just transfer. Inheritances are subject to the principle of transfer, which includes voluntary exchange and gift. Thus, the person on whom an inheritance is bestowed has a claim to this inheritance on the condition that the testator himself had a right to the property, that is to say, the two criteria of the claim have not been violated. Nozick's argument is meant to be historical, in the sense that an unjust acquisition—no matter how far in the past—renders all later transfers of the goods through exchange or gift likewise unjustified and liable to be undone. What matters to the status of inheritances under property law is that the principle of transfer demands the completely unlimited transfer of gifts. Every government redistribution is rejected as illegitimate (Nozick 1974, 168). Nozick explicitly pointed out that for his entitlement theory, aspects of equality as the final state were irrelevant, nor could equality of opportunity serve to justify redistribution (1974, 233ff.). Only the individual's preference for equal opportunity could lead to his redistributing his wealth as an autonomous decision, by making it available to charitable purposes; coercion, however, was illegitimate.[62]

3. The third argument is directed against the goal of implementing material equality of opportunity itself.[63] Inheritance, according to the argument of Milton and Rose Friedman (1980), for example, is merely one of the "accidents of birth" alongside different talents and highly varied physical attractiveness.[64] But how would we seriously attempt to create an equality of talents, intelligence, or looks? And since that is obviously impossible, the question arises why we should do so with material advantages. The reason "Because we can!" is inadequate for the Friedmans from an ethical perspective, because it would institutionalize the discrimination against advantages of wealth vis-à-vis advantages of biology. Hence, attempts at creating equal starting positions were suspected of satisfying merely motives of envy and should therefore be abandoned altogether.[65]

The character of the American discourse on inheritance has changed since the 1970s in this direction. Arguments that regard inheritance taxation as normatively and functionally problematic are now much more in the foreground. The connection between the concentration of wealth, social problems, and inheritance taxation, discussed in public discourse in the early twentieth century, now plays only a subordinate role. Instead, greater emphasis is placed on the dysfunctional economic consequences of high inheritance taxation and on protecting the rights of owners to transfer their wealth. In the process, opponents of inheritance taxation are able to defend their position with arguments that claim the common good and do not come under the general suspicion of representing plutocratic enrichment strategies. Within conservative discourse, the estate tax was presented increasingly as a threat to the private disposition over property and economic incentive, and thus as one cause behind the economic problems that became more acute especially after 1973.

The Reform of the Estate Tax

It was within this changed political climate that pressure to reform the estate tax grew. Reform also seemed indicated by various systemic problems in the existing law. For example, the exempt amount of $60,000 had been unchanged since the thirties. Because of the erosion in the value of money caused by inflation, the real exempt amount had declined, and at the same time there was a bracket creep. There was also a need for change with respect to the tax system, in two ways: first, the unequal taxation of estates and gifts was unsatisfactory (gifts continued to be taxed at only 75% of the estate tax rate); second, there was the possibility—which the wealthy continued to use—of circumventing the estate tax at least in part through so-called generation-skipping trusts. Gifts and these trusts, along with the tax-free payout of life insurance policies (Eisenstein 1956, 251–52), constituted the primary tax loopholes. These problems were discussed within the Department of the Treasury from the end of the 1960s, and in 1969 the department presented a report with a set of proposals for legislative reform.[66] This report became the basis of the estate tax reform of 1976, the prelude to the wave of reform that has continued to this day, and the terminus of which may well be the abolition of the estate tax.

The two reforms in 1976 and 1981 revised estate taxation in such a way that the goal of redistributing wealth, which had been in the forefront since the New Deal, clearly receded into the background. That is not yet so clearly apparent in the law of 1976, but in retrospect we can classify it as a preliminary step to the crucial reform of 1981. The tax reform law of 1976 abolished the different taxation rates for estates and gifts and integrated them into a unified scale; along the way, the exempt amounts were also standardized.[67] The second major change was the introduction of a tax for generation-skipping trusts, which was supposed to ensure that an estate would be subject to the estate tax once in every generation.[68]

The most important step away from the goal of wealth distribution, however, came with the increase in the exemption in 1976 and the simultaneous cut in the top tax rates. The filing requirement was gradually raised in five steps to $175,625 by 1981.[69] The top tax rate was cut to 70% for estates over $5 million; at the same time the basic tax rate was raised from 3% to 18%. Through the reduced taxation of especially large estates and the increased rate for small estates (though with a simultaneous increase in the filing requirement), the taxation of inheritances after 1976 tended to be distribution neutral.

Looking at the debate over the reform of the estate tax carried on in Congress in 1976 (table 5.5), one detects fundamental changes from the debates in the first third of the twentieth century. The first striking fact is that nearly all arguments support the reform of the estate tax, that is, they support an increase in the exemption, a reduction in tax progression, and special regulations for small businesses and the inheritance of farms. Compared to the distribution of arguments in the earlier debates, this was a dramatic shift.

When it comes to the reasons offered by representatives in support of the legal reform, what stands out compared to the earlier debates is the much stronger orientation toward economic arguments. The cut in the estate tax burden is justified largely with the relief this would provide to closely held businesses and farms. The special emphasis on family businesses—especially in agriculture—is found in the argumentation of the opponents of the estate tax since 1976 and has become increasingly prominent over time. The lack of liquidity by smaller business, most of which are run as joint partnerships, and the greater difficulties they have raising capital, the argument goes, threatens their continued survival if the generational transfer entails a substantial drain of funds from tax obligations. This was the first time that small family wealth moved into the foreground as a point of reference in the discourse over the estate tax in the United States. The estate tax was now branded as the unfair taxation of entrepreneurial initiative.[70] By contrast, the argument about the concentration of large dynastic fortunes, which had dominated the discussion over the estate tax until the 1940s, had all but faded away. This reorientation was also reflected in tax policy: in 1976, it was decided to allow closely held businesses to extend the payment of the estate taxes over a period of fourteen years (Johnson and Eller 1998, 86).

Hereafter, the argumentative structure was shaped by arguments over the economic efficiency of the tax burden, and no longer by questions of justice and adequate revenue. Family-oriented arguments were heard now and then, but in aggregate they continued to be of little importance. Moreover, unlike in Germany and France, the family appears in the American discourse over inheritance taxation largely in its function as an economic unit of production. Opponents of reform in the 1976 debate placed primary emphasis on

TABLE 5.5
The 1976 Estate Tax Reform in Congress: Reasons
Offered by Speakers for Their Position

	Support for Estate Tax Reform	Opposition to Estate Tax Reform
Reasons inherent in the law	20.9	
Reform necessitated by "bracket creep"	17.8	
Other inherent legal reasons	3.1	
Fiscal reasons	3.1	52.9
Maintaining the level of fiscal revenues		52.9
Curtailing the tax take of the federal government	3.1	
Political reasons	6.4	23.5
Privileges from the effortless acquisition of wealth		5.9
Acceptance of social inequality	0.6	
Tax equity	2.7	17.6
Free disposition over property	1.0	
Strengthening national interests	2.1	
Economic reasons	59.5	23.6
Promoting small farms	27.2	11.8
Effects on family businesses	22.6	
Greater equality in the distribution of wealth	1.7	11.8
Avoiding the breakup of land and businesses	5.9	
Other economic reasons	2.1	
Familial reasons	8.9	
Preserving the wealth within the family	6.3	
Providing for family members	1.7	
Family cohesion	0.9	
Other reasons	0.7	
	N = 287	N = 17

Note: Figures are percentages. The debate took place between 9 March and 1 October 1976; a total of thirty-three speakers participated.

preserving tax revenues, but the relative importance of arguments aimed at tax equity and a more equal distribution of wealth continues to reveal the structure of earlier estate tax debates in Congress. On the whole, though, the structure of the debate manifests a profound shift in the balance of power within the discursive field. The liberal economic current, which rejects the interference in private property rights through inheritance taxes out of considerations of economic efficiency, is dominant. A previous comparable situation existed at best during the 1920s under President Coolidge and his secretary of the Treasury, Andrew Mellon.

The tax reform of 1976 was only the first step toward the much farther reaching reform of 1981. The Economic Tax Act of 1981, part of President Ronald Reagan's tax reform, the core of which was a reduction of the top income tax rate to 50%, enacted another increase in the exemption, while the progressive nature of the estate tax was scaled back further. Specifically, the reform stipulated that the filing requirement would be raised to $600,000 by 1987 in six annual steps. Moreover, transfers to a spouse were made tax exempt.[71]

The immediate effect of raising the filing requirement and making spouses tax exempt was a reduction in the proportion of estates that owed any taxes at all. Whereas that number had stood at 7.65% of all deaths in the United States in 1976, in 1987 it had dropped to merely 0.88%.[72]

The third change brought about by the Economic Recovery Act was a further reduction of the estate tax progression. Here, too, legislators introduced a graduated plan that reduced the top rate from 70% to 50% by 1988, while at the same time cutting the size of the estate that fell into this bracket from $5 million to $2.5 million.[73]

The effect of this reform was to make smaller estates entirely exempt from taxation (after 1987, spouses could bequeath up to $1.2 million tax free) and to provide noticeable relief for large fortunes over $3 million (after deducting exemptions). It is clear that with this reform, the goal of redistributing wealth through estate taxation was abandoned. In the 1981 report by the Ways and Means Committee on the proposed tax changes, redistribution motives played no role whatsoever. Instead, as in 1976, the report referred to the protection of family businesses and to the cut in the income tax, with which the estate tax should be aligned (Hudson 1983, 28).

The scaling back of the estate tax—begun in 1976, taken further in 1981—was also continued by the reform of the estate tax law in 1997. At that time, under Democratic president Bill Clinton, Congress decided to raise the filing requirement further in seven steps to $1 million by 2006. The top tax rates were left unchanged. Additional special allowances were made for family businesses (Johnson and Mikow 1999). The fiscal consequences from the cut in the top tax rate and the raising of the exemption since 1976 can be seen from the decline in the percentage that the estate tax revenue accounts for of total tax revenues: from 1.3% in 1980[74] it dropped by nearly half to 0.7% in 1987.[75]

The Abolition of the Estate Tax?

Currently, annual revenues from the estate tax are a little over $20 billion.[76] This means that the estate tax accounts for around 1.4% of total tax revenues. By the end of this decade, had the tax rates that existed until 2001 continued, tax revenues would have risen to $50 billion a year. In the United States, the estate tax is assessed on only around 2% of yearly deaths; 98% of all estates are not taxed thanks to the high exemptions. The effective tax rate for taxable returns stands at an average of 17% of the value of the estate (Gale and Slemrod 2001). However, half of the estate tax that is raised is paid by the largest 5.4% of estates that are subject to taxation (Johnson and Mikow 1999, 107ff.). In other words: half of the revenue of the estate tax is collected from only one-tenth of 1% of all estates. Merely the 467 largest of the taxable estates in 1999, each of which had a taxable value of more than $20 million, paid just under $5.5 billion (24%) of the entire tax revenue (Internal Revenue Service 2001). The estate tax is thus paid chiefly by the estates of superrich testators, whose heirs would, conversely, derive the most benefit from the abolition of the estate tax.

In the reforms of the estate tax since 1976, the top tax rate was almost cut in half. Moreover, even before the decision of 2001, the increase in the exemption shielded the vast majority of estates from the tax, while special relief was granted to family businesses and family farms (Johnson and Eller 1998, 86ff.). Still, even after the reforms of the seventies and eighties, the Republican Party, especially, demanded ever more vociferously the complete abolition of the estate tax. Beginning in the midnineties, there have been various bills to abolish the tax; at the end of the nineties, opponents garnered majorities in both houses of Congress, but President Clinton vetoed the bill. The repeal of the estate tax might succeed with President Bush in the White House. The clearest indication is the Economic Growth and Tax Relief Reconciliation Act of 2001, which phases out the tax by the year 2010 (although it will return in 2011 unless Congress takes action before then) (Brownlee 2004, 217ff.; Graetz and Shapiro 2005). Since the passage of this bill, Republicans have been trying to find a majority for a permanent repeal of the estate tax, but so far they have not succeeded in the Senate. The compromise that could emerge is a further reduction of the progression rate and an increase in the exemption. However, the current size of the budget deficit reduces the maneuvering room for a further reduction of the estate tax. Democratic senators estimate that a repeal of the estate tax would cost the government $78 billion a year (on average) in lost revenues.

On an argumentative level, the debate in April 2001 continued the debate of 1976. It is therefore possible to speak of a phase in the discourse over the taxation of estate in the United States that began around 1970 and has continued to the present. At the same time, the nearly even distribution of arguments for and against the repeal of the tax and the high number of participating speakers reveal the degree to which inheritance taxation has once again assumed an important place in the political controversies in the United States.

If one looks at the distribution of arguments marshaled by the representatives (table 5.6), the dominance of economic ones is striking. In this regard the trend of 1976 has grown stronger. It is particularly noteworthy that three out of four arguments by opponents of the estate tax invoked economic reasons. The points of reference are chiefly family businesses and farms that are supposedly threatened by the estate tax. A new argument was that the estate tax posed a particular threat to businesses run by women and minorities. These are often family businesses with weak capitalization, it was said, which is why they are especially hard hit by the drain of capital from the estate tax. Leaving aside the blatant instrumentalization of these groups of entrepreneurs in the discourse (the existing regulations on the taxation of estates protects against these kinds of threats), this is the first time they received special attention in the controversies over the tax.[77] The tax cuts found also strong public support at least during the first years of the Bush presidency (Bartels 2005).

The supporters of the estate tax also based their arguments strongly on economic considerations. They deny that the estate tax posed a threat to the survival of family businesses; in fact they even see it as protection for small companies. After all, the abolition of the estate tax would only help the already financially strong large companies, who would acquire additional competitive advantages. In addition, defenders of the tax marshal fiscal arguments. The repeal of the tax, they maintain, would lead to reduced tax revenues, and that would entail cuts especially in education and social spending. This makes the repeal of the estate tax into a question of tax equity—only the superwealthy are given relief.[78]

As the law stands right now, the estate tax would return one year after its phaseout with the rates as they were in 2000. But since the tax decisions of 2001 there are efforts under way in Congress to push through the final abolition of the estate tax.[79] Abolition would be in line with the reforms since 1976 and would simultaneously represent a turning point in American tax law. Michael Graetz noted as early as 1983 that the decline in the fiscal importance of the estate tax provides an argument for its repeal. The minor revenue from the tax, combined with the administrative expenses of collecting it and weak public support for the tax, is making the estate tax a matter of indifference to budget politicians (Graetz 1983, 271). Very much in this spirit, the law professor John E. Donaldson (1993) justified the repeal of the existing estate tax by pointing out that the tax does not achieve any of its stated goals: redistributing wealth, contributing to the tax revenues, or contributing to the progressivity of the tax system. The argument of minor fiscal importance is dubious, however, since the estate tax revenue makes

TABLE 5.6
The Estate Tax Reform in Congress in 2001: Reasons
Offered by Speakers for Their Position

	In Support of a Repeal of the Estate Tax	Opposed to Repeal of the Estate Tax
Reasons inherent in the law	3.2	
Other reasons inherent in the law	3.2	
Fiscal reasons	8.0	24.7
Preserving budget revenues	4.8	24.7
Reducing the federal government's tax take	3.2	
Reasons related to the political order	8.0	25.2
Privileges from the effortless acquisition of wealth		0.5
Acceptance of social inequality	0.8	
Tax equity	4.4	22.8
Free disposition over property	2.0	
Reduction in charitable giving	0.8	1.9
Economic reasons	77.8	49.2
Promoting small agricultural holdings	16.8	22.3
Effect on family businesses	25.5	24.2
Equality in the distribution of wealth		2.3
Avoiding the breakup of land or businesses	6.8	
Preserving jobs	14.7	
Providing economic support to women and minorities	2.8	
Other economic reasons	11.2	0.4
Familial reasons	1.2	
Preserving wealth within the family	1.2	
Other reasons	0.8	
	N = 251	N = 215

Note: Figures are percentages. The debate took place on 3 and 4 April 2001; a total of eighty-four speakers participated.

up no less than 9% of discretionary spending from tax revenues, and the tax basis is presently expanding through the death of the generation that accumulated considerable wealth during the prosperous postwar decades (Gates and Collins 2003, 92).

It is interesting, however, that the targeted abolition of the estate tax has led to a renewed controversy within the American public. This reflects yet another change in the political discourse on the inheritance of wealth that has predominated since the 1970s, a change that is simultaneously continuous with the inheritance-critical discourse that has been firmly rooted since the Revolution. One might possibly interpret this as the first sign of another "great transformation" in ideas about the economic order. What is evident in the political public and in the social sciences is a renewed critical interest in the estate tax. In the spring of 2001, a group of prominent wealthy Americans, among them Warren Buffett, George Soros, and William Gates, Sr., voiced their opposition to the repeal of the estate tax in a public appeal. In this appeal, signed by more than a hundred wealthy Americans and published in full page ads in newspapers, they argued that the repeal of the tax would be "bad for our democracy, our economy, and our society" (Appeal 'Responsible Wealth,' Internet; Graetz and Shapiro 2005, 168ff.). The repeal would bring benefits to wealthy Americans at the expense of the lower social classes, would make it harder to finance social programs, and would have a negative impact on giving to charitable organizations.[80] This places the group squarely in the American tradition that defends the unlimited individual accumulation of private property, while at the same time rejecting the private bequeathal of large fortunes. The appeal forms a line of continuity to Andrew Carnegie's 1889 essay "Wealth," in which he called for the introduction of steep inheritance taxes and philanthropic engagement on the part of the wealthy. A newspaper interview with Warren Buffett reveals the meritocratic-individualistic understanding of property that forms the backdrop:

> We have come closer to a true meritocracy than anywhere around the world. . . . You have mobility so people with talents can be put to the best use. Without the estate tax, you in effect will have an aristocracy of wealth, which means you pass down the ability to command resources of the nation based on heredity rather than merit. (*New York Times* 14 February 2001)

The preservation of the estate tax has been opposed at the same time by an initiative under the name NoDeathTax.org. It includes renowned economists and supports an appeal by Milton Friedman. As mentioned above, Friedman already rejected the estate tax back in the 1970s. The appeal opposes what it calls the "death tax" by listing its negative effects on the savings rate and capital accumulation, the double taxation of income that has already been taxed, the small amount of revenue derived from the tax, and its failure to reduce the concentration of wealth.

Economic and legal discourses in the 1990s and the first years of the new millennium also attest to a new interest in estate taxation and confirm the tradition of egalitarian liberalism (Alstott 1996; Holtz-Eakin 1996; Gale and Slemrod 2001; Murphy and Nagel 2002; Gates and Collins 2003).[81] These public controversies reflect the—to this day—controversial character of inherited wealth within American society.

However, ideas about confiscating wealth in every generation and redistributing it in an egalitarian fashion, which were characteristic of Orestes Brownson, for example, hardly play a role any longer in the discourses. Brownson and also the Populists were guided by the ideal of a property-owner society modeled after Jefferson's republicanism, though it was increasingly out of sync with the actual economic developments since industrialization. The debates over inheritance law in the late nineteenth and early twentieth centuries often picked up this image of society. At the end of the twentieth century, the proponents of an egalitarian liberalism were guided by a model of society that no longer rejected on principle the intergenerational perpetuation of an unequal distribution of wealth, while at the same time demanding corrections to the distribution of wealth, however. This is most evident from John Rawls's *Theory of Justice* (1971). At the time of its publication it had barely any influence on the discourse over inheritance taxation, but by now it has become an important point of reference for the liberal position. Rawls defended the institution of inheritance and demanded intervention only to the extent that the concentration of wealth undermines freedom and fair equal opportunity:

> The unequal inheritance of wealth is no more inherently unjust than the unequal inheritance of intelligence. It is true that the former is presumably more easily subject to social control; but the essential thing is that as far as possible inequalities founded on either should satisfy the difference principle. Thus inheritance is permissible provided that the resulting inequalities are to the advantage of the least fortunate and compatible with liberty and fair equality of opportunity. (1971, 277)

The reference to Rawls's position in the contemporary discourse on inheritance law indicates that egalitarian liberalism has undergone a learning process, as a result of which it has let go of the notion of an egalitarian society of property owners normatively without relinquishing the demand for corrections to the distribution of wealth.

The question which party will prevail in the current political clashes in the United States is open. The discourse over the normative status of unearned wealth, which has accompanied American history for more than 200 years, continues. The United States, much more so than the two European societies, stands within a political tradition for which the acquisition of wealth by inheritance, without any personal merit or effort, is deeply problematic.

5.2. "Sense of Family" versus Social Justice: The Inheritance Tax in Germany

A comparison of the institutionalization of the estate tax in the United States with the introduction of the Reich inheritance tax in Germany reveals close chronological, fiscal, and political parallels: (1) The inheritance tax in Germany was introduced on the Reich level in 1906, thus around the same time as the estate taxes in the United States; at the same time, various German states were also levying inheritance taxes. (2) The immediate cause for the introduction of the tax was a fiscal crisis produced by the rising military expenses and legal limits to the broadening of the tax base, more precisely, the prohibition against the levying of direct taxes by the Reich. (3) In the last third of the nineteenth century, Germany, too, saw a growing strength in the forces of political reform that were pushing for a more just distribution of economic wealth. The concurrence of fiscal crisis, political reform movements, and the introduction of the inheritance tax creates a context similar to the one I have identified for the United States.

And yet, there are important differences between Germany and the United States with respect to the institutionalization of inheritance taxation and the discourses surrounding it.

1. Institutionally, there is a difference in the system of taxation. In Germany, the tax is assessed as an inheritance tax and not as an estate tax, which creates the possibility of shaping the tax rates and the progressivity of the tax to reflect the degree of kinship between the testator and the heirs. The inheritance of direct family members—especially spouses and children—can be either exempted from the tax or taxed at only a low rate. And in fact, in Germany close family members of the deceased pay lower taxes, and for a long time children and spouses were entirely exempt. In addition, the progressive rates of the German inheritance tax are—aside from two brief exceptions—consistently much lower than in the United States.

2. The discourse over inheritance taxation in Germany is based on very different arguments: front and center for opponents—and to a limited extent even for proponents—of inheritance taxation are arguments rejecting it as illegitimate interference in family wealth and predicting destructive consequences for the family; the tax was contrary to the "sense of family." Proponents of the tax in Germany base their arguments largely on the goal of social justice, to which the tax is supposed to contribute by financing the social policies of the state. The primary concern is to generate state revenues to correct, through policy, the social problems resulting from the unequal distribution of property and unequal abilities to generate income on the market. In contrast to the United States, the social reformist position is result-oriented. Promoting equal opportunity, against the harmful political consequences from an excessive concentration of wealth, and redistributing wealth—arguments that had such great importance in the American discourse—are hardly relevant in Germany.

In this section I will examine how the inheritance tax debate in Germany carried on since the *Vormärz* period (1815–48) differs from the American debate, and I will try to show to what extent important structural differences in German inheritance taxation, especially the institutionalization of the inheritance tax and the low rates for direct family members, can be explained by the divergent understanding of the function and social consequences of inherited wealth. I shall begin by outlining the legal-political debate on inheritance taxation and bring out its specific characteristics. Against this background I shall then discuss the parliamentary controversies over the introduction of inheritance taxation in the Reichstag at the beginning of the twentieth century and the subsequent development.

Inheritance Taxes and the Social Question

In Germany, the public discussion over inheritance taxation and its economic and social consequences commenced in the 1830s and grew more intense especially in the last third of the nineteenth century. First in the run-up to the Revolution of 1848 and then especially after 1879, a growing number of publications appeared on this topic, and questions about the tax interference in the private transmission of wealth *mortis causa* became a prominent theme of legal and political discussion. The backdrop to all of this was initially not the general financial needs of the states, but the social dislocations— encapsulated in the phrase "the social question" and, in the beginning, associated chiefly with pauperism—caused by the structural economic changes in the wake of the beginning process of industrialization. From the 1840s on, inheritance taxation is discussed in Germany in connection with the financing of the state's social policies, a goal that was different from that in the United States. Where the radical liberal reformers in the United States in the early nineteenth century wished to use inheritance taxation to create *equal starting conditions* for the distribution of private property, reform in Germany was intended to support the active intervention by the state in an effort to solve the growing social problems. This orientation of the discourse on inheritance taxes persisted in the second half of the nineteenth century and also structured in crucial ways the parliamentary controversies in the early twentieth century.

However, much as in the United States, the inheritance tax had little initial parliamentary importance in the nineteenth century. Most German states had introduced a succession tax in the nineteenth century.[82] Prussia played a particularly important role in this, because its system of inheritance taxation served as the model not only for many of the individual states, but also for the inheritance tax of the German Reich introduced in 1906.[83] The stamp duty enacted by Prussia in 1822 already contained two of the principles essential to later inheritance tax laws: first, the differentiation of tax rates in accordance with the degree of kinship between the heir and the testator; second, the calculation of the level of the stamp on the basis of the value of the inheritance. Ascendants and descendants were exempted from the tax, as was the wife if she inherited jointly with her deceased husband's legitimate children (Meynen 1912, 14).[84]

The existing succession tax was hardly controversial in the Prussian parliament. Tax rates were moderate, and the exemption for direct family members meant that an estimated 75% of inherited wealth escaped taxation. However, a debate on the reform of the inheritance tax law that was carried on in the Prussian *Landtag* in 1872 already reveals the arguments that came to dominate later debates in the Reichstag and placed special emphasis on the need to protect the nuclear family. The discussion revolved around the repeal of taxation on spouses, which was supported by the speakers nearly unanimously on the grounds that it represented an illegitimate interference in the family: it was too damaging to the sense of family "if precisely at the moment in which the family is in mourning, the state approaches the heirs with its demands for money" (Meynen 1912, 15). Pious restraint by the state on this matter amounted to giving up the better part of the possible revenues from the inheritance tax.

Inheritance taxation became important in the legal-political discussion in the *Vormärz* period. In the 1830s, the topic was initially taken up by liberal economists and jurists as well as early socialist reformers. The economists Ludwig Heinrich von Jakob (1837), Johann Gottfried Hoffmann (1840), and Karl Heinrich Rau (1832) adopted the critical stance of Adam Smith and David Ricardo toward the taxation of inheritance. They used Smith's economic argument that the inheritance tax impeded the private accumulation of capital, though they also invoked the need to protect the family.[85] At the same time, they regarded minor inheritance taxes of the kind found in Prussia as unproblematic. For example, the economist Karl Heinrich Rau, the teacher of Adolph Wagner, argued that the payment of an inheritance tax was not harmful to the formation of capital if it could be made from the interest income. If it affected the capital itself, it would have negative incentives for savings (Rau 1997 [1832], §237). Hoffmann was also critical of the inheritance tax, though he concluded that the existing levy in Prussia was acceptable because it had been "enacted with much moderation and leniency" (Hoffmann 1840, 426). Heinrich von Jakob used the family-related argument:

> The only thing in favor of a levy on inheritances is that it can be paid without difficulty by those who are subject to it; but if this circumstance alone could justify it, no property would be safe from the law any longer. Moreover, it is exceedingly burdensome if it falls upon the income of those who previously lived only with difficulty off the wealth that is now diminished, or who are placed into a difficult position through the death of the testator who was also the person supporting them. (Jakob 1837, 186, qtd. in Schanz 1901, 640)

The economists influenced by Smith and Ricardo played hardly a role in the subsequent German debate. The utilitarian writings of Jeremy Bentham and John Stuart Mill aimed at limiting the right of inheritance exerted a far greater influence on the liberal intellectuals in the 1840s. For Bentham, the unlimited right of inheritance represented a violation of the utilitarian ethical principle of maximizing the sum of the utility of all members of society, because it led to an unproductive concentration of wealth and to the unjustified enrichment of distant relatives.[86] Because inheritance law was for Bentham positive law, the state could limit it on the grounds of utility. Bentham's student John Stuart Mill took this a step further with his proposals for a steep inheritance tax. But unlike Bentham and Mill, German social reformers were not concerned with creating equal starting positions, but with corrective social policies.

In Germany, the critical positions of the utilitarians were discussed chiefly under the rubric of escheat, meaning the determination of a state share of inheritances, which amounted to de facto taxation. The right of intestate inheritance was to apply only to direct family members, while the state would enter into the inheritance instead of collateral relatives. One of the proposals envisaged a right to inheritance on the part of the state even if a last will was present.[87] Just as in the United States and in France, the crucial basis in legal theory for the state's interference in inheritance law lay in its designation as positive law.

The discussions over the state's right of inheritance and the use of the resulting revenues for social policies began during the pauperism crisis of the 1840s. In 1842, the Swabian jurist Paul Achatius Pfizer, one of the most important liberal thinkers of his time, justified the state's right of inheritance in his *Gedanken über Recht, Staat und Kirche* (1842, "Reflections on Law, State, and Church") by pointing to the state's growing tasks in social policy—and *not*, as Orestes Brownson and Thomas Skidmore, for example, did in the United States, by invoking the goal of achieving the most equal distribution of property possible in order to realize equality of opportunity.[88] The emerging inequality of property, so Pfizer, could pose a threat to social order, and this was something the state had to take action against in its social policy. At the same time, his proposal was linked to the protection of the family. The nuclear family as "a community of property owners" should retain the unrestricted right of inheritance, though "mere collateral relatives should not be accorded a statutory right of inheritance, and the right of disposing over their estate should at least be restricted for the unmarried and those without children" (1842, 65). In this way, the state was to be given the funds "to support the numerous class of those without property and inheritance not only temporarily, and with somewhat more than the bare necessities" (65–66).

The legitimacy of the state's right of inheritance is derived from the assumed obligation of the state to care for its citizens.[89] Welfare support was necessary because the crisis of poverty raised the specter of revolution. This social policy backdrop to Pfizer's argumentation shines through again and again in the debate over escheat in the *Vormärz* period.

For example, Theodor Hilgard—a legal official who had emigrated to the United States during the *Vormärz* (Strunck 1935, 24)—proposed, in his tract *Zwölf Paragraphen über Pauperismus und die Mittel, ihn zu steuern* (Twelve Paragraphs on Pauperism and the Means of Regulating It) (1847), a clear limit to the right of intestate inheritance, under which collateral relatives beyond the fourth degree would no longer possess that right, and of bequests to cousins as well as aunts and uncles, the state would receive one-fourth and one-third, respectively. The state would be a co-heir even if a will existed, at half the rates that applied to the statutory succession. Hilgard wanted to use the proceeds to set up an inheritance fund that would support emigration, poor relief, and redistribution to the impecunious. The suggestion by Hilgard was developed in greater detail by the Munich journalist Karl Brater in his booklet *Die Reform des Erbrechts zu Gunsten der Nothleidenden* (The Reform of Inheritance Law for the Benefit of the Suffering, 1848). A little later, the Weimar *Staatsrat* Gottfried Stichling published a tract (1850) that put forth less radical demands, though it also affirmed a right of inheritance for the state and offered social policy goals as justification.

All of these authors were concerned—in part also against the backdrop of the threat of social unrest—with generating financial resources the state could use to alleviate the worst poverty, whereby the right of inheritance of direct family members was acknowledged across the board:

> However, the individual's right of disposition by last will and the family's statutory right of inheritance must remain as a firm rule and two basic pillars, from which the greatest possible development of human individuality pursues its goals and against which the claims of the state encounter their definitive limit. (Stichling 1850, 504–5)[90]

The connection between inheritance taxation and social policy created in the 1840s a discursive nexus that would accompany the inheritance tax debate in Germany to this day. The "social question," which pushed itself increasingly to the forefront of the sociopolitical discourse in the second half of the nineteenth century, continuously generated new proposals on how inheritances by collateral relatives could be used for social policies.

The connection between the state's obligation to provide welfare services and the limitation on the inheritances of what were referred to as "laughing heirs" was consistently maintained. Twenty-five years after Hilgard, this is evident, for example, in the proposal put forth by the economist Karl Umpfenbach (1874): the right of intestate inheritance should end with the fourth degree of kinship, and testamentary freedom should be limited in such a way that only half of the estate could be passed to collateral relatives, with the rest bequeathed at best with a lifetime interest. The "people's inheritance" that fell to the state should then be used for education:

> This people's inheritance is intended for training and educating those members of a generation who are unable by their own means to achieve in the first place

the harmony of productive capacity and personal improvement that is in accord with the level of culture.' (Umpfenbach 1874, 49)

Family and State in the Inheritance Tax Discourse

This kind of proposal is interesting because it characterizes a specific situation of transformation. Social reformers were well aware that the emerging industrial society was creating social frictions that necessitated corrective intervention. Redistribution in the spirit of solidarity was supposed to reduce poverty, and the state's assumption of the expenses of education and training was supposed to create the possibilities of earning a living for the lower social strata. While the reformers opted for a government social policy as an institutional structure to correct market outcomes, they were also hesitant, because redistribution must not impair the supportive solidarity within the expanded nuclear family. The passing down of wealth within the family fulfilled an important social function of providing support, with no thought yet given to the state taking on this function—for example, through the introduction of pension insurance. That is why the proposals for the most part dispensed with inheritance taxes up to the third or fourth kinship group. This meant, though, that the succession tax would generate at best very little revenue that was hardly sufficient to fund social policies.[91] Among the social reformers of the mid–nineteenth century we find in this regard an unresolved conflict between familial solidarity and state social policy, a conflict that did not yet become politically explosive. In retrospect, one can already discern the future fundamental conflict in the German inheritance tax discourse: on the one side is the protection of the wealth of the (expanded) nuclear family; on the other side is the demand that inheritances be used as the financial basis for the state's social policy. In this clash, the wealthy instrumentalized the family-related arguments to protect their own interests. But the factual reference point in the German discussion of the inheritance tax is always *familial wealth in its function of providing for surviving family members.* In the United States, by contrast, the reference point was *large fortunes and their potentially harmful effect on democracy.*

The last quarter of the nineteenth century saw a shift in emphasis in the development of socio-reformist concepts for state intervention in the private inheritance of wealth: the role of the state in the pursuit of social welfare goals was accentuated more strongly, while at the same time the concern about the threat to the family from the inheritance tax receded into the background. It was especially writers from the Historical School who argued along these lines. The Historical School turned away from classical economics not only methodologically by criticizing the notion of universal economic laws, but also by emphasizing the ethical goals of economic policy, which led to the recognition of the necessary role of the state in regulating relationships of economic exchange. The critical attitude toward the laissez-faire of classical economics linked them to a social reform program whose realization was intended to help overcome the contemporary tendencies toward anomie within society. Reform of inheritance law was one element of that program. The representatives of the Historical School adopted both the notion of the state's right of inheritance and the introduction of a progressive inheritance tax.

In his *Rede über die soziale Frage* (Speech on the Social Question, 1872), Adolf Wagner, the most prominent economist of the younger Historical School, while demanding the preservation of the private right of inheritance, supported a right of the state to inherit at the expense of more distant degrees of kinship, and advocated a progressive inheritance tax graduated according to the size of the inheritance and the kinship relationship, whose goal should be a fairer distribution of the tax burden (Wagner 1872, 37). Wagner regarded the preservation of the right of private inheritance as "absolutely necessary economically and ethically for the family unit and the economy" (37), thus adopting the liberal economic argument as well as the orientation toward the family that is characteristic of the German discourse. But in contrast to the proposals from the 1840s, this did not stop Wagner from calling for the taxation also of descendants and spouses. The starting point for Wagner's argumentation (1880, 476ff.) was the change in the functions of the family brought about by the processes of modernization, which caused the tasks of the family to shift increasingly to the state:

> The smaller . . . the legal and practical importance—and in particular the civil-law obligations—of the family unit toward the individual becomes, the more the latter "emancipates" himself from the family, the more purely private wealth is legally considered individual wealth and economically functions de facto as such, the more certain obligations, of rendering aid, supporting the poor and so on, pass to the state, in other words, the more individualism takes hold in the life of the people in the place of the strict family and gender order: the more justified in principle, and the more necessary and just in practice, does the participation of the public body, especially the state, in inheritance become, the more justified is a system of expansive inheritance taxes. (Wagner 1880, 477–78)

Comparable positions from the circle of the Historical School were advocated from 1870 on by the likes of Wilhelm Roscher (1886, 308ff.), August von Miaskowski (1882a, 1882b), Julius Baron (1876), Hans von Scheel (1877b), Albert Schäffle (1895, 418ff.), Heinrich Geffken (1881), and A. Eschenbach (1891), and they increased the pressure of reform for a heavier taxation of inheritance in the German Reich.[92] At the same time, the political conflict over inheritance taxation grew more acute, because the justification of the state's right to interfere in bequests even to close relatives of the testator ran counter to the interests of those who owned wealth. Opponents of the inheritance tax in Germany always pointed primarily to the function of inheritances in providing for surviving family members and to the threat the tax posed to family unity. They succeeded in preserving the supportive function of the family as a point of reference in the discourse, and in mobilizing this principle against a state policy of redistribution.

The Inheritance Tax among Early Socialists and the Social Democrats

A second thread of the inheritance tax discourse that had a social reformist orientation emanated in the nineteenth century from Socialists and Social Democrats. It was reasonable to expect them to put forth a demand for a redistribution of inherited wealth that was much more radical than what the liberals or the Historical School proposed. It is therefore surprising that such demands came only from the early Socialist currents, which virtually ceased to have any influence in the second half of the nineteenth century.

The demand for a confiscatory limit to the private right of inheritance found support first in France among the Saint-Simonists. Since the early German socialists referred to Saint-Simonism, I will briefly sketch this position here.[93] According to Saint-Simon, economic wealth is created by productive, gainful work. The unequal distribution of wealth, especially through the privileges of social estate and birth, blocked the property-less strata of the population from realizing their productive potential. That is why Saint-Simon's student Saint-Armand Bazard proposed a complete abolition of the right of inheritance and the transfer of the assets to the state. Personally acquired wealth was to remain in private ownership. Prosper Enfantin, another student of Saint-Simon, less radically wanted to repeal the inheritance right only of collateral relatives and introduce an inheritance tax for direct relatives. Revenues from these measures should make it possible to abolish indirect taxes and establish a fund for educational tasks and other goals aimed at the common good (Strunck 1935, 15ff.). The Saint-Simonists were thus not concerned with equality as such, but with the abolition of a system of income distribution based on privileges of birth and replacing it with one oriented toward merit and ability. Realizing this intention would presuppose radical restrictions on the right of private inheritance. These ideas of equality show a clear overlap between the early Socialists and the reform movements of the 1830s and 1840s in the United States. However, in contrast to the American reformers, the equal distribution of property among the students of Saint-Simon was not aimed at the redistribution as *private property*, but at greater *communal property*, which would be put at the disposal of those who were able to use it productively.

This is also true for the early German Socialist Wilhelm Weitling, who incorporated the proposal for a radical reform of inheritance law into his reformist tract *Das Evangelium des armen Sünders* (The Gospel of the Poor Sinner, 1843). Weitling's demands included the abolition of the private right of inheritance and its conversion into a communal inheritance (1968 [1843], 410).[94] The early Socialist position in Germany achieved its greatest political influence, however, in the *Communist Manifesto* (1970 [1848]) written by Marx and Engels, whose catalogue of demands included the abolition of the right of inheritance.

All this makes the subsequent development of the Socialist position on inheritance law surprising. The introduction of steep inheritance taxes did not become a prominent political goal. Marx and Engels withdrew their call for the abolition of the right of inheritance not long after the publication of the *Manifesto*,[95] and it also ceased to play a role in Social Democracy after 1860 (Hennicke 1929, 106ff.). Although the party programs of the SPD contained the call for higher inheritance taxes and a limit on the right of inheritance for distant relatives, they never demanded its abolition. Marx himself gave a lecture on inheritance law in 1869 at the Fourth Congress of the Communist International in Basel. In it, he objected to the early Socialist position by arguing that the demand for the abolition of the right of inheritance inverted cause and effect: the real lever for social change was the abolition of the private ownership of the means of production, not the elimination of the symptomatic consequences of the existing property law. Moreover, inheritance law was not an issue for the working class, which had nothing to pass on anyhow. If the abolition of the right of private inheritance were elevated into a major political issue in spite of this, "it would be sure to raise an almost insurmountable opposition which would inevitably lead to reaction" (Marx 1869).

Within the Social Democratic Party, only the more moderate demands for an increase in the inheritance tax and a limit on intestate succession found support.[96] The crucial considerations behind this were tactical as well as programmatic. Tactically, the Social Democrats in the 1890s assumed that it was precisely the decision *not* to redistribute wealth that could contribute to the collapse of the capitalist system.[97] The increasing concentration of wealth would undermine the stability of the capitalist order, which is why reducing that concentration was in fact not in the interest of a revolutionary political strategy. Moreover, the redistribution of property—through changes to the inheritance law, for example—played only a subordinate role for the Social Democrats, because they did not wish to fritter away their energy at several political fronts (Schröder 1987, 289ff.).

Another indication for the restraint of German Social Democrats when it came to pursuing redistributive goals through inheritance taxation was the reserved response to the Rignano plan.[98] This plan, which envisaged a gradual confiscation of inheritances through three generations, was translated from French (1904) into both English (1924) and German (1905). The proposal attracted a lively discussion in the United States, in France, and especially in England (Chester 1982, 67ff.; Erreygers 1997). In Germany, not only did the plan meet with little resonance in the inheritance law debate as a whole,[99] but the Social Democratic leadership took note of it with some reserve. In his forward to the German translation of the plan (1905), Eduard Bernstein, who in his program of "Socialist revisionism" had advocated the evolutionary transformation of capitalism, pointed to the important role that private property had for the accumulation of wealth in a society, and believed that a radical limitation on the inheritance of wealth was justified only if the ownership of capital was separated from the productive function.

The call for the introduction of a progressive inheritance tax was for the Social Democrats in the later empire part of their general tax policy, which was aimed at reducing indirect taxes in order to provide relief to the lower income strata. To make up for the loss of revenue from a cut in these taxes, direct taxes should be introduced—especially an income tax, but also a succession tax—which would place a burden on the ownership of wealth. The goal of this tax policy was greater tax equity, but not the redistribution of wealth. A dissertation at the University of Heidelberg at the end of the 1920s commented rather laconically about the attitude of the Social Democrats toward inheritance taxation:

> This emphasis on a lack of interest [toward the inheritance tax] is something the party retained later. It always strove to assume the stance of an outside critic. This stance was taken, for one, out of tactical considerations; second, from the beginning the party was at pains to note that the inheritance tax was not a tax of socialism—neither an element of its system nor an instrument for bringing it about. (Hennicke 1929, 107–8)[100]

The Inheritance Tax in Parliamentary Debate

How did the intellectual discourse about the reform of the inheritance tax enter into parliamentary debates in the Reichstag and the structure of the laws on inheritance taxation that were enacted? This is the question I will pursue in this and the next two sections. It will become clear that while the debates over the introduction of a Reich inheritance tax in the German Reichstag that began at the end of the nineteenth century were prompted—as in the United States—by the increasingly difficult fiscal situation, the discourse and structure of the inheritance taxation that was passed differed in specific ways from the American estate taxation. These specific characteristics are found consistently from the inheritance tax laws and the first inheritance tax debates in the Reichstag in the middle of the 1890s, down to the most recent debate in the Bundestag in 1996. Only two brief exceptions occurred in the crisis years of 1919–1922 and 1946–48, when inheritance taxation departed from the otherwise consistent pattern.

The Fiscal Background

The introduction of a Reich inheritance tax first became a topic of parliamentary debate in the Reichstag shortly after the establishment of the Reich.[101] But it was only in the 1890s that the Reich inheritance tax became an important topic in parliament. The backdrop to this was the fiscal situation.

The growth in the tasks of the centralized state, and especially the armament policy that had begun in the 1890s, led to a rising need for revenue on the part of the Reich. At the same time, the possible sources of income were constitutionally limited. In the federal financial constitution after 1871, the Reich had access to revenue from state-run enterprises, from various consumer taxes, tariffs, and the contributions by the individual states (called *Matrikularbeiträge*).[102] The Reich was barred from levying direct taxes, which led to a weak fiscal position overall.

The armament policy had serious fiscal consequences, because the expenses of the Reich, alongside the initially small outlay for social security, were concentrated in the area of defense. The size of the financial need depended largely on the defense budget, which accounted for about 80% of Reich expenditures at the beginning of the century and showed a sharp absolute rise as a result of the naval buildup (Nipperdey 1990, 172; Wehler 1995b, 1034–35). This created a situation that was very similar to that in the United States: a prohibition of direct taxes against a backdrop of a rising need for funds, especially from defense spending. Since the armament policy in Germany received support across the party spectrum, all the way to the Left Liberals (Wehler 1995c, 1134), the debates were heavily focused on the question of financing. Analogous to the United States, the German tax controversy revolved around the question of whether the consumption taxes should be raised further or whether new sources of taxes should be created for the Reich through the introduction of direct taxes (including the inheritance tax). At the back of this controversy stood the question about how to distribute the tax burden.

The introduction of a Reich inheritance tax was demanded primarily by the SPD, though it received support also from the Left Liberals as well as the Center Party. In 1893, August Bebel introduced the call for a Reich inheritance tax in the Reichstag and justified it on the grounds that it would make possible a cut in indirect taxes (Reichstag, S.B., 27 November 1893, 116). In Minister of Finance Miquel's negative reaction there already appeared the consistent argumentative structure of the opponents of the inheritance tax in Germany, with its focus on preserving family wealth undiminished. In order to generate a meaningful amount of revenue, Miquel maintained, the inheritance tax would have to be levied also on the inheritances of children and spouses. This would affect especially the middle classes, which usually suffered a loss of the testator's income in spite of the inheritance (Reichstag, S.B., 27 November 1893, 126–26). The taxation of descendants and spouses ran counter to "a natural sense of justice in Germany" (Reichstag, S.B., 15 January 1894, 660). The bill by the Social Democrats was rejected.[103]

In the budget debates between 1894 and 1905, delegates from the Left Liberals, the Center Party, and the SPD repeatedly called for the introduction of the Reich inheritance tax and in so doing exerted growing political pressure for tax reform. But it was only the budget bill for 1906 that finally contained a proposal for the introduction of a succession tax. The increasingly precarious fiscal situation of the Reich, especially after the first Naval Supplementary Bill of 1900 and the economic crisis after 1900, made the development of new tax sources imperative. The naval bill had stipulated that the costs must not lead to higher burdens on the lower social strata, and the Social Democrats were not willing to accept further hikes in consumption taxes unless they were accompanied by taxes on income and property. The Conservatives were more likely to accept the inheritance tax than the income tax. But another reason why the inheritance tax was a good candidate for boosting revenues was the fact that, with the exception of Alsace-Lorraine and the Hanse cities, the states de facto made little use of this tax source. For example, in Germany in 1901, only 0.48 marks of inheritance tax was collected per capita, while in England it was 9.17 marks and in France 4.12 marks (Schanz 1906, 196). There was thus fiscal maneuvering room in this area, though the government could use it only over the opposition from those who owned property.

To implement the inheritance tax, however, the government had to overcome not only the resistance of conservative interest groups, but also the opposition of the individual states, who were loathe to forgo the income from the inheritance tax and also saw their position of power vis-à-vis the Reich weakened by strengthening the hand of the latter in tax policy. The tax law presented in 1905, which ultimately led to the introduction of the Reich inheritance tax, eliminated the resistance of the individual states through a deal that promised to reduce the financial obligations of the states toward the Reich.[104]

The Introduction of the Reich Inheritance Tax

The draft of a finance law presented to the Reichstag in the fall of 1905 contained a total of five tax laws, including the inheritance tax law. The challenge was to close a financing gap the Tax Commission had put at 200–220 million marks (Begemann 1912, 90) in a budget of 1.1 billion marks. In the debate of 1906, the front lines ran between the Social Democrats, the liberal parties, and the Center Party on one side, who supported a Reich inheritance tax, from which the SPD wanted to generate the greatest possible share of revenues, and the conservative parties, on the other side, who favored raising consumption taxes and thereby rendering the inheritance tax superfluous.[105] The commission set a target level of 72 million marks for the revenue from the inheritance tax, a third of which was to flow to the individual states, which means that 48 million marks of the inheritance tax revenue could be given over to the Reich budget.[106]

In the deliberations that began on 6 December 1905, nearly all speakers talked about the relationship between the states and the Reich in the distribution of the inheritance tax. The reason most frequently given for rejecting the tax was that the Reich inheritance tax interfered in the tax authority of the federal states (table 5.7). However, that question was no longer a bone

TABLE 5.7

The Debate over the Introduction of the Reich Inheritance Tax, 1905–6: Reasons Offered by Speakers for Their Position

	Opposed to the Inheritance Tax	In Favor of the Inheritance Tax
Reasons inherent in the law	35.8	19.8
Tax interferes in the powers of the federal states	24.4	
Legal tradition	0.6	
De facto acceptance of the law	1.9	0.6
Reference to legal practice in other countries	5.7	17.4
Other reasons inherent in the law	3.2	1.8
Fiscal reasons	5.8	27.6
Tax revenues	5.8	27.6
Political reasons	14.7	38.8
Rejection of privileges derived from the effortless acquisition of wealth		1.2
Principle of meritocracy	2.6	3.0
Principle of equality		1.8
Tax equity	5.1	23.2
Free disposition over property	3.8	
Reference to public opinion	0.6	2.4
Other reasons related to the political order	2.6	7.2
Economic reasons	31.3	13.8
Consequences for the development of the economy	3.2	2.4
Effects on small farms	20.5	3.6
Effects on family businesses	2.6	
Equality in the distribution of wealth and land	0.6	7.8
Land fragmentation, excessive debts	4.4	
Familial reasons	12.1	0.0
Preserving wealth in the family	1.3	
Providing for family members	4.4	
Family cohesiveness	6.4	
	N = 156	N = 167

Note: Figures are percentages. The debate took place between 6 December 1905 and 19 May 1906; a total of forty speakers participated.

of contention between the states and the Reich, since the commission's proposal accommodated the interests of the states by limiting the *Matrikularbeiträge*. The controversy between the parties thus revolved chiefly around the inheritance tax rates—and thus around the revenue to be raised by the tax—and their application to the spouse and children of the testator.

The Social Democratic speakers were aiming for the highest possible inheritance tax so as to create fiscal leeway to cut the consumption taxes. The envisaged reorientation of the tax system was justified chiefly with the argument of tax equity. By contrast, the equality in the distribution of wealth and the rejection of the effortless acquisition of wealth played a much smaller role in Germany compared to the debates in the United States over the introduction of the inheritance tax in that country in 1909 and 1916.

During the first reading of the bill, August Bebel referred to the inheritance tax as the "decency tax" (*Anstandssteuer*) (Reichstag, S.B., 7 December 1906, 159), and pointed to the much higher inheritance tax revenue in England. Bebel's argumentation concerned the fair distribution of the tax burden:

> The person who owns property is the one the state must look after the most, the one it has to defend the most, and in the degree to which the costs of defending the income and the property of the haves rise, the haves should also contribute to the outlays of the state and the Reich in accordance with their property. That is their damn duty and obligation. (159–60)

Bebel called for including spouses and descendants to boost the tax revenue and to close the gap in the budget without raising the indirect consumption taxes. His justification is not only fiscal in nature; he also invoked the declining importance of the family unit, which, he maintained, was increasingly losing its social and economic function.[107] This argument had been introduced into the political debate long before by Adolph Wagner (1872), and it shows how the process of functional differentiation produced by industrialization exerted pressure in the political discourse on the existing institutions of inheritance law. It is in this sense also that one can interpret the Social Democrats' rejection of tax benefits for agricultural property and of the intended tax privileges for the church, foundations, and the high nobility (*Landesherren*, the kings and counts who ruled the individual states). The Social Democrats were aiming for greater tax equity by taxing social strata with high income and wealth more heavily and by abolishing tax privileges.

In the second reading of the bill, the Social Democrats introduced an amendment that defined the inheritance tax as an estate tax with rates between 2% and 16%.[108] The estate tax would have also taxed the inheritances of descendants and surviving spouses, which would have generated substantially higher revenue, but was criticized as a violation of the "sense of family." The Social Democrats intended to raise 290 million marks with the tax (Reichstag, S.B., 9 May 1906, 3050), which would have completely closed the funding gap in the budget while also leaving room to cut the indirect taxes. The basic position of Social Democratic tax policy becomes clearly visible once more: the goal was to replace indirect taxes with direct taxation of income and property.[109]

In justifying the motion, Eduard Bernstein first pointed to the character of inheritances as "effortless income," which legitimated the transfer of part of the estate to the state. Bernstein also discussed the question about the concentration of capital, emphasizing, first, that capital formation was no longer as dependent on individual private fortunes as it had been in the early phase of industrialization, because businesses were increasingly organized as joint-stock companies. Second, he spoke of the excessive concentration of wealth as a "social danger," arguing that inherited wealth had a degenerative effect and—with reference to the United States—that private fortunes could exert a corrupting influence (via foundations, for example) on the arts and sciences.[110]

On the conservative side, as well, the question about the distribution of the tax burden was front and center. The difference was that conservatives did not invoke a fair distribution of wealth; instead, they argued that inheritances deserved to be protected because they were family property, and that family farms were under threat.[111] An exemplary case is the argumentation by the Prussian minister of finance, Freiherr von Rheinbaben, during the first reading of the bill. He was especially opposed to including spouses and descendants, a move that ran counter to the German legal understanding of property as family property:

> Gentlemen, in German lands, in most areas, there prevails the notion that it does not accord with the sense of family, the father's obligatory care for his wife and children, if the little that he has worked to acquire during his life is afterwards in part taken away from his children. (Reichstag, S.B., 7 December 1905, 167)[112]

In spite of inheritance, the financial situation of the family generally worsened after the death of the earner because of the loss of income. Moreover, taxing descendants and spouses could not bring in a lot of revenue, because it had to remain low; it was therefore not a suitable means of boosting the income of the Reich. Another argument by the Prussian minister of finance also emphasized protection of the family: he justified the demand for lower taxation of real property on the grounds that it was much more difficult to evade taxes on landed wealth. An equal taxation of both types of property could be achieved only by taxing land at a lower rate. For if one wanted to prevent tax evasion in the case of stocks or cash, for instance, this would lead "to an all-but intolerable intrusion into the most intimate family relationships" (Reichstag, S.B., 7 December 1905, 167–68). In addition, von Rheinbaben maintained that the taxation of descendants was especially onerous for the transmission of farms. Taking over a family farm became an unattractive proposition and led to the undesirable exodus of farmers from the land. This was a link between economic and family-related arguments, one that can be found to this day in the reasons put forth by those who reject inheritance taxes. The consequences of the tax for family businesses has been one of the most widely used arguments since the 1970s.

Also family-related is the argument put forth by the Conservatives that immediate family members often contributed to the growth in the testator's property, "which is why one can speak only to a limited extent of the acquisition of genuinely foreign wealth" (Hauptverband der Deutsch-Konservativen 1909, 39). In aggregate, the Conservatives advanced not only family-related arguments against inheritance taxation, but the protection of family wealth and (agricultural) family businesses was for them the central factor legitimizing their rejection of the inheritance tax.

The reference to the consequences that inheritance taxation would have for agricultural enterprises already points to the special place that agrarian interests had in the political conflict over the inheritance tax. The German Conservative Party, the most vehement opponent of the tax, made itself the champion of these interests, which is hardly surprising considering that the party's social basis lay in the landowning Prussian nobility. Against the wishes of Finance Minister Stengel, special tax breaks for agrarian land were incorporated into the law.[113] The lobbying for this preferential treatment of agrarian interests was done by the organizations representing rural landed property, especially the Farmers' League, the Chambers of Agriculture, and the German Agriculture Council (Hoffmann 1907, xxxi; Hennicke 1929, 8ff.).

The opposition to inheritance taxation by the representatives of agricultural interests represents another striking difference from the inheritance discourse in the United States, where around the same time it was precisely the Populist movement, with its strong agrarian imprint, that spoke out in favor of a thorough redistribution of wealth. The explanation for this lies in the structural differences of agriculture in the two countries and in the divergent groups that expressed themselves in the political interest associations. Agriculture in the United States was at this time strongly characterized by family farms, which found themselves in an existential crisis in the 1890s; as a result, the populist movement had its social basis chiefly in the family farms of the Midwest and the South. By contrast, large estates were still widespread and political dominant in the eastern parts of Germany. Large landowners exerted enduring influence in the organizations representing agrarian interests, especially in the Farmers' League, which was in turn very closely linked to the German Conservative Party (Puhle 1967, 67ff. and 213ff.). They rejected the inheritance tax as a threat to family-run agricultural enterprises. However, this argument must be seen as interest-guided political rhetoric, for factually it was not correct. Because of their low value, most family farms would not have been affected by the inheritance taxation in the first place (May 1909). Yet this political strategy was possible only because the legitimizing reference point for inheritance taxation in Germany was chiefly the threat to small-scale family wealth, and not, as in the United Sates, concentrated large fortunes.

In the end, the inheritance tax that was adopted in June 1906 against the votes of most conservative delegates differed but little from the draft presented in the fall of 1905. The amendments that went much further, especially those proposed by the Social Democrats, failed to find a majority in parliament. The representatives of the Center Party took a positive stance toward inheritance taxation out of social policy considerations, but they supported the government's bill only because it did not contain any tax on spouses and children. As far as the delegates of the Center Party were concerned, the tax revenues that could be raised and a more just distribution of the tax burden spoke in favor of the inheritance tax. And they justified the exemption for the inheritance of descendants also against the background of the familial understanding of property:

> Many of my political friends who join me in the principled position that the wealth of families should be seen as holistic—a legal view that has resulted, in nearly all inheritance tax laws of the most varied states of the German Reich, in the exclusion of taxation in cases of succession to descendants—share the same view that with the same right and complete consistency, the reversion of the inheritance portion of children to the parents must remain tax exempt, because we are dealing with a principle, with the preservation of the unity of family wealth. (von Savigny, Reichstag, S.B., 10 May 1906, 3058)

For Liberals, too, the family argument assumed an important place in the rejection of the taxation of children and surviving spouses: "The sense of family means the preservation and basic pillar of our civic society," argued the National Liberal delegate Heinrich Westermann (Reichstag, S.B., 10 May 1906, 3062). Within the liberal parties, only the Left Liberals supported an expansion of the tax to children and spouses.

The passage of the law established on the Reich level in Germany an inheritance taxation that has existed ever since continuously and unchanged in its structure. The explicit model for the law was the Prussian inheritance tax law of 1873. The tax was conceived as an inheritance tax; the rates were differentiated according to the degree of kinship to the testator. The inheritance of spouses and children, an estimated 80% of inherited wealth, was exempted from the tax. The progressive nature of the tax meant that large fortunes were taxed more heavily.[114] Parallel to the inheritance tax, a gift tax was introduced with the same rates.[115]

The Failed Introduction of the Estate Tax in 1909

The actual revenue from the inheritance tax was far below the expected sum of 72 million marks. Only 26.3 million marks in inheritance taxes were raised in 1907, and 45.6 million in 1908 (Begemann 1912, 98; Statistisches Reichsamt 1930, 39).[116] At the same time, the fiscal situation of the Reich deteriorated with the economic crisis that began in 1907, and which necessitated another tax reform to boost the state's income. The government's proposals for tax reform were made public at the end of 1908, and they put the added tax income that was necessary at 500 million marks. This sum was to be generated chiefly by raising or introducing indirect taxes—especially the tobacco tax, the tax on alcoholic beverages, and the tax on gas and electricity, though a raise in inheritance taxation was also contemplated (Reichstag, S.B., Anlagen, vol. 248, p. 21), and 100 million marks was to help close the gap in the Reich budget.[117] To realize this plan, the government pursued four initiatives, the most important of which was the introduction of an estate tax. In addition, bills were introduced that put a limit on the degree of kinship in intestate law (right of the state to inherit), imposed a military tax that was levied on individuals who had not done military service, and increased the Reich's share of the inheritance tax revenue from two-thirds to three-quarters. It is worth taking a closer look at the debate over these bills, since the estate tax and the limit on intestate inheritance right invariably clashed with the familial notion of property and had to produce especially vehement disagreements.

The estate tax was to exist alongside the inheritance tax and indirectly tax also the descendants and spouses of testators, who had been exempt from the 1906 inheritance tax. Because the estate tax could be seen as the final burden imposed on the deceased, family members would receive a smaller inheritance, to be sure, but formally they were not being taxed. The explicit model for the introduction of an estate tax was England (Reichstag, S.B., Anlagen, 248:22), which was known to derive substantially higher revenues from the taxation of inheritances and was repeatedly invoked as an example by supporters of inheritance taxation. The justification for the proposed bill sought to preempt the expected political resistance to the new tax:

[The government does not fail to grasp] that such a tax amounts to a considerable sacrifice especially for the peasant farmer who does not dispose over substantial capital and, under certain circumstances, would have to take out a mortgage to pay the tax; therefore, the draft bill, as already the existing inheritance tax, makes extensive allowances for agrarian interests. However, there is no indication that such a tax, where it exists, as in England, France, Austria, Alsace-Lorraine, and the Hanse cities, has unsettled the sense of family. That it runs counter to Germanic law and German understanding, because no real succession occurs in the transmission from father to children, would be true only if the owner of the property were not allowed to dispose of the amount beyond the obligatory portion also during his lifetime or in case of his death. (22–23)

The bill called for the taxation of estates valued at more than 20,000 marks, beginning with a basic rate of 0.5%. The top rate of 3% would apply to estates valued at over one million marks (Reichstag, S.B., Anlagen, vol. 248, Anl. 997, p. 3). This put the rates far below the estate duty in England. The target was a yearly revenue stream of 84 million marks (May 1909, 230). In addition, through the military tax that was connected with the estate tax, the estate of testators who had not done any military service would be taxed at an additional 1.5%.

The introduction of the bills was followed by protracted and testy negotiations in the commission, at the center of which stood the proposed estate tax. The "vehement agitation from agrarian circles" (Begemann 1912, 110) saw in the estate tax the threat of a confiscation of wealth aimed against the agricultural sector, and it marshaled once again the well-known family-oriented arguments. The fact that the estate tax did *not* consider the kinship relationship between the testator and the heirs was regarded as a breach with the familial understanding of property in Germany, as well as a departure from the tax system. It is no accident that the opposition to the introduction of the estate tax was especially pronounced. In the parliamentary debates over the government's proposed inheritance tax bills of 1909, the German Conservative Party was once again the most vehement opponent of the bills, supported by organized agrarian interests and the conservative papers. The estate tax plans encountered "the fiercest resistance above all from conservative, Catholic, and agrarian circles . . . , who saw themselves affected in their understanding of family and basic economic interests" (Wischermann 1994, 191).

The outcome of the vote was not determined by the expected opposition stance of the Conservatives, however, but by the wavering and disapproving position of the National Liberals and the Center Party, who based themselves chiefly on the argument that the tax interfered in familial property. While most delegates of the Center Party had voted for the introduction of the inheritance tax in 1906, they no longer supported the proposed bills of 1909 that would have made also descendants and spouses subject to taxation. Within the Center Party, the voices who believed that the inheritance tax threatened the interests of agriculture and landed property and posed a danger to the family had the upper hand over representatives of voters from the working class, who were in favor the tax (Hennicke 1929, 68ff.). Only the Social Democrats and the Left Liberals voted in favor of the estate tax. Crucial for the Left Liberals, who were united in the Freisinnige Fraktionsgemeinschaft (Free-Liberal Parliamentary Group), were both social aspects of a just tax distribution and a notion of equality that included the use of tax policy to bring about a more balanced distribution of wealth. It is here that we are most likely to find, within the German spectrum of parties, a liberal-egalitarian concept of property that is characteristic of the United States. Already in 1906, the Left Liberals had opposed the tax exemption for territorial rulers as well as the preferential treatment of the church and agrarian interests (table 5.8).[118]

The arguments of the opponents of the estate tax focused on the principle of differentiation according to kinship proximity and claimed that the law would impose intolerable burdens, especially on farmers. This reveals once more the importance of the agrarian organizations, who had already achieved that in the proposed bill, the estate tax would fall much less heavily

TABLE 5.8
The Debate over the Introduction of the Estate Tax and Escheat, 1908–9:
Reasons Offered by Speakers for Their Position

	Opposed to the Estate Tax	In Favor of the Estate Tax
Reasons inherent in the law	24.3	27.6
Tax interferes with the authority of the federal states	3.1	
Legal tradition	6.3	2.5
De facto acceptance of the law	7.0	
Reference to legal practice in other countries	3.9	16.8
Other reasons inherent in the law	4.0	8.3
Fiscal reasons	7.0	13.6
Tax revenue	7.0	13.6
Political reasons	26.6	51.6
Rejection of privileges derived from the effortless acquisition of wealth		1.7
Principle of meritocracy	6.2	5.9
Tax justice	5.5	30.5
Free disposition over property	3.9	0.8
Recourse to public opinion	7.9	11.0
Other reasons related to the political order	3.1	1.7
Economic reasons	25.0	5.9
Consequences for the economy	2.4	1.7
Effects on small farms	16.3	
Effects on family businesses	3.9	
Greater equality in the distribution of wealth and land		2.5
Social consequences	2.4	1.7
Familial reasons	18.3	0.8
Providing for family members	3.5	
Preserving wealth within the family	3.1	
Family cohesion	11.7	0.8
	N = 129	N = 118

Note: Figures are percentages. The debate took place between 19 November 1908 and 5 July 1909; a total of twenty-nine speakers participated.

on agricultural land than on other kinds of assets.[119] This preferential treatment of agrarian interests led to clashes not only within the commission, but also in the scholarly literature on the estate tax law.

One example is the essay by R. E. May, "On the Struggle over the Estate Tax," published in the *Finanzarchiv* in 1909. Using financial-statistical calculations, it demonstrated that agricultural enterprises would be affected much less by the estate tax than the agrarian interest groups were claiming in the political discussion. According to May (1909, 247), agricultural landholdings would have to generate only 12% of the estate tax revenue, and the vast majority of farms would not be affected at all by the estate tax because of the exemptions.

These arguments, which questioned the factual truth of the opposition's position, especially that of the agrarian organizations, had no decisive influence on the parliamentary process. Although various parliamentarians on the finance commission criticized the reduction of the tax burden on agricultural land called for in the bill as unjustified preferential treatment for special interests, the twenty-eight-member commission rejected the bill on 2 March 1909 with only six yes votes from the Social Democrats and the Freisinnige Fraktionsgemeinschaft (Reichstag, S.B., Anlagen, vol. 256, Aktenstück 1446). The government responded with a bill that would have changed the inheritance tax law of 1906 and made the children and spouses of testators subject to taxation, at rates between 1% and 4%. On 24 June 1909, parliament rejected this bill, as well, with a vote of 194 to 186 (Reichstag, S.B., 24 June 1909, 8834).

A short time later, on 5 July 1909, the state's third bill dealing with inheritance law also failed, with a clear majority opposed. With this law, the government had tried to restrict the right of intestate inheritance to the first and second *Parantel*, and, moreover, to grant a right of prior inheritance only to grandparents (third *Parantel*). If the degree of kinship to the testator was any more distant, and if there was no will, the state would fall heir to the estate. The *Parantel* limitation was at this time established in several other legal systems (see Holthöfer 1987, 127ff.). In Germany, as well, this legal initiative could draw on a long history of legal and political reflections on this issue. Escheat had been discussed since the 1840s within the context of social policy, and the first draft of the BGB that was presented in 1890 called for limiting the right of intestate inheritance to the third *Parantel* (Holthöfer 1987, 133).[120]

The idea of a limit on *Parantel* was revived again in the tax debate of 1909. It was expected that this would raise an additional 25 million marks. The government justified the proposed law with the changing role of the state: "It is impossible to still invoke the mere fact of blood kinship on behalf of an unrestricted right of inheritance on the part of relatives at a time when the state has long since taken the place of the family unit, which offered the individual security and welfare (*Fürsorge*)" (Reichstag, S.B., Anlagen, vol. 248, Anlage 998, p. 12). This argument reveals precisely the shift in the understanding of social welfare that was already evident in the reform texts of the 1840s and later in the writings from the circle of the Historical School: the provider of welfare and assistance was no longer the family, but the state. But it was only now, against the backdrop of the state's growing need for revenue, that the potential for conflict came to the fore. Tax revenues had to be increased to finance the state's expanding functions, which in turn necessitated a stronger tax interference in private property, a move that was difficult to justify and legitimate.

In the struggles over how the burden would be distributed, the various interest groups sought to legitimize their position by selectively invoking elements from the inheritance discourse. The Social Democrats and Left Liberals invoked chiefly the value of justice. The conservative opponents of inheritance taxation, by contrast, instrumentalized the family principle. Even though structural changes had already hollowed out this principle, it retained considerable legitimizing weight within the German inheritance discourse, and it could be played as a reliable trump card by those who opposed the estate tax and escheat.

The argument about the potential destruction of the sense of family was repeatedly put forth by opponents of the bill during the parliamentary debate in the summer of 1909. The strategy was to reject the limitation on the right of inheritance as an unjustified usurpation by the state. For example, Adolph Gröber of the Center Party argued as follows: "Gentlemen, in every family property there is more or less a piece of the work of the ancestors, and it is therefore the necessary consequence that one should let the family enter into the inheritance" (Reichstag, S.B., 5 July 1909, 9073). The family and its protection in the German (Germanic) legal tradition were regarded as an absolute good, and the bill was seen as the gate by which the state would push its way into the family. The conservative camp even spoke of "inheritance theft" and "the threat of socialism."

By succeeding in making the bill appear hostile to the family, opponents of escheat put supporters on the defensive. Against the backdrop of the dominance of the familial conception of property, the arguments of both sides could—or had to—refer chiefly to the protection of the family as the normative yardstick. This moved the development of family structures and the treatment of collateral relatives within the tradition of German inheritance law into the center, while pushing questions of tax justice to the margins. Even those who favored the limitation on *Parantel* in intestate inheritance law were forced to move in the realm of family-related arguments by pointing to the declining importance of family bonds and to the limitations on the right of inheritance in the German legal tradition. One example is the SPD delegate Arthur Stadthagen:

> Some speak of the Germanic sense of family and so on, of allowing the relatives down to the last degree to inherit. Well, the old Germanic *Feldgemeinschaft* [collective ownership of agricultural land] speaks for our principle. The place of

the family economic community has been taken today by the larger community, the province, the state, and the Reich. The old Germanic family community is precisely opposed to inheritance down to the hundredth degree. (Reichstag, S.B., 5 July 1909, 9078)

With the rejection of the bill on escheat, all initiatives in the late empire to raise the revenues from the inheritance taxation by taxing the inheritance of children and spouses, and to limit the statutory inheritance right of distant collateral relatives, had failed. Yet another attempt in 1913 to introduce the limitation on *Parantel* in intestate inheritance law also failed to muster a parliamentary majority (Reichstag, S.B., Anlagen, vol. 301, Anlage No. 874). That this parliamentary blockage of the introduction of escheat was highly controversial is revealed by an appeal published on 27 December 1912 in the journal *Grenzbote* under the title "In Support of the Reich's Right to Inherit"; it was signed by seventy-five individuals from public life, primarily jurists and economists like Schmoller, Sering, Zorn, Brentano, Delbrück, Harnack, and Stammler (see Holthöfer 1987, 133).

The "propertied classes," however, succeeded in diverting the tax increases to indirect taxes. This represented a repeat of the picture of the political situation in Germany in the late empire that we have already encountered in the discussion over the *Fideikommisse*: the conservative elites are able to block reforms even against considerable and growing opposition. At the same time, sociopolitical tensions continue to increase—and are then discharged in the revolution of 1918.

Inheritance Taxation after the Revolution

The nexus between war or defense spending and inheritance taxation existed in Germany as in the United States. It is evident in the introduction of inheritance taxation in many individual states following liberation from Napoleonic occupation, and in the passage of the law on the Reich inheritance tax in connection with the naval policy at the turn of the century. At the same time, the inheritance tax was supported by reform-oriented leftists and liberal parties as a contribution to a more just tax structure—though in contrast to the United States, very little on the grounds that it contributed to a redistribution of wealth. The conservative parties opposed the tax.

As a result of the radical change in Germany's political structure following the November Revolution, the subsequent development of the tax in the postwar period was very different from that in the United States. After World War I, there was in fact no political pressure to abolish the tax. Instead, the takeover of the government by the Social Democrats, the Center Party, and the Liberals, combined with the dramatic financial situation in Germany, led to an increase in inheritance taxation.[121] The coalition between the Social Democrats and the left-liberal German Democratic Party that governed after the revolution brought together the two most vocal advocates of an increased taxation of inheritances during the empire. The Center Party, the third member of the coalition, had moved noticeably to the left before the revolution under the leadership of Matthias Erzberger and was now also in favor of expanding inheritance taxation.

Erzberger's finance and tax reform that was passed in September 1919 focused strongly on the taxation of inheritances to improve state revenues. An increase in the succession tax and the introduction of an estate tax were intended to achieve additional income of 470 million marks for the Reich budget (van der Borght 1920, 196). To achieve this, the rates of the existing inheritance tax were raised, and the inheritances of children and spouses were made subject to taxation. They were assessed in the first tax bracket, with rates fixed between 4% and 35%. If distant relatives or individuals not related to the testator were the heirs, the progressive rate rose to as high as 70% for bequests over 1 million marks. In addition to the inclusion of children and spouses in the succession tax and the heightened progressivity, additional income was to be generated by taking into consideration the wealth that the heir already possessed. If the heir had assets of more than 100,000 marks, the tax rose to a top rate of 90% (Troll, Gebel, and Jülicher 1999, 6). Moreover, the National Assembly in 1919 passed an estate tax, which had been rejected by parliament in 1909.[122] All told, as a result of the new laws, inheritances were taxed on average at an estimated 15%; assuming that a succession takes place every thirty years, this amounted to a burden of 0.5% on property per year (van der Borght 1920, 197–98).

The leftist parties did not think that the increase in the rates and the introduction of the estate tax in 1919 went far enough. They demanded that the estate tax should constitute the central tax burden on property by bringing in at least twice as much in tax revenue. In the debate in the summer of 1919, the fiscal and economic situation was clearly in the foreground. The Social Democratic delegate Wilhelm Keil, for example, called for raising the total amount derived from inheritance taxation to between 1.5 and 2 billion marks. To that end, the inheritance tax for distant relatives was to be increased to 100% (Reichstag, S.B., 20 August 1919, 2652). Behind these radical demands stood clearly the altered balance of political power of the period of the revolution. Among the leftist parties, inheritance taxation was now no longer merely an instrument for bringing about greater tax equity; instead, inheritance law was also seen, on the basis of Hilferding's tax theory, at least as an indirect instrument for socializing property (Hennicke 1929, 129; Merk 1934, 44). This radicalization is reflected in the distribution of arguments used to justify the increase in inheritance taxation in the debate in 1919 (table 5.9). Thus, the arguments over tax equity declined by two-thirds compared to the debate of 1908–9 (table 5.8), while arguments aimed at the equality in the distribution of property were invoked nearly five times more frequently. Added to this were the arguments aimed at the socialization of property through inheritance taxation. Here a comparison with the United States is once again of interest. Unlike in the United States,

TABLE 5.9

The Debate in 1919 over the Introduction of the Estate Tax and the Increase in the Succession Tax: Reasons Offered by Speakers for Their Position

	Opposed to the Proposed Bills	In Favor of the Proposed Bills
Reasons inherent in the law	2.6	3.2
De facto acceptance of the law	2.6	
Reference to legal practice in other countries		3.2
Fiscal reasons	2.6	21.0
Tax revenues	2.6	21.0
Political reasons	26.3	51.6
Effects on social morals	15.8	11.3
Tax equity	2.6	9.7
Free disposal over property	5.3	
State's fiscal crisis caused by the war justifies the laws		29.0
Other reasons related to the political order	2.6	1.6
Economic reasons	61.2	24.2
Consequences for the economy	42.1	3.2
Effects on small farms	7.9	1.6
Breakup of businesses	5.3	
Greater equality in the distribution of wealth and land		11.3
Socialization of productive capital	5.3	6.5
Social consequences	2.6	1.6
Familial reasons	5.2	0.0
Providing for family members	2.6	
Family cohesion	2.6	
	N = 38	N = 62

Note: Figures are percentages. The debate took place on 8 and 9 July 1919 and on 20 August 1919; a total of fourteen speakers participated.

the goal of the redistribution that the leftist parties in Germany pursued during the revolutionary phase by means of inheritance law policy was not a more balanced distribution of private wealth, but the *socialization of property*. Among the leftist and left-liberal parties, privileges derived from the "effortless" acquisition of wealth played no special role; instead, the issue was private property as such.

The radical ideas were found only in the parties of the Left, but the entire party spectrum in the revolutionary period was more open to inheritance taxation. The Conservatives, refounded as the German National People's Party (Deutschnationale Volkspartei) no longer rejected the taxation of spouses and children on principle, but they voted against the commission's draft because it called for an excessively high taxation (Posadowsky-Wehner, Reichstag, S.B., 9 July 1919, 1430). The delegate Oskar Maretzky from the National Liberal German People's Party justified his opposition with family-oriented and economic arguments:

> Not only will this law undermine thrift, the sense of family, the work aimed at caring for the family, . . . but it will go far beyond this and put an end to the productive drive that led us to economic greatness before the war. (Reichstag, S.B., 20 August 1919, 2556)

The overwhelmingly economic argumentation by opponents of the inheritance tax constituted a clear change in the structure of the discourse compared to the prewar period. And the economic arguments also no longer referred chiefly to the effects of the laws on family businesses, but to the economic system as a whole. The high inheritance taxation, it was argued, could lead to a socialization of private property. More than half of the arguments of the opponents of the proposed laws invoked their economic consequences. Fears about a change in the economic system were not unjustified, as is evident from the contribution to the debate by the Center Party, which had a strong workers' wing. Not only did the Center Party under Erzberger vote for the taxation of spouses, which it had still opposed in 1909, but like the Social Democrats it also welcomed inheritance taxation as a first step toward socialization (Erzberger, Reichstag, S.B., 8 July 1919, 1376ff.). The left-liberal parties supported the government's proposals as well, though they had already been open to inheritance taxation before the war. They saw in it, first, the realization of the social goal of balancing out differences in wealth and creating more equality of opportunity, and, second, a necessary measure to deal with the fiscal crisis (Reichstag, S.B., 20 August 1919, 2652).[123]

Further reform was enacted as early as 1922, and it took back many of the far-reaching measures of the 1919 laws. For example, the estate tax was repealed (though a wealth tax was introduced the same year), and the progressivity of the inheritance tax was noticeably scaled back. How strongly the familial notion of property reasserted itself in this reform is evident not only from the repeal of the estate tax, but also from the *structure* of the changes in the progressivity of the inheritance tax: the top rate in the first tax bracket was cut in half, while it was left at 70% for the most distant relatives and for nonrelated heirs. Moreover, spouses were once again exempted from the tax, with a few exceptions (Troll, Gebel, and Jülicher 1999, 7).[124] Crucial to these changes was the Center Party, whose opposition had already blocked the introduction of escheat in 1919.

The massive increase in the taxation of inheritances at the beginning of the Weimar Republic can be easily explained with the changed constellation of political power and the fiscal crisis. The propertied could now be taxed more heavily to finance the state's expenses. But the political upheaval following the November Revolution was able to influence the legislation on inheritance taxation in such a profound way for only a short period of time. The reforms were undone only a few years later. This meant the return of the inheritance tax policy that had long prevailed in Germany—with lower tax progressivity and lower tax rates or tax exemption for descendants and spouses. The law of 1919 was merely a brief interruption in this general pattern.

The Final Structure of the Inheritance Tax

With the reform of 1922, the institutionalization of the inheritance tax in Germany was largely complete. The wording of large sections of the tax law of 1922 is largely congruent with the German inheritance tax law in force to this day (Troll, Gebel, and Jülicher 1999, 7). All subsequent reforms dispense with the estate tax, and the succession of relatives has remained unrestricted. The additional tax burden on propertied heirs was abolished in 1923 (Wischermann 1994, 180). At most the taxation of spouses, which was reintroduced in the finance reform of 1925 for marriages without offspring, can be seen as a systemic change. This introduced a motive of population policy into inheritance taxation, though it had existed once before in the Prussian succession tax between 1822 and 1873.[125] After 1951, a spouse was generally subject to the inheritance tax and was privileged only through special exemptions.[126] In that regard, a—at least moderate—taxation of spouses was enshrined over the long term, and the same is true for the children of the testator.

To this day, changes to inheritance tax law since the reforms of the early 1920s have dealt substantially with tax rates and exemptions, questions of valuation, and the placement of categories of kinship in specific tax brackets. The simultaneous influence of exemptions, tax rates, tax bracket, and valuation of assets makes it difficult to assess the long-term development of the burden on wealth from inheritance taxation in Germany. On the whole, though, it can be said that the inheritances especially of close family members were consistently taxed at a very moderate rate in Germany. Exceptions were only the period immediately after the revolution (1919–22) and the years from 1946 to 1948, when the inheritance tax was regulated by the law of the Allied Control Council. Otherwise, the top rates in the first tax

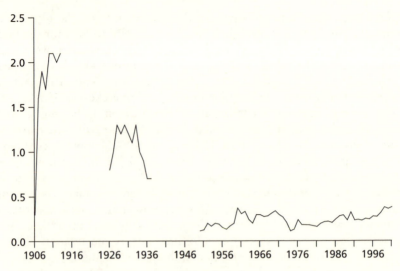

Figure 5.3 Inheritance tax as share of total tax revenues in Germany, 1906–2001 (in %)

Source: Statistisches Bundesamt.

bracket have been moving since 1925 within a range of 15% to 38%, the entry rates between 2% and 7%.[127] This is a marked difference from the tax treatment of estates in the United States, with its top rates of up to 77%. Of interest for a comparison with the United States is the Control Council Law of 1946, which was enacted by the victorious powers, all of whom taxed inheritances much more strongly than the German Reich had. In the Control Council Law there was only one tax bracket with a progressivity that ranged from 14% to 60%. The tax had to be paid also by spouses and children of the testator for their inheritances (Troll, Gebel, and Jülicher 1999, 9). These were the highest inheritance tax rates ever applied in Germany to close family members.

Inheritance Tax Debates in the Federal Republic

In the Federal Republic, three phases can be distinguished in the taxation of inheritance after 1949, which show at least a shift in emphasis: a first phase of low inheritance taxation between the 1950s and 1973, at the rates of 1925; a second phase from 1974 in which large fortunes were taxed more heavily; a third phase from 1996, when the progressivity of the rates was scaled back again by the conservative-liberal government. Inheritance taxation in the Federal Republic continued to reflect the family-oriented conception of property. In fact, the latter was even enshrined in the Basic Law, whose guarantee of property as well as special protection for marriage and family establish direct legal limits on increases in inheritance taxation. The differentiation between the property of the living and the transfer of property *mortis causa* consistently found in American legal discourse did not establish itself in Germany. Thus, even confiscatory inheritance taxes would be constitutionally permissible in the United States—but not in Germany.

It is hardly possible to speak of a political battle over inheritance taxation in the Federal Republic after 1945. The topic did not lead to any important parliamentary debates, and it played hardly any role in the scholarly literature.[128] It was only in the foundational period of the Federal Republic and once again in the 1960s that the question of how to deal with inheritance preoccupied liberal social theory and economics at least at the margins.

In the 1940s, two neo- (or ordo-) liberal economists, Alexander Rüstow (1949) and Wilhelm Röpke (1948), placed themselves within the liberal tradition skeptical of inheritance, a tradition that resolved the contradiction between inheritance and equality of opportunity through radical restrictions on the private right of inheritance.[129] Rüstow saw a developing tension between, on the one hand, a laissez-faire capitalism denounced as plutocratic, and the spreading Communist polities, on the other. The two social forms were mirror images when it came to their freedom-threatening consequences. Already in the 1930, Rüstow had begun to develop the theory of neoliberalism. Unlike what today's use of the term might suggest, it did not imply the demand for the most unrestricted market possible, but containment of the dysfunctionality caused by the market with the help of state intervention. The promise of justice of the market economy was to be fulfilled through state intervention against tendencies toward concentration that were inherent in the free market. Rüstow speaks of a liberal interventionism, "which interjects itself not as impeding intervention contrary to the laws of the market, but as concordant adjustment intervention in line with the effective direction of market laws in order to ensure that they operate as smoothly as possible" (Rüstow 1949, 35). The creation of material justice in the starting position was to implement real meritocratic competition. "The inherited inequality in starting position is the critical element of institutional structure by which feudalism lives on in the market economy and turns it into plutocracy, the rule of wealth" (1949, 55). Rüstow proposed a reform of inheritance law that included a strongly progressive inheritance tax as well as an egalitarian program of redistributing the productive wealth in every generation.[130] These proposals are close to the egalitarian liberal tradition in the United States, but they had no effect on the development of inheritance taxation in Germany.

Picking up on this neoliberal critique of inheritances and the debate over concentration processes in the economy that was carried on in the 1960s in economics (Jostock and Ander 1960), Klaus Peter Kisker (1964) examined the question of using inheritance taxation as an instrument for the redistribution of property. His finding: the existing inheritance taxation had no effect of any sort on the distribution of property. Kisker drew up a proposal for a taxation that could have redistributory effects. His normative point of reference was the goals of a just distribution of wealth (1964, 14) and equality of opportunity (1964, 189) in society. His proposal had no influence.

Parliamentary debates on inheritance taxation that are worth mentioning occurred in connection with the legal reforms in 1973 and 1996.[131] In the reform of inheritance tax law in 1973, questions concerning the valuation of real property and tax relief for small and medium-sized inheritances were front and center. Parliament agreed to raise the exemptions while simultaneously raising the top tax rates, which meant that larger inheritances were taxed more heavily.[132] The possible increase in the inheritance tax had drawn attacks from the opposition in the election campaign of 1972.[133] The heavier taxation of large fortunes is in line with the Social Democratic positions during the empire and the Weimar Republic. The new tax rates produced a doubling of tax revenues by 1976 (Troll, Gebel, and Jülicher 1999, 2). Because of the relief for smaller inheritances through an increase in the exemption, the reform led to a heavier burden on large inheritances. This development was the exact reverse of what was happening in the United States, where around the same time, though starting from a much higher tax level, a scaling back of the progressivity of the tax was discussed and then implemented beginning in 1976.

Looking at the debate in the German Bundestag in 1973, however, one finds once again that redistributive goals played no role (table 5.10). Rather, Social Democratic speakers put forth chiefly arguments of social justice and spoke of a measured increase in the burden on large fortunes. When it came to justifying the change in the law, arguments about boosting the state's revenue—which had been so important in the Weimar Republic—no longer played any role. Moreover, it is striking that family-oriented arguments were now put forth by the SPD to defend the proposed bill. They used it to justify an increase in the exemption. What is surprising is that the opposition parties of the Christian Democratic Union/Christian Social Union largely supported the reform. Although their speakers called for another increase in the exemption and rejected the higher valuation of real estate, they approved of the higher top tax rates, which seemed to the delegate Zeitel, for example, "still acceptable for reasons of distributive justice" (Bundestag, S.B., 6 December 1973, 4117). The argumentation is close to that of the Center Party at the beginning of the twentieth century. Family-oriented arguments appear with the CDU/CSU largely in connection with family businesses. Little of the trenchancy that marked the clashes over this topic during the empire and the Weimar Republic was left by 1973.

This is also true of the last debate to date on the topic of inheritance taxation in the German Bundestag. In a decision of 22 June 1995, the Federal Constitutional Court had declared that the preferential treatment for real property was unconstitutional and had called upon the federal government to make statutory changes in the taxation of property and inheritances. On the basis of the guaranteed right of inheritance, the right of relatives to inherit, and the special protection of marriage and the family

TABLE 5.10
The Debate over Reform of the Succession Tax in 1973: Reasons Offered by
Speakers for Their Position on Whether to Raise Tax Progressivity and
the Exemption

	Opposed to the Proposed Bill	In Favor of the Proposed Bill
Reasons inherent in the law	27.3	3.2
Simplification of the tax system		3.2
Inflation necessitates reform	9.1	
Constitutionality of the law	18.2	
Fiscal reasons	0.0	3.2
Tax revenues		3.2
Political reasons	9.1	54.8
Rejection of privileges derived from the effortless acquisition of wealth		16.1
Tax equity	9.1	38.7
Economic reasons	54.6	22.6
Consequences for the economy	9.1	6.5
Effects on small farms	27.3	12.9
Effects on family businesses	9.1	
Equality in the distribution of wealth		3.2
Social consequences	9.1	
Familial reasons	9.1	16.2
Providing for family members		13.0
Preserving wealth within the family	9.1	3.2
	$N = 11$	$N = 31$

Note: Figures are percentages. The debate took place on 22 February 1973 and 6 December 1973; a total of nine speakers participated.

that are contained in the Basic Law (e.g., Löhle 2001), the Constitutional Court also demanded that in the case of smaller estates, inheritances for family members should be exempt. In addition, the inheritance tax should be limited in accordance with the so-called principle of half-division (*Halbteilungsgrundsatz*) in such a way that the individual liable for the tax is left with the substantially larger portion of the estate. Finally, the government should ensure that the survival of medium-sized enterprises is not threatened by the inheritance taxation (Troll, Gebel, and, Jülicher 1999, 19). The decision by the Federal Constitutional Court defines the limits to the taxation of inheritances in a noticeably more restrictive manner than courts have done in the United States, for example. The characteristic familial conception of property is a factor also in the decision by the highest court—for it was only the inheritances of those in the first tax bracket that had to remain largely exempt from the tax.

The changes enacted in 1996 switched the valuation of real estate from the probate valuation method (*Einheitswertverfahren*) to the net income value method; although this led to a higher valuation, it was usually still below the market value. Since this higher valuation of real property would have increased the inheritance tax burden, the law boosted the exemptions for immediate family members. Today, spouses are entitled to an exemption of 307,000 euros, children up to 205,000 euros, grandchildren still up to 51,200 euros. The tax brackets were reduced to three and the tax rates were cut. In the first tax bracket, rates are currently between 7% and 30% (previously: 3%–35%), in the most unfavorable third bracket, they are between 17% and 50% (previously: 20%–70%). This scaling back of the progressivity of the tax provided relief above all to large inheritances.[134] Smaller inheritances are taxed at a lower rate because of the higher exemptions, though once the exemption threshold is exceeded, the tax burden on smaller amounts is higher than before. In addition, the favorable tax treatment for the transmission of business assets was further expanded.

The reform of 1996 reversed the trend of 1974 toward the higher taxation of large inheritances. However, the tax relief that was sought by the government in 1996 was not to be achieved by reducing the overall revenue from the inheritance tax. In fact, because of the higher valuation of real estate, it was expected that the revenue would actually increase. Since the wealth tax has not been assessed since 1997, the intention was only to reduce the total tax revenue from the two taxes on wealth.

The parliamentary debate on the revision of the inheritance tax law was shaped by the dictates of the Federal Constitutional Court, which provided the chief reference point for the speakers of all parties. Once again, the fiscal consequences of the reform played only a subordinate role. Both the tax relief for small family fortunes and the protection of family businesses were in principle uncontroversial, though the concrete legal form they would take was contested. In this debate, as well, we see the continuity of family-related argumentation, which was put forth this time chiefly within the context of the economic consequences of the inheritance tax (table 5.11). The speakers of the coalition parties regularly employed economic arguments about promoting economic growth and securing jobs. The Social Democratic demand to raise the progressivity of the tax was put forth by Ottmar Schreiner, though it played only a subordinate role (Bundestag, S.B., 9 September 1995, 5912).[135] The great importance of the equality arguments in the debate is due to the contributions by the PDS

TABLE 5.11
The Debate over Reform of the Succession Tax 1995–96: Reasons Offered by
Speakers for Their Position on Raising Tax Progressivity and Exemptions

	In Favor of Reducing Inheritance Tax	Opposed to Reducing Inheritance Tax
Reasons inherent in the law	22.9	33.4
Constitutionality of the law	20.8	25.0
De facto acceptance of the law		2.8
Other reasons inherent in the law	2.1	5.6
Fiscal reasons	6.3	5.6
Tax revenues	6.3	5.6
Political reasons	18.8	41.7
Abolition of privileges		5.6
Principle of meritocracy		11.1
Principle of equality		13.9
Tax equity	16.7	11.1
Free disposition over property	2.1	
Economic reasons	46.0	19.6
Consequences for the economy	8.4	2.8
Effects on small farms	2.1	2.8
Effects on family businesses	29.2	2.8
Equality in the distribution of wealth		5.6
Preservation of jobs/social consequences	6.3	5.6
Familial reasons	6.3	0.0
Preserving wealth within the family	2.1	
Family cohesion	4.2	
	N = 48	N = 36

Note: Figures are percentages. The debate took place between 5 September 1995 and 12 December 1996; a total of sixteen speakers participated.

(Party of Democratic Socialism). For example, the connection between the principle of meritocracy and inheritance was brought up by the PDS speaker Barbara Höll, who invoked Walter Eucken (Bundestag, S.B., 14 June 1996, 9916). Gerda Hasselfeldt of the CSU responded with the argument that property had a performance-enhancing function (9916). The goal of the PDS, which introduced a bill of its own that called for the introduction of an estate tax, as well, was to use the inheritance tax also as an instrument for the redistribution of wealth (Bundestag, S.B., 14 June 1996, 12057). The Greens demanded that the additional revenue from the tax, which they estimated at 2 billion marks, be spent on providing a basic level of social protection, which placed them—consciously or unconsciously—in the nineteenth-century tradition of a direct link between inheritance taxation and social policy (Bundestag, S.B., 12 December 1996, 13415).

In the midnineties, the discourse on inheritance taxation in Germany was in line with the developments in the United States.[136] There, too, the exemption of small to medium-sized family fortunes and the protection of medium-sized businesses assumed a key role in the debate, a development that had already begun back in the 1970s. This focus in the inheritance tax debate is difficult to explain on substantive grounds. After all, both in the United States and in Germany there have long existed special regulations for the transmission of business assets, which largely remove the burden of the inheritance tax, especially from smaller businesses (Busch 2002, 64ff.). Inheritance taxes effectively paid by businesses amount to no more than 300 million euros or a little more than 10% of the overall revenue from inheritance taxation (Lehmann and Treptow 2006). Nevertheless, further tax relief for businesses stands at the center of another reform of inheritance tax law currently under way in Germany. What this focus tends to reflect is the high legitimacy that measures aimed at freeing entrepreneurial initiative from what is alleged to be excessive governmental interference have enjoyed in the discourse over economic policy during the last twenty-five years.

In contrast to the United States, the reduction in inheritance taxation in Germany hardly led to any larger clashes over legal policy, and to date the topic has not been rediscovered by political discourse. Seen against the backdrop of my interpretation of the fundamental thrust of the inheritance taxation discourse in the United States and in Germany, that comes as no surprise. The goal of creating greater equality of opportunity by redistributing wealth plays virtually no role in Germany's political culture, where the protection of family wealth is in the foreground. The "unearned" acquisition of wealth is hardly subjected to a critical assessment in the public political arena. Since the 1920s, inheritances in Germany have played merely a secondary role for the goal of achieving social justice through tax policy. The latter focused on other contested areas, especially the income tax and indirect taxes. This has remained true to this day, even though nearly two-thirds of Germans believe that the inheritance tax should be raised (Infratest Dimap 2002). Still, impulses for reform can be mobilized at most via the argument of tax equity. Resolutions by Bündnis 90 Die Grünen and the SPD's party congress in Bochum in 2003 could be indications that the topic of inheritance taxation may yet become more important in the political debates against the backdrop of the existing fiscal problems and the transformation of the welfare state. However, the resistance to interference in "family wealth" that is grounded in the familial conception of property *and* the minor importance of the tax in total tax revenue provide no reason to expect that inheritance taxes will play a *significant* role in reform processes in the future.

5.3. DESTRUCTION OF NATIONAL WEALTH? THE PROGRESSIVE INHERITANCE TAX IN FRANCE

In France, too, the period from the late nineteenth century into the 1930s was the key phase in the political conflict over inheritance taxation. During this time, the succession tax—already introduced in the late eighteenth century—first underwent a thorough reform. Subsequently, the topic was repeatedly the subject of parliamentary and public debates until the 1930s. It was only afterwards that the controversies lost their political importance. Although this development appears at first glance to parallel the political clashes over the inheritance tax in Germany and the United States, I will show in this section that the controversies over the inheritance tax in France on the whole were less important and display a different internal structure than in the other two countries. Those differences include, apart from the longer continuity of inheritance taxation in France by the central government, a reduced importance of motives of redistribution and social justice in the inheritance tax discourse, a critical assessment of progressive taxation against the background of a special interpretation of the principle of equality, and the linkage between inheritance taxation and questions of demography.

Inheritance Taxes in the Nineteenth Century

When the inheritance tax in France was finally restructured in 1901 and thus adapted to the needs of a modern tax system after years of parliamentary debate, a succession tax on a national level had already existed for more than a century. The centralized organization of the French tax system and the taxation that had existed since the Revolution help to explain why the fundamental legitimacy of inheritance taxation was much less a topic of political controversy than in Germany and the United States. The conflict between individual states and the federal government that was characteristic for Germany and the United States played no role in France.

The Revolution already saw passage of the inheritance tax law that was modified but remained structurally unchanged until the end of the nineteenth century, and important elements of which have remained valid to this day. The law of inheritance taxation that was drafted by Talleyrand and then approved by the National Assembly on 5 and 19 December 1790 as part of the *Droits d'enregistrement*[137] replaced the *centième denier* introduced in 1703 by an edict of Louis XIV, which had imposed a payment of 1% on all property transfers, though transfers to direct ascendants and descendants were exempt (Stourm 1912, 248; Dupeyron 1913, 74ff.; Christmann 1939, 66ff.). The law of 1790 developed this levy in the direction of a differentiated succession tax by including also movable property and making the tax rate dependent on the degree of kinship with the testator.[138] What this meant was that in France, all heirs and all types of property were subject to inheritance taxation as early as 1790.

The inheritance tax law was reissued a few years later, on 22 Frimaire VII (12 December 1798), with altered tax rates but without any changes to the structure of the tax. This law remained in force throughout the entire nineteenth century. However, various amendments between 1816 and 1850 raised the tax rates and differentiated the kinship classes further.[139] These changes were amendments, not fundamental reforms. Of structural significance is only the bill of 18 March 1850, which abolished the different taxation of real estate and movable property. This change took account of the changed importance of the two types of property in the advancing process of industrialization in the nineteenth century. Movable property was an increasingly relevant part of private wealth, and its lower rate of taxation privileged one class of property owners.

However, there were three provisions of the law that remained controversial. In the course of the nineteenth century, they repeatedly became the subject of parliamentary clashes and eventually led to the reform of 1901: (1) the nondeductibility of outstanding mortgages from the value of real estate used for the purpose of taxation; (2) the basis used in calculating the taxation of lifetime interest rights; (3) the introduction of tax progressivity. Of particular importance was the question of the progressive nature of the tax, because here the interests of property owners clashed with the state's interest in generating tax revenues.[140] That is also why the central focus of the present section will be on the question of tax progressivity. However, since this discussion took place within the context of the other two issues until passage of the inheritance tax law in 1901, I will begin by taking a brief look at them.

1. According to the law of 1798, debts and other encumbrances on real estate could not be deducted in calculating its value for the purpose of taxation (Schanz 1901, 134ff.). The reason is that the tax was categorized as a transaction tax, which, unlike property taxes, is levied on the gross value. However, it also reveals that French inheritance taxation developed out of feudal dues (Christmann 1939, 69). Throughout the nineteenth century this regulation was repeatedly denounced as a fiscal injustice with negative economic consequences. Various parliamentary initiatives beginning in the middle of the nineteenth century sought to change it, without success.[141] The reform attempts led to nothing, because a substantial decline in revenues was predicted and because deductibility would create new possibilities for tax evasion (Dupeyron 1913, 81ff.; West 1908 [1893], 24). The result of the

nondeductibility of debts is that real estate carrying a high debt load is proportionally taxed much higher, even though it is much less able to absorb it. This can have economically dysfunctional consequences, in two respects: first, there is an incentive not to burden real capital with debts, which deprives the economic process of investment capital and slows economic growth. Second, to the extent that mortgages were taken out to cover shortfalls in income during an economic crisis, the relatively higher tax burden increased the danger of excessive debt. In the late nineteenth century, French agriculture found itself in a sustained crisis, which led to loss of income, debts on landed property, and a wave of selling with substantial loss of value for real estate (Haupt 1989, 207ff.). This crisis explains why at this time more and more bills to reform the deductibility of debts with respect to the inheritance tax were introduced in parliament.[142]

2. A second peculiarity of nineteenth-century French inheritance tax law was the excessive taxation of lifetime interests (*usufruit*). According to the law of 1798, the heir of the property had to pay the full inheritance tax and the beneficiary of the lifetime interest had to pay half that amount again (Shultz 1926, 35). This meant that the bequest in the form of a lifetime interest was taxed at 1.5 times the usual inheritance tax rate. Only the law of 1901 introduced a provision that abolished this added tax burden and divided the tax between the owner and the beneficiary.[143]

3. These two peculiarities of French inheritance tax law are important for the questions concerning the level of the tax and tax progressivity because they were linked together. The deductibility of debts and the reduction of tax rates on inheritance in the form of a lifetime interest were widely recognized demands. However, in the absence of other changes, meeting these demands would have led to significant losses in tax revenue. The 1894 bill on the reform of inheritance law estimated that these losses would amount to 81 million francs, which was equal to more than 40% of the revenue from the inheritance tax.[144] Since the inheritance tax accounted for about 5% of total tax revenue in France, budget politicians could not simply forgo this income stream. That is why the proposals put forth in parliament since 1849 for a switch to the net principle in assessing the value of real estate came with suggestions on how the expected shortfall in revenue could be made up: in 1849 through the introduction of progressive tax rates, in 1871 through the additional levy of an income tax, and in 1889 and in the bill that was eventually adopted in 1894, progressive taxation once again.

Inheritance Taxes in Political Discourse

French inheritance tax policy had a different character than its German and American counterparts. First clues come from the classification of the inheritance tax as a transaction tax and the "framing" of proposals for a progressive structure of the tax within the context of the reform of the deductibility of debts and the calculation of the tax for lifetime interest. The inheritance tax that had existed since 1790 was a long-established source of revenue alongside the land tax, the door and window tax (a kind of income tax), the trade tax, indirect taxes, and other transaction taxes. The proportional inheritance tax was seen as a "conventional" tax source and was not linked to any ideas pertaining to the policy of wealth distribution. Politically, it was hardly contested.

In France, there was a broad political consensus not to use tax policy as a way of redistributing wealth. All parties except for the Socialists signed on to this consensus during the Third Republic. But at least until 1924, the Socialists as a governing party, as I will discuss in greater detail below, were always bound into a coalition with moderate republican parties. Moreover, their policies had to give much greater consideration to the interests of the rural population than the SPD, for example, had to in Germany.

I intend to show that during the key phase of the inheritance tax reform between 1895 and 1935, as well, the goals of redistributing property and using inherited wealth as a source of revenue for the state were only of secondary importance to a policy in France that was aimed at social justice. Finance politicians justified increases and the progressive structure of the inheritance tax with the necessity for greater tax revenues to cover the budget, and normatively they invoked chiefly the principle of a taxation in accordance with the means (facultés) of the citizens. The inheritance tax was seen as a tax that should be given a structure that was neutral in terms of redistribution policy, and that derived its legitimacy from the state's efforts to protect property.[145] The progressive taxation that was introduced in 1901, and had very high rates between 1917 and 1926 (which is explained by the state's fiscal crisis), derived its legitimation from the principle of an equal tax burden on the citizens.

Reforms of inheritance taxation ran into considerable opposition as soon as the suspicion was aroused that they amounted to a substantial interference in private property in the interest of redistribution. This suspicion attached especially to progressive taxation. Although motives of social justice and redistribution were articulated by the Socialist Party, for example, they played a comparatively subordinate role in the discursive field. The egalitarian tradition so important in the United States, which saw the effortless acquisition of property and dynastic wealth as morally problematic, was of very little importance in France. Likewise, the connection made in Germany between inheritance taxation and social justice played a rather minor role in France. To the extent that political goals *were* linked with the inheritance tax in France beyond the generating of revenue, they were largely in the field of population policy and not social policy or the promotion of equal opportunity.

This might come as a surprise, because France in the early nineteenth century saw what was perhaps the most influential radical critique of the effortless acquisition of wealth. But the early socialism of the students of Saint-Simon, who called for the abolition of private property, played no more a part in the inheritance tax debates in the late nineteenth and early twentieth centuries than did the socio-reformist tradition of Catholicism or the criticism of the dynastic transmission of property articulated by the solidarism movement.

Invoking the teachings of Saint-Simon and Bentham's utilitarianism, Prosper Enfantin and Saint-Armand Bazard demanded the abolition of the private right of inheritance (Bouglé and Halévy 1924 [1829]). In so doing they went beyond Bentham, who had suggested expanding escheat so as to limit bequests to collateral relatives. Bazard and Enfantin, however, maintained that only the distribution of property by a central agency would place it into the hands of the most capable members of society. Inheritances should thus first pass to the state, which would then distribute them based on who was best able to use the assets (means of production) productively. This radical proposal was soon criticized within the Left itself. Enfantin revised his demand in a later work (1970 [1832]) by calling only for the abolition of bequests to collateral relatives and an inheritance tax of 20% for descendants and ascendants. Charles Fourier, in a letter in 1831, called the demand of the Saint-Simonists that the right to inherit be abolished an outrage (see Erreygers 1997, 28), and Proudhon (1995 [1860]), who became a representative of the National Assembly in the revolution of 1848 and whose work influenced some of the French Socialists at least until World War I, categorically rejected the abolition of inheritance rights on the basis of his critical attitude toward the state. He saw the inheritance tax as the continuation of feudal structures, with the state merely taking the place of the feudal power. According to Proudhon, inheritance taxes were unfair to the family, were based on the presumption that the generations were independent of each other, and were economically harmful. Proudhon's verdict against inheritance taxation aimed at a redistribution of wealth was categorical:

> The abolition of inheritance in favor of the state would be tantamount to a governmental communism, the worst of all tyrannies, a kind of pantheism, in which only an impersonal will to glorify an abstract idea governed, fed, sustained, and exploited individuals, but in which there was no society beyond the family, no family beyond individuals. (Proudhon 1995 [1860], 150)[146]

Between the Saint-Simonists, with their early demand for the abolition of the right of inheritance, and Proudhon, who strictly rejected serious interference in inheritance law in favor of the state, we find in France in the mid-nineteenth century reform-oriented writers who did want to retain the principle of private property, but who at the same time wanted later inheritance law to create more balanced starting conditions for all members of society. One example is the economist Eugéne Buret, who published *De la misère des classes laborieuses* (On the Misery of the Working Class) in 1840—a book that Friedrich Engels a short time later referenced in his own work on the condition of the working class in England—in which he proposed a reform of inheritance law. Buret's point of departure was the positive law character of inheritance law and the utilitarian premise that the law of property should be based on the principle of the greatest social utility. Buret (1840, 386) explicitly rejected the radical reform proposals of the Saint-Simonists, proposing instead that the state should share in all inheritances at a rate equal to the statutory portion of a child. He justified this proposal by pointing out that the individual was socially embedded within the family and society:

> A human being is not merely a child of his family, he is also a child of the society in whose midst he was born, child of his nation, which has paid with its blood for the soil that every property owner cultivates, whence it guarantees to him the use of the same and offers all the advantages of civilization which are not the work of him who profits from them, but of the entire nation. (1840, 388–89)

Buret calculated that as a co-heir, the state would acquire 200,000 hectares of land every year, which could be distributed to 50,000 families, who could live independently from it. Evident in this proposal is the fear of a proletarianization of the French population, and, conversely, the normative grounding of a model of society based on the broad distribution of property. That Buret was already writing during the transition phase from an agrarian to an industrial society is reflected in his expectation that the state's portion of the inheritance would contain, alongside land transfers, also co-ownership rights to industrial enterprises. Those he intended to distribute in the form of stocks to the workers, who would thus receive another means of livelihood in addition to their wages (1840, 390), one that would free them at least in part from proletarian dependency. Redistribution through inheritance taxation was to be done for the purpose of *property creation*, and not, as in the German discourse, to provide social welfare or to improve education.

A similar position, linked with a much more pronounced skepticism toward the state, was developed by the philosopher François Huet. In 1853 he published, under the title *La Règne Social du Christianisme* (The Social Reign of Christianity), a theory of property in which he combined private property rights with the commandment of fraternity. Huet, who was a professor in Ghent until the late 1840s and then moved to Paris (Cunliffe 1997, 707; Cunliffe and Erreygers 2000), can be assigned to the liberal and social tradition of French Catholicism, which was pushed onto the defensive after the takeover of power by Napoleon III. A campaign against his allegedly subversive views forced him to resign his professorship. In his theory of property, he was concerned with distributive justice between the generations within a social order based on private property. He rejected social inequality based on dynastic wealth, because it led to hereditary wage dependency and thus threatened individual liberty. Huet, too, was thus following the normative ideal of the individual and independent occupation of farmers or artisans. In the same vein he rejected the socialization of property as envisaged by Marx or Louis Blanc, because it would lead to dependency on the state and military despotism. Huet defended private property and, in a limited form, also the right of parents to pass inheritances to their children. However, inherited property itself must not be handed down further. Upon the death of the heir it should pass to the state, which would use it every year to pay "start-up capital" to all members of society who were between fourteen and twenty-five years old (Huet 1853, 274). This would achieve a greater equality of starting conditions. The social inequality that arises in society as a result of the different use of this start-up capital does not pose a problem in Huet's eyes, since it was the product of the free decisions of individuals. This proposal resembles the ideas developed a little earlier in the United States by Thomas Skidmore and Orestes Brownson. Private property was to be linked to the principle of equality of opportunity and individual economic independence, whereby the connection between the Christian ethic of fraternity—expressed in the idea of redistribution—and of individual freedom that is anchored in the right of property was central to Huet's "liberal socialism" (Cunliffe 1997).[147] In the Third Republic, as well, social Catholicism rejected the rule of the free market and sought to strengthen the cohesion of society and point to a way out of the instability of proletarian life by promoting small-scale ownership (Caron 1991, 432).

The positions that were critical of inheritances found an indirect parliamentary expression during the Revolution of 1848. In July 1848, the finance minister of the transitional government, Michel Goudchaux, introduced in parliament a bill for the progressive taxation of inheritance. He grounded it in the character of inheritances as the effortless acquisition of wealth and in the guarantee of property by the state, which justified a progressive taxation:

> Progressive taxation seems to adapt itself naturally to the subject of inheritance: the goods acquired in this way are the not the fruits of the labor and intelligence of the person who harvests them; he owes them to the accident of birth, indeed, at times also to the whims of private affection. It is only just if the heir or recipient of the bequest, to whom society grants the use of this blessing of fate, pays a fee to the state, which should be higher, the higher the inheritance or the generous gift. (Bill of 3 July 1848, Assemblée Nationale, c. r., 322)

This bill, which envisaged maximum tax rates for inheritances over one million francs ranging from 6% for the testator's children to 20% for nonrelated heirs,[148] had no chance of becoming law against the rapidly recovering conservative forces (Fénolhac 1919, 43). The conservative member submitting the report, de Parieu, spoke out vehemently against the tax in his parliamentary report in September 1848, arguing that it violated the principle of proportionality.[149] Here we see the subsequently influential argumentation put forth by opponents of the progressive inheritance tax, who believed that progressivity violated the principle of tax equity. If the tax is the price for the protection of property by the state, does progressive taxation not amount to punishment for the formation of capital? The backdrop for the debates over progressive inheritance taxation was the constitutional question over the exact meaning of the vague formulation in the Declaration of the Rights of Man and Citizen of 1789 that taxation should be based on the means (*facultés*) of the citizens.[150] Property owners insisted on the principle of proportionality and saw in the principle of progressive taxation a revolution that threatened the social order. Progressivity would lead to the emancipation of the proletariat, feared de Parieu, and thus violate the neutrality of the state in the pursuit of the common good (see Schnerb 1973, 136).

A debate took place in parliament in January and February 1849, and the government's bill was eventually rejected. The members of parliament who defended the bill put forth as justification chiefly the expected additional tax revenue of 30 million francs (Assemblée Nationale, c. r., 3 July 1848, 321). Redistribution arguments and those relating to social justice, the principle of equality, and the rejection of the effortless acquisition of wealth played a comparatively minor role (table 5.12).

The content analysis of the debate of 1848 reveals a specific discursive structure among opponents of the tax. Much more so than was the case in the United States or Germany, they argued on the basis of the principle of the free disposition over property. Moreover, they challenged the fairness of progressive taxation. In France—as in the Germany, but unlike the United States—family-oriented arguments were marshaled against the progressive inheritance tax. Striking is the high ratio of economic arguments among the opponents of the succession tax. In Germany and the United States, economic arguments acquired a similar weight only after World War I and in the New Deal, respectively. In those countries, economic arguments became important only when the debate revolved around the introduction of extremely high inheritance tax rates. By contrast, the threat that the proposed, low progressive rates were already seen to pose to the French economy became the preeminent argument of the opposing camp. Central reference points for the opponents of inheritance tax in the French discourse were the preservation of the "nation's wealth"—the totality of property in private hands—and the status of the *propriétaires*.

The Inheritance Tax in the Third Republic

After this first attempt to introduce a progressive inheritance tax in France, it took nearly half a century before the subject returned as a topic of parliamentary debate. In the political debate on inheritance taxation that was carried out more intensely in the last decade of the nineteenth century, the reform plans of the early Socialists, of Buret, and of Huet were hardly mentioned any more. There was a much greater—though predominantly oppositional—recourse to the writings of John Stuart Mill that were critical of inheritances.

The 1890s saw the rise of the social reform movement of Solidarism, which was given its most influential theoretical formulation in the 1896 book

TABLE 5.12

The Debate over Progressive Inheritance Taxation in the National Assembly in 1849: Reasons Offered by Speakers for Their Position on the Introduction of Progressive Inheritance Taxation and the Equal Treatment of Movable Property in the Taxation of Inheritance

	Against the Progressive Inheritance Tax	In Favor of the Progressive Inheritance Tax
Reasons inherent in the law	8.2	8.6
Inheritance law is positive law		8.6
De facto acceptance of the law	2.7	
Other reasons inherent in the law	5.5	
Fiscal reasons	5.5	42.9
Tax revenues		42.9
Reducing the tax revenue	5.5	
Political reasons	32.7	37.3
Rejection of privileges derived from the effortless acquisition of wealth	1.4	8.6
Principle of equality		2.9
Tax equity	9.5	25.8
Free disposition over property	12.2	
Consequences for democracy	9.6	
Economic reasons	44.5	11.4
Consequences for economic development	6.6	11.4
Effects on small farms	20.3	
Land fragmentation, excessive debt	14.9	
Familial reasons	9.5	0.0
Providing for family members	1.4	
Preserving wealth within the family	8.1	
	N = 74	N = 35

Note: Figures are percentages. The debate took place between 15 January and 1 February 1849; a total of fourteen speakers participated.

Solidarité from the pen of the radical Republican Léon Bourgeois, parts of which connected to the earlier social reform movements. This politically important movement, which would probably be characterized as communitarian today, advocated stronger state regulation on the basis of the liberal economic system. Unregulated economic liberalism, it was said, led to the oppression of the poor by the rich and thus endangered individual freedom. Human beings are always part of the social community to which they owe their rights, which is why there was a positive obligation to give something back to society. The argument was directed against an unrestricted right of property and the principle of state noninterference in liberal economic theory. The "debts" of the individual towards the community imposed the obligation to pay dues to society in accordance with an individual's ability to do so. The demand was for the establishment of social welfare institutions, a guarantee of a minimum subsistence, free education, and also interventions in inheritance law (Bourgeois 1902 [1896], 155). Specifically, Bourgeois called for the introduction of an income tax to finance the state reforms, though, revealingly enough, not for a higher inheritance tax.[151] One reason for this could be that the taxation of inheritances was at best ambivalent within the context of the French discourse about the meaning of the concept of solidarity. Inheritance within the family itself was seen as the expression of an act of solidarity (Baudrillart 1857; 1883, 258), which would be threatened by interference in the right of private inheritance. For Baudrillart, the irony of Socialist demands for limits on the right of inheritance lay precisely in the fact that they sought to achieve a society based on solidarity by destroying the solidarity that was "naturally" present within the family.

A higher inheritance tax was demanded around the same time by Émile Durkheim (1992 [1957]; 1984 [1893]). His social theory showed a strong convergence with that of Solidarism, though without sharing the latter's normativism. Durkheim emphasized the social embeddedness of the individual in modern societies, and on this basis he advocated the idea of a "liberal corporatism" (Gülich 1989). For Durkheim, the institution of inheritance established social stratification, which allowed the conclusion of unfair contracts and thus endangered the cohesion of society. Durkheim called for a reform of inheritance law that would begin by abolishing the inheritance rights of collateral relatives:

> Such a limitation to the right of disposal is in no way an attack on the individual concept of property—on the contrary. For individual property is property that begins and ends with the individual. (1992 [1957], 216–17)

Here Durkheim was linking up with the self-conception of the Third Republic as a "Republic of Talents."[152] The intent behind his suggested reform of inheritance law was to abolish privileges linked to status and replace them with meritocratic principles. A person's property should strictly mirror what he or she had accomplished for society. The moral consciousness of society would thus move increasingly in the direction of moral individualism.

Durkheim predicted that this moral development would also render inheritance to children ever more meaningless. Even restrictions on testamentary freedom would then encounter hardly any resistance (1992 [1957], 217). Like Huet, Durkheim was an enemy of state-owned property. The inheritance should not pass to the state, but to intermediary institutions, namely, the occupational groups, which alone were able to create the necessary bonds of solidarity in modern society. The reform was aimed at strengthening civil society, and—like Le Play earlier—it was critical of the strong fixation of French society on the state.

In a later work, in the second foreword to *The Division of Labor in Society* (1984 [1893], Durkheim took a more critical position on the limitation of private inheritance rights. For one, he maintained that even the creation of complete equality of opportunity was no guarantee for the establishment of fair contractual relationships. Only the definition of the rights and obligations of the actors of an occupational field, toward each other and toward the community, could create justice in social relationships. Moreover, Durkheim now believed that a significant reform of inheritance law would endanger the institution of the family (1984 [1893], lv). Here he was revealing his sociological skepticism toward egalitarian liberalism: in weighing the repercussions of a radical reform of inheritance law, it was not enough to give normative consideration to enhancing equality of opportunity; the consequences for the intergenerational bonds of solidarity within families had to be taken into account as well.

We thus find in nineteenth-century France a line of critical engagement with the private right of inheritance that stretches from the Saint-Simonists to Durkheim. However, this tradition played hardly any role in the political reforms in the political controversies of inheritance law in the late nineteenth and early twentieth centuries. Early on, influential leftist theoreticians were critical of or even opposed to the use of inheritance taxation as an instrument of redistribution. The social reformers of Catholicism were interested in a broad basis of property, but not in the goal of a general redistribution of wealth. While the Solidarism movement sought greater social justice, inheritance law reform also played a subordinate role, and a redistribution of wealth was explicitly rejected. The liberal economists that were dominant in France followed Adam Smith in consistently rejecting the progressive inheritance tax. Nearly all works on economics around the turn of the century took a critical view of inheritance taxation. Already in the middle of the nineteenth century, liberal economists defended the private right of inheritance above all with the argument that it was the precondition for economic incentive. Without that kind of incentive, land would not be brought under cultivation, factories would not be built, and savings would not be accumulated (Puynode 1859, 21; Steiner 2004, 12ff.). The sort of influential advocacy for inheritance taxation that came in the United States from institutional economics and in Germany from representatives of the Historical School did not exist in France.[153]

The Inheritance Tax within the Context of Economic History and the
History of Mentalities in France

How can one explain the minor importance of inheritance taxation as an instrument of social reform within the political debates in France? Three interconnected factors come into play: (1) the property structures in France in the late nineteenth century, with a stronger emphasis on agricultural property; (2) the valuation of capital and of real estate as central sources for the wealth of the French nation; and (3) the consequences of the relationship between state and society for tax policy.

1. Landed property continued to play an eminent role within French society of the late nineteenth century. Because industrialization proceeded more slowly in France, a larger share of the population was engaged in agriculture than was the case in Germany, for example. In 1906, 43.6% of those gainfully employed were farmers; in Germany it was only around a third (Haupt 1989, 225; Wehler 1995b, 685). Only in the 1930s did the number of industrial workers in France surpass those employed in agriculture. Moreover, the pattern of industrialization in France was characterized more heavily by small industries in the rural areas, which meant that urbanization moved at a slower pace compared to Germany. Even industrial workers themselves frequently still owned land they worked and that offered a fallback during times of industrial crisis. The result of these structural peculiarities taken together was that the rural population was also for the parties of the Left more important in the political process in France than in Germany, where the Social Democratic leadership defined its policy clearly in line with the needs of the urban industrial proletariat. The social basis that German (and British) Social Democracy found among workers in large-scale industrial enterprises was smaller in France. French farmers "clung to the land which their ancestors had wrested from the feudal lords in heavy struggles during the great Revolution and most of them were therefore conservative in attitude" (Bloch 1972, 191). Moreover, France did not have the close link between the Socialist Party and the union movement that was characteristic of Germany and especially England. In their political programs, the unions and the Socialist Party in France had been making concessions to the small farmers since the 1890s by accepting private property and merely recommending to the farmers that they organize their farms into cooperatives. By contrast, German Social Democrats called for the direct transition from large-scaled landownership to collectivized soil. The greater importance of small-scale agricultural holdings in France and the French pattern of industrialization provide clues why the taxation of inheritances was not an important goal in France, even for the parties of the Left. The nobility as well as the agrarian and small-town middle-class population exerted critical influence in the parliament of the Third Republic, though that influence steadily declined (Bloch 1972, 257; Haupt 1989, 212). This constellation lacked the political

and structural basis for making radical inheritance tax reform into a serious issue.

2. This explanation related to the structure of the economy is joined by one from the history of mentalities having to do with the role of private wealth in the self-conception of French society. In the nineteenth-century society of notables, landed property was an important marker of social prestige. Land was for the nobility and the bourgeoisie a preferred investment vehicle for capital during the nineteenth century, because it offered security against industrial crises, and because the lifestyle of the *propriétaire* was held in high regard (Tulard 1989, 230ff.). A preindustrial economic mentality was able to persist in the society of notables (Haupt 1989, 173), a mentality that propped up the dominant agrarian character of French society and elevated the way of life of the *propriétaire* into a prevailing normative ideal also among the bourgeoisie. Especially prior to 1870, some entrepreneurs thus gave up their factories after they had acquired a sufficient amount of wealth in order to live without working. Before 1914, France had half a million people of working age who had no occupation but lived off the income of their capital. This social class of rentiers persisted until 1945 (Haupt 1989, 209). To be sure, because of the structural change in the composition of property, the growing importance of movable wealth, and the agrarian crisis, landed property played a decreasing role. However, the social type of the property owner, with partial imitation of the lifestyles of the aristocracy, remained attractive in French society far into the twentieth century—down to the lower middle class. Landed property functioned "as a life buoy, as it were, of French society, which gave it stability and lift in times of crisis. Property, family connections, and power not only established the preeminent status of the notables, but eventually also asserted themselves as social models beyond this class, shaping the behaviors and desires of white-collar employees, farmers, lawyers, and renters" (Haupt 1989, 198). Within this normative context, which can be understood as the product of the relationships between bourgeoisie and aristocracy after the French Revolution,[154] the French bourgeoisie gave rise to a dominant entrepreneurial type. His "basic motivation of business was social rather than economic: to insure the continuity of the family and its social predominance rather than to produce the greatest amount of goods" (Hoffmann 1960, 4).

Although the bourgeoisie supported the transformation processes of industrialization, it did so merely within the parameters of a strongly hierarchical model of society and the recognition of the outstanding importance of the family. In the cultural self-conception of a social order that was based on property and rather conservative, the inheritance of wealth was highly significant, because it both symbolized, and allowed individuals to attain, long-term stability. This explanation from the history of mentalities makes clear why the demand for the redistribution of wealth through inheritance taxation encountered vehement opposition in France. We are dealing here not only with the interests of farmers and large landowners, but also with the normative self-perception of the central social strata of French society, who thought of themselves as *propriétaires*, a perception that began to dissolve only in the twentieth century. In the debates over inheritance taxation, this self-conception manifested itself in the repeated assertion of how important savings were to the French, and the fear that this could be undermined by inheritance taxation. The accumulated private property (*fortune nationale*) was the sacrosanct foundation of French society, the basis of its stability. Around 1900 we repeatedly hear the proud assertion that France was the capital-richest country in Europe. Progressive inheritance taxation, so went the typical argument of André Dupeyron (1913, 229), would destroy this foundation, because "by devaluing the land and driving savings increasingly toward more productive and more readily concealed movable assets, it accelerates the exodus from the land, thus creating the danger of turning the French into a people without roots and without ties to a specific place, eventually extinguishing the love of nation." The unrestricted transfer of wealth was seen as the guarantor of the stability of French society. This contrasts with the self-conception of both American and German society. In the United States, the dynastic transmission of wealth came under especially critical scrutiny. In Germany, the forces of the landowning nobility were tied up in defensive battles over the preservation of a social model oriented toward preindustrial social structures, but they were unable to provide a normative model of society that would have attracted the consensus of a broad spectrum of political actors.

3. Questions of taxation were historically freighted in France. Many of the local social controversies in the ancien régime revolved around the often brutal manner in which agents of the state collected taxes. The Revolution of 1789 was triggered in the final analysis by a fiscal crisis, at the center of which were the tax privileges of the nobility and the clergy. Against this backdrop, the question of what kind of taxation was appropriate to the means (*facultés*) of the citizens and was respectful of equality played an important role in all political systems after 1789. So important were taxation principles to the Revolution that a provision was even incorporated as Article 13 in the Declaration of the Rights of Man and Citizen in 1789: "A common contribution is essential for the maintenance of the public forces and for the cost of administration. This should be equitably distributed among all the citizens in proportion to their means."

Their great political importance in the history of the ancien régime and the Revolution turned matters of taxation into an exceedingly sensitive area of French politics down into the twentieth century. The orientation toward the principle of equality was predominant, which in regard to tax questions was interpreted largely as a proportionality of the tax burden. The normatively enshrined neutrality of the state vis-à-vis the private interests of the citizens delegitimized the pursuit of redistributive goals by way of tax policy. Although during the Revolution the Jacobins and the movement of the *Egaux*, for example, called for creating greater social equality through progressive taxation and contributing to tax equity by reducing indirect taxes, these views did not prevail politically over the long run (Ardant 1965, 71ff.).[155] While the "parties of the movement" in the nineteenth century appropriated progressive taxation as one of their issues, such a tax system was not institutionalized until the twentieth century. To this day, as I will discuss below, French inheritance taxation contains strong proportional elements. The hostile attitude toward progressive taxes becomes clear in the failure to introduce inheritance taxation during the Revolution of 1848 and then again at the end of the nineteenth century, when Republican forces and the Socialists were gaining strength (Ardant 1965, 77ff.). Moreover, unlike in the United States, when it came to achieving social justice through taxation, even the reforming forces did not believe that this goal depended specifically on inheritance taxation, but more generally on a reduction of inequalities in income and wealth. In this regard, the French situation is comparable to the German one.

The vehemence with which demands for a progressive tax system in France were rejected even at the end of the nineteenth century can be seen from the fact that at this time it was not only conservative politicians who still derived proportional taxes from the principle of equality asserted in 1789 and depicted progressive taxes as a violation of this principle. It was repeatedly argued that the central principle of the Revolution, legal equality, demanded that citizens participate in tax levies in exact proportion to their income and wealth and that there be no privileges for or discrimination against individual groups. Taxes derived their legitimacy from the services that the state provided its citizens in return. In this context, inheritance taxation can be justified as payments for the costs incurred by the state in protecting property. However, a special imposition on wealth acquired without effort would constitute an injustice against the principle of equality, which would violate the strict neutrality of the state vis-à-vis particular interests.[156] This shows how the legacy of tax conflicts during the ancien régime still influenced tax debates during the Third Republic. Expressed in terms of tax theory, the French inheritance tax discourse was oriented toward the concept of horizontal equality, while vertical equality was regarded with skepticism. This was an expression of the autonomy of the French state with respect to the interest groups of civil society, that the state accommodated the interests of the wealthy when it came to inheritance taxation. The irony of this constellation is especially evident in comparison with the United States, where the state never possessed this autonomy vis-à-vis particular interests, and where private means were used to influence tax laws (Steinmo 1993), while at the same time a taxation of estates was institutionalized that affected precisely the great fortunes with a steep progressivity.

Part of the explanation for why it proved so difficult to modernize the French tax system in the Third Republic is also the fear at the time over an excessive expansion of the state's power (Hoffmann 1960, 15). Although the question of whether or not the state was too powerful was contested among the political groups, it is clear that both the use of the principle of equality to justify limiting taxation to proportional taxes and the tightly constrained justification for tax levies created a discursive context that made the introduction of progressive inheritance taxes in France politically difficult.

When the political demands for a reform of inheritance tax law grew louder in the late nineteenth century—largely because of the unresolved issue of the deductibility of debts in calculating the inheritance tax—and the introduction of a progressive taxation was in the offing, strong opposition arose. The latter is documented in numerous, chiefly legal and economic, publications from that period. Unlike in Germany and the United States, the majority of those who came to their position from the social sciences rejected progressive inheritance taxation (Bonnet 1879; Déhon 1898; Michaux 1885; Noël 1884, 1902). Neither the early Socialist position nor Durkheim's social-liberal view played a role in the discourse. In terms of party politics, progressive taxation was called for by liberal political groupings and by the Socialists, though without any mention of redistributive goals. For the Socialists, as well, although they demanded that larger inheritances be taxed more heavily and smaller inheritances avoid the tax through exemptions, their concerns related largely to fiscal policy, as is evident from the speech of the Socialist delegate Jean Bon in the estate tax debate of 1917 in the National Assembly:

> The goal of the tax system is only—and let me repeat this once more—the tax system; it is sufficient unto itself. A good tax system is one that demands for national and social necessities from the citizens precisely the share that corresponds to their wealth. (Bon, Annales de la Chambre des Députés, Débats Parlementaires, Session ordinaire de 1917, 12 December 1917, 1:3538)

The Inheritance Tax Reform of 1901

How did inheritance taxation in France develop against this social, political, and normative backdrop? I have already pointed out that the most contested question of the political debate of the 1890s was the introduction of tax progressivity. Bills providing for a progressive taxation of inheritances were introduced in 1888 by the Finance Committee—though no debate on it took place in parliament—as well as in 1890 and 1891 by various parliamentarians and in 1894 by the government, which eventually led to the reform of 1901 (Fénolhac 1919, 52–53). The justification for the bill of 1891 makes clear that progressive taxation was to be introduced largely because of the difficult fiscal situation, not out of the desire to redistribute private wealth (see Coutot 1925, 19). In the Finance Committee, the representative submitting the report, Dupuy-Dutemps, justified the principle of progressivity on the grounds that it would improve tax revenues on the basis of means (*facultés*):

> Transforming the proportional tax into a progressive tax is justified, for two reasons, namely justice and utility. Our tax system is dominated by the principle

that the tax to be paid by every citizen corresponds precisely to his share of the expenses of the state, and that each citizen must pay his share of the expenses of the state in accordance with the size of his wealth. (Assemblée Nationale, c. r., Commission Report, 10 November 1894, 415)

Although the report of the commission quoted John Stuart Mill at length, it explicitly rejected his justification for restricting the inheritance of wealth, which was aimed at equality of opportunity. Finance Minister Raymond Poincaré defended the right of inheritance as part of the right to private property, and the only legitimate grounds for taxing inheritances was "payment for services rendered to the heirs by the state" (415). Poincaré rejected progressive taxation in principle because it went against the proportionality of the tax burden, though he made an exception for the inheritance tax. With inheritances, the obtained benefits of wealth were disproportionately higher, the greater the inheritance. Most members of the commission shared that opinion. The progressivity of the inheritance tax "is also an expression of a justice system through which the maxim of the French Revolution is adequately implemented, namely: 'Every citizen owes the state a share that corresponds with this wealth,' because the tax capacity is not measured proportionally to income—or, more generally—to wealth, but rises progressively with it" (416).

Finance Minister Poincaré supported the inheritance tax bill largely because of the additional revenue it would generate. Since the late 1880s, the Radicals and the Socialists had been steadily gaining ground in elections and could now begin to turn their ideas on taxes into policies. Léon Bourgeois (the author of the aforementioned book *Solidarité*), the Socialist leader Jaurès, and moderate Republicans like Joseph Caillaux advocated the introduction of a tax system based on the principle of progressivity. Thus, in France, as well, reform movements provided the backdrop for the debate over the restructuring of the French tax system between 1895 and 1917 (Callet 1962). The policy was shaped largely by the moderate forces of reform of the Radicals and the radical Socialists, to whom the taxation of property presented at the same time a dilemma, because it stood in conflict with a right to private property that was regarded as absolute (Ardant 1965, 82).

More strongly than in Germany, the political spectrum in France, including the forces of reform, emphasized that private property was worthy of protection and rejected a right of the state to interfere with property to effect a redistribution of wealth. Tax-based interventions in private property had to justify themselves against the principle of proportional taxation. Even the defenders of progressive taxation argued that this tax principle allowed for taxation based on the means of the individual. They did not argue with goals of redistribution. The content analysis of the debate of 1895 makes clear that neither the rejection of unearned wealth through inheritances nor reference to the principle of equality was put forth as an argument with any frequency (table 5.13). The strict separation between self-earned property

TABLE 5.13

The Debate over Progressive Inheritance Taxation in the National Assembly, 1895:
Reasons Offered by Speakers for Their Position

	Opposed to the Progressive Inheritance Tax	In Favor of the Progressive Inheritance Tax
Reasons inherent in the law	18.2	15.0
Standardization of the tax system	2.8	3.0
Legal tradition		3.0
De facto acceptance of the law	9.3	1.5
Reference to the legal practice in other countries	5.0	7.5
Other reasons inherent in the law	2.1	
Fiscal reasons	12.3	12.1
Tax revenues	2.2	12.1
Reducing tax revenues	10.1	
Political reasons	25.5	43.8
Rejection of privileges derived from the effortless acquisition of wealth		1.5
Principle of equality	1.4	3.0
Tax equity	12.9	22.7
Free disposition over property	1.4	
Recourse to public opinion	2.2	
Consequences for democracy	7.8	16.6
Economic reasons	43.7	28.7
Consequences for economic development	10.0	7.5
Effects on small farms	23.0	19.7
Capital flight	7.2	
Equality in the distribution of wealth	0.7	1.5
Social consequences	2.8	
Familial reasons	0.7	0.0
Providing for family members	0.7	
	N = 139	N = 66

Note: Figures are percentages. The debate took place between 9 and 22 November 1895;
a total of twenty-four speakers participated.

and the effortless acquisition of wealth, which was so characteristic of the United States and which explains why inheritance taxation could become a centerpiece of the political controversies during the Progressive Era, was largely absent in the French debate. Instead, both advocates and opponents of the tax advanced economic and fiscal arguments. In addition, questions of tax equity played an important role for advocates. They saw in the tax— that is, the greater burden on wealthy citizens—a factor that provided stability for the democratic political system. Opponents invoked reasons inherent to the law and asserted the lack of legal acceptance and the arbitrary nature of the tax. Family-oriented arguments barely made an appearance. Once again, what is noticeable about the French debate compared to the debates in Germany (1905–6) and in the United States (1916) is the much greater emphasis on economic arguments. The tax had to be acceptable especially with respect to its economic consequences. The bill introduced in the Chamber of Deputies in the fall of 1894 was passed in 1895, but the Senate dragged out its approval until 1898, because it rejected the progressive taxation of inheritances. It took another three years to iron out the differences between the two legislative bodies. The new regulations came into force only with the Tax Law of 1901 (West 1908 [1893], 24). The law implemented three important reforms: it introduced a system of progressive inheritance taxation, allowed for the deductibility of debts from the assets that formed the basis for calculating the tax, and established a new way of calculating the value of lifetime interests.

According to the new law of 1901, the tax rates for children varied between 1% and 5%, for spouses between 3.75% and 9%, and for nonrelated heirs (tax bracket 7) between 15% and 20.5% (Graeff 1925, 33).[157] What was retained, therefore, was the higher tax for spouses than for children introduced since the Revolution, an important difference from German inheritance taxation. In Germany, spouses and children were initially exempt from the inheritance tax, and to this day spouses enjoy tax privileges through especially high exemptions vis-à-vis the children. Another element that stands out in France compared to Germany is the higher taxation of collateral relatives. For siblings, who paid rates between 4% and 11% in Germany according to the law of 1906, the French law set rates of 10% to 13.5%.[158] At the same time, the French tax is at this time far less progressive than the German and discriminates less—by way of tax rates—on the basis of the blood relationship between the heirs and the testator. Another peculiarity of the French inheritance tax law of 1901 was that no exemptions were granted for smaller inheritances. The principle of equality was enforced without exceptions also against smaller bequests.[159]

Tax Progressivity as a Threat to National Wealth

The law of 1901 made France the first of the three countries under examination to have a progressive inheritance tax. Progressivity made it possible to adjust the inheritance tax revenue with much greater flexibility to budgetary needs through changes to the tax rates. Two developments are then crucial to the further course of inheritance taxation in France down to the 1930s: first, the drastic increase in inheritance taxation between 1910 and 1926, when inheritances were taxed at up to 80%; second, the close link between inheritance tax and population policy.

In the public debate over the inheritance tax, the opponents were clearly in the preponderance. Already during the deliberations over the law of 1901, those opposed to progressive taxation had warned that the principle of progressivity would be used after its introduction for constant tax hikes. Shortly after passage of the law, the very influential conservative economist and financial journalist Paul Leroy-Beaulieu, who stood in the neoclassical tradition, wrote in *L'économiste français* (2 March 1901, 262): "The progressive tax is a deregulated, unconstrained tax, which means that in a certain respect it amounts sooner or later to confiscation."

The subsequent development reveals just how justified the conservatives were in their fears about further tax increases. As early as 1902, Louis-Lucien Klotz, a representative of the Radicals and the future finance minister, proposed a drastic hike in the tax rates for especially large estates. Inheritances over 100 million francs should be taxed at up to 7.5% for direct descendants and up to 55% for nonrelated heirs. This proposal failed to garner a majority (Shultz 1926, 38). However, additional levels of progressivity were introduced in 1902, as a result of which inheritances over one million francs were taxed more heavily.[160] Rising state expenditures, especially for military purposes, brought growing pressure for further tax hikes. France had no income tax—it was introduced in 1914 (Callet 1962)—and the Socialists, whose influence was growing, demanded that inherited property carry a heavier burden with tax increases. Against this backdrop, Finance Minister Poincaré proposed, during the debate over the 1907 budget, raising the taxes on inheritances over 10,000 francs. Moreover, additional levels of progressivity should be set for inheritances over 50 million francs. Revenue was to rise by 60 million francs, that is, about 20%. The proposal was rejected by the Budget Commission (West 1908 [1893], 30–31).

By 1910, the budget situation had become so dire that the inheritance tax was finally increased. Under the new law, direct descendants were taxed at up to 6.5% and nonrelated heirs at up to 29% (Al-Omar 1959, 78–79). In addition, further kinship classes were differentiated in the direct line (Dupeyron 1913, 102).

This increase in tax rates met with decided opposition from economists. In the revised edition of his book on finance, published in 1912, the renowned economist René Stourm spoke out against the "disastrous march of tax progression" (1912, 250), which was destroying the national wealth:

> The higher rates, which would represent a systematic exploitation of the
> national wealth, can no longer be defended, for they would destroy the entire

object of the tax. The exceptional revenues during the initial period would be followed, year after year, by unproductivity and ruin. Only the enemies of property and of the social order could desire such a regime, which is unanimously rejected by both theory and practice. (238)

The progressive tax would negatively influence savings behavior as the basis of capital formation, which is why Stourm maintained that the most one could justify was a proportional taxation of inheritances equal to their yield of one year. Stourm rejected the theories of Mill and Saint-Simon in favor of limiting the transfer of wealth *mortis causa*. He argued that inheritances were justified precisely under utilitarian criteria, for they stimulated acquisitiveness and savings and contributed to the preservation of the family. Edgar Allix (1927, 674) sounded the same note in his standard work on finance: "The state devours the wealth of the land by using every year part of the national wealth to cover ongoing expenses." The preservation of property was clearly in the forefront also in André Dupeyron's work on inheritance taxation that was published in 1913. The inheritance tax rates, he maintained, would lead to the destruction of the national wealth, and Dupeyron even saw the tax as posing a threat that capital would be completely socialized (1913, 225). France's wealth depended on the savings behavior of its citizens. The inheritance tax, however, would prevent savings and interfere with the activities of agriculture and businesses. Dupeyron argued—paraphrasing Adam Smith—that the state would spend the money it took in largely on unproductive goals; hence the inheritance tax constituted "a threat to public wealth" (227). In Dupeyron, moreover, there are overtones of a clear opposition to mobile capital and urbanization, which would be further promoted by the especially high burden on landed property (where the possibilities of tax evasion were much less) and lead to the uprooting of the population. This motive of the threat of deracination had already played an important role in the mid–nineteenth century in the discussion in France over inheritance taxation and testamentary freedom. In contrast to Germany, the emphasis is less on the function of inheritances in providing support and maintenance within the family, and more on the continuity of the family that transcends the individual. This motive was already evident in Le Play in the model of the *famille souche*, though it can also be interpreted as an expression of the French bourgeoisie's previously mentioned orientation toward aristocratic ways of life.

The second argument against progressive inheritance taxation advanced by critics concerned the protection of the family. In Stourm's eyes, the tax destroyed families: "If the wealth were dissolved in every generation, the sense of permanence, which is essential to the preservation of families, would also be destroyed" (1912, 235). For Dupeyron, the tax is a "calamitous assault on the family, which, as the true social unit and elementary organism, must be saved with all legitimate means in order to put a stop to the disorganization of society" (1913, 231). Gabriel Fénolhac, who was writing after the war and took on the whole a more positive attitude toward the inheritance tax, argued that differentiating the tax according to the degree of kinship was useful "for preserving the cohesion of the family and of good social order" (1919, 51).

The emphasis on the protection of the national wealth (*fortune nationale*) is a specifically French orientation in the discourse about inheritance taxation; family-focused arguments show a distinct similarity to the German discourse. However, unlike in Germany, the family was defended not as an absolute principle, but much more in a context that balanced the interests of the family and the state, and in relationship to the actual structures of the family. This suggests a more modern notion of the family. When escheat was moved from the twelfth to the sixth degree in 1917 in an effort to generate additional revenue from the inheritance tax, this was accepted also by the opponents of progressive inheritance taxation: family structures, it was acknowledged, had developed into less comprehensive kinship systems, and the law had to reflect this (Coutot 1925, 28). Inheritance taxation had its basis "in the development of the family, which for many years has been increasingly limited to parents and children" (Canal 1921, 16). However, the Socialists demand in 1917 that escheat be extended to the third degree was rejected, because this would harm the family as the basis of social organization. The conception of the family that is focused more strongly on the nuclear unit is also evident in the breakdown of revenues from the inheritance tax. In the 1930s, a third of the revenue was collected from the taxation of collateral relatives (Christmann 1939, 81). In Germany, in contrast to France, all proposals to introduce a right of the state to inherit were consistently rebuffed as contrary to the family spirit. Here the conception of the family, which took its cues from the Germanic legal notion of the clan, encompassed even the most distant relatives; any restriction was seen as a breach of this principle. This difference between the two countries cannot be explained on the basis of the actual differences in family structures in France and Germany in the early twentieth century (see Kaelble 1991, 41ff.), because the heavier taxation of collateral relatives in the French system has existed since the late eighteenth century and is found to this day in the tax rates, even though the family structures have grown to be very similar.

The Goal of Inheritance Tax Policy with Respect to Population Policy

Another specifically French characteristic of the inheritance tax discourse in the first third of the twentieth century was the connection between tax policy and population policy. As I already pointed out in the second chapter in connection with the reasons for unlimited testamentary freedom put forth by Frédéric Le Play, the connection between provisions of inheritance law and the birthrate became a theme in France. After the collapse of the

Second Empire, France's low birthrate compared to other countries became a topic of growing public discussion, and one that led to social mobilization. In 1896, Jacques Bertillon founded the Alliance nationale pour l'accroissement de la population française, which called for political reforms to boost the demographic dynamic. The group demanded a multitude of measures aimed at favoring families with many children: higher taxes for families with fewer than three children, shorter military service, financial support for large families, the linking of state subsidies to the number of children, and even changes to the voting system, such that an additional vote could be cast for each child (Spengler 1979 [1938], 234ff.). This movement expresses once again the tradition that French social policy has a stronger orientation toward family policy and population policy (Kaufmann 2001, 928ff.). This natalist movement had a nationalistic imprint. An abundance of children was a factor of national strength, especially with respect to the more populous neighbor Germany. Because inheritance taxation was linked to population policy, inheritance tax policy combined with nationalism.

One demand put forth by Bertillon was to reduce the inheritance tax for large families. This measure was intended to compensate for the additional expenses these families would incur in educating their children: "The state thus takes away from them that part of their wealth which would have been used by necessity for the education of children" (Coutot 1925, 27). Tax politicians argued that a lower inheritance tax for families with more children would compensate for the higher burden from consumption taxes, which is why this was an equitable measure (Canal 1921, 60).

This demand, however, was controversial, largely because the lower birthrate—especially compared to Germany—could be seen, following Le Play's argument, as the response to the real division provided for in the Civil Code: in order to leave their children a piece of land of sufficient size to provide a livelihood, families of small farmers were having fewer children (Haupt 1989, 94). The higher inheritance taxes for families with only one or two children, it was argued, would lead to an exodus from the land, because the land would have to be sold to pay the tax debt. The hoped-for effect of a boost to the birthrate would therefore not happen (Spengler 1979 [1938], 236; Dupeyron 1913, 107–8). The sociologist René Worms, too, saw in the link between the number of children and inheritance taxation chiefly a means of generating more tax revenue, while he discounted its effectiveness in boosting the birthrate (1917, 203).

Although the question of the consequences of higher inheritance taxation was controversial among advocates of an active population policy, demographic arguments began to influence the parliamentary debates on the inheritance tax from 1907 on (Faure 1922). For example, the bill on inheritance tax reform put forth by Finance Minister Cochery in 1910 called for higher inheritance taxes if the testator had only one or two children: for one child an additional inheritance tax of 50% would be assessed, for two a tax of 20%.

Although parliament rejected this proposal, the link between inheritance taxes and the number of children remained a topic of parliamentary debate. And in 1917 this idea was in fact put into practice with the introduction of an additional estate tax, the amount of which would depend on the number of children.

Inheritance Taxation and Financial Crisis: The Postwar Period

If one follows the development of inheritance taxation in France from the fundamental reform in 1901 to the 1920s, one finds a picture similar to that in Germany. The growing financial need of the state, the costs of the war, and later the economic crisis in the postwar period led to drastic increases in inheritance taxes, to the point where almost confiscatory rates were briefly reached. As was the case in Germany and (with qualifications) in the United States, the beginning of World War I meant for France that the already difficult situation of public finances became much worse. Between 1913 and 1918, annual state expenditures rose from 4.7 billion francs to 58.5 billion francs, of which only 6.8 billion was covered by tax revenues (Shultz 1926, 79–80). After the war, France had a national debt of 175 billion francs (Bloch 1972, 270). In this situation, the fortunes acquired without effort through inheritance were seen increasingly as a source of additional revenue.

At this time, the French tax system still relied heavily on indirect taxes. Because of the decline in consumption during the war, revenues from these taxes could not be raised sufficiently. The income tax instituted shortly before the war was set up to have low rates and had not yet been tested (Respondek 1918, 107). Transaction taxes, which included the inheritance tax, traditionally played a large role in French tax policy. Already before the war they made up one-fourth of tax revenues. It was not until 1917 that the French tax system underwent a comprehensive reform and was adapted to the fiscal needs of wartime.

Immediately after the outbreak of the war, the Socialists called for limiting the right of intestate inheritance to the third *Parantel*, the introduction of an additional wealth tax, and an increase in inheritance tax rates. The parliament rejected all of it. However, an increase in inheritance taxes was passed at the end of 1917. Beginning in 1918, the inheritance tax was 1%–12% for direct descendants, 10%–26% for siblings, and 25%–36% for nonrelated heirs.

The finance law drawn up by Finance Minister Klotz on 31 December 1917 not only increased the progressivity of the inheritance tax, but also introduced an estate tax (*taxe successorale*) and progressivity in the gift tax. The estate tax amounted to a departure from the French system of inheritance taxation, which, like the German system, had rested since the late eighteenth century on the taxation of the inherited shares of the estate.[161] In France, as in Germany, the model for an estate tax was the English "estate duty;" evidently, there was a kind of institutional learning from other legal systems. However, the fact that the lifespan of this tax was brief in both Germany and France can be interpreted as the result of the eventual dominance of culture-bound, path-dependent institutionalization.

Although the French estate tax leaned heavily on the English model, the introduction of the tax already reveals an interesting difference from English and American estate taxation. While no attention was paid to the family situation of the testator in England and the United States, France institutionalized the estate tax precisely as an instrument of family or population policy. The progressivity of the tax was based not only on the size of the estate, but also on the number of children.[162] For example, according to the law of 1917, no estate tax was due if the testator was survived by at least four children.[163] If there were no children, the assets had to be taxed at the highest rate; each child lowered the relative tax burden on the estate.[164] Alongside fiscal considerations, this demographic aspect stood in the foreground of the debate over the bill in the National Assembly in December 1917. The Socialists demanded an increase in progressivity for large estates and the introduction of an exempt amount for small inheritances.[165]

A dramatic increase in inheritance taxation occurred after the end of the war. The development parallels that in Germany. France had exhausted itself financially to achieve its military victory. The finance policy of the French government in the postwar period sought to solve this problem with the help of substantial reparations payments by Germany. But while Germany was in fact contractually obligated to render these reparations, actual payments remained far below expectations. However, in expectation of the revenue from reparations, France "prefinanced" the country's rebuilding and the social security for disabled veterans. The shortfall in German payments led to a worsening inflation crisis that lasted until 1926, when the French government, under the reelected Raymond Poincaré, switched to a rigorous policy of austerity (Schmale 2000, 256–57).

Already in June 1919 a bill that would have raised inheritance tax rates for siblings as high as 65% and for nonrelated heirs as high as 80% barely failed in parliament. The same fate befell a proposal put forth by the Socialists at the beginning of 1920, which would have granted the state an obligatory share equal to the inheritance of a child. Following the law on the obligatory portion in the Civil Code, this would have amounted to a share of the inheritance of 50% if the testator had no children, and to one-third if there was one child. This proposal ran into vehement opposition in the public discussion. The fear—as always—was that private wealth would be reduced and that this law would have negative consequences for economic ambitions and for savings behavior (Nicolau 1922, 128–29).[166]

The significant change in the Finance Act of 1921 was a further increase in the progression rates for the succession tax: for children of the testator they could go as high as 17%, for siblings 44%, and for nonrelated heirs 59% (Shultz 1926, 84). Although the Right rejected these tax increases, which were intended to raise an additional 170 million francs in tax revenue; they regarded it as a victory that Finance Minister François Marsal did not yield to pressure from the Socialists to grant the state the inheritance portion of a child (Bloch 1972, 275).[167]

In combination with the estate tax, the high inheritance tax rates could amount to a complete confiscation of the inheritance. To prevent this, the Finance Act of 1921 stipulated that the taxation of inheritances could not exceed 80% in aggregate (Al-Omar 1959, 80–81).[168] But 1921 did not yet represent the high point in the taxation of inheritances. In 1924, following the takeover of the government by the leftist cartel, tax rates were increased another 20%, though the limitation of a maximum tax of 80% on inheritances was retained.

The continual rise in the tax progression since the introduction of the progressive succession tax in 1901, and especially the increase after World War I, was a response to the grave financial crisis in France, which did not abate until the second half of the 1920s. Although the Socialists originally demanded the heavy taxation of inheritances and the introduction of a capital tax, most of the increases in the inheritance tax came under the government of the National Bloc. They were the result not of a "leftist" finance policy, but of the dire fiscal situation. Under the government of the leftist cartel, France experienced a massive crisis of inflation, which, after the return to power by Poincaré, was resolved—at least temporarily—by a complete change of course in finance policy. Poincaré restored confidence in the French economy with a consistent austerity policy. As a result, capital that had been moved to other countries returned, and a balanced budget was achieved in 1926 (Schmale 2000, 257).

In the process, Poincaré's government immediately reduced the tax burden on inheritances, no doubt also to send a signal against the flight of capital. In the law of 3 August 1926, which took effect in January 1927, the top rate for inheritances over 50 million francs in the first tax bracket was lowered to 12.5% (down from 30%), and in the least favorable bracket to 47% (down from 71%). It was especially the heirs of large fortunes who benefited from the reduction in progression (Al-Omar 1959, 84). Moreover, the maximum rate of 80% that could be imposed on inheritances was drastically cut: in the direct line for spouses to 25%, for collateral relatives up to the third degree to 35%, and for other heirs to 40% (Al-Omar 1959, 84).[169] This ended the phase of extremely steep inheritance taxation in France. It was limited to the fiscal emergency after World War I, and it did not amount to a lasting reorientation of French inheritance tax policy. As a remnant of the phase of high taxation, the estate tax was abolished again in 1934 and folded into the succession tax (Al-Omar 1959, 99). At the same time, the demographic goal was now integrated into the succession tax itself. Henceforth, tax rates were based on the number of children left behind by the testator.

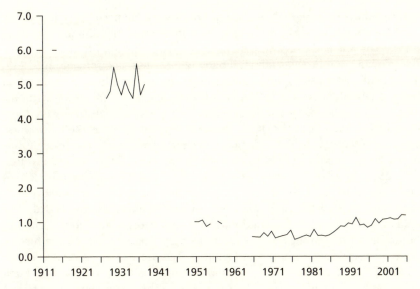

Figure 5.4 Inheritance and gift tax as share of total tax revenues in France, 1913–2006 (in %)

Source: OECD Revenue Statistics.

Inheritance Taxation since the Mid-1930s

The repeal of the estate tax in 1934 ended the forty-year-long key phase in the development of French inheritance tax policy. The rapid reduction of tax rates after the stabilization of the financial situation in 1926 reveals that the increases between 1910 and 1926 had been emergency measures. They were measures of fiscal policy that did not—except in the perspective of the parties of the Left—follow any political ideas about a redistribution of wealth. On the contrary: the high inheritance taxation was seen as a threat to the foundations of the French economy, because it led to massive capital flight (Allix 1927, 675) and thus endangered the national wealth. Although the taxation of inheritance remained in place, France, unlike the United States, did not again witness similarly steep increases in progression after the tax cuts of the 1920s. France was less affected by the worldwide economic crisis than Germany and the United States; moreover, within the political discourse in France, inheritance taxes were hardly seen as an instrument for redistributing property so as to prevent the dynastic concentration of wealth. Even the government of the Popular Front in the mid-1930s did not pursue an inheritance tax policy with redistributive goals. For one, Prime Minister Léon Blum believed that the mandate of the Popular Front was not strong enough for radical social reforms (Hazareesingh 1994, 240); for another, this reflects the rather weak interest of the Socialists in even using inheritance taxation as an instrument of social reform.

Up to the 1950s, the inheritance tax rates were changed every few years. In the midthirties, the progression was increased, in 1938 the tax was boosted by 8% and the progression for very large fortunes raised to pay for the growing military spending. Following further tax reforms in 1939, 1940, and 1948, rates could reach 88.6% in the tax tables for nonrelated heirs of inheritances over 150 million francs, but these rates were fictitious. The limits on the maximum tax remained in place, though they were loosened in 1940 (25% in the direct line and between spouses, 40% for close collateral relatives, 50% for distant collateral relatives). Even an extraordinarily large inheritance passed down by parents was never taxed at more than 25%. In 1948, the rates were raised once again for collateral relatives and at the same time reduced in the direct line for families with many children, but in 1949 the rates were already cut again across the board. The system with limits on the maximum rate and a differentiation of the tax burden according to the number of children was largely given up in a further tax reform in 1959. Children and spouses were now taxed at rates between 5% and 15%, siblings at 40%, and distant collateral relatives at 60% (Moniteur-Documents 1961, 11). According to the current law, inheritances in the direct line and between spouses are taxed at rates between 5% and a maximum of 40%, inheritances to siblings between 35% and 45%, to collateral relatives to the fourth degree at 55%, and all other heirs at 60% (Leveneur and Leveneur 1999, 11–12).

If one compares French inheritance taxation with its German counterpart, one sees a convergence over time. Experiments with estate taxes were given up fairly quickly in both countries. The demographic goals institutionalized in French inheritance law between 1917 and 1960 eventually disappeared almost completely. Today, differences exist chiefly in the higher taxation of collateral heirs in France, for whom a proportional tax with a relatively high rate exists. This continues to reveal a conception of the family in France that is more strongly tailored to the nuclear family and the orientation toward the principle of proportionality, which is a product of history.

5.4. Conclusion

Inheritance taxation in the United States, Germany, and France shows a clear chronological convergence: it was in the early twentieth century that all three countries introduced a system of taxation that has remained essentially in place until today. Before that we find inheritance taxes with mostly only minimal rates, exemptions for close relatives, and either no or only minor progressivity. In Germany and the United States, those taxes were levied only on the level of the states. The reasons for this nearly parallel modernization of the inheritance tax systems can be found in the almost contemporaneous expansion of the tasks of the centralized state and the appearance of social reform movements pushing for "just" taxation. Tax justice was to be achieved primarily through the reduction of indirect taxes and the introduction of progressive income and inheritance taxes.

However, because the fiscal problems existed in similar form in all three countries, the problem of generating higher tax revenues *cannot* explain the *different structure and shape* that inheritance taxation took. The structural differences are as follows: in the United States, inheritance taxation is institutionalized as an estate tax. The blood relationship of the heirs to the testator plays no role. Beginning in the 1930s, tax rates reached progressive levels that led for large fortunes to what was at least nominally almost confiscatory taxation. This changed only in the 1980s, and to this day the nominal progression of the estate tax in the United States is significantly higher than in the two European countries. This makes inheritance taxation one of the very few areas in which a state institution in the United States has a stronger redistributive underpinning than in the European countries.

In Germany, inheritance taxation was introduced as a succession tax, and the direct relatives of the testator—spouse and children—were only hesitantly included in the taxation. Compared to the United States, the progression of the inheritance tax—leaving aside the exceptional years 1919–22 and 1946–48—was much lower, especially for close relatives, and the maximum it reached in the various laws was no more than 38%.

In France, inheritance taxation was likewise institutionalized primarily as a succession tax, even though an estate tax was levied on top of it between 1917 and 1934. Except for the years between 1917 and 1926, tax progression was much lower than in the United States. Characteristic for France is the very high taxation of collateral relatives from the second degree, and the pursuit of demographic goals with inheritance taxes in the period between 1917 and 1960.

Beginning in the early nineteenth century, different discourses on how to assess the inheritance of wealth emerged in the three countries: in the United States, the debates over estate taxation revolved, for one, around the question of the legitimacy of inherited wealth, and the taxation of inheritances was justified as a way of creating greater equality of opportunity. For another, the perpetuation of dynastic wealth was seen as a potential threat to the democratic foundations of the polity. One can trace this line of argumentation from the Revolution down to the most recent controversies over the abolition of the estate tax. Opponents of the estate tax, meanwhile, put forth chiefly economic arguments that point to the possible threat to capital accumulation; since the 1970s, they have insisted very strongly on the negative consequences of estate taxes for small businesses and farms.

These characteristics are reflected in the debates in the U.S. Congress. Proponents of the tax justify state interference in the transmission of wealth, first, with the goal of higher tax revenues, and, second, with the argument of tax equity. The tax is supposed to generate additional revenue, and estates are seen as a legitimate tax source. However, among American supporters of inheritance taxation an important role is also played by the rejection of privileges derived from "unearned" wealth and, connected with this, the goal of greater equality in the distribution of wealth. Among opponents of the estate tax, arguments inherent in the law have played a central part. This makes it possible to argue against the tax on a formal level without creating the impression that one is merely defending the particular interests of a rich oligarchy of wealth. The parliamentary discourse underwent a profound change in the 1970s, when the negative economic consequences of the estate tax for small businesses and farms moved front and center. Economic arguments play a far more important role among both opponents and supporters of the tax than they did in the debates in the first half of the twentieth century. Family-oriented arguments have little significance for either side. Even the discussion about family businesses that has moved increasingly to the fore in the United States since the seventies concerns their economic viability, not the continuity of wealth within the family and the function of family assets in providing for family members.

In the debates that have been carried on in Germany since the pre-1848 period over the inheritance tax and escheat, the redistribution of wealth and the goal of preventing the concentration of wealth have played a far smaller role than in the United States. Inheritance law as an instrument for the redistribution of wealth was discussed at most among early Socialists and then again immediately after the revolution of 1919—but not with the (liberal) goal of redistributing it *as* private wealth, but of socializing property. Proponents regarded the taxation of inheritances chiefly as a source of state resources that could be used to realize sociopolitical goals. Revenue from the inheritance tax was to be used to solve social problems—fighting poverty, promoting education, supporting emigrants, and, most recently, financing a basic income. Inheritance taxes make a contribution to achieving greater social justice—their justification, to highlight the difference from the United States, is focused more on results than opportunity. The tax finds its justification in the ability of heirs to pay it. The role of the state is not limited to the function of a redistribution agency; rather, by deciding on the use of the funds, it intervenes in social relationships.

The second characteristic of the justificatory system of the German inheritance tax discourse lies in the prominent place of family-related arguments among opponents of the tax. They see the tax as an interference in familial wealth that is hostile to the family. Opponents invoke the "family spirit" and thereby delegitimize especially the taxation of children and spouses. Initially, they were not taxed at all in Germany, and to this day the inheritance tax that is levied on them is moderate compared to the other two countries.[170] Although today the concept of a "sense of family," which was a central concept of the German inheritance tax discourse until the 1920s, is no longer used, the orientation toward family wealth is still evident. The arguments now point to the protection of the family in accordance with Article 6 of the Basic Law.

In France, the inheritance tax was never at any point in the political discourse seen as an important instrument of social reform—except by the Utopian Socialists and occasionally by other social reformers. That is even true of the Socialists, for while they did advocate a higher tax progression, their goal was merely a more just taxation, not a redistribution of wealth. In the French inheritance tax discourse, concern over the threat to national wealth was clearly in the forefront, and opponents of progressive inheritance taxation consistently had the upper hand. They were able to interpret the principle of equal taxation in a way that provided the legitimation for proportional taxation. This does not mean that the share of the inheritance tax of total tax revenues in France is lower, but the tax is not aimed specifically at large fortunes. One peculiarity of the French taxation of inheritances was the intention of using this tax to boost the birthrate.

The debates over the taxation of inheritance carried on Germany, France, and the United States since the nineteenth century show different discursive structures, each of which displays long-term continuity. If one looks more closely at the specific differences in the way inheritance is taxed, what stands out is the connection between the country-specific tax regulations and the respective tax discourse: the exemption by and large of immediate family members in Germany and the family-oriented conception of property; the strong tax progression and the high taxation of inheriting children in the United States and the individualistic-meritocratic conception of property with its distrust of the dynastic concentration of wealth; the strong orientation toward property and stability in France and the nearly complete absence of an inheritance tax discourse focused on social reform. This correspondence suggests that the systems of justification expressed in the political discourse did in fact influence the codification of the law. The connection to political actors lies in the fact that the systems of justification lend cultural legitimacy to concrete institutional structures of inheritance taxation and thereby influence the chances that certain proposed laws will in fact be adopted. The political actors are steered toward certain goals and the corresponding strategies for implementing them. The resonance of the reform proposals within the context of the prevailing discursive field influences their chances of success in the legislative process. Although the connection between justificatory systems and the structure of inheritance taxation cannot be proved in the strict sense of a causal explanation, correlations pointing in this direction are evident.

In all three countries, inheritance taxation makes up only a small part of the total revenue from taxes. At the end of the 1990s it stood at 0.7% of total revenue in Germany, at 1.8% in France, and at 1.4% in the United States (Bach and Bartholmai 2002; Büttner, Scheffler, and Spengel 2004).

Since the introduction of modern tax systems in the early twentieth century, the lion's share of tax revenue is generated by profit or income taxes on companies and private individuals and by indirect taxes. Inheritance taxation cannot be developed into an equally important source of taxes. One reason is that the tax cannot be higher than the capital appreciation if one wants to maintain the basis of the tax over the long term. A second reason is that a substantial expansion of inheritance taxation would run into political opposition from property owners and would also have some unwanted economic consequences. Even though opponents far exaggerate the economic repercussions of inheritance taxes, there is reason to expect that at least a drastic increase in the tax would lead to a reduction in the capital basis for investments through increased consumption and capital flight. Regardless of whether it is to be used to generate income to fund social policy measures or to promote equality of opportunity—these predictable consequences set boundaries to inheritance taxation. This means that, the problematic status of the inheritance of wealth in a meritocratic society notwithstanding, its utility as an instrument of reform is limited. That is one reason why—except briefly in crisis-ridden upheavals—none of the three countries under examination taxed inheritances in such a way as to cause a lasting redistribution of property. The private transmission of wealth by inheritance is not only the expression of the political power of property owners, but also part of the incentive structures that produce the well-being of society. In spite of these limitations, the differences in the actual form of the tax in Germany, France, and the United States, especially the differences in tax rates, point to considerable maneuvering room.

Chapter 6

CONCLUSION: DISCOURSES AND INSTITUTIONS

MODERN SOCIETIES see themselves as meritocracies. The achievements and contributions of individuals, as measured by market success, are the most important normative criterion used to justify social inequality. But how can inherited wealth be reconciled with this self-conception of modern societies?

The hereditary transmission of private wealth from one generation to the next runs counter to the self-conception of modern societies, a problem that was widely discussed especially in the nineteenth and at the beginning of the twentieth century. With societies now facing the transfer of the enormous wealth accumulated during the postwar period, the institution of inheritance is becoming once again a topic of political debate and controversy. This applies especially to inheritance taxation. Parliamentary debates on inheritance law reform and a plethora of legal, philosophical, and sociological treatises document how important the regulation of the transfer of wealth *mortis causa* is to social policy in the three countries I have examined. These contentious debates look at inheritance from the normative perspective of how to justify the "unearned" acquisition of wealth, and in connection with the effect that inheritance law is presumed to have on a society's economic productivity, the cohesion of its families, and its demographic trend.

In this book I have looked at the four most important clashes over inheritance law policy in Germany, France, and the United States, as well as at the concrete development of that law: the fight over freedom of testamentary disposition, the regulation of familial claims to an inheritance in statutory inheritance law, the abolition of entails, and the taxation of inherited wealth. The comparative perspective and a time frame of more than two hundred years have made it possible to discern long-term developments in inheritance law and to identify the differences among the three countries. Analyzing the discourse over inheritance law has allowed me to bring out the connection between the development of inheritance law and the "orders of justification" (Boltanski and Thévenot 1991) concerning the treatment of "unearned wealth" that have prevailed in these countries. The goal of this study was twofold: first, to lay out the chief issues in the discourse on inheritance law—the intent here was to provide clues for understanding how the relationship between the individual and the community has evolved in the modernization process; second, to show the link between the patterns of justification for inheritance law and the actual, concrete shaping of the elements of that law.

This concluding chapter summarizes the important findings of the study. Above all, however, I will discuss theoretical reflections that explain the development of inheritance law; in the process, I will specify how the explanatory approach I have pursued here holds up against alternative explanations of institutional development.

The Development of Inheritance Law in Germany, France, and the United States

One can discern shared structural elements and parallel trends in the inheritance law of Germany, France, and the United States. In all three countries there exists a private inheritance law that grants to the testator, on the basis of testamentary freedom, the right to dispose of his or her property *mortis causa*. At the same time, the rights of the testator are constrained by the rights of close family members to portions of the estate. The rights of the surviving spouse and of illegitimate children, in particular, have expanded over the past two hundred years. By contrast, the right of legitimate children to a reserved portion of the estate has changed very little. Privileged rights of inheritance based on ascriptive status markers were abrogated in all three countries: inheritance by primogeniture, the unequal treatment of sons and daughters, and entailed estates that supported the economic basis of the nobility's political power have all been expunged from the law. In addition, progressive inheritance taxes, by which a portion of the estate is remitted to the state, have existed in all three countries for about a hundred years.

At the same time, a closer look at the actual development of inheritance law in the three countries reveals considerable differences in the way the law has been shaped. For example, the testator's freedom of disposition is far broader in the United States than in Germany and, especially, in France. The most salient distinction lies in the possibility of disinheriting one's children under U.S. law. France, by contrast, has real partitioning of the estate among the heirs. Differences are also found in the development of the legal status of the surviving spouse and illegitimate children. The legal status of the widow was first strengthened in the United States; when it comes to the rights of illegitimate children, today only the laws of some states in the United States recognize differences from those of legitimate children. While the constraints on property were abolished in all three countries, this was done at very different times. Estates are taxed progressively in Germany, France, and the United States, but a comparative examination of tax tables shows considerable divergences in the actual tax: a steeply progressive taxation of estates in the United States, which reflects the goal of equal opportunity and the desire to prevent the formation of dynastic wealth; a particularly low tax imposed on close family members in Germany, which reflects the perception of estates as family wealth; a likewise low taxation of large estates in France, which is derived from the principle of equality and the desire to protect "national wealth."

Explaining the Development of Inheritance Law

But how can one explain the commonalities and differences in inheritance law in Germany, France, and the United States? The hypothesis put forth in the present study asserts that a comprehensive explanatory model must include above all the symbolic systems that made the specific stipulations of inheritance law in each country seem particularly problematic or appropriate. To explain the development of inheritance law, it is not enough to study the demands concerning its economic functions and how these have changed, or to point to interest groups and their relative strength. Why is that?

At first glance, a functionalist model that starts with economic conditions and how they have changed seems a plausible theoretical framework for explaining the evolution of inheritance law.[1] One example of this theoretical approach is the study by Carole Shammas, Marylynn Salmon, and Michael Dahlin (1987), one of the few monographs on the development of inheritance law based on a long-term study. This study interprets the stages in the reform of inheritance law in the United States since colonial times as adaptations to changing economic conditions under the respective regimes of family capitalism, corporate capitalism, and state capitalism. In other words, the changing economic demands on inheritance law are supposed to explain the law and its development.

What justifies such an economic approach is its reference to the connection between legal institutions and economic efficiency. Institutions are social mechanisms of coordination that must *also* be measured by their contribution to the shaping of economic incentives. Institutions must be "functionally fit" (Offe 1996, 199ff.). Institutional regulations considered economically dysfunctional come under pressure to change. However, one cannot infer from this general assumption that legal institutions do in fact adapt flexibly to changing economic demands.

Considerations of economic efficiency no doubt play a significant role in the debates about inheritance law. Analysis of parliamentary debates has shown that proposed laws are often justified by goals of economic growth and that this mode of justification has become increasingly important. Institutional developments like the abolition of entails can also be interpreted from a perspective of economic efficiency. But other aspects of the development of inheritance law remain incomprehensible on the theoretical basis of economic explanation. This is particularly evident if one takes a comparative approach. Why is the principle of real partitioning implemented in France after the Revolution, while in the other countries it is rejected as economically detrimental? Why are different levels of inheritance taxes adopted in the three countries? How could the legal institution of entail persist in Germany even under the conditions of a highly industrialized economy? From the perspective of economic institutionalism, inheritance law in all three countries should converge. In the long run differences should disappear, unless the different legal rules are equally efficient or the economic conditions of the three countries are so distinct that they require different institutional designs to perform efficiently.

Yet an empirical examination of the development of inheritance law shows that although efficiency is indeed a central argument in justifying proposed laws, the development of the law itself can be understood only in part as a creation of efficient legal structures. For one, rules remain nearly unchanged over long periods that saw fundamental economic changes; for another, inheritance law in Germany, France and the United States does not converge. Why does this resistance against presumably more efficient rules of law exist?

One reason is presumably the uncertainty over how to implement efficiency institutionally. This is evident, for example, in the question over the effect of inheritance law on individual economic motivation. While it can be argued that the possibility of leaving property to children might be an incentive for testators to accumulate wealth, it can also be maintained that the effortless transfer of wealth corrupts the acquisition-oriented values of the children and is thus economically inefficient. In the debate over inheritance law it was liberal commentators especially who repeatedly warned against this consequence and derived from it the demand that large inheritances be confiscated. Motivating and demotivating effects of inheritances can cancel each other out and are therefore useless as a criterion for making a decision on this issue. The systematic point here is that the uncertainty and inconsistency of economic consequences of concrete provisions of inheritance law often do not allow actors guided by the efficiency criterion to identify economically efficient institutional designs in advance (Beckert 2002). The efficiency of inheritance law can be judged, if at all, only after the fact. However, the divergence of forms of institutionalization in the three countries speaks against economic institutionalism.

Second, an analysis of the development of law simply in terms of efficiency seems too narrow. Economic explanations of the development of the law marginalize aspects of distributive justice.[2] These aspects, however, play a prominent role in the debates on inheritance law in all three countries, as do the normative self-conception of these societies as meritocracies, the legacy of legal traditions, and the anticipated consequences of specific legal provisions for the stability of familial and political structures. A multitude of goals is linked with the shaping of inheritance law. Institutions, one could say by way of generalizing, must be not only "functionally fit," but also "morally supported" (Offe 1996, 199ff.). In his sociology of law, Max Weber (1978 [1922], 1:333) pointed out that the law guarantees the most varied interests, which is why legal orders can prove resistant to economic change. A purely economic model of explanation is theoretically not complex enough because it leaves out the influence of other socially important goals. At most it can be merely an empirical finding that economic motives predominate in the development of inheritance law. The present study has shown that other goals pursued through the regulation of inheritance law also enter into the evolution of the law.[3]

An alternative approach would be to move the role of interest groups to the foreground in explaining the development of inheritance law. Collective actors differ in the power available to them, which they use to implement their interests in the political process (Märtz 1990; Wilson 1990). Institutions, understood as mechanisms for regulating the distribution of scarce resources in society, can be analyzed as a product of power relations between conflicting social interest groups. The interest group approach dispenses with an evolutionary or teleological model of institutional efficiency: institutional designs can be inefficient because actors attempt to maximize their individual interests (rent seeking) with no regard as to the effects on the total welfare produced in society (social maximizing). Thus, the interest group approach offers an explanation for why economically inefficient regulations of inheritance law can prevail even in the long term.[4]

The interest group approach contains an additional aspect for explaining the development of law by including the role of actors interested in its codification. Every change of inheritance law requires a majority of the legislature or the approval of the executive or both. Interest groups clearly try to influence this legislative process. Linking the explanation of institutional development to actors provides this approach with an essential advantage over the above-mentioned economic functionalism.

Still, acknowledging the importance of interest groups is not already tantamount to saying that the development of inheritance law and the legal differences that exist among the three countries can in fact be explained through the differing strengths of interest groups. Not only is it extremely difficult to measure the strength of interest groups (Wilson 1990, 10ff.), existing comparative studies also point to the unsolved problem of "why interest groups with similar organizational characteristics (including measures of interest group 'strength') and similar preferences could not always influence policy in the same way or to the same extent in different national contexts" (Thelen and Steinmo 1992, 5). Moreover, it also remains unexplained why institutions show such a clear continuity over the course of history, even though the political regime and the structure of the state change fundamentally (Dobbin 1994, 10).

While there is no doubt that interest groups influence the development of inheritance law, the empirical findings of this study can be attributed only in part to the divergent power of interest groups. What *can* be explained is the close link between the dissolution of entails and political revolutions. Likewise, the introduction of progressive inheritance or estate taxes in all three countries is connected with the growing strength of social reform movements that pushed for tapping great wealth to finance rising governmental expenses. At the same time, property owners succeeded in preventing the effective redistribution of property by means of an inheritance tax. Finally, the very existence of the right to bequeath property privately can be interpreted as an expression of the power relationship between property owners and those segments of the population who do not own wealth. But the present study shows that an explanation of the development of inheritance law cannot build solely on the strength of interest groups. For one, interests cannot be understood independent of ideological convictions. Why do property owners like Andrew Carnegie or Warren Buffet support high inheritance taxes? Why does the critique of bequeathing property come mainly from liberals, while the topic is of secondary significance for social democratic parties? For another, the limitations of the interest group approach become especially evident from a comparative perspective. For example, using the assumption that the interests of the affluent classes were much more weakly represented in the United States through much of the twentieth century than in Germany to explain why much higher inheritance tax rates were enacted in the United States would be problematic. The unequal treatment of illegitimate children in the United States and the possibility of disinheriting children can also hardly be explained by divergent resources in the political process.

Discursive Fields and the Development of Inheritance Law

This critical examination of economic functionalism and of the interest group approach does not lead to the conclusion that the development of inheritance law should be examined independent of its compliance with economic demands and independent of the distribution of political power. Institutions derive their legitimacy also from how they are seen to be fulfilling their intended functions. Moreover, institutions are contested as rules and mechanisms for distributing scarce resources among social groups. Yet comparison of the development of the law in the three countries has revealed that these approaches do not comprehensively explain the development of inheritance law. What is lacking, according to the thesis put forth in this study, is the reference to the actors' normative and cognitive concepts of how inheritances can be legitimated, and which institutional reforms can lead to the declared goals of regulating "unearned wealth."

I examined these symbolic orders and their development by looking at the legal, sociological, and parliamentary debates on inheritance law. The starting point was that political actors see the problem of inheritance law within culturally formed orders of justification. The perception of possible functions of inheritance law and of the effects of specific provisions of inheritance law emerges, like the interests of social groups in specific rules of inheritance law, through the constitutive filter of these discursive fields. Following Durkheim (1995 [1912]), we can speak here of classification systems that organize patterns of perception socially and thus draw cognitive and normative boundaries. The symbolic orders themselves, so I have argued, influence the development of inheritance law. The significance of culture lies in the general systems of meaning underlying the fundamental views of social order and action strategies that prevail in social groups (Dobbin 1994, 2; Lamont and Thévenot 2000; Swidler 1986). This approach thus pays attention to the expectations with which actors determine what is problematic about bequeathing wealth, what can be seen as a fulfillment of goals, and what means can be used to achieve these goals. The discursive fields influence how the interests of social groups are defined and structure views of causal relations as well as the action strategies derived from them. In this sense, national traditions as reflected in the structures of expectation of the political actors lead to specific perspectives on the problem of inheritance law and at the same time suggest specific strategies for resolving it, while other strategies are not even considered as serious alternatives.

The background to such an understanding of the role of culture, which is closely linked with the "new sociological institutionalism" (Powell and DiMaggio 1991; DiMaggio 1994), lies in an interpretation of instrumental rationality distinct from economic theory. Economic theory assumes a concept of rationality according to which actors make optimizing decisions based on their respective preferences. This excludes the questions of how the preferences of the actors actually emerge and how they change. What is also implied is the—at least probabilistic—grasp of causal relationships, because that is the only way decision-makers can calculate which action strategy is in fact optimal for achieving their goals. That this assumption is problematic is evident from unintended side-effects or the failure of intentional rational strategies, all of which points to the problem of uncertainty produced by complexity and novel decision-making situations (Beckert 2002). This can be illustrated once again with the supposed motivation effect of inheritances. Different representatives of the same social groups, and all having the goal of their children's welfare in mind, have argued both that the right to bequeath property should be unlimited and that it should be strictly circumscribed.

The goals that link actors with the codification of inheritance law, and the strategies they deem effective for achieving these goals, emerge in a cultural context that can encompass a group or society as a whole. The assumption that action goals and strategies are socially constructed makes it possible to examine how the *specific* demands made by actors are constituted, even when "optimal" strategies cannot be deduced unambiguously. If one is unwilling to regard these specific demands as accidental and thus leave them unexplained, one can analyze them as dependent upon the culturally mediated interpretation of causal relationships, rational strategies, and existing conditions of action.

The link between action goals and strategies and the cultural context is evident in the discourses on inheritance law. These discourses introduce into the analysis another level of collective representation besides the legal code itself. Comparable legal rules do not necessarily allow us to infer identical cultural perceptions, since the motives of the actors remain invisible behind these rules. This is one limitation in Durkheim's otherwise important intuition that the development of the law could be examined as an indicator of changes in the forms of social integration.

By including discourse, the analysis can be connected to both the recent developments in comparative cultural sociology (Lamont and Thévenot 2000) and the discussion of frames in the literature on social movements. Comparative cultural sociology shows that cultural repertoires are not equally available for actors in different situations and various national contexts. Which evaluative schemata are relevant as *limits of meaning* can be seen only on the level of forms of interaction. Research on social movements uses the concept of *frames* to explain constructions of meaning through movement activists. The resonance of a structure for the perception of social problems depends on the general political culture that provides social actors with a kind of "grammar" (Gamson 1988; Gerhards and Rucht 1992; and Snow and Benford 1988). These structures of meaning, however, are never unambiguous and must always be reproduced in the dialogical interaction between signs and actors (Steinberg 1999, 738ff.).

The constitutive, a priori assumptions of actors about how to deal with "unearned wealth" can be observed in the orders of justification I have described. They influence not only what actors consider the fulfillment of the functional requirements of inheritance law, but also which strategies or institutional forms they prefer for obtaining this goal. What I am talking about, therefore, is a fundamental orientation in how individuals think about the institution of inheritance, which *itself* helps to structure the definition of the interests of political groups and thus influences the development of the law.

Orders of Justification of Inheritance Law

The differences between the symbolic orders expressed in the discourse on inheritance law were discussed in detail in the main chapters of the book. Briefly summarized, the following characteristics emerged: in all three countries, one camp in the debate has advocated the position of unlimited rights of inheritance. Testamentary freedom is to be as comprehensive as possible, and taxation of inheritances is rejected. This position is grounded chiefly in the principle of the freedom of private property and in economic concerns about the negative effects that interference in the private autonomy of the testator could have on capital accumulation and the family.

In all three countries, this view is opposed by positions critical of the transmission of wealth. Those who advocate them call for restrictions on the freedom of the testator in order to regulate the division of inheritances within the family, or for limitations on the private transfer of property *mortis causa* through taxation. The interventions they seek as well as the justifications for these interventions show different national patterns. In Germany and France, the consequences of inheritance law for the family assume a special relevance. The main argument in Germany has been that limiting testamentary freedom is necessary to protect the family against the rise of an immoral individualism. An important argumentative point of reference in France during the Revolution was that limiting the arbitrariness of the testator would lead to greater equality in familial relations and at the same time counteract patriarchal despotism in the family. Later, under the impact primarily of the works of Frédéric Le Play, unlimited testamentary freedom was seen in France as the precondition for maintaining stable family relations. Especially in Germany, moreover, family and state were discussed as alternative loci for claims to support based on the principle of solidarity. According to one side, interventions in the right of inheritance led to the destruction of the family as a community of solidarity. Such interventions were justified, according to the other side, because the family is no longer able to provide significant support, a function that has increasingly been taken over by the state.

In Germany, inheritance law has been connected to social policy from the first half of the nineteenth century to the present. Taxing "unearned wealth" was expected to help solve the "social question." The normative concept has been "social justice," which demands contributions to carry out a redistribution of wealth in the spirit of solidarity. In France, meanwhile, the principle of equality has played a dominant role in discourse on inheritance law since the Revolution. It provides the backdrop for the limits on testamentary freedom, the institution of real partitioning, and resistance to the progressive inheritance tax. Moreover, in France a connection has been drawn between inheritance law and population development ever since the Revolution, but especially in the wake of the publication of Frédéric Le Play's works. In the United States, too, ever since Independence, the dynastic bequest of wealth has been considered critically in terms of its consequences for society. Not only are inheritances seen as contradicting the meritocratic self-conception of American society, since they question the principle of equality of opportunity; they are also rejected because the dynastic concentration of wealth is perceived as a source of danger to democratic political structures, and because the effortless acquisition of wealth through inheritances could corrupt the (Protestant) values of the heirs.

The relevance of these symbolic orders for explaining institutions is revealed by correspondences between the structure of the normative problematization of inheritance law and its actual institutional expression. Such connections were demonstrated in the book: the high progression-rate of the American estate tax during most of the twentieth century, which concurs with the critical position opposed to the dynastic perpetuation of wealth; the long existing exemption of close family members in German inheritance tax and its comparatively low rates even now, which reflect the connection between inheritance and family in the legal and political discourse; the limitation on testamentary freedom in France, which has its correspondence in the pronounced significance of the principle of equality in the French discourse on inheritance; the tax relief for testators with many children in French inheritance tax law, which has its counterpart in political discourse in the link between inheritance law and the demographic trend.

These congruencies reveal a connection between the normative structures of the problematization of "unearned wealth" and inheritance law. The detailed discussions in the four main chapters have made clear, however, that the normative structure can be only *one* factor explaining the development of the law. The only sensible approach is to pursue the assertion that cultural idioms affect the actors' conceptions of goals, definitions of interest, and concepts of rationality, which in turn influence the chances that proposals for a reform of inheritance law will actually be implemented. For the introduction of progressive inheritance taxes, which took place in all three countries in the early twentieth century, cannot be explained without paying heed to the increased financial need of the modern state and the political power of social reform movements. Similarly, the repeal of entails in all three countries has a direct temporal connection with the establishment of republican forms of government. Hence, to explain the development of inheritance law, the respective structures underlying the problematization of "unearned wealth" must always be seen in connection with economic and political conditions. The explanatory model I am after therefore links cultural idioms with interests and perceived functional requirements.

Functions, Interests, and Culture in the Development of Inheritance Law

But how can functions, interests, and cultural idioms be brought together in a model of the development of inheritance law? The first basic theoretical decision is to develop such a model from a perspective of action theory. This means that institutional structures and their changes must be explained with respect to the decisions of actors. Theoretical approaches that marginalize the role of actors by starting from teleological assumptions of historical development, functionalist reasoning, and structuralist theories, are rejected.

Action theory shifts the focus onto the political carrier groups (Weber 1978 [1922]) that shape legal institutions. The primary groups analyzed in the present study are politicians, jurists, and other competent participants involved in debates in the public sphere. These three groups relate to the legislative process with different degrees of immediacy. Politicians shape statutory law in the legislative process. Jurists exert a direct influence on the interpretation of the law through the administration of justice and indirect influence on legal reforms through expert opinions. The members of the third group, which consists essentially of social scientists and philosophers, exert indirect influence on legal reforms as competent expert participants in the public discourse. The discussion of inheritance taxation, in particular, also looked at social reform movements as a source of political influence on the development of inheritance law.[5]

In examining political carrier groups, the study connects closely to the interest group approach. At the same time, however, this approach is transcended, since the question of the constitution of interests and their conversion into action is reflected in terms of cultural sociology. My approach argues that actors always move in a culturally predetermined field of legitimate normative conceptions of goals, social values, and specific perceptions of causal relationships. This background, which can be analyzed as a discursive field, represents for the actors a *backdrop to their actions*, one that is relevant in practical action, but at the same time is hardly reflected upon consciously. This background of a priori assumptions enters into the process by which actors articulate their interests and becomes itself a "resource" in the political debate. Communicated through the carrier groups, existing conceptions of legitimacy and perceptions of causal relationships influence the structures of inheritance law. The different symbolic orders through which the transmission of wealth is perceived themselves become an explanatory factor in the development of inheritance law that can be reconstructed by means of action theory. This is significant, because the consideration of culture becomes sociologically meaningful only through its connection to social groups whose influence shapes processes of institutionalization in practical terms (see Wuthnow 1987 and 1989). References to vague "national characteristics" or the "national spirit" would be much too unspecific to contribute to a concrete explanation of inheritance law.

However, the relationship between interests, cultural idioms, and functions—which are synthesized into political positions of the carrier groups in the discourse on inheritance law—must itself be specified more precisely. How are interests related to the functional consequences of specific provisions of inheritance law? How are interests and values linked? How do values influence the perception of functional consequences? What is the relationship of legal reforms to existing institutional structures?

A first step in answering these questions consists in explicating the concept of interest. Here we can pick up on Max Weber's (1978 [1922], 1:333) insight that "interest" must not be equated with economic interest. Rather, according to Weber, the law guarantees "the most diverse interests" (333). By examining discourses on inheritance law, I have shown in this book in what way questions of family cohesion, the consequences of inheritance law for the political and economic order, and the normative problematization of "unearned wealth" are significant in the context of meritocratic societies for the actors that shape inheritance law.

However, it is not only the formulation of interests that is subject to cultural influences. The same is also true of the way in which the consequences of specific provisions of inheritance law are perceived. It was precisely through a comparative perspective that I was able to show in this study that actors in various national contexts expect completely different consequences from the same institutional regulations. The vast majority of actors in the German discourse on inheritance law in the nineteenth century believed that the expansion of testamentary freedom would endanger the family, while in France observers expected that the same measure would protect the traditional family. Legal institutions operate in a sphere of causal relationships that is complex and often incomprehensible to the actors. This lack of clarity opens the way for radically different interpretations, some of which may be motivated by special interests (which actors might want to conceal), while others reflect culturally based frames of interpretation.[6]

Finally, there is the question concerning the significance of existing legal rules for the development of inheritance law. Against the interest group approach, representatives of historical institutionalism point to the significance of path dependence in explaining the stability of *existing* institutional designs in the respective countries; accordingly, they examine the significance of institutions in explaining political results (Hall and Taylor 1996; Thelen and Steinmo 1992). Existing institutions are critical for the chances of actors to implement their political and economic interests. Existing institutions are inertial because the distribution of resources tends to produce the kind of political decisions that reinforce them. The term *path dependence* thus identifies an important *descriptive* category, which calls attention to the self-reproducing, idiosyncratic nature of institutions and makes long-term national differences of institutional structures appear self-evident. I have characterized this in the present study as the *longue durée* of inheritance law. However, there are two problems that attach to the concept of path dependency as an *explanatory* category. On the one hand, there is the danger of ascribing to institutions not only an influencing, but also a determining role (Beckert 1999b; Thelen and Steinmo 1992, 15), which diverts attention completely from the significance of political actors. Thus, institutional theory becomes a theory of structure that dispenses with the contingent decisions of actors—except at "critical junctures"—to explain macrosocial processes of development. On the other hand, an objectivist view at institutions is encouraged, which ascribes "thingness" (Dobbin 1994, 9) to institutions and disregards their social construction. However, institutions can influence action only when the actors accept them as self-evident and their behaviors are guided by the assumption that the institutional rules are valid. Thus, institutions must be anchored in the thoughts of the actors and they reproduce only through rule-conforming *agency*. This process of institutional reproduction through agency suggests an explanation for the inertia of institutions that is not completely dependent on the distribution of resources and emphasizes the significance of routines, symbols, and scripts. Institutions operate as cognitive frameworks that provide components for agency from which interpretations of situations and strategies of action are derived.[7] This implies, however, that their reproduction is not to be explained independent of symbolic orders.

Stability and Change of Orders of Justification

The discursive guidelines of inheritance law turn out to be amazingly stable over the more than 200-year period studied. One can trace them especially well until the 1930s, for until then, inheritance law was a constant topic of political discourse. Since then, inheritance law has played only an intermittent role, which makes it harder to pursue the development of discursive structures. However, in current debates, especially in the discussion in the United States about the estate tax, many of the guidelines that had already crystallized two hundred years ago still appear. But what are the mechanisms through which the classificatory arrangements can be reproduced over such a long period? If the explanation of the development of inheritance law proceeds from social carrier groups and assigns a place to symbolic orders, the reproduction of these collective representations must be explained through their connection with the actors. A complete explanation of the persistence of the orders of justification underlying inheritance law requires a detailed analysis of the carrier groups. Here I limit myself to five elements that are significant:

1. For one, there are cognitive and normative "sunk costs." The way in which legal scholars and social scientists perceive the problems connected with an area of law always refers to the "sedimentary products of the works of their predecessors" (Bourdieu 1983, 69, in Schultheis 1999, 77). What this means is that any analysis falls back on the already existing views of the problems connected with inheritance law, and these views provide a predetermined structure to the perception of the problems. References to written sources can resume even after long interruptions.

Of course, this does not mean that it is impossible to deviate from existing perspectives. But existing argumentations do have a position of cognitive privilege, since they connect more easily to the political discourse. This is evident from the repeated references in parliamentary debates to rules of inheritance law in other countries. The speakers cite these rules either with a critical intent to assert a difference between "their own" and a "foreign" law that should be rejected, or, if they refer positively to the rules of foreign law, the opposition often delegitimizes the proposal as "culturally alien." The argumentative deviation can thus contribute to reinforcing "one's own" traditions. Another pattern in the reaction to outside argumentative contexts is ignorance. For example, the American institutionalist Richard Ely's adoption of Bluntschli's family-oriented arguments simply fizzled out in the American discourse on estate taxation and thus remained ineffective.

2. This self-referentiality of discursive structures is also reinforced by the increasing differentiation of society and the accompanying unfolding of institutional idiosyncrasies. Legal discourses, but also other discourses in the social sciences, become ever more closed-off semantically and thus increasingly immune to social changes. "The force of the purely logical legal

doctrines let loose, and a legal practice dominated by it, can considerably reduce the role played by considerations of practical needs in the formation of the law" (Weber 1978 [1922], 2:459). Actors perceive the problems associated with the bequest of property based on legal doctrines and close themselves off from reforms that contradict their logic. A good example is the debate between Romanists and Germanists in German legal thinking in the nineteenth century. Another example is the debate over the justification of the transmission of property derived from natural law or positive law.

3. This inner logic of the legal discourse—and to a limited extent also of other social-science disciplines—spreads into parliamentary debates, as well. Many politicians are themselves lawyers—or have some other academic education—and have therefore been shaped by the perspectives on the issue of inheritance law mediated by the institutions in which they were trained. It can be assumed that these perspectives exercise a stabilizing influence on the political perception of the problem.

4. Moreover, it can be shown that existing law itself claims "an enormous power of definition concerning all subjects of the social world" (Schultheis 1999, 72). Not only do discursive patterns influence the development of law, but the reverse is also true, that is, existing law influences the perception of the problem of inheritance. This applies in Germany to the protection of property rights under Article 14 of the Basic Law in conjunction with the protection of the family under Article 6, which are always cited as solid points of reference by opponents of inheritance taxation. The same is true of the real partitioning of property stipulated in the Code Civil, which became a fixed point of reference for republican forces. When it became necessary to make this legal proviso more flexible, this could be achieved politically only by hollowing out the regulation while leaving it formally untouched. Thus the path dependence of the law is also to be seen in connection with the cognitive power of existing law.

5. Finally, the social representation of the regulation of inheritance law is embedded in the broader political culture. This embeddedness leads to the stabilization of discourses on inheritance law also when social structures undergo changes that lead to new demands on inheritance law, because the broader cultural idioms exert pressure toward coherence. For example, the French ideology of "familialism" suggests a specific relationship between the state and family and the role of population policy, which is then *also* translated into the politics of inheritance law (Schultheis 1999, 77–78). Similarly, the problematization of equality of opportunity in American political culture is definitely not limited to inheritance law, but also touches on university admission policies, the labor market, and gender policy.

However, the importance of more general discursive contexts also provides a clue to the causes behind the change in discourses on inheritance law and the legal transformation that goes along with it. The change in inheritance law discourses or their sudden surge in importance can be consistently connected with profound political and social experiences of crisis.

This is true of the bourgeois revolutions at the end of the eighteenth century, of the experiences of social crisis during industrialization, and of the transformation of the guiding economic ideas in the 1970s. This points to a link between experiences of "collective effervescence" (Durkheim) and institutional change, which must be seen simultaneously in connection with processes of cognitive transformation. The experience of crisis dislocates existing routines and makes the conscious reconceptualization of the situation necessary.

Recently, Mark Blyth (2002) laid out a theory of endogenous institutional change, which proceeds from the notion of uncertainty and accords central importance to ideas. In situations of profound crisis, the actors are confronted by uncertainty about causal relationships, and this uncertainty must be digested in a process of interpretation before new institutional structures can be erected on the foundation of collectively shared ways of seeing:

> [T]he destabilization of institutions may produce uncertainty, and while such uncertainty may manifest itself in effects . . . , neither the causes of nor the solutions to such uncertainty are given by the conditions of the collapse. Agents must argue over, diagnose, proselytize, and impose on others their notion of what a crisis actually is before collective action to resolve the uncertainty facing them can take meaningful institutional form. (Blyth 2002, 9)

This picks up directly on the critique of Durkheim's sociology of religion that was articulated by Hans Joas (2000), who argued that Durkheim, in his theory of institutions, paid too little attention to the process of the discursive interpretation of effervescent collective experiences of crisis. My analysis of the development of inheritance law in France, Germany, and the United States, however, has shown that only a few situations saw the emergence of completely new interpretations of causal relationships, of the problems that needed solving, and of the values to be pursued. One example is the change, in the late nineteenth century in the United States, in the perception of the role of the state in guaranteeing equal opportunity (Huston 1993). In the vast majority of cases we find an upsurge in positions that already exist in the discursive field and are able, within a short period of time, to achieve ideological hegemony, though without eliminating the opposing position from the field once and for all. Revolutionary France saw the victory of the idea that equality in family relationships should be promoted through the introduction of an inheritance law based on the principle of equality and through limits on testamentary freedom. However, the losing side achieved renewed prominence in the 1850s, when these very regulations of inheritance law were held responsible for the crisis of the family and the country's demographic trend, which was seen as deeply problematic. In the United States, the conflict between the importance of inheritance law to the normative idea of equality of opportunity, and its importance to the principle of the free disposition over private property and economic development, can be traced back to the revolutionary period. During the transformative situations of crisis—at the end of the nineteenth century, in the 1920s, the 1930s, and the 1970s—we can observe a change in which interpretation held sway. For example, the analysis of the discourse on inheritance taxation in the United States in the 1970s revealed that this issue was perceived much more strongly under the aspect of economic efficiency and less so from the perspective of equality of opportunity. This goes hand in hand with a refocusing of fiscal and economic policy discourses in the same direction. This change in the "master frame" also affected the debates over inheritance taxation. However, these arguments of the opponents of inheritance taxation had dominated the debate at least on one previous occasion, namely in the 1920s. At the same time, the discussions in the late 1990s show that the arguments about equality of opportunity did not simply vanish. Rather, they continue to be put forward, especially in academic debates, with those championing them trying to adjust to the challenges from the economic arguments.

The interpretations of situations of crisis, which alone create the prerequisites for institutionalizations, are thus in no way arbitrary. Rather, they reflect a country's discursive field, a field that appears very stable over the long term. The positions contained within this field, one can presume, are especially easy to mobilize because of their cognitive grounding. This helps to explain why we find at most weak tendencies for a convergence of inheritance law discourses in the three countries.

Here and there in the development of inheritance law one can also detect change induced from the outside. This change is triggered by external legal intervention. Examples are the German areas that remained under the influence of the French Code Civil even after the Wars of Liberation of 1813–15, and the suddenly very high inheritance tax introduced by Allied law in Germany after World War II. In the long run, however, these deviating developments were reversed.

Individual, Family, and Society in the Development of Inheritance Law

The examination of the development of inheritance law and the guiding problems in each of the three countries was linked with a question of social theory. To what extent does the development of inheritance law reflect a tendency toward individualization, understood as the increasing disembedding of the individual from social obligations? What development of the relationship between individual, family, and society (state) can be seen in the evolution of inheritance law and the discourses on this area of the law?

By addressing processes of individualization, this study connected with one of the crucial questions of Émile Durkheim (1984), but also of social theory in general. In and of itself, however, Durkheim's methodological intuition to use the evolution of law as an indicator for examining the change in the relationship between individual and community in the modernization process contains no evidence about this process. That evidence emerges only from Durkheim's interpretation of the development of law that he examined. Durkheim read in it the retreat of the collective consciousness and at the same time a change in the structure of social solidarity. For him, modernization means the development of "moral individualism." With this concept, Durkheim expressed that the "liberation" of the individual from the clutches of the community does not reflect a reduction of societal influence on the individual, but rather a *change* in the way that society exercises moral power over the individual that moves the rights of the individual to the center.

This concept also entailed concrete expectations about the development of inheritance law. Durkheim (1992 [1957], 1984 [1893]) predicted severe restrictions on the right to bequeath property, because the understanding of property would develop toward a concept of *individual* property rights, which expired with the death of the property owner. Public opinion would object with growing vehemence to the ascriptive privileging of a few members of society through inheritance. This reflects the convictions of many republicans in the Third Republic that social institutions should follow meritocratic principles. The transmission of wealth contradicts this principle because it leads to unequal starting positions and the heir is spared the need to prove his abilities in competition. Durkheim linked the increasing individualization also to the institutional implementation of the principle of achievement. Indirectly this expectation also shaped Talcott Parsons's (1954) discussion of inheritance. Inheritance as a social institution of modern societies plays almost no role in Parsons's theory. That is because Parsons read the structures of modern society largely from the situation of the American middle class in the mid–twentieth century, and for *its* social position, inheritances played virtually no role. But to see this class as paradigmatic for social theory is misleading inasmuch as the relevance of inheritances is thus excluded from the theory, although they might be significant for the reproduction of social inequality. This insight into the history of theory may help explain why sociology largely refrained from dealing with the topic in the second half of the twentieth century.

In any case, if one looks at the development of inheritance, Durkheim's and Parsons's meritocratic expectations came true only in part. They are evident in the equality of sons and daughters and the extension of inheritance rights to illegitimate children. The strengthening of the legal position of the surviving spouse is also a rejection of the dynastic principle of blood kinship. Moreover, American social reformers, in particular, wanted to create the social preconditions of individual equality of opportunity by taxing large estates. But in none of the three countries were inheritances redistributed with the result of creating more equal individual starting conditions. Durkheim made an error of prognostication by seeing the private right of inheritance as a relic in the process of dissolving.

A completely different theoretical approach—though one that can also be characterized as based on the assumption of individualization—marks Max Weber's description of the development of inheritance law. He perceived a tendency of increasing individual rights of disposal on the part of the testator (Weber 1978 [1922], 2:370ff.) and, conversely, the curtailment of family considerations and state intervention in the transfer of wealth *mortis causa*. This, too, provides only an incomplete theoretical framework for the findings of the present study of the development of inheritance law in Germany, France, and the United States. In none of the three countries was testamentary freedom expanded during the period under investigation. While the statutory portions for family members of the deceased were different in the three countries, they hardly changed for the legitimate children of the testator. They were expanded for the surviving spouse as well as for the illegitimate children who had previously been largely excluded from intestacy law. Although the extension of the rights to a statutory portion—the topic of controversy especially in France and Germany—was directed against the dynastic interlinking of noble families, at the same time it reinforced new forms of the family. That the changes of inheritance law aimed not at individualism, but at a *change* in family solidarity, becomes even clearer if one looks at the discourse on testamentary freedom. For even proposals to expand testamentary freedom could at times be intended to strengthen the family as a counterbalance to tendencies toward individualization. This was true for family researchers like Wilhelm Heinrich Riehl and Frédéric Le Play, who wanted to protect the unity of the extended family with unlimited testamentary freedom. The family was to function as a shelter for the individual against the excessive vagaries of modern economic life.

An impetus toward individualization is evident, at best, several centuries earlier, during the transition from the Middle Ages to the early modern period, when testamentary freedom known from Roman law was gradually introduced under pressure from the church. Other developments of inheritance law are ambiguous with respect to the increased autonomy of the testator. The dissolution of entails can be interpreted as confirming Weber's thesis in that the heirs can dispose of the landed property. At the same time, the testator can no longer decide to which persons of the next generation the property should pass, and he cannot shield it from alienation. The prohibition thus limits the freedom of the testator and reduces individual property rights.[8] The inheritance tax, meanwhile, through which the state appropriates part of the bequeathed property, clearly disconfirms the expectation of Weber's version of individualization theory. Here, too, the trend goes toward reducing individual power of disposal by expanding fiscal intervention in property.

The comparative examination of the development of inheritance law and the accompanying discourses show no unambiguous tendency of an expanding individualism, neither in Durkheim's definition nor in Weber's. Instead, what we find are processes that balance the interests of the family and testator, on the one hand, and the familial sphere and the state, on the other. These processes of negotiation take place within the respective contexts of cultural idioms. The result is a political compromise involving economic, political, and familial matters, as well as the inertia of existing legal institutions. This process is more precisely grasped with the phrase "embedded individuality" than with Durkheim's concept of "moral individualism," for the development of inheritance law shows that the individual is by no means the *sole* moral reference point. Instead, it is the individual within his familial and social contexts. The latter also include the economic and political implications of inheritance law.

In *what kind of* compromises the tension between the individual, the family, and society (state) is institutionalized thus seems to be much more open than sociological approaches of individualization or economic institutionalism allow. This is reflected in the varied development of inheritance law in the three countries and in long-term differences.

When it comes to social theory, one can draw from all of this the conclusion that the contingency of social processes of institutionalization must be placed front and center. The evolution of the law seems to be the result of concrete processes of negotiation that are conducted as political, legal, and general intellectual discourses, which are carried on against the backdrop of the perception of functional demands, power positions, existing institutional structures, and cultural identities. The development of institutions is fundamentally undetermined, and the capacity of society to exert influence upon itself must be accounted for conceptually. The process of modernization does not undergo evolution in the sense of a movement toward increasingly efficient institutional forms or increasing individualization. Instead, it seems more plausible to speak of "multiple modernities" (Eisenstadt 2000), which emphasizes the inertia of independent traditions and at the same time leaves room for contingent processes of change.

THE METHOD OF CONTENT
ANALYSIS OF PARLIAMENTARY DEBATES

The findings about the argumentative structure in the discussions over inheritance law, presented in the text in the form of tables, are based on a content analysis of parliamentary debates.[1]

The analysis involved key parliamentary debates on three of the four controversies over inheritance law discussed in this book. I tried to encompass the longest possible chronological period in order to provide a good sense of the developments over time. Since the contested topics became relevant to the legislative process at various times, the debates I analyzed have different chronological focal points. Moreover, not all issues became the subject of parliamentary controversies in all three countries. This is especially true of the United States, where only the federal estate tax falls within the legislative purview of Congress. All other areas of inheritance law lie within the legislative competency of individual states, but their legislative bodies did not produce stenographic records of their debates. The best comparative perspective is afforded by the debates over inheritance taxation, which were carried on in all three countries at about the same time and are documented by stenographic records.

To reduce the amount of material that had to be analyzed, I considered only the debates in one of the two parliamentary houses. My choice fell on the lower house, because its debates reflected a broader range of attitudes that existed within the political constituency. Given the prevailing electoral systems, this chamber had a more democratic legitimation in the two European countries, at least in the nineteenth century. In Germany, the upper house, the Bundesrat, is a body that represents the interests of the states and their executive branches.

A total of thirty-six debates were coded. Some of the debates were not extensive enough for further processing; others dealt with themes that are not considered in this book (e.g., the form of the testament). The body of the book evaluates seventeen debates: seven German, four French, and six American debates. The chronological and thematic distribution can be seen from appendix table 1.

All speeches of a given debate were coded. As a debate I defined the various readings of a single bill, which is why the period of the debate often stretches over several months.

The coding of the debates first recorded general data, such as the name of the speaker, the date of the speech, the speaker's party and religious affiliation, gender, social status, occupation, and origin (electoral district). There are many gaps when it comes to religious affiliation, since the relevant parliamentary records in France and the United States for the most part do not take note of it, and it is often also impossible to infer it from the information that is provided. When coding occupational affiliation, if several professions were indicated, I chose the profession at the time of the speech or closest to it chronologically.

APPENDIX TABLE 1
Country, Date, and Thematic Area of the Debates Subjected to Content Analysis

	Germany	*France*	*United States*
Testamentary freedom		1790–91	
Entails	1848, 1914	1826	
Inheritance taxes	1905–6, 1908–9, 1919, 1973, 1995–96	1849, 1895	1909, 1916, 1926, 1935, 1976, 2001

Next I coded the individual arguments (positions) that were put forth by the speakers for or against a bill or individuals sections of a bill. One example is the position "in favor of the introduction of an inheritance tax." The unit of coding is thus the individual argument. This unit of coding is linked to the existence of sentences that, alone or in aggregate, assume the structure of an argument. An argument that was repeated several times by the same speaker in one speech was coded for each repetition. If the same argument appeared several times in the same sentence, it was coded only once. However, if a sentence contained several different arguments, all of them were coded. "Several arguments" can mean either one argument that is given more than one justification, or several arguments that are put forth with the same justification. Quotes by other individuals that were used by a speaker in argumentation to bolster his or her position were also coded. Titles and comments by hecklers were not coded. Only the arguments of a speech that pertained to the topic of inheritance were coded. All other themes were ignored. In total, 5,640 arguments were coded.

Codes were assigned to the individual arguments. Codes were also assigned to the justifications for the argument, that is, for the semantic expressions with which speakers justified their positions. Since new positions and justifications continually appeared in the debates, the code system was constantly expanded during the coding process and was completed only when the coding itself was finished. In my discussion of the results, I grouped the highly differentiated categories into units. Because numbers were rounded up or down, the results in the tables do not always add up to exactly 100%.

The system of categories for the arguments is structured hierarchically. The first part concerns the topic within the inheritance law discourse addressed by the argument. There are three main categories, each with subcategories. The respective themes are found in the subcategories.

The second part of the system of categories concerns the speaker's assessment of the topic. One example would be the justification for the position "in favor of the introduction of an inheritance tax" by the statement "because it leads to a more just distribution of taxes." The system is broken down into two main categories. Below them are subcategories, which are in turn subdivided into the concrete value-positions or functional justifications of the speakers. Only the concrete justifications were coded, not the main categories or subcategories.

The coding was carried out by two assistances trained in this method. The reliability of their results was tested variously by having the same text passage coded by both assistants, and the results were found to be highly congruent. Differences emerged mainly in the evaluation of whether or not a specific sentence constituted an argument that should be coded. The code of the argument theme and of the argument justification of every coded argument was noted in the original text. The arguments were coded only after the entire passage in which they occur had been read; this was done to prevent arguments from being taken out of context and thus wrongly interpreted.

Acknowledgments

1. For the founding fathers of sociology, the transfer of property by bequest was an important issue, as can be seen in the works of Weber (1978 [1922]); Durkheim (1992 [1957], 1984 [1893]); and Simmel (1992 [1908]). This interest largely disappeared in the 1930s. A renewed interest within German sociology is reflected in the works of Kohli (1997, 1999); Kosmann (1998); Lauterbach and Lüscher (1996); Lettke (2003); Lüscher (2002); Szydlik (1999); and Willenbacher (2003). Inheritance is a rather marginal topic also in American and French sociology, though more interest has developed recently (Gotman 1988; Spilerman 2000). Somewhat more research on inheritance has been done in the fields of economics, legal studies, and history.

Chapter 1: Introduction

1. For Émile Durkheim's sociology of law, see Gephart 1993, 321ff.

2. Sociologists like Ferdinand Tönnies, Talcott Parsons, and Robert Park agreed with Durkheim on this. The subject also plays an important role for theories of modernization that developed later, and it shapes current sociological debates on the nature of modern societies.

3. That bases of legitimation of social rules also emerge discursively can be seen in Durkheim's work itself (1992 [1957]), namely in the reference to the role of professional groups, in the debate on the state and democracy, as well as in the discussion of the binding effect of words in contract theory. But this idea is hardly developed systematically.

4. On the issue of the division of estates, Weber also rejected a purely economic explanation of institutions of inheritance law: "Economic factors originally determined to a large extent whether a property was inherited by one person or principal heir or whether it was divided. This practice varies with economic influences, but it cannot be explained solely by economic factors, and especially not by modern economic conditions" (Weber 1978 [1922], 1:377).

5. The literature about social movements uses the closely related concept of "frames." Framing also concerns the specific meaning a fact obtains in the perception of actors. An excellent theoretical discussions of the concept and its development in discourse theory can be found in Steinberg 1998, 1999.

6. For a discussion of the concept of discursive fields, see Spillman 1995.

7. Limitations exist here primarily for the United States, where only questions of inheritance tax are decided at the federal level, while other areas of inheritance law are left to the individual states. However, for the most part, there are no stenographic records of the legislative sessions of the individual states.

8. In France, the state's inheritance right took effect after the twelfth degree of kinship, since 1917 after the sixth (Rieg 1971, 84). In the United States, it exists in a

few states. In Germany, it was not introduced, but was the subject of parliamentary and political debates.

9. The reason one must speak of purely *social* privileging is that while different degrees of intelligence and physical attractiveness also bestow advantages that are independent of effort and achievement, these are largely the result of nature.

10. The distribution of wealth has been studied far less than the distribution of income (Wolff 2002, 1). International comparisons, especially, are notoriously difficult, given different methods for collecting data. Still, the data that is available provides at least a general idea of the structure of wealth distribution in the United States, Germany, and France. The *income and consumption sampling* on which the data for Germany is based does not encompass the richest and the poorest households, which means that the actual inequality of distribution is not adequately recorded. The wealth statistics reveal that in 1989, the top 0.6% of households owned 25% of all the wealth (Bedau 1998, 111). For a review of the literature on wealth research see Spilerman 2000.

11. For an account of the development of the distribution of wealth in France in the twentieth century that looks at the distribution of inheritances see Piketty 2001.

12. Arondel, Masson, and Pestieau (1997, 104). For Great Britain, Wedgwood (1928) showed, on the basis of data from the publicaly accessible register of inheritances, that the vast majority in a sample of heirs to large fortunes of the 1920s had themselves made substantial inheritances. This finding was confirmed in later studies by Harbury (1962) and by Harbury and Hitchens (1979). A rather anecdotal account of the importance of inheritances for the distribution of wealth within American society is offered by Phillips (2002, 114ff.).

13. The economic literature lists a variety of motivations for the transmission of property: accidental bequest, which arises from the uncertainty of the time of death (Davies 1982); altruistic bequest, where the parents' concern for the welfare of their children explains the transfer *mortis causa* (Becker and Tomes 1979); strategic bequest, where the parents seek to secure the caring attention of their children in old age through the promise of an inheritance (Bernheim, Shleifer, and Summer 1985); paternalistic bequest, where the parents use the expectation of an inheritance to influence how their children live their lives (Modigliani and Brumberg 1954); dynastic bequest, a concept that goes back to Schumpeter and posits an intergenerational desire to accumulate wealth (Masson and Pestieau 1997). See also Jürges 2001.

14. The sort of effects that the private transmission of wealth has on the motivation for economic action is difficult to determine empirically. Wisman und Sawers (1973, 423–24) have shown that very diverse motivations exist for the formation of wealth and the accumulation of capital. Alongside the motivation to leave an inheritance behind, old-age provisioning and child-raising, as well as prestige, power, and social status play a role, which is why even confiscatory inheritance taxes would reduce the formation of wealth only in part. It can also be argued that incentives for saving can be created through instruments other than inheritance. For example, in the American context, Haslett (1986, 147) lists the restrictions on consumer credits, higher taxes on consumption, and state subsidies for investments as means for creating better incentives for investment. However, Wismann and Sawers, referring to a study from the 1960s, also note that the inheritance motif gains in importance as a motivation for the accumulation of wealth with rising income and advancing age. For additional empirical literature on motivations for saving and bequeathing wealth see Hurd and Smith 2002; Jürges 2001; Lauterbach and Lüscher 1996; Lüth 2001.

15. Gallo and Gallo (2001) have shown that the psychological damage caused by the parents' wealth can even create the need for psychotherapeutic help.

16. On a macroeconomic level, the connection between the inequality of wealth distribution and economic growth is also important for an economic assessment of inheritances. Although many economists see an unequal distribution of wealth as something positive, since it points to incentive structures that reward differences in individual achievement, that view is not without controversy. It can also be shown that strong inequality hampers growth. On this see the review of the literature by Aghion, Caroli, and García-Peñalosa (1999).

17. See also Phillips 2002, 116ff.

18. For France see Déprez 2002.

19. In actuality, however, the income from inheritance taxes rarely accounted for more than about 2% of total tax revenues in Germany, France, and the United States.

Chapter 2: The Right to Bequeath

1. However, Leipold (1997, 14) also notes: "It is almost self-evident that testamentary freedom cannot be unlimited, if one simply takes into consideration the idea of the family's right of inheritance. . . . It would be highly inconsistent if the property constraints within the framework of marriage and the closest family were subordinated completely to the property owner's free decision on the occasion of his death."

2. In the absence of an inheritance law, property would become ownerless upon the death of the owner and could be appropriated by those who stake the first claim to it. The question of the ownerlessness of property upon the transfer of property *mortis causa* was discussed especially within legal philosophy in the late eighteenth century. See, for example, Kant (1965 [1797]), §34–6, and appendix 7.

3. This is already evident in the first reform, the abolition of the nobility's special inheritance law involving primogeniture and the preferential treatment of sons (Decree of 15 March 1790). This established legal equality between the nobility and commoners in inheritance law. To be precise, the reform actually began with the decree of 4 August 1789, which abolished the feudal system. This also rendered the inheritance law pertaining to the nobility's landholdings meaningless. However, inheritance law as such is not mentioned in this decree, which is why the beginning of the reform of inheritance law is more appropriately dated to March 1790. The relevant article of the decree reads as follows: "All the privileges, feudal and noble rights pertaining to the abolished estates, the rights of the firstborn and of male offspring to feudal tenures, landholdings, and noble landed property, as well as the unequal distribution on the basis of the status of the individuals, are abolished" (qtd. in Aron 1901, 472). The decree concerned feudal rights as a whole, which reveals that this reform of inheritance law was seen as part of the social transformation of the ancien régime. The decree, however, did not yet touch on the question of testamentary freedom; it merely broke the nobility's privileged position in inheritance law and subordinated it to the principle of equality. As long as the testator could violate the principle of equality by circumventing customary law or establishing certain provisions in the will, this principle could not be enforced in practices relating to inheritance; doing that required limitations on testamentary freedom.

4. The bill introduced in November 1790 called for (*a*) the complete equality in the legal division of the inheritance, (*b*) the abolition of the distinction between

inherited and acquired wealth, between real estate and movable property, and between bourgeois and noble property, and (c) the absolute validity of the principle of representation in the first line, in the side line up to and including nephews. The principle of representation means that a relative who is next in the succession to the inheritance in the direct line takes the place of the heir ahead of him or her if the latter is already deceased. For example, if a daughter who has children dies, they move up to take their mother's place in the line of succession (see Lingenthal and Crome 1894–95, 1:29 ff.). At the request of Mirabeau, the discussion of the proposed bill was postponed by the constitutional assembly, because it did not contain any provisions about the institutions of substitution and testamentary freedom (Aron 1901, 476). In response, the committees presented the bill again in March 1791, now supplemented with a law that was supposed to regulate testamentary succession.

5. As in Germany one hundred years later, the harmonization of the law was an important concern of the reforms of the inheritance law during the revolutionary period (Dainow 1940, 677). Unlike in Germany, though, the revision of civil law after the French Revolution was linked with the interest in fundamental political reforms aimed at implementing the principle of natural equality.

6. Unless otherwise noted, the translations of French quotes are those of the translator of this volume.

7. To make the principle of equality the central focus of inheritance law and to limit testamentary freedom was by no means an innovation of the Revolution. Rather, the ideas of inheritance law reform that were crucial in the Revolution and the critique of the existing systems of inheritance law can be traced back in part as far as the sixteenth century. Long before the Revolution, it was already apparent in France "that the mental development was oriented toward the idea of equality" (Aron 1901, 462). In the *Lettres persanes* (No. 119), Montesquieu had already rejected the nobility's privileges in inheritance law as "destructive of the equality of the citizens."

8. Written law applied to about one-third of the territory of the French state; customary law prevailed in the other two-thirds (Giesey 1977, 271).

9. The *légitime* was fixed at one-fourth of the statutory portion of the inheritance. In the sixteenth century, the *légitime* became also the common element of customary law in the northern part of the country (Dawson 1980, 39ff.).

10. This distinction was abolished with the revolutionary legislation.

11. Unequal inheritance rights between sons and daughters had been institutionalized in some *coutumes,* however (Aron 1901, 451).

12. Contrary to what one might have expected, in the debate on testamentary freedom in April 1791 there was no clear correlation between the region a speaker hailed from and his position on the issue. While Cazalès, as a delegate from the region of *droit écrit*, demanded unrestricted testamentary freedom, various speakers from areas with a Roman legal tradition spoke out *in favor* of limits on that freedom. A weak link exists between a speaker's region of origin and the demand that an equal division of inheritance be enshrined in the law.

13. In the Declaration of the Rights of Man and the Citizen of August 1789, property was described as a natural and inalienable right, and the constitution adopted by the National Convention in 1793 likewise counted "equality, liberty, security, and property" among the inalienable basic rights.

14. On the conception of property in France in the eighteenth century see also Sagnac 1898, 21ff. and Botsch 1992.

15. By no means all theorists of the law who conceive of inheritance law as a civil law simultaneously see also property law as civil law. Pufendorf and, building on him, Blackstone embrace the natural law justification of property as an institution that precedes society, but they see inheritance law as civil law. Especially in the United States, the differentiation between the legitimation of property in natural law and the grounding of inheritance law in positive law has continued to this day as the basis of laws concerning the taxation of inheritances.

16. Montesquieu had described the increasing inequality in the social development, but at the same time pointed out the way to abolishing it: "In the state of nature, indeed, all men are born equal, but they cannot continue in this equality. Society makes them lose it, and they recover it only by the protection of the law" (Montesquieu 1899 [1748], 1:111).

17. Here we can distinguish once again between two conceptions of property: the concept of the *limits to property* rests "on the idea of the state's responsibility toward the weaker segment of society" (Botsch 1992, 226–27) and was advocated by Robespierre, for example. Going even further, various popular movements during the Revolution, in particular, propounded a concept of *égalité des biens*, which was aimed at an actual equal distribution of property or called for the abolition of private property (216ff.), and invoked Rousseau. The best-known advocate of this conception of property was undoubtedly Gracchus Babeuf, the leader of the movement of the *Egaux* who was executed in 1799. This movement also influenced the ideas of the early socialists (Ritter 1996, 28–29; Schunck 1994, 178–79), thus extending its influence far beyond France. See chapter 5.

18. A content analysis of the debate shows that nearly 95% of the arguments put forth by the twelve deputies who participated touched on these two issues. Nearly 80% of the arguments dealing with testamentary freedom called for restrictions on it. The principle of equality in *statutory inheritance law* met with broad support also in the constitutional assembly. Likewise, the abolition of substitutions was hardly controversial. [The French term *substitution* refers to the legal institution corresponding to entail in common law.—TRANS.]

19. In the bill that was discussed, the share of the estate that a testator could pass on in his will was limited to one-fourth of the estate, if the testator did not leave behind more than three children. Only if there were no heirs in the direct line would he be allowed to dispose over half of his wealth in his will. In his speech, Mirabeau actually demanded that the share of the estate that could be disposed of in a will be reduced further, to 10%.

20. The speech was delivered by Talleyrand, since Mirabeau was already on his deathbed. It is controversial which parts of the speech were written by Mirabeau himself (see Darrow 1989, 1). This speech was repeatedly referred to in later debates over inheritance law in the French parliament.

21. This idea was articulated especially clearly in the same debate by Robespierre, who at the same time also established the link between inheritance law and the principle of equality: "The property of the man must be returned to the common good of society after his death. It is solely in the public interest that society hands it over again to the descendants of the first owner: in the process, however, the public interest is guided by the principle of equality" (Robespierre, Assemblée Nationale, 5 April 1791, 563).

22. Robespierre, who also made this connection between the unequal distribution of wealth, political inequality, and the destruction of liberty, introduced yet

another argument against testamentary freedom, which was mentioned again and again in later debates on inheritance law. This was the moral corruption caused by the unequal distribution of wealth: "Equality is the source of all political well-being; the unequal distribution of wealth, however, is the source of all political evil; it alone causes man to envy his fellow man and makes him into the tool of his ambition, the plaything of his passions, and is often the accomplice in his criminal doings. Wealth gives birth to the destructive qualities of luxury and prosperity, in that beneficiaries as well as the envious are corrupted by it" (Robespierre, Assemblée Nationale, 5 April 1791, 563).

23. The juxtaposition of the values of liberty and equality is a dominant theme in many debates over inheritance law. As I have shown above, in the French Revolution, however, these values were *not* antagonistic—at least for the republicans—but were interconnected.

24. Constraining paternal despotism was a strong reason why Mirabeau called for limits on testamentary freedom: "It is the fathers who have created these testamentary laws, though in creating the same they thought merely of their imperium, while forgetting their fatherhood." (Mirabeau, Assemblée Nationale, 2 April 1791, 513). Mirabeau himself was the second-born son of a noble family who was disinherited by his father (Tschäppeler 1983, 55). In Germany, Hegel (1991 [1821]) criticized the despotic power of the father created by testamentary law.

25. Cazalès, the spokesman for the defenders of testamentary freedom, even threatened that the regions of the country with written law would break away (see Hedemann 1930, 75).

26. The wording of the law was as follows: "All existing unequal treatment between the legal heirs produced, whether it is different treatment of firstborn and later-born, the distinction between the genders, or the customary exclusion in the direct or lateral line, is abolished. All heirs of the same degree enter into the succession to property accorded to them by the law in equal shares; if a legitimate claim exists, a division into equal shares will take place for every descendant" (Art. 1 of the Law of 8 April 1791, Assemblée Nationale, 650).

27. Results of the content analysis of the debate.

28. Correlations with a speaker's social background (nobility or bourgeoisie) are not evident, one reason presumably being that in the National Assembly some noblemen were elected on the list of candidates of the bourgeoisie (e.g., Mirabeau).

29. The crucial sentence of the law reads: "[T]he possibility of disposing over one's property, whether in the case of death, during one's lifetime, or through contractual gifts in the direct line, is abolished; this is being done in consequence of the fact that all descendants possess an equal right to the division of the property of their ancestors" (Law of 7 March 1793, qtd. in Eckert 1992, 186).

30. Another concern voiced by delegates was that the Revolution itself would change testamentary behavior: fathers could use their last will to disadvantage sons who had joined the Revolution (Gotman 1988, 84).

31. If the testator had no direct descendants but only siblings and ascendants, he could freely dispose over half of the estate.

32. After the adoption of the constitution in Year VIII (1800) there existed a three-chamber system of the legislative branch, consisting of the a State Council that drafted the bills, a Tribunate that debated them, and the Legislative Body (Corps Législatif) that finally voted on the laws. There was also a Senate that could repeal laws as unconstitutional. This fragmentation paralyzed parliament and served to

secure the power of the first consul, that is, of Napoleon. The electoral process of the constitution provided for a multitiered process of selecting candidates; it gave rise to a proposed list from which the Senate chose the members of the Corps Législatif and the Tribunate (Schunck 1994, 189; Tulard 1989, 188–89).

33. A first draft for a uniform code of civil law was presented as early as 1793 under the aegis of Cambacérès. However, this version, like three subsequent ones, was not viable politically (Dainow 1940, 678ff.).

34. Therein lies an important difference from Germany's Civil Code (Bürgerliches Gesetzbuch, BGB). The Code Civil knows only legal heirs (*héritiers*), and testaments establish merely bequests. Moreover, children do not inherit from their parents; rather, the law appoints them heirs (Lingenthal and Crome 1894–95, 1:47). Because the children (or other entitled persons) inherit the obligatory share directly, they are in a stronger position than they would be under German law, which grants them merely the position of a creditor vis-à-vis the testamentary heir (see Rieg 1971, 89).

35. This "state-interventionist tendency" (Fehrenbach 1974, 25) in the conception of property appears, with respect to testamentary freedom, already in Mirabeau's speech of 1791: "Society thus has the right to deny its members, on a case-by-case basis, the possibility of disposing over their property as they see fit" (Mirabeau, 2 April 1791, 512).

36. The political goals of Napoleon's policy on primogeniture are examined in chapter 4.

37. Of course, the importance of the principle of equality can be read not only from the limitation on testamentary freedom, but also from the equal status of sons and daughters and the abolition of primogenitures and substitutions.

38. See, among others, Baudrillart 1857; Courcelle-Seneuil 1865; Dupuit 1865; and Legoyt 1857.

39. The dominance of the state over the family is also evident in French adoption law. Here the importance of blood kinship was reduced and the actual affirmation of the family introduced as the foundation of kinship relationships. This happened much earlier in France than in Germany. The family is thus legally shaped according to the political conception of the state (cf. Frank 1999, 212).

In contrast to Germany, where the family appears as the end of lawmaking, in France the family is seen much more strongly as an instrument to attain the desired structures of the political community. However, this conception can also be found in Hegel, whose arguments about the limitation on testamentary freedom were influential for the legal-philosophical discourse in Germany in the nineteenth century (see the discussion further below). For Hegel, the family was only the first stage of morality, which found its highest form in the state. This connection between family and political structure was *not* adopted into inheritance law in Germany as part of the reception of Hegel. However, Hegel already developed "the concept of a modern constitutional state [*Rechtsstaat*] . . . that consciously made the guidance of social development and the promotion of its citizens through a social policy and administration its goal" (Ritter 1996, 25). This idea of the welfare state became especially influential for the discourse on inheritance law in Germany.

40. The clearest position in opposition to Le Play on the question of the consequences of testamentary freedom for the stability of family structures was probably assumed by Ernest Cornulier de Lucinière, who, in his 1878 book *Etudes sur le droit de tester* highlighted precisely the antifamily character of the last will.

Cornulier de Lucinière saw in testamentary freedom an expression of the despotic organization of the Roman family. It was nothing other than the right to disinherit a family, and he placed it on a par with divorce and incest. His attack on testamentary freedom culminated in the charge that a testament was a kind of blasphemy, in the wake of which envy, jealousy, and legal proceedings would increase within the family (see Tschäppeler 1983, 51–52). In the German discourse, testamentary freedom was likewise associated for the most part with a hostility to the family. Testamentary freedom was linked with an exaggerated individualism that was rejected. However, the editor in charge of inheritance law on the first commission of the German Civil Code, Gottfried Schmitt, shared Le Play's view that testamentary freedom would in fact protect the family (see Schröder 1981, 86ff., and the next section). The contradictory proposals on how to regulate testamentary freedom from writers who pursued the goal of preserving traditional family structures provide an exemplary illustration that when it comes to inheritance law, clear institutional implementation cannot necessarily be deduced from goals. In the political discourse we find contrary strategies, each of which claims that it alone can attain the goal of the welfare of the family.

41. In the German debate on testamentary freedom, Bruns (1882, 161) called Le Play a representative of a "highly conservative position," which is clearly simplistic. See also Brentano 1899.

42. Montesquieu, as well, had already highlighted the connection between inheritance law and demographic development (1899 [1748], vol. 2, chapters 21 and 28).

43. Assemblée Nationale, 5 April 1791, 573.

44. For example, the inheritance law in Belgium was comparable to that in France, but that country had higher birthrates (Brentano 1899, 137).

45. The extent of the fragmentation of French agriculture becomes apparent in a comparison with England, where in 1870 the 2,184 most important landowners held 50% of all landed property. In France, the wealthiest 50,000 landowners held one-quarter of the landed property (Zeldin 1973, 148).

46. During the French Revolution, this argumentative connection was already made by those groups who envisaged the social picture of a republic of small landowners (Botsch 1992, 215).

47. See also section 5.3.

48. On the connection between the wealth of the church and gift law in France see Marais 1999.

49. In the United States, as well, fear of an excessive concentration of power was an important motivation behind the reform of inheritance law in the eighteenth century, and, a hundred years later, behind the estate tax. However, in contrast to France, the point was *not* to secure the state's preponderance of power, but to diffuse power as broadly as possible within civic society as the foundation of democracy.

50. On this see chapter 4.

51. Brentano (1899), in his strict rejection of Le Play's proposals, does not do justice to this aspect. Brentano saw in the resumption of the discussion over testamentary freedom a continuity to those restorationist forces in the Chambre des Pairs who had tried in vain in 1826 to reintroduce primogeniture in France (see chapter 4). To him, the difference was merely one of means. While for Le Play testamentary *freedom* was the means for an undivided transmission of agricultural landholdings and the strengthening of paternal authority, the proponents of primogeniture thirty-five years earlier had chosen legal *coercion*. Lujo Brentano (1899, 118–19)

interpreted this argumentative development as a rhetorical adaptation to the contemporary demand for freedom in economic life, which signaled a development of the "feudal-romantic program of the restoration period into modern patriarchy."

52. This puts me at odds with the interpretation of Tschäppeler (1983, 67), who sees the question of equal treatment of heirs as the essential issue in the controversy. I believe this can be attributed to Tschäppeler's inadequate differentiation of German and French conflicts over inheritance law. In the period after the French Revolution, the political discourse in Germany was overwhelmingly skeptical toward the idea of social equality. To be sure, the demand for the legal equality of citizens did play an important role for the bourgeoisie in the early nineteenth century, in the prerevolutionary period, and in the revolution of 1848–49. However, for the workers' movement, the concept of social equality had greater importance only in its early phase (1830–50), whereas later "it no longer played a crucial role in the German workers' movement as an ideal sociopolitical concept" (Dann 1975, 1041). After 1870, the concept of equality hardly "appears any longer in the form of a positive slogan in the sociopolitical clashes" (1044). Here a clear difference from France is evident.

53. Historically, the strict right of kinship inheritance was initially loosened by the church, which demanded portions of the estate for the salvation of the deceased's soul. The "free portion" allowed for the disposition over a share of the wealth for purposes of the church and the common good (see Merk 1934, 15; Tschäppeler 1983, 33; Wegmann 1969, 4). This is interesting insofar as it calls attention to the role of the church in individualization processes.

54. The two justifications for inheritance law are loosely connected to the position one takes on testamentary freedom and intestacy law. Proponents of an individual justification of the law of private inheritance tend to accord more space to the testamentary dispositions of the testator, whereas jurists who derive the justification from family law take a more critical view of the last will and subordinate it to the law of intestate inheritance. However, this connection is only a loose one, because in legal-philosophical terms, it is possible to justify testamentary dispositions on the basis of family law, as well as intestacy law on the basis of an individual conception of property.

55. His argumentation was later adopted by William Blackstone, through whom it has exerted a substantial influence on American legislation regarding inheritance law to this day.

56. "When the parents die, their rights in the sensible world—and hence their rights to property—cease to exist altogether. Should children inherit equal shares of their parents' intestate estate? Should parents have the right to make wills? And how free should parents be to give their property to those who are not family members? How extensive should the legal formalities be? To what extent should parents have the rights to disinherit their children? Answers to these questions depend solely on the state's positive laws, which decide such matters on political grounds. There are no *a priori* grounds for deciding them" (Fichte 2000 [1796], 318, §60).

57. This notion of inheritance law is also evident in the General Law Code (Allgemeines Landrecht). While the redactors recognized testamentary freedom as a natural law, they did not see a justification in natural law for the obligatory portion. The obligatory portion was only adopted because it did not contradict natural law and already existed in Prussia (Samter 1879, 252).

58. This is noticeable, for example, in the rejection of the principle of an egalitarian division of the inheritance by the German social scientist Wilhelm Heinrich Riehl.

Riehl examined the Palatinate, which stood under the law of the Code Civil in the nineteenth century, and commented on French inheritance law: "In the Palatinate, the French idea of the unrestrainedness of the individual has become so firmly established among the people that not only have family conditions acquired a completely altered form because of it, but social and economic conditions are also heading toward a complete transformation. Here the urge of each individual person to stand completely freely on his own feet has led to a fragmentation of landholdings, indeed, to a continuing fragmentation of all economic livelihoods, a fluctuation of all wealth and ownership, that is without parallel in Germany. The conditions are most intimately connected with the slackened spirit of family" (1889 [1855], 218).

59. According to Hegel's philosophy of law, inheritance law is not anchored in natural law, but in positive law, more precisely, in family law. In this regard Hegel is basing himself on Fichte (2000 [1796], 318), who had rejected the notion that inheritance law could have a justification derived from natural law.

60. For an interpretation of Hegel's argumentation on testamentary freedom that regards it as much more liberal see Welker 1982.

61. For example, Hegel writes the following in §180 of his *Rechtsphilosophie* (1991) [1821], which deals with testamentary freedom: "To make this arbitrariness the main principle of inheritance within the family was, however, part of that harsh and unethical aspect of Roman law referred to above."

62. For a critical assessment see Villey 1974, 144.

63. This assessment of Roman law held sway not only in legal philosophy, but also among practical jurists, as is evident, for example, in an essay of 1834 by the *Kammergerichtsassessor* Georg Friedrich Gärtner: "To be sure, the principles of the oldest German law were completely opposed to this Roman law of inheritance, which has its roots in the principle of arbitrariness, even though limitations were set for the latter at the time of its expression" (Gärtner 1834, 399–400,. qtd. in Schröder 1981, 449).

64. For a detailed discussion see Schröder 1981; Tschäppeler 1983; Welker 1982.

65. Between 1824 and 1835, Gans published a monumental, four-volume work on the development of inheritance law.

66. This position is also very evident in the conservative Swiss jurist and politician Johann Caspar Bluntschli: "Natural inheritance law is merely the continuation of natural family law. The heirs of everybody are already marked as such by nature. According to a long-standing view, the will of the testator has no influence on succession. As the old legal saying goes, God makes heirs, not man. Every person's heirs are already known during his lifetime; his descendants, or his parents and their descendants, if he has no children, or his grandparents and their children and grandchildren, if no one from the family of the parents is still alive, are his heirs. The original inheritance law is therefore always and of necessity a statutory inheritance law and family inheritance law" (Bluntschli, 1879, 238).

67. We read this in Röder: "Above all, a right of inheritance belongs to those who already before the death had a closer right with respect to the material assets left behind, because only they were most intimately bound to the deceased— through all of life and in all his purposes and needs—into one and the same closer circle of life, such as marriage and family, by the bond of personal love and gratitude" (1860 [1846], 524).

68. See Klippel 1984, 165–66.

69. I do not mean to suggest that the family played no role in the French discourse on inheritance law, but the justification for the limitation on testamentary freedom was not derived from the fact that inheritance law was grounded in family law.

70. This patriarchal picture of the family was invoked far less in justification of testamentary freedom in Germany than it was invoked in France, and it was also openly criticized: "At this point one really needs to ask whether such pecuniary fear is indeed a suitable means of family discipline" (Bruns 1882, 171). Conversely, the motive of abolishing paternal arbitrariness is especially given as an argument for limiting testamentary freedom in Germany. While that is also true for France, especially during the revolutionary period, the argument plays only a subordinate role to that of the natural equality of the children. From this one could draw speculative conclusions about different normative notions of the structure of family relationships in the two countries.

71. See also Leveneur and Leveneur (1999, 5): "the family was seen as the germ cell of the nation."

72. The Leipzig legal philosopher Heinrich Ahrens (1808–1874), who was a delegate at the National Assembly in Frankfurt in 1848, also highlighted the connection between inheritance law and community that transcended the family. In his two-volume work *Naturrecht oder Philosophie des Rechts und des Staates* (1870–71, 6th ed.), Ahrens places testamentary freedom next to statutory inheritance law, though his argument for testamentary freedom was not based on the law of individual disposition over private property, but referred to man's character as a creature of reason. Testamentary freedom allowed the testator to "promote the true and the good," for example, by supporting charitable foundations and thus fulfilling moral obligations (see Schröder 1981, 444–45).

73. See also the theories of property by Gustav Schmoller, Valentin Mayer (1871), and Rudolf von Ihering (1877).

74. See also the discussion in chapter 3.

75. I am referring to the Prussian Rhine province, to Alsace-Lorraine (after 1871), to Bavaria and Baden west of the Rhine, which had introduced the Code Civil in German translation as Badisches Landrecht in 1809 (Mertens 1970, 4).

76. As in France a hundred years earlier, the introduction of a civil code was supposed to overcome the legal fragmentation in the German Reich. However, the issue was not a *reform* through a change in the existing private law, but merely harmonization between the various parts of the country. These parameters of the task are especially important and consequential, because it did not permit the process of lawgiving to be seen as a mandate for reform.

77. The deliberations took place between May 1886 and June 1887.

78. I discuss these authors in detail in chapter 5.

79. Mertens (1970, 87ff.) emphasizes especially the influence exerted by the agrarian lobby on the elaboration of inheritance law in the draft of the Civil Code.

80. However, the commission certainly did not push this legal modernization forward consistently. The feudal institutions of entails, feudal tenure, and family estates were not touched by the Civil Code and left to the regulations of state law. On this see chapter 4.

81. The debate is so unproductive that I have dispensed with coding it for content analysis.

82. See chapter 5.

83. The National Socialists did, however, pass laws dealing with inheritance law. They included especially the Reich Farm Law (Reichshöfegestz) and, of course, restrictions on the inheritance rights of selected populations groups—especially the Jews—that were justified on racial-ideological grounds.

84. This is not true for the right to inherit farms.

85. This grounding of the debates over testamentary freedom within controversies over social policy would also explain why economic consequences hardly played a role in these debates in the nineteenth century.

86. This is true comprehensively only since the pension reform in 1957. Added to this is the fact that agriculture, where the limitations on testamentary freedom had great economic importance, became less relevant, while in most German states, special inheritance laws for agricultural property prevented division by inheritance.

87. See the report by Martiny (2002) for the Sixty-Fourth Meeting of German Jurists.

88. For a detailed discussion of this issue see the following chapter.

89. To the extent that inheritance law in the United States had also received less attention from *Congress* than it did in the two European countries, this must be attributed also to the common-law tradition.

90. As another explanatory element one can surmise that common law, by virtue of being law that is not enacted by the state, does not move conflicts over legal policy so strongly into the light of the public political arena; instead, conflicts are fought out much more in the legal decisions of the courts. An analysis of this supposition would require an examination of court decisions on questions of testamentary freedom.

91. Inheritance law in the United States is not federal law. Rather, each state has its own inheritance law. I will try to bring out the shared aspects of these laws. More detailed accounts are given only for Pennsylvania. The inheritance law of Louisiana is an obvious exception. Because of its history as a French colony, Louisiana has a civil law code (Louisiana Code) that was developed on the basis of the French Code Civil. What I say about American inheritance law therefore does not apply to Louisiana. Of special relevance with respect to inheritance law are also the legal differences among the nine community property states (Arizona, Idaho, California, Louisiana, Nevada, New Mexico, Texas, Washington, and Wisconsin). In these states, the property of spouses is considered joint property. There are no dower rights, but the surviving spouse automatically inherits half of the common property acquired during the marriage (Simes 1955, 17). Since most of the wealth is usually generated during the marriage, widows are usually better off in community property states than they are with dower rights in common-law states. See also chapter 3.

92. The only rights that children can assert against complete disinheritance are based on homesteading laws and "family allowances," which guarantee maintenance in case of indigence. Between 1682 and 1688, Pennsylvania had a law making it illegal to disinherit a wife and children (Shammas, Salmon, and Dahlin 1987, 30).

93. Empirical studies on the question of the disinheritance of children in the United States are discussed by Rosenfeld (1979, 1982). They show that this possibility is not used very often by testators, appearing in only 10% of testaments.

94. The American jurist Lewis Simes (1955, 7) expressed this difference thus: "To most American lawyers, the idea of restricting inter vivos gifts of chattels in

favor of children or parents is definitely shocking. They feel that any such system goes too far in sacrificing alienability."

95. Dower and curtesy rights varied in the colonies and later in the states, though they were oriented towards the stipulations I describe. For a more detailed account see Shammas, Salmon, and Dahlin 1987.

96. This right of choice was introduced first in the southern states and spread to the North only in the course of the nineteenth century. The reason for it was that slaves were movable property (Shammas, Salmon, and Dahlin 1987, 69–70).

97. In some cases, courts even decided that widows had no dower right to such uncultivated land, because it was not producing any income (Horwitz 1977, 56–57).

98. The first homestead law was enacted in 1893 in Texas (Simes 1955, 18).

99. See also the following chapter.

100. These reforms are discussed in chapters 3 and 4.

101. This corresponds closely to one passage of the speech by Pétion de Villeneuve in the inheritance law debate in France in April 1791: "This does not mean that I claim that a completely equal distribution of property is possible; rather, I would like to suggest that one must counteract early on and with the greatest care this enormous inequality in distribution, which destroys the relationships between people and is the most dangerous plague of societies" (Archives Parlementaires, 24:614).

102. On the political side see also Benjamin Leigh, in Peterson 1966, 337ff.

103. See also Kent 1971 [1826–30], vol. 4.

104. Before that, in a few states the widow, if the landed property had allegedly been sold by her husband without her consent, had usufruct rights vis-à-vis the new owner (Friedman 1966, 360–61 and 430–31; Horwitz 1977, 56). This made the alienability of real estate more difficult, since a buyer could not be sure whether or not the land he was acquiring was burdened by dower rights.

105. "The difference between the two forms of co-ownership was technical, but not unimportant. If two persons owned land in common, each had a separate, distinct, undivided share. Each could sell, give away, or divide his interest. A joint tenancy carried with it the right of survivorship; if one tenant died, the other automatically succeeded to the property. A joint tenancy, then, was a sort of last-man club in land. It was suitable for family lands; less so, for lands of people dealing at arm's length with each other in the market" (Friedman 1985, 234–35).

106. This is in line with the observation by Max Weber (1978 [1922], 2:691–92), who noted that the extent of testamentary freedom in the United States could be compared only to that in the Roman Republic. In Rome, the disinherited had the chance to acquire land in the conquered territories.

107. One exception is a text of judge Edward A. Thomas, who called for limitations on testamentary freedom in 1886: "A general statute providing that, except for especial reasons, each child shall receive share and share alike, would not only appear to be the most equitable in by far the majority of instances, but would promote family concord and happiness, and would diminish family feuds and litigation to a remarkable extent" (1886, 367).

108. A particularly pointed formulation of this tension comes from Robert Dahl: "We Americans have always been torn between two conflicting visions of what American society is and ought to be: To summarize them oversimply, one vision is of the world's first and grandest attempt to realize democracy, political equality, and political liberty on a continental scale. The other is a vision of a country where

unrestricted liberty to acquire unlimited wealth would produce the world's most prosperous society. In the first, American ideals are realized by the achievement of democracy, political equality and the fundamental rights of all citizens in a country of vast size and diversity. In the second, American ideals are realized by the protection of property and opportunities to prosper materially and to grow wealthy. In the first view, the right to self-government is among the most important of all human rights, and, should they conflict, is superior to the right to property. In the second, property is superior, self-government the subordinate right" (Dahl 1985, 162–63).

109. See chapter 5.

110. For example, Nussbaum's remarks (1937, 184) that the great testamentary freedom in the United States served to perpetuate the American industrial aristocracy and to keep farms intact holds true only against the backdrop of the experiences of the late nineteenth century, though not for the early nineteenth century.

111. This distinction between France and Germany does not mean that the family plays a lesser role in French inheritance law. However, in France the rights of the family are derived from a supraordinated principle (equality), while in Germany the family is the direct reference point for the restrictions placed on inheritance rights.

CHAPTER 3: EQUALITY AND INCLUSION

1. On the motivations behind the bequeathal of wealth from an economic perspective see, among others, Masson and Pestieau 1991.

2. This is also confirmed by the fact that in spite of broad testamentary freedom, testators do not fundamentally depart in their decisions from the rules of intestacy law (Parsons 1954, 184; Shammas, Salmon, and Dahlin 1987).

3. Intestacy law determines how the property of a decedent who has left no (valid) testament should be distributed.

4. France and many American states have a law by which the state inherits ahead of distant collateral relatives. Practically, however, this is of little significance.

5. On this see Farber 1973; Goody, Thirsk, and Thompson 1976; and Kosmann 1998, 24, for additional literature.

6. The phrase "conjugal family" refers to the unit of parents and children. Another term for it is "descendant family of the first degree."

7. This chapter, unlike the others, is not broken down by country, but by areas of the law. This approach seemed preferable, given that the chapter examines three regulatory areas of statutory inheritance law.

8. Exceptions to this were the entails that existed in Germany until the early twentieth century, which were usually passed along in accordance with primogeniture succession, and the peasant *Anerbenrecht* (right to inherit an undivided farm). See chapter 4.

9. Debates about primogeniture succession (which was derived from feudal law) had been going on in Europe since the sixteenth century (Shammas 1987, 156).

10. This rule was presumably derived from the Old Testament, where the double portion for the eldest son is given as a rule of inheritance in Deuteronomy. Jewish and Islamic law also knows the rule of a double portion for the eldest son or sons in general.

11. Exceptions were Connecticut, New Jersey, and North Carolina.

12. Knight (1992, 164ff.) sees equal division of inheritance as arising from greater negotiating power on the part of children vis-à-vis their parents in commercial

and industrial economies. In conditions of a subsistence economy, children depended on their parents, who controlled the land. Parents preferred the eldest son, because he was most valuable to them. In an economy based on commerce and industry, on the other hand, children had alternative options of employment and could therefore demand equal division of inheritance from their parents. I believe this explanation is inadequate. Why, for example, did England, the most strongly industrialized country in the nineteenth century, change its primogeniture rule only in 1925, thus being a clear laggard in the development of the law?

13. It is interesting to note, however, that sons continued to receive preferential treatment among very wealthy testators. This agrees with the finding of Parsons (1954, 186–87) that inheritance practices depend on social class. For the upper class, according to Parsons, the principle of patriarchal succession is still valid. The model of multilineal symmetry is found especially in the middle class. One interpretation could be that in the middle class, inherited wealth is seen more as support for the success that is to be attained by personal achievement, because children cannot become independently wealthy through bequests, as the inherited wealth is too little.

14. The strengthening of claims to solidarity by the spouse against the transmission of wealth by inheritance, and the simultaneous weakening of such claims by distant collateral relatives, can also be seen in the development of the structure of the tax rates in inheritance taxation. See chapter 5.

15. If there were relatives in the second class, the spouse was entitled to half of the estate; if there were relatives of the fourth class, the spouse was entitled to the entire estate.

16. The restriction of *dower* rights to real property became increasingly problematic, because as the economy developed, the composition of property shifted more strongly to personal property, as a result of which the share that widows received of their husband's estates shrank (Shammas, Salmon, and Dahlin 1987, 69).

17. Only in South Carolina and Georgia did widows have claim to full property in intestacy law. In South Carolina, the widow received the dower in fee simple; in Georgia she had the choice between a child's portion in fee simple or a life-estate in one-third of the real property (Shammas, Salmon, and Dahlin 1987, 69).

18. Another important motivation behind settlements came from fathers, who by taking the rights of control from the husband wanted to protect the property their daughters brought into marriage against the husband (Friedman 1999, 50).

19. See Dahlinger 1918 for the influence that activists of the women's movement exerted on the legislation in Pennsylvania in the middle of the nineteenth century.

20. See Avery and Konefsky 1992 for a historical example from the early nineteenth century in Massachusetts, which reveals the importance that regulations of the property rights of married women had for family life and the survival of a farm.

21. If the decedent has no surviving spouse, the sequence of succession in the intestacy law of Pennsylvania is as follows: children, parents, siblings, grandparents, half each to the maternal and the paternal side (with representation through the direct descendants), and finally the uncles and aunts of the decedent or their children. If the decedent leaves none of these relatives, the estate falls to the state (Aker 1998, 7). In contrast to Germany, Pennsylvania, along with about half of the other states (Shammas, Salmon, and Dahlin 1987, 166) and France, does not have an unlimited kinship succession.

22. The class system is also called the Justinian inheritance system and is distinct from the system of classes (*Parantelordnung*) that is used in German law. For the

differences in detail see Ferid and Sonnenberger 1987; 490ff.; Rieg 1971, 81–82; Mertens 1970, 41ff.; Leipold 2000, 32ff.

23. This system of distinguishing between different kinds of property could also help to explain why real property was held in such high esteem in France. Under the property relationships of the *communauté légale*, real estate that was acquired through inheritance remained securely in the testator's bloodline.

24. As a first step, in 1866 the surviving spouse was granted the copyright to literary and artistic works. In 1873, widows of men who had been deported as punishment received the lifetime interest to one-quarter of the estate alongside the children, and to half alongside other relatives. In 1891, changes to the spousal inheritance law in the Code Civil generalized this regulation to all deaths with one surviving spouse. The restriction that the lifetime estate was terminated upon remarriage was abolished in 1917. In 1925, the right of a lifetime estate was extended to the entire estate if the only heirs were collateral relatives. In 1930, the surviving spouse was granted a property share of one-half of the estate if the decedent had no other relatives in the paternal or maternal line. The claims of relatives who were entitled to inherit alongside the spouse were cut back further in 1957. In 1958, the spouse was accorded the status of a *héritier* and was given preference, as an heir, to the usual collateral relatives, which means he or she was, in a sense, placed in the system of inheritance classes between the third and fourth class. The reform of 1972 further expanded the surviving spouse's usufruct rights vis-à-vis the relatives. Henceforth, the spouse received a lifetime interest in half of the estate alongside the testator's parents and children (Holthöfer 1982, 983ff.; 1987, 158ff.; Leveneur and Leveneur 1999, 128ff.; Rieg 1971, 85–86).

25. From the perspective of legal systematics, it is notable that inheritance law in the Code Civil is linked with property law. It is dealt with there as a form of acquisition of property. The German BGB, by contrast, emphasizes the connection to family law by placing inheritance law as the fifth book of the BGB right behind family law (fourth book) (Rieg 1971, 79).

26. The eminent moral significance of illegitimate children is also evident from the fact that legal quarrels over paternity and support were in some cases criminal proceedings as late as the early twentieth century. The crime consisted of causing an illegitimate birth (Hauser 1997, 937; Krause 1967, 497; Robbins and Deak 1930, 326).

27. In that sense the exclusion of illegitimate children from the family structure is simultaneously the expression of the limitation of paternal power (Weber 1978 [1922], 1:372).

28. Specifically: "If the same has not made a testamentary disposition, has left no legitimate or adopted or legitimized offspring, or has either recognized the child in a public document or was declared by a decision of the court during his lifetime to be the father of the child, even if the decision become legally binding only after his death, or paternity was derived from an oath imposed on the mother or her representative" (Zürn 1892, 117).

29. However, this still placed illegitimate children ahead of the surviving spouse.

30. Under German law, it was even irrelevant to the acknowledgment of an illegitimate child by the father whether the latter was in fact the biological father.

31. Article 340 continued to apply after 1912 to children that were the product of adultery or incest (Robbins and Deak 1930, 322).

32. In view of the strong influence that the Catholic Church in France exerted on legislation dealing with the family, the view of Marianne Weber (1907, 325), who saw a frivolous backdrop to the unequal treatment, seems implausible: "No other civilized country of the present has—allegedly in the interest of female morality—endowed the sexual wantonness of the man with such a carte blanche." One goal of Article 340 seems to have been to prevent paternity suits, which were numerous in the ancien régime and often led to social scandals as well as wrong judgments (Robbins and Deak 1930, 321–22).

33. This right also existed already in Roman and canon law.

34. In Arizona, North Dakota, and Oregon, however, all legal distinctions on the basis of the parents' marital status were already abolished in the 1920s and 1950s (Krause 1967, 505; Robbins and Deak 1930, 327).

35. The important formulation of Justice William O. Douglas in *Levy v. Louisiana* in 1968 was as follows: "Illegitimate persons are not 'nonpersons.' They are humans, live, and have their being" (see Hauser 1997, 905).

36. This principle states: "No state shall . . . deny to any person within its jurisdiction the equal protection of rights." It does not mean that no unequal treatment of any kind is permissible between groups of people; however, it must be shown that this treatment is in the larger interest of the state. The law may not apply only to part of a larger group whose members are alike with respect to the purpose of the law; moreover, the goal of group formation itself must be permissible (Krause 1967, 483ff.).

37. At the same time, common law establishes strict criteria for determining the nonmarital status of the child. If the mother of the child was married at any point during her pregnancy, the child is considered legitimate (Jones et al. 1985, 679).

38. Of course, this argument loses validity with the new scientific methods of determining paternity, for example, through a genetic test. Since Supreme Court decisions have allowed unequal inheritance rights during the last thirty years largely on the basis of protecting property, there is reason to believe that the availability of more secure methods for determining paternity will place growing pressure on this weaker legal status in the Supreme Court (Hauser 1997), and that a further legal equalization for illegitimate children will take place also in the United States.

39. However, only a small number of states have actually introduced the UPC.

40. It might also explain why illegitimate children have remained to this day an important topic in social policy in the United States (Bennett 2001; Solinger 1992).

41. Of course, this does not apply to the heirs of extremely wealthy testators.

CHAPTER 4: POLITICAL STRUCTURE AND INHERITANCE LAW

1. The BGB (§§2109, 2162–63, 2210), however, prohibits the appointment of a successor for longer than thirty years. American law has the "rule against perpetuities," which limits tying up property to twenty-one years after the death of the last heir who was alive at the time of the testator's death. In France, Articles 897 and 1048–50 of the Code Civil permit only substitutions of one degree.

2. This legal institution had different names in the three countries. In Germany, the term *Familienfideikommiss* or simply *Fideikommiss* was used; French law spoke of *substitution*; in the United States the term *entail* was common. I use *entail* when speaking about this form of property in general, and the United States, in particular; the German and French terms are used in discussing those countries.

3. Entails also made their way into nineteenth-century literature. Examples are E.T.A. Hoffmann's *Das Majorat*, Achim von Arnim's *Die Majoratsherren*, Balzac's *Les Paysans* and *Le Curé de Village*, and Jane Austen's *Pride and Prejudice*.

4. In Prussia there was also the possibility of setting up monetary entails. These were strongly reminiscent of the "trusts" known to Anglo-Saxon law, in which the holder of the trust can dispose only over the income generated by the assets of the trust. However, socially important and politically controversial was chiefly the establishment of entailed estates, by which landed property was permanently removed from the market mechanisms of exchange. Whenever the present chapter speaks of entails (*Fideikommisse* in Germany, *substitution* in France), it is always referring to this binding of real property. Monetary entails are of only secondary importance (see Heß 1990, 157ff.).

5. In the United States, entails came from English law, where they had been a legal institution in use since the thirteenth century (fee tail), grounded in the law De donis conditionalibus (Orth 1992, 37). However, after Henry VIII had passed a law under which entails could be confiscated by the crown in cases of high treason, and when entails also became easier to dissolve beginning in the fifteenth century, a different institution to restrict the disposability of real property came into use in England. Referred to as "strict settlement," under this arrangement the testator left the usufruct of the property to the son, but installed the as-yet unborn grandson as the owner. Once the grandson reached the age of majority, he transferred the property to his father, though on the condition that he would in turn bequeath it to his grandson and grant his son usufruct rights. This meant that landed property could de facto not be sold. The rule, however, was based on strong custom and therefore presupposed the willingness of subsequent generations to perpetuate the property relationships. See Felix 1903, 107–8.

6. In fact, the connection between Christian and Islamic law can be traced back another step. The *wakf* evolved as an Islamic legal institution through contact of the Islamic legal world with Christian-influenced Byzantine law after the conquest of Byzantium. In the Christian Byzantine Empire there existed monastic foundations that had exactly the same purpose: protection against the possible confiscation of their property by the emperor (Bayer 1999, 56ff.).

7. The law of entail was developed in Germany in the seventeenth century, especially by Philipp Knipschildt. For an account of the legal-historical development of the right of entail in Germany see Bayer 1999; Eckert 1992; Gerber 1857; Lewis 1868; and Söllner 1976.

8. These included mandates in the Herrenhaus (Upper Chamber), the *Landtag* (state parliament), the *Kreistag* (district assembly), or, in France, the Chambre des Pairs. For example, in 1912, 121 holders of entails sat as delegates in the Herrenhaus in Prussia (Heß 1990, 186).

9. It was this arrangement that made the entail acceptable to later-born children, in the first place. At the same time, however, this led to the inefficient allocation of state and ecclesiastical offices, since they were distributed according to ascriptive criteria and could not be handed out according to merit (Felix 1903, 113).

10. Entails were outlawed in the various states in the United States at different times. Most states had enacted prohibitions before 1800.

11. On the importance of French laws to the German states in the early nineteenth century, see the following section.

12. In letters to his brother Joseph, Napoleon recommended, as a way of securing power, the granting of majorats to trusted followers, who would thereby be obligated to loyalty: "Introduce the Civil Code in Naples, and at the end of a few years all the fortunes not attached to you will be destroyed, and any that you wish to preserve will be consolidated. That is the great advantage of the Civil Code. . . . It consolidates your power, for by its means all wealth not in the form of gifts by trust disappears, and no great families remain except those you transform into fiefs. That is why I recommended a Civil Code, and why I established it" (Napoleon, 5 June 1806, in Thompson 1934, 149).

13. Weber (1978 [1922], 2:692), too, argued that Napoleon's legislation concerning majorats was chiefly motivated by politics, and that it served the goal of placing the distribution of social power in the hands of the government.

14. These estates were located not only in France. Rather, with the help of majorats, Napoleon sought to establish also in the conquered territories a class of privileged aristocratic landowners as a way of securing political loyalty. Majorats were also found on German soil until 1814, for example in the newly created Kingdom of Westphalia; after the victory over the French forces, these were converted into entails in accordance with the German law (Berding 1973; Fehrenbach 1974).

15. An important difference between the entails of the ancien régime and the Napoleonic majorat also lay in the fact that the holders of majorats lacked seigneurial rights (see Stein 1959 [1850]).

16. In the *Lettres persanes*, Montesquieu had likewise argued that the right of primogeniture was a brake on population growth (see Bayer 1999, 175–76).

17. In my view, the clash over entails confirms Wehler's thesis (1995a) of partial modernization. However, I do not mean to suggest that the thesis is valid as an overall assessment of the development of German history in the nineteenth century. Many historical works (most recently Anderson 2000) have shown that such a German *Sonderweg* cannot be empirically verified in many regards. Of course, this does not rule out the existence of strikingly backward aspects of the political order, which also include the law of entails.

18. In his *Critique of Hegel's "Philosophy of Right,"* Marx (1970 [1843]) discussed Hegel's treatment of entails. Marx saw this legal institution as proof of the alienation of the owner, since he could not decide on the use of the property; instead, his will became itself "the property of the property." See also Bayer 1999, 296ff.

19. According to the ALR, a landed entail had to yield an annual net income of at least 2,500 thalers (Eckert 1992, 94). Later, the sum was set at 7,500 marks (Weber 1904, 505).

20. In the ALR that applied to net income of 10,000 thalers (Eckert 1992, 94). Later, the sum was set at 30,000 marks (Weber 1904, 505).

21. Discussed in detail in Bayer 1999, 235ff.

22. In the process, Müller also brings in the topos of the clash between individualistic Roman law and socially oriented German law (Müller 1992 [1809], 246ff.) and the critique of the liberal theory of equity of exchange.

23. In the debate, Alexander von Bally and Freiherr von Vincke, members of the right-wing parliamentary fraction Café Milani, were staunch supporters of *Fideikommisse*. The speakers of the Right Zentrum (Beseler, Langerfeldt, Lette, Reichensperger, Salzberger), on the other hand, were more varied in their comments. Some joined the call for the dissolution of *Fideikommisse*, though it is especially within this parliamentary group that we find speakers who did not wish to abolish

Fideikommisse immediately, but wanted to let them continue for a transition period or exempt the ruling nobility from the prohibition. The deputy Beseler also put forth arguments for an *Anerbenrecht* for farmers (i.e., the right to inherit an undivided farm). The representatives of the Left Zentrum and of the left groupings Nürnberger Hof and Donnersberg (Löwe, Mohl, Mölling, Zimmermann) advocated the prohibition of *Fideikommisse*, fiefs, and primogenitures, without mentioning any transition periods for their dissolution.

24. Beseler opposed the dissolution of *Fideikommisse* with the family-oriented argument that it represented legal relationships "that are closely connected with the inner bonds of families" (Beseler, 4 July 1848, in Wigard 1848, 1:687).

25. Count von Schwerin, who belonged to the conservative Café Milani, distinguished himself in the debate between fiefs and entails, supporting the abolition of feudal relationships while rejecting the abolition of *Fideikommisse* as an unjustified interference in private law (Wigard 1848, 6:2548). The high nobility was thus indicating at least a limited willingness to accept reform, though this must also be seen as a tactical concession given the political atmosphere at the time. The argument based on property law was also put forth by Alexander von Bally (another member of the Café Milani) and the delegate Carl Georg Beseler in defense of entails. And those speakers who wished to tolerate *Fideikommisse* only for a transition period (Langerfeldt, Reichensperger) for the most part justified this with arguments intrinsic to the law itself, that is, on the grounds of legal security and legal coherence.

26. See, for example, the comments by the delegate Hermann (29 September 1848, in Wigard 1848, 3:2335).

27. Exceptions were Frankfurt am Main and Oldenburg (Merk 1934, 28).

28. This creates an interesting parallel to the original spread of entails in the sixteenth and seventeenth centuries. At that time, they were a protection against *political* uncertainty; in the late nineteenth century they were a protection against *market* uncertainties.

29. During debate in the Prussian parliament in 1852, the delegate Veit had drawn a connection between the individual and the bourgeois order of the state as well as the family and the aristocracy: "The contrast between the bourgeois and the aristocratic-medieval notion of property and family life is brought to bear on the question of family entails. The bourgeois notion proceeds from the individual, while the aristocratic one proceeds from the family, which it seeks to preserve above all else" (Prussia, *Verhandlungen der Ersten Kammer* 1851–52, 1:183 and 185, qtd. in Eckert 1992, 519).

30. This connection continued to play a role in the debates in the late empire period. Otto von Gierke (1892) saw the German idea of the tribal possession expressed in the *Fideikommiss*. However, von Gierke also noted critically that some family members would be excluded from the inheritance by *Fideikommisse*. Similarly Max Sering (1904, 64) in his commentary on proposed entail law in Prussia in 1903: "By contrast, supporters of an anticapitalist agrarian reform advocate making it potentially easier to establish entails in order to remove landed property from the increasingly emerging tendency of its subordination to the rule of capital."

31. Bayer 1999, 307ff.

32. Bayer 1999, 336ff.

33. The ethnologist Heinrich Riehl (1889) believed it was necessary to expand *Fideikommisse* to farms (*Anerbenrecht*) as a way of counteracting the fragmentation of the soil and supporting the family structure of the "whole house."

34. Consequently, the commission clashed only over the question of whether regulations pertaining to *Fideikommisse* should be incorporated into the new civil law code. While the redactor in charge of property law, the Prussian *Obertribunals-rat* Reinhold Jahow, came out in favor of including them in an expert opinion he wrote in 1878, the redactor for inheritance law, Gottfried Schmitt, rejected them.

35. In some parts of the state, the law on *Fideikommisse* was regulated by the General Law Code of Prussia of 1794, in other parts of Prussia by the common law or the Rhenish law. On entail law in Prussia at the end of the nineteenth century see Zürn 1892, 47ff.

36. Heß (1990, 159ff.) has shown on the basis of statistical data, in part as a secondary analysis, that the holders of *Fideikommisse* did not play an eminent role either economically or politically. Because of extensive cultivation, the productivity of the land they worked was below average, only a minority of estates (37%) were operated by the holders themselves, the holders created costs for the state because of their tax privileges, their effect on the development of the population tended to be negative, and only a minority of those holders and their family members who were active in the military or in state service went beyond the lower rungs on the career ladder. This data points to an important discrepancy between the rhetoric of conservative politicians about the function of entail holders as pillars of the state and their actual roles. See also Weber 1904.

37. The argument that the nobility were a pillar of the state was also invoked by Otto von Gierke, Carl Stüve, and Wilhelm Roscher, though some of these authors at the same time came out in favor of reforming the law on *Fideikommisse* to bring it in line with the market. That position was opposed by Weber (1904, 563ff.).

38. Of course, the irony was, as Max Weber aptly noted (1904, 565), that entailed estates, in particular, employed many Polish agricultural laborers, which is why the alleged goal of the ethnic policies could not be achieved.

39. This provision went back to a recommendation from Max Sering (1904, 68), though he had called for merely a ten-year period of ownership.

40. In view of an uncertain power balance in the Chamber of Deputies, the intended reform of the law of *Fideikommisse* was repeatedly postponed and delayed in the parliamentary process, with the conditions for its successful passage deteriorating. In 1913, the Freisinnige Partei threatened to have the Reichstag intervene in the Prussian legislative process. The fact that the law was still being debated during the war led to an additional loss of legitimacy, given the much more important economic and social problems the country was facing. Moreover, the government was eager to preserve the "truce" (*Burgfrieden*) with the liberal and leftist parties. The effort surrounding the entail law was now interpreted increasingly as the purely particularistic defense of its interests on the part of the aristocracy and was publicly rejected. While the bill proposed in 1917 did contain important provisions limiting *Fideikommisse* and thus accommodated the critics, it was already too late for a reform.

41. On the dissolution of *Fideikommisse* see, among others, Oberdiek 1934.

42. However, it would appear that (some?) aristocratic families are practicing a succession modeled after *Fideikommisse* to this day in order to preserve property in one piece (see *Frankfurter Allgemeine Zeitung*, 31 August 2002, 11).

43. The role that entails played in the middle colonies (New York, New Jersey, Pennsylvania, and Delaware) is not entirely clear. In New York, for example, structures that were much like feudal estates dominated the eastern side of the Hudson River from the late seventeenth into the early nineteenth century. These enormous

holdings were in the hands of a few families, some of whom entailed the land. Not all holdings were treated that way, however, and it seems to have been the common practice to dissolve an entail by a decision of the state assembly if the economic situation made it necessary to do so (Kim 1978, 173ff.). Entailment was outlawed in New York in 1782. In the case of Pennsylvania, Shammas, Salmon, and Dahlin (1987, 95) conclude: "Our will samples from Bucks County in the colonial period and the 1790s show that, even then, fathers almost never entailed the land they devised to their children."

44. However, even after the Revolution, not all states were consistent in enacting prohibitions of entails. For example, Pennsylvania did not outlaw entails until 1855 (Shammas, Salmon, and Dahlin 1987, 95). And as late as the beginning of the twentieth century, the possibility of entailing property existed in Illinois, Colorado, Massachusetts, and Arkansas, for example, although the holder could easily convert landed wealth into free property (Morris 1927, 25ff.). This led to the continued legal existence of this institution in a few states and, because of frequently divergent interpretations, to sporadic court battles over entailed property as late as the early twentieth century (see *Columbia Law Review* 15:618, "Notes"). However, these were legal niceties of no consequence to the question about the entailment of property as a socially significant legal institution.

45. Entails were outlawed in Virginia (1776), Georgia (1777), New York (1782), North Carolina (1784), Kentucky (1796), and New Jersey (1820) (Morris 1927, 26–27).

46. This can be deduced from the fact that in some wills even movable property was supposed to be bequeathed in tail. Since that was legally not possible at all, it points to faulty knowledge of the law on the part of those drawing up the will. However, in a few colonies it was possible to inherit slaves in tail (Hughes 1976, 116).

47. However, in eighteenth-century Europe, fiefs were still a very widespread form of property entailment.

48. The historiographic importance of the finding that entails were so pervasive is that the American Revolution did in fact lead to profound social changes and did not remove merely symbolic relics from Europe's feudal past. The latter view was advocated in the influential book by Louis Hartz (1955, 67): "It is the fact that feudal relics such as primogeniture abolished by the American revolutionaries were indeed relics—which explains the nature of their abolition."

49. In the mid–nineteenth century, George Fitzhugh (1967 [1854]) proposed that Virginia bring back primogeniture succession and entails. However, his proposal was more like an *Anerbenrecht* (right to inherit an undivided farm), because Fitzhugh suggested an upper limit of "five hundred acres of land and thirty negroes" (192) for entails and spoke out critically against possible tendencies toward aristocratization. In contrast to Germany and France, this kind of position toward the entailment of property is a rare exception in the discourse on inheritance law in the United States.

50. Another example of the importance of economic pressure on the legal institution of entailing property in the colonies is the development in Georgia. When the colony was founded in 1732, it was envisaged that every settler would receive fifty acres of land, though entailed in such a way that it could be bequeathed only to a male heir and was also inalienable. The goal was to force the settlers to work the land themselves instead of either leasing or selling it. In response to pressure from settlers, this limitation on property was first loosened and then abandoned in 1750.

Georgia was also one of the first states in 1777 that enshrined the prohibition of entails in its constitution (Hughes 1976, 76ff.).

51. One example is the article "Primogeniture and Entail" published in 1849 under the byline T.G., in which the author virtually celebrates the abolition of these institutions in the United States and invokes France and England as negative examples.

52. This maximum duration of a trust is fixed in Anglo-Saxon law by the "rule against perpetuities."

CHAPTER 5: SOCIAL JUSTICE THROUGH REDISTRIBUTION?

1. There are two ways of taxing the wealth that is passed down. The tax can be assessed on the estate itself, as is the practice in the United States, in which case the tax is an estate tax. But the tax can also be assessed on the heirs for their share of the estate, as is done in France and Germany, in which case it is an inheritance tax. In the following discussion, I have used *inheritance taxation* when talking in a general sense that includes both kinds of taxes.

2. On the distribution of wealth see the introduction.

3. As already noted in the introduction, scholars disagree about the share that inheritances have in the unequal distribution of wealth. All we have are model calculations with a range from 20% (Modigliani 1988) to 80% (Kotlikoff 1988).

4. Mill's proposal at the same time reveals an ambivalence in liberal thinking: what he wished to limit was not the right to bequeath property, but only the right to inherit it. No restrictions should be placed on how the owner disposed of his property, including bequests *mortis causa*; the right to make bequests was for Mill an integral part of the right of property. That was also why he opposed the inheritance law introduced in France after the Revolution, which prescribed equality among the children (Mill 1976 [1848], 227). However, for Mill, different from Locke, the right *to inherit* property was not part of the principle of individual property, which is why restrictions on *inheritance* did not conflict with property law.

Mill did take into account parents' obligation to provide for their children. Parents must provide the education and the means by which their children will be given a fair chance in practical life. When the parents die, these obligations must continue to be met out of the estate. But beyond this claim to support, children, in Mill's view, have only a limited right to wealth acquired effortlessly via an inheritance, since it would free them from the exertion of work. Children should inherit only an amount sufficient to guarantee a "moderate independence" (1976 [1848], 889). And "if there are no heirs either in the descending or in the ascending line, the property, in case of intestacy, should escheat to the State" (223).

5. This argument was later also advanced by David Ricardo (1977 [1817], 96).

6. The argument about the destruction of capital bases is strongly tied to agricultural production and to the organizational structures of companies prior to the "managerial revolution," which is why today it is put forth almost entirely in connection with family businesses.

7. In terms of tax theory, the justification for levying inheritance taxes rests on three foundations: the raising of tax revenue for the state, the redistribution of wealth, and a contribution to progressive taxation that is intended to achieve tax equity (Graetz 1983; Schanz 1901, 171ff.).

8. A utilitarian organization of inheritance taxation is guided by the social utility function that maximizes the sum of individual utility. Rawls's difference principle

moves the question of inequality front and center. The taxation must be oriented toward improving the situation of the most disadvantaged actor. However, Rawls's theory also covers those institutional reforms that lead to additional inequality, as long as the new distribution produces an improvement for the most disadvantaged actor.

9. See, for example, the argumentation by Stiglitz (1978), who demonstrated in an econometrical model that the estate tax can lead to an *increase* in the unequal distribution of income and wealth.

10. One could speculate that the enormous resistance to inheritance taxation might also have psychological causes. Given the finality of life, there may be something comforting in the idea that one can continue to be materially present among the living by bequeathing property.

11. The obligatory payment of dues upon the transfer of property *mortis causa* can be historically traced back as far as 700 B.C.E., to ancient Egypt. It played a role both in Roman law (*vicesima hereditatium*) as well as for the feudal societies of the late Middle Ages and the early modern period (*laudemium* and *Erbkauf* [inheritance purchase]) (Schanz 1901; Shultz 1926). In the societies I am examining, inheritance taxation in the modern sense begins in the nineteenth century. However, only the late nineteenth and early twentieth centuries saw the emergence—at around the same time in Germany, France, and the United States—of systems of inheritance taxation that have essentially been in force until today.

12. In the estate tax, the value of all the property left behind by the testator forms the basis of the taxation. By contrast, in the inheritance tax, the wealth inherited by the heir forms the basis of the tax. The difference in method has important consequences for the possibility of differentiating the tax rates according to the degree of kinship of the heirs as well as for an assessment of the progressive rates. For arguments against a differentiation of inheritance taxation based on the closeness of the kin relationship see Tait 1966.

13. In the United States, inheritance taxation exists simultaneously on the federal and the state levels, though it uses different methods. On the federal level, the tax has been since 1916 a pure estate tax that is assessed on the assets of the testator. Many states also levy an inheritance tax, the rate of which is based on the wealth that is inherited and differentiated according to degrees of kinship. State inheritance taxation was introduced at various times, though much earlier than the federal estate tax. For example, in 1826 Pennsylvania was the first state to levy a tax on bequests to collateral relatives (collateral inheritance tax). This tax remained in existence and was developed further as a source of revenue, which is why it comes as little surprise that the question of introducing a federal estate tax in the early twentieth century triggered vehement clashes between the federal government and the states. Since in the United States the taxation of inheritances is the only part of laws relevant to inheritance that is institutionalized on the federal level, I will deal in this section primarily with the federal estate tax. Given the existing record of the congressional debates, it is also possible to perform a content analysis of these debates.

14. Thomas Paine had called for the introduction of a 10% inheritance tax, with the proceeds used to finance social welfare programs to combat poverty (Dippel 1976, 212).

15. This is not true for Owen, who was part of the early socialist movement and took a more ambivalent stance toward private property. On this see the discussion below on early socialism in France and Germany.

16. The legal basis for this line of argumentation is found in the civil law grounding of inheritance law (see chapter 2), which has practical legal significance especially when it comes to legal challenges to the legitimacy of inheritance taxes. Courts upheld the taxation of inheritances with this argument. As long as the transmission of wealth is taxed, the inheritance tax can be set as high as one wishes without violating the constitutional guarantee of private property. For example, in *Eyre v. Jacob* (1858), Judge Lee justified the legitimacy of the inheritance tax with the civil law status of inheritance law: "The right to take property by devise or descent is the creature of the law and secured and protected by its authority. The legislature might if it saw proper, restrict succession to a decedent's estate ... or it may tomorrow, if it pleases, absolutely repeal the statute of wills and that of descents and distributions and declare that upon death of a party, his property shall be applied to payment of his debts and the residue appropriated to public use" (qtd. in Chester 1982, 37). In the decision about the constitutionality of the federal inheritance tax introduced in 1898 (*Knowlton v. Moore*, 1900), Supreme Court justice White argued likewise: "The right to take property by devise or descent is the creature of the law, and not a natural right" (qtd. in Chester 1982, 57).

17. The strong support for inheritance taxation by the Transcendentalists did not mean, of course, that the tax met with unanimous approval in the early nineteenth century. After the introduction of inheritance taxation in Pennsylvania in 1826, for example, the State Assembly received a large number of petitions by individual citizens and local assemblies demanding that the tax be rescinded. In response, a parliamentary commission examined the constitutionality of inheritance taxation. It concluded that the tax was not an illegitimate interference in private property and recommended that the tax be retained. The commission based its argumentation on Blackstone and his categorization of inheritance law as positive law. Given the civil law character of inheritance law, society was at liberty to set the rules on how the property of the deceased would be used. Since the state granted civil law, it also had the right to intervene in the transmission of wealth *mortis causa* by means of a tax. See the *Journal of the Thirty-Seventh House of Representatives of the Commonwealth of Pennsylvania*, vol. 2, 1826–27, Document 280, 695ff. Additional examples of petitions to the assembly in opposition to the inheritance taxes are also found in the protocols. See especially the years 1826–28.

18. In Pennsylvania, for example, spouses, parents, and direct offspring—provided they were not born out of wedlock—were exempt from the inheritance tax in the nineteenth century. The law of 1826 introduced a tax of 2.5% on the estate if its value exceeded $250. In 1846, the rate was increased to 5% (West 1908 [1893], 98). It was only in the twentieth century that inheritance taxation was expanded. In 1917, Pennsylvania introduced an inheritance tax of 2% for direct heirs (Shultz 1926, 127). Since 1961, inheritance tax rates have fluctuated between 6% and 15%, depending on the relationship to the testator, but independent of the size of the estate (Bookstaver 1982, 720). The motivation behind the imposition of inheritance taxes was not to redistribute wealth, but to tap into a source of tax revenue—a small source, since inheritance taxes in Pennsylvania accounted for merely around 2% of total tax revenue.

19. The stamp tax enacted by Congress in 1797 was intended to finance military clashes with the French navy and the suppression of Spanish troops in the southwest (Paul 1954, 6; Hudson 1983, 10). The tax was levied on receipts for legacies and shares of personal estates and the probate of will. The tax varied slightly

depending on the size of the inheritance, though it did not exceed 0.5%. Moreover, the first fifty dollars were tax exempt; widows, children, and grandchildren were entirely exempt from the stamp tax. The introduction of this levy did not lead to any documented controversies in Congress. The tax took effect on January 1798 and was repealed four years later. In 1815, Secretary of the Treasury Alexander Dallas proposed an inheritance tax to finance the war against England. Other war taxes had already been introduced, and presumably the only reason why Dallas's suggestion, which was intended to raise an additional 3 million dollars, was not implemented was that the signing of the Treaty of Ghent meant the end of the war was imminent (West 1908 [1893], 88–89). The pattern of inheritance taxation in times of war continued in the Civil War. Beginning in 1862, a tax of 0.75%–5% was imposed on estates over $1,000, depending on the heir's relationship to the testator. For surviving spouse was exempt from the tax. Lineal descendants, lineal ancestors, as well as siblings were in the lowest rate; the highest rate was payable by collateral relatives in the fifth kinship order, by strangers, and by institutions (West 1908 [1893], 89). In 1864, the legacy tax was raised to rates between 1% and 6%, and for the first time a tax was also levied on bequests of real estate. Assuming a complete inheritance of private wealth every thirty-two years and taxation at the lowest rate of 1%, this tax should have generated yearly revenues of $5 million (West 1908 [1893], 92). However, the actual revenue was much less: in 1865–66 it was only a little over $1 million though by 1869–70 it had risen to more than $3 million. This amounted to just under 1.7% of total tax revenues (92). Evidently the shortfall had to do with ineffective administration of the tax or at least the initial absence of penalties for failure to submit the required statements. The inheritance tax law was repealed in July 1870, after the justification of war financing no longer existed.

20. An altered justificatory context was already apparent when inheritance taxation was introduced to finance the war against Spain in 1898. Republicans on the one side and Democrats and Populists on the other clashed over the question whether the war should be financed by federal debt or higher taxes (Ratner 1967, 230ff.). Democrats and Populists rejected financing by means of a bond as taxation of the masses for the benefit of the privileged classes, and in its place they called for an income tax. The introduction of an inheritance tax was the result of a compromise between the Senate and the House. The regulations of the inheritance taxation introduced in 1898 were modeled largely after the law of 1862. However, a new feature was the fact that rates rose progressively with the size of the estate. Rates between 1% and 5% applied only to estates of up to $25,000 and rose in four steps to three times that if the value of the estate exceeded $1 million. The highest progressive rate—i.e., 15%—applied to the least favorable degree of kinship and to religious, charitable, and educational institutions. However, religious, charitable, and educational institutions were subsequently exempted from the tax. Congress passed a law to that effect on 16 May 1902 (see C.R., 16 May 1902, 5564–65). Estates under $10,000 were tax exempt. If one looks at the revenue from this tax, it is evident that—as had been the case during the Civil War—the receipts from the estate tax rose year by year. The highest share of total tax revenues was reached in 1902–3 at just over 2.3% (West 1908 [1893], 96). Still, most of the war costs were financed through bonds, which is why the compromise should be seen as a victory for the conservative position (Ratner 1967, 237), although the taxation of inheritances was also adopted.

21. Prior to the ratification of the Sixteenth Amendment in 1913, the introduction of an income tax was virtually impossible, and this created growing financing problems for the federal budget. The Sixteenth Amendment allowed Congress to levy taxes on income without having to divide up the revenue between the federal states. The federation was thereby placed on an entirely new foundation in terms of fiscal policy.

22. The Populists were able to exert direct parliamentary influence in the 1890s, when the People's Party they founded was able to send representatives to Washington through electoral victories especially in the South and the Midwest. Between 1890 and 1896, the People's Party established itself as the most influential third political power in the United States. The party did not include the call for inheritance taxation in its campaign platform.

23. For Roosevelt, as for his successor, the Republican William H. Taft, the inheritance tax had higher priority, presumably for pragmatic reasons: it seemed easier to enact, as there were no constitutional concerns about it, and the conservatives saw it as the lesser of two evils.

24. See also the similarly critical thoughts by J. K. Vanderbilt (Keister 2000, 251).

25. Weber had already pointed to the connection between the Protestant ethic and "that theory of certain American millionaires: their earned millions should *not* be left to the children. Doing so would only deny them the moral task of having to work and earn for themselves" (Weber 2002 [1920]: 239.89.

26. This rejection of the state as the "heir" to the wealth expresses not only an Anglo-Saxon distrust of the state, but also the connection in Carnegie's thinking to the social Darwinism of his contemporary and acquaintance Herbert Spencer (Hansen 1992, 106). Carnegie connected the thorough acceptance of the meritocratic principle with an elitist understanding of social reform. Carnegie called for the establishment and administration of philanthropic foundations during the lifetime of the wealthy because he believed that they possessed special qualities, as evidenced by their entrepreneurial success. For that reason he was best qualified to decide what sort of use of the funds would serve society.

27. On this see also Aldrich 1996, 59–60.

28. To this day, wealthy Americans often spend significant amount of their money on philanthropic purposes. For example, it has been estimated that charitable giving in the United States amounted to $143.9 billion in 1995 (Eller 2001, 174).

29. Other economists at the time who called for a progressive taxation of inheritance were Edwin R. Seligman (1894, 1925 [1895]) of Columbia University, and Max West, who in 1894 published the first American book with a survey of the historical development of inheritance taxation.

30. See also Ely 1891, who discusses Bluntschli's writings on inheritance taxation and, apparently under the influence of the German debate, places much greater emphasis on the rights of the family. For Ely, a higher inheritance tax must protect the rights of the wife and children, which is probably uncontroversial in normative terms, but is hardly ever mentioned as a position in the American debate on the inheritance tax. Ely studied in Halle, Berlin, Geneva, and Heidelberg, where he also obtained his doctorate. Beginning in 1881 he was professor of political economy at Johns Hopkins University.

31. Paul (1954, 108), as well, believed that the passage of the estate tax in 1916 was made possible largely by the public political discourse: "The estate tax enacted

by the 1916 act was a manifestation of a grass roots movement which had been visible for discerning eyes for a good many years."

32. Resistance to the inheritance tax can be seen, for example, from the lawsuits—surely motivated by the Supreme Court decision of 1895—that were filed in an attempt to have the inheritance tax declared unconstitutional. These included *U.S. v. Perkins* (1896), *Magoon v. Illinois Trust and Savings Bank* (1898), and the already mentioned *Knowlton v. Moore* (1900).

33. As early as 1894, the House and the Senate agreed on the introduction of an inheritance tax as part of an income tax in the National Revenue Act, but the Supreme Court declared the act unconstitutional, and it was annulled in 1895 (Myers 1969 [1939], 123ff.; West 1908 [1893], 94). The passage of the income tax law of 1894 is remarkable also for the fact that this was the first time the taxation of inheritances was enacted independent of war expenditures. This reflected the beginnings of a new understanding of estate taxation: under the impact of social-reformist protest movements, it was seen increasingly as a potentially *permanent* source of funds to finance the tasks of the federal government and thus made part of the comprehensive restructuring of government revenues. The decision by the Supreme Court did not target the unconstitutionality of the inheritance tax, but the Court saw no way to separate the income tax from the inheritance tax in the National Revenue Act of 1894 and therefore annulled the law as a whole (Hudson 1983, 12).

34. Influenced by the success of the People's Party, the Democratic Party advocated the introduction of an income and an inheritance tax on the federal level beginning in the middle of the 1890s.

35. Towards the end of the nineteenth century, it was not only the political discourse over the inheritance tax that was on the rise. The tax was also expanded in a number of states. In 1890, only nine states imposed an inheritance tax. In the 1890s alone, an additional eighteen states introduced an inheritance tax, which meant that by 1902, twenty-seven of the forty-five states were taxing inheritances (Ratner 1967, 354). By 1921, all but three states had introduced an inheritance tax. The three exceptions were Alabama, Florida, and South Carolina.

36. In the end, the tax was abolished in 1902—but only after heated debates and under massive influence from the Ways and Means Committee and its Republican chairman, Sereno Payne. Pressure also came from various states, who saw their own revenues from the taxation of inheritances threatened. See, for example, the resolution from the Wisconsin State Assembly (C.R., 1 March 1901, 3264).

The Democratic representative Oscar Underwood—who would be a candidate for the presidency in 1912—sought to separate inheritance taxation from other war taxes. In February 1900, Underwood even called for reducing the exempt amount for estates by half, though he failed to win a majority in Congress (C.R., 15 December 1900, 335ff.). The background to this move was the decision of the Supreme Court in *Knowlton v. Moore* (1900), which declared that the inheritance tax of 1898 was constitutional, but which defined as the basis for the tax not the estate, but legacies. As a result, the exempt amount of $10,000 was multiplied by the number of heirs, and the treasury lost millions in tax revenues (Ratner 1967, 246).

37. The budget proposal for 1909 included an inheritance tax. It was a moderate tax, with rates between 1% and 3% for immediate family members, and 5% for collateral relatives. The model was the inheritance tax in New York. With this proposal, Payne was trying to secure a majority for the budget in Congress without introducing an income tax, as demanded by the Democrats. However, the Senate

rejected the inheritance tax and dropped it from the budget bill, especially on the behest of Senator Nelson W. Aldrich. Instead, a tax on corporate profits was levied for the first time. In the debate, Payne argued that the budget needed additional financing of $20 million (with total revenues of $320 million), and that the inheritance tax was the best alternative to cover it. The proposed taxation of corporate earnings could endanger the recovery of the economy following the collapse of 1907, while the introduction of an income tax would be blocked by the Supreme Court (C.R., 23 March 1909, 194–97). Moreover, Payne maintained, the inheritance tax was a fair tax and also easy to collect: "What easier tax to pay than this [the inheritance tax]? A man gets a legacy, a stranger perhaps to the testator, a clear gain to him; why should not he pay a part of that to the support of the Government?" (Payne, in C.R., 23 March 1909, 196). The discussion over the inheritance tax in Congress was characterized more by technical details and especially the question of how it would relate to the inheritance taxation by the states than by principled disagreements. Most speakers supported the introduction of the inheritance tax. The conflicts in the debate arose over the income tax and the question of reducing indirect taxes and import tariffs.

38. A second report by the commission, written by commission members John R. Commons, a student of Richard T. Ely's, and Florence Harriman, was less radical, though it also proposed a tax of 15% on estates over $1 million, and an even higher rate for bequests to collateral relatives (Commons and Harriman 1916, 224).

39. Legal scholars, too, were calling for an inheritance tax. See Montgomery 1916.

40. In England, the richest 2% of the population owned about 71% of the wealth in 1909, while the lowest 65% owned merely 1.7% (King 1915, 96).

41. The Sixteenth Amendment allowed only the taxation of income by the federal government, not of wealth.

42. $150 million as opposed to the $29 million that was assumed would be taken in by the inheritance taxes of the states. However, the projected revenue from the estate tax that was made the official basis was much lower. $17 million were expected for fiscal year 1917, and yearly revenues of $54 million for the federal government following the complete introduction. The actual income from the estate tax was (in rounded figures) $6 million in 1917, $47 million in 1918, and $82 million in 1919 (C.R., 23 February 1926, 4425). The difference from the projections is explained by an increase in the tax rates in 1917 and 1918.

43. This argumentation was also pursued by Charles R. Grisp, for example, though presented in a less radical manner. See C.R., 6 June 1916, 10532.

44. This very high exempt amount was intended to preserve smaller estates for taxation by the states (Paul 1954, 108). The tax rates set up in 1916 remained in force for only six months. Against the backdrop of rising war costs, the Revenue Act of March 1917 raised them by 50% (Ratner 1967, 380). Over the strenuous objection of the Senate, a special wartime estate tax was also enacted, which led to a doubling of the 1916 rates. The introduction of two additional progressive levels raised the tax on estates over $10 million to 25%. Ratner (1967, 375) notes that the taxes to finance World War I, in contrast to the previous war financing, had to be borne much more strongly by high-income earners and the wealthy: "The contrast with the tax distribution of the Civil and Spanish-American wars was proof of the progress in fiscal justice and democracy made by the pre–World War I generation." Still, the United States financed also World War I largely with loans. The budget for 1917–18 had $4 billion of tax revenue, contrasted to $15 billion of new debt.

45. In the fall of 1918, the House of Representatives even approved another increase in tax rates by 50%, which would have taxed estate over $10 million at 40%; this bill, however, failed to garner a majority in the Senate (Ratner 1967, 396). The political sentiment hostile to inheritance is also evident from initiatives in various states (including Mississippi and Illinois) that sought to "cap" inheritances (Chester 1982, 68ff.).

46. An adapted version of Rignano's book was translated in the United States in 1924 by William Shultz, who moderated the plan somewhat to reduce the accumulation of capital in the hands of the state. This, he argued, made the plan more compatible with American values and ideas (see Chester 1982, 67ff.). The Rignano plan was also discussed in Germany and France (translation 1904) and thus offers a good opportunity to compare the reactions in the three countries. It was in England, however, that the plan found its greatest resonance until the late 1920s. The backdrop to the discussions included also the debts of the European states after World War I; tapping inheritances was considered to help pay off these debts. On the discussion over Rignano's plan see Erreygers 1997, 36ff.

47. Other economists who favored an inheritance tax in the postwar period were John A. Ryan (1920) and E.R.A. Seligman (1925 [1895]).

48. Understandable enough, opposition to maintaining the estate tax was especially vehement from representatives of states that were seeking to benefit from tax competition. Florida, for example, had passed a constitutional amendment prohibiting the levying of an inheritance tax. Democratic representative Robert A. Green from Florida was therefore a decided opponent of the estate tax on the federal level, which, he argued, contributed to weakening the states (C.R., 16 December 1925, 959–60).

49. In addition, Congress agreed to refund the taxes paid under the higher rates introduced in 1924, as a result of which $250 million was refunded to seven families of heirs alone (Paul 1954, 139; Ratner 1967, 429).

50. In addition, a lifetime exemption of $50,000 was introduced along with a yearly exempt amount of $5,000.

51. The Finance Committee of the Senate had also justified the tax hikes of 1934 with the goal of preventing the unwanted concentration of wealth (Hudson 1983, 20).

52. The gift tax at a rate of 75% of the respective estate tax rate was retained.

53. See figure 5.1. The sharp rise to 10.8% in 1936 is attributable, however, to President Roosevelt's announcement of further increase in inheritance taxation, which led to a surge in gifts.

54. However, the tax law passed in 1934 reduced the exempt amount by $10,000. The exempt amount was then raised to $60,000 in 1942, while the levels of progression and the tax rates were left unchanged (Paul 1954, 322). This meant that smaller estates especially were taxed less heavily.

55. See the discussion in Paul 1954, 185ff. The best contemporary book that was sympathetic to Franklin D. Roosevelt's policy is Myers (1969 [1939]). The essay by Percy Phillips (1937) represents the critical view of the new tax rates. Phillips believed that the heavy taxation of estates threatened the capital base especially of family businesses, which would lead to the sale of these businesses to pay the tax bill and to the diversion of investments into more liquid instruments such as annuities, with potentially negative economic consequences that were long-lasting or even irreparable (1937, 114–15).

56. There was no significant change in the tax during this period. Only the exempt amount for spouses was raised in 1948, the purpose being largely to establish legal equality between community property states and common-law states (Hudson 1983, 25; Paul 1954, 495ff.). The adjustment led to the de facto reduction in rates, because the presence of a spouse meant that half of the estate escaped taxation, and the progression for the taxable estate was also less (Eisenstein 1956, 242).

57. The law itself does not contain the final abolition of the estate tax. According to the current bill, the tax will return one year after its expiration with the tax rates of 2000.

58. See also Chester 1982, 51. The metaphor of the lottery is misleading with respect to inheritances, because there is no random transfer of wealth *mortis causa*, with every player having the same chance. Rather, from a sociological perspective it is precisely the intergenerational reproduction of social inequality that is important (see Bourdieu 1983, 183).

59. In the period 1934 to 1950, the share of taxable estates was never higher than 1.5%. Between 1954 and 1976 it rose to as high as 7.65% in 1976 (Johnson and Eller 1998, 85). The reason was the unchanged exempt amount of $60,000, a threshold that more and more estates passed because of inflation and growing prosperity. Another explanation, though it appeared in the literature only later, refers to the changed perception of the wealthy (Friedman 1999): inherited riches are today not perceived chiefly as an unfair distribution of wealth; instead, even the have-nots derive benefit from watching the wealth of others as conveyed by the media.

60. In his book *Generating Inequality* (1975), Lester Thurow argued that, contrary to the liberal self-conception, the distribution of wealth in the United States was in part the result of what were in the final analysis random profits from transactions in the financial markets (random walk theory), and in part the result of inheritances unrelated to merit. Thurow estimated that half of all fortunes over $1 million were based on inheritances. Brittain (1978), drawing on an analysis of data from the Internal Revenue Service, arrived at the same conclusion. The difference between the meritocratic basis for justifying an unequal distribution of wealth and the actual causes behind social inequality then suggest that the meritocratic principle should be enhanced through an effective tax on inheritance.

61. Of course, the economic justification of the institution of inheritance neglects the problem that it is impossible to determine an economically optimal rate of investment (Tullock 1971, 472), which means that one cannot simply argue with a maximum of investments.

62. In his book *The Examined Life: Philosophical Meditations*, first published in 1989, Nozick advocated an entirely different position. The desire to leave something to another person is an expression of the bond between the testator and the recipient. The donor "has earned the right to mark and serve her relational bonds by bequeathal" (Nozick 1989, 30). However, Nozick now sees the social inequalities arising from inheritances as unjust and therefore argues in favor of limited bequeathals. His suggestion is for an arrangement under which "taxes will subtract from the possessions people can bequeath the value of what they themselves have received through bequests." In this way, an inheritance "could not cascade down the generations" (30–31). For Nozick, only the property that is personally acquired or created is an expression of the testator's person, the bequeathal of which can be an expression of affection and familial bonds and is thereby justified. We can detect a clear proximity to the argumentation of Eugenio Rignano (1905, 1924). The

argument from property law found in *Anarchy, State, and Utopia* no longer plays a role in this line of reasoning.

63. However, Tullock (1971, 24–25) denies outright that inheritances lead to unequal starting positions. However, this argument is an exception even among politically conservative commentators, one that is not shared even by Hayek (1960, 89).

64. This argument was first put forth by Friedrich von Hayek, who wanted equality to be understood merely as equality before the law and who saw in the principle of equal opportunity unequal treatment: "From the fact that people are very different it follows that, if we treat them equally, the result must be inequality in their actual position, and that the only way to place them in an equal position would be to treat them differently" (1960, 87). Even if one considered a more just distribution within society as desirable, this did not justify the application of discriminatory coercion. Hayek and Friedman discuss material inheritance on the one hand within the context of other influences like talents and personal attractiveness, but on the other hand they also connect it to the question of the functional role of families for the interests of society. If one believes with Hayek that the family is an important institution in forming attributes and abilities that are desired by society, one can also acknowledge that the transmission of standards and traditions is closely linked to the continuity of wealth (1960, 111).

65. Orestes Brownson (1978b [1840], 79) had tried to refute this argument by pointing to the special character of material inheritance, namely that it was created in the first place through the legal regulation of the rules of inheritance. Another approach was taken by Michael Levy (1983, 549–50), who pointed out that talents, intelligence, and abilities represented merely human capital, the usefulness of which could manifest itself only through the work of those who possessed it, which made it different from material inheritance, which creates advantages for the owner without his active participation.

66. United States Treasury Department 1969.

67. Henceforth, gifts were counted against the exempted amount in calculating the estate tax, minus an annual gift exemption of $3,000.

68. Until then, it was possible, for example, to transfer wealth into a trust for the benefit of a great-grandchild, with the income from the trust going to the grandchild during his or her lifetime. Although a gift tax was due when such a trust was set up, no additional taxes were due upon the death of the grandchild. The tax newly introduced in 1976 was intended to close this loophole and henceforth taxed the assets upon the death of the grandchild at the rate that would have applied if the testator had transferred the wealth not to the great-grandchild, but to the grandchild.

69. The tax reform of 1976 abolished the existing regulations on exemption and introduced two new categories. One was the unified credit, which was deducted from the gift tax and from the estate tax. The other was the filing requirement, which stipulated the value of the gross estate for which an estate tax declaration had to be filed. The gross estate comprised all assets of the estate *before* deductions for liabilities, exemptions for bequests to the spouse (until 1981), bequests to charitable organizations, as well as funeral expenses and costs for the administration of an estate. With the unified credit of $192,800 (1987), a taxable estate of $600,000 could be passed on without the heirs having to pay an estate tax. Because of the difference between gross estate and taxable estate, more than half of the estates for which a filing was due ended up owing no taxes.

70. The sustained importance of this argumentation is also evident in the reasons offered by the Republican senators Jon Kyl and Jesse Helms for a bill they introduced in 1995 calling for the complete repeal of the estate tax: "Hard working American men and women spend a lifetime saving to provide for their children and grandchildren, paying taxes all the while. . . . when the purpose of that hard earned saving is about to be achieved, families discover that between 37 percent and 55 percent of their after-tax savings is confiscated by Federal inheritance taxes. . . . In order to pay these taxes, many small businesses must liquidate all or part of their assets" (http://thomas.loc.gov., Family Heritage Preservation Act, 27 March 1995, 628).

71. The intention behind this decision in terms of legal policy was to regard the assets of spouses as a kind of joint ownership property, where a wealth transfer subject to taxation occurs only when it passes to the children or another person (Hudson 1983, 24). Special exemptions for bequests to the surviving spouse were established as early as 1948, initially with the intention of ensuring the equal treatment of estates from common-law states and community property states.

72. By the end of the 90s, the number had gone up again to about 2% (Johnson and Eller 1998, 84).

73. In addition, the yearly gift exemption was raised to $10,000. Moreover, gifts to pay for tuition and health care costs were exempted entirely from the gift tax (Johnson and Eller 1998, 78).

74. The figure for 1980 includes the gift tax, though.

75. Graetz (1983, 262) estimates that as a result of the 1981 tax reform, the wealth subject to taxation declined by 70% and the tax revenue raised to one-third of what it would have been if the regulations of 1976 were still in force.

76. The inheritance tax revenue of the states amounted to an additional $4.382 billion in 2000.

77. The intense lobbying for an abolition of the estate tax has been described by Gates and Collins (2003, 52ff.), and by Graetz and Shapiro (2005). The authors show, with the help of examples, that the clearly false claims about the consequences of the estate tax for family businesses were used to influence public opinion.

78. The controversy in Congress ran along party lines. Nearly 90% of the arguments against the estate tax came from Republicans, while the same percentage of arguments presented by the Democrats called for retaining the tax. A clear correlation can also be found with religious affiliation. Most Catholic and Jewish representatives supported the estate tax, while two-thirds of the Protestant representatives opposed it. However, religious affiliation correlates strongly with party affiliation, and it is likely that party membership is the truly decisive variable. A less pronounced relationship exists with respect to gender. But two-thirds of all the arguments presented by female representatives are in favor of the estate tax, while that is true for only 45% of the arguments presented by their male colleagues. This ratio corresponds exactly with party membership. When it comes to professional and occupation affiliation, the analysis shows that the tax is rejected above all by self-employed representatives, entrepreneurs, farmers, publishers, and members of the teaching professions. Overwhelming support for the tax comes from members of the legal professions.

79. A bill to that effect was passed by the House in April 2002 but failed to make it through the Senate in June 2002 (see *New York Times*, 19 April 2002 and 13 June 2002).

80. Foundations, which published their own appeal for the preservation of the estate tax, expect yearly donations to decline between $5 billion and $6 billion if the tax is abolished (United for a Fair Economy, Internet). The importance of estates for the high level of American charitable giving can be illustrated with the following numbers: in 1999, about $14.5 billion in bequests flowed from estates to charitable organizations. Of the 467 largest estates with a taxable value of more than $20 million, 261 (56%) of the testators left parts of their assets to charities; the total amount was $6.8 billion or $26 million per testator (IRS, Estate Tax Returns Files in 1999, Internet). One research study, based on data from 1992, assumes that the repeal of the estate tax would lead to a 12% decline in bequests to charities, which, in 1999, would have amounted to a total loss of $1.7 billion (Joulfaian 2000).

81. McCaffery (1994) opposed the estate tax from an egalitarian-liberal perspective. Steep inheritance taxes, he argued, would fuel consumption. However, for a liberal society it was the open display of wealth that was a special provocation, not so much the differences in the ownership of wealth. Instead of taxing inheritances, a progressive consumption tax without an inheritance tax should be introduced. Ann Alstott (1996) answered McCaffery that it was precisely the potential for social and political embodied in the ownership of property that was problematic for the liberal social order.

82. The inheritance taxes in the German states were for the most part introduced in the early nineteenth century. Before that, the feudal system of dues had already known payments on the transfer of land *mortis causa*, such as inheritance purchase and the *laudenium* that had to be paid by vassals upon entering into an inheritance. The first real inheritance tax in Europe (after the fall of the Roman Empire) was introduced in the Netherlands in 1598. Here, too, the issue was the financing of war costs—in this case the war against Spain (Meynen 1912, 14). For a comprehensive overview of the development of inheritance taxation since antiquity see Schanz 1900–1901. The expansion of inheritance taxation in the early nineteenth century finds its explanation in the financial woes of the German states after the Napoleonic wars (Schanz 1901, 587). For example, the tax was introduced in Hesse in 1808, in Mecklenburg-Schwerin in 1809, in Württemberg in 1810, in Schaumburg-Lippe in 1811, in Saxony in 1811, and in Prussia in 1822 (Schanz 1901; Shultz 1926, 52). When the inheritance tax was introduced on the Reich level in 1906, all German states taxed inheritances, with the exception of the principality of Waldeck (Schanz 1906, 195).

83. In terms of the system of taxation, the succession tax that is levied in Germany today is largely identical with the stamp duty on inheritances introduced in Prussia in 1822, with the exception of progressivity, which was added later. This shows once again the long-term continuity of regulations pertaining to inheritance law.

84. If that was not the case, a stamp of 1% was stipulated. The taxation of spouses is a great exception in this early phase of inheritance taxation. It was justified on the grounds that a widow who did not have to provide for children had fewer expenses. Half a century later, in the discussion over the Prussian inheritance tax law of 1873, delegates rejected the taxation of spouses nearly unanimously as inimical to the sense of family. According to the law of 1822, the taxation of collateral relatives took place on four steps and was moderate, with rates between 1% and 8%. One interesting regulation was the exemption of 400 thalers for bequests to the deceased's domestics (Schanz 1901, 600). Even the Reich Inheritance Tax Law of 1906 still included special exemptions for bequests to the testator's domestics.

The law of 1873 also provided for a differentiated gradation of tax rates according to degrees of kinship, which were categorized into tax brackets. Tax rates ranged from 2% for siblings to 8% for nonrelated heirs. Children were exempt from the tax. Interesting is the differentiation in the case of illegitimate children, who did not enjoy the exemption. If they were acknowledged, they had to pay a 4% inheritance tax; if they were unacknowledged, they were treated like nonrelated heirs (*Anlagen zu den stenographischen Berichten über die Verhandlungen des Hauses der Abgeordneten der 3. Session der 11. Legislaturperiode*, vol. 1, Aktenstück No. 362). The Prussian inheritance tax law was amended in 1891 and 1895.

The stamp law was supplemented in 1867 by a decree that applied to all regions united with Prussia in 1866. In May 1873, the law was cast into a new form by the Prussian *Landtag* as an actual inheritance tax law, by which the stamp law became valid for all parts of Prussia. This move freed the law from the dues character of the stamp tax, originally introduced for documents, and brought a number of legal specifications (see the "Denkschrift des Hauses der Abgeordneten" in *Anlagen zu den stenographischen Berichten über die Verhandlungen des Hauses der Abgeordneten*, 3. Session, 11. Legislaturperiode, 1872–73, vol. 2, Aktenstück No. 12). The amendment is important, because it modernized the legal systematics. The only essential change in content lay in the repeal of the taxation of the spouse, which was welcomed by all speakers in the general debate on 29 November 1872. Until 1872, the tax stood at 1% and was only imposed if the spouse did not inherit concurrently with her husband's legitimate children (the expectation of the law was that the husband would die first). The primary controversy in the debate revolved around a rise in the taxation of collateral relatives, which was intended to compensate for the loss of tax revenue from the elimination of the tax on spouses. The parliamentarian Richter also criticized the exemption of bequests to churches and charitable foundations that had been introduced in 1867, using as an argument not only the loss of tax revenue, but the threat it posed to the principle of property itself: "The wealth of the dead hand contradicts the principle of private property, the principle on which our entire social and political order rests" (*Stenographische Berichte über die Verhandlungen der Häuser des Landtags, Haus der Abgeordneten*, vol. 1, 12 November 1872–21 January 1873, session of 29 November 1872, 225).

85. Smith, too, had argued against inheritance taxation with reference to the family. The death of the father usually entailed a loss of income for the family, which is why a tax on the remaining capital was "cruel and oppressive" (Smith 1978 [1776], 387). Only if the children were already economically independent was a taxation of inheritances justified.

86. In his *Principles of the Civil Code*, he spoke out in favor of limiting inheritances so as to create greater equality: "When property by death of the proprietor ceases to have an owner, the law can interfere in its distribution, either by limiting in certain respects the testamentary power in order to prevent too great an accumulation of wealth in the hands of an individual; or by regulating the succession in favor of equality in cases where the deceased has left no consort, nor relation in the direct line, and has made no will. The question then relates to new acquirers who have formed no expectations; and equality may do what is best for all without disappointing any" (Bentham 1864, 122).

87. The discussions about the state's right of inheritance influenced the parliamentary discourse especially in the deliberations over the BGB. The second draft of the BGB as well as the version presented to the Reichstag envisaged limiting the

right of intestate succession to the first four kinship groups. However, the Reichstag incorporated the unlimited right of inheritance into the BGB. In 1909 and 1913, the Reichstag debated bills concerning the state's right of inheritance that were intended to change the regulations in the BGB. These bills failed to garner a majority, however (Holthöfer 1987).

88. On exception in the German discourse is Carl Julius Bergius (1865), who was deeply sympathetic toward England's political system and British liberalism. With reference to Mill, Bergius saw the task of inheritance taxation as limiting the concentration of wealth: "However, to counteract the accumulation of very large fortunes in the hands of those who do not acquire it by personal effort, it might be advisable to establish a limit for what a person may acquire through gift, bequest, or inheritance. Inheritances and bequests that exceed a certain amount are there very suitable objects of taxation" (Bergius 1865, 253).

89. Pfizer thus does not argue from open resentment against the aristocracy, something that is clearly visible in Mill.

90. A similar proposal was also floated by the Swiss jurist Bluntschli (1856), whose position was also discussed in Germany and the United States.

91. Even if the protection of the wealth of the nuclear family is given up, over the long term private property would be an inadequate tax basis to fund social policies in their entirety, since the tax could be levied at most on the growth in wealth in every generation. But the recognition of the true costs of an expansive social policy emerged only with the expansion of the institutions of the welfare state, which had to be financed largely from taxes on income and consumption or insurance contributions.

92. The interest of the Verein für Sozialpolitik in the topic of inheritance continued into the 1930s. The last important work was a three-volume, nationally and internationally comparative compendium on the inheritance of agricultural landed property after World War I, edited by Max Sering and Constantin von Dietce (1930).

93. For a more detailed discussion see the section on France. On early socialism see also Ritter 1996, 28ff.

94. Weitling put this idea this way in his *Garantien der Harmonie und Freiheit* (Guarantees of Harmony and Freedom, 1842): "For millennia, the property of the wealthy has passed to their children through inheritance, like the poverty of the poor to theirs. Would it not be possible to reverse this for once? No! For it would not improve anything if this or that worthy man is given a fortune; only if nobody gets one, or, which is the same thing, if everyone is the heir of all the land" (Weitling 1955 [1842], 34).

95. In the preface to the second German edition, Marx and Engels distanced themselves from the catalogue of demands and thus also from the demand for the abolition of the right of inheritance.

96. See the Eisenach Program of 1869 and the Erfurt Program of 1891, which called for an income tax, a wealth tax (the latter only in 1891), and a progressive inheritance tax. The indirect taxes were to be abolished.

97. This idea was articulated, for example, by Bebel in 1893 in the Reichstag (Reichstag, S.G., 27 November 1893, 114–15).

98. On the Rignano plan see the previous section on inheritance taxation in the United States.

99. But see later Schumpeter (1928, 113), who was restrained in his comments about the plan, and Kisker (1964, 137ff.), who dismissed it as insufficiently radical.

100. From a Marxist perspective, inheritance law was criticized once again in 1929 by Karl Renner, the future president of Austria. Renner judged the right of private inheritance in modern capitalist societies to be "antisocial," because it contributed nothing to the development of production. As a rule, inheritances were merely a consumption subsidy for the heirs and fulfilled no social function for society. See Renner 1965 [1929], 164ff.

101. In 1872, during the discussion over the Prussian inheritance tax law, a few delegates in the Prussian *Landtag* floated the idea of shifting the taxation of inheritance to the Reich level. In 1877, Prussia presented this proposal to the Bundesrat. It was rejected by the commission appointed to study it on the grounds that the varying codifications of inheritance law by the individual states (before the introduction of the BGB!) would make a uniform taxation impossible. The real reason, however, was probably that the states were not willing to forgo the revenue from the inheritance tax.

102. The *Matrikularbeiträge* were apportioned fees that the federal states transferred to the Reich to cover its costs. The income still included reparation payments from the war against France and loans granted by the Reich.

103. However, the National-Liberal delegate Bassermann (Reichstag, S.B., 11 January 1894, 590) already formulated an assessment that held true later on: the majority situation in the Reichstag would change in such a way that the financing of the rising state expenditures through indirect taxes would become less and less feasible, which was why the Reich inheritance tax would have to be introduced sooner or later.

104. To the individual states, the federal contributions had become a growing and unpredictable burden, because the portion of the Reich budget that was not covered by taxes and levies had to be financed up to a certain level by the individual states. Since the individual states at the same time were entitled to that share of Reich revenue which was above the fixed budget revenues, they were able to benefit from this setup during economically stable times. However, in the economic crisis that had been ongoing since the beginning of the century, accompanied by rising expenditures by the Reich for its armament policy, the states were confronted not only with reduced tax revenues, but also with higher obligations toward the Reich. To that extent, the states had a substantial interest in reducing the *Matrikularbeiträge*, or at least fixing them at a specific level. The inheritance tax that was levied by the states was used as a negotiating point to reach that goal: should the Reich inheritance tax lead to a drop in revenues for the states, this should be compensated for by revising the *Matrikularbeiträge* (Begemann 1912, 90). The bill debated in the Reichstag stipulated that the *Matrikularbeiträge* should be capped at 24 million marks. In the law that was passed, the *Matrikularbeiträge* of the states that exceeded this level were merely deferred.

105. On the financial reforms of this time see also Witt 1970.

106. The 24 million marks were nearly equal to what they took in from this tax (1901: 27.3 million). Moreover, they were given the right to levy additional inheritance taxes of their own, which meant that there would be no loss for the states. The rates for the proposed tax were between 4% and 10%, depending on the degree of kinship with the testator. The inheritance of spouses and children would remain exempt. The rates would rise progressively, and at the top end would double for inheritances over 500,000 marks.

107. See also Bernstein 1906, 38.

108. The top rate would apply to estates over 10 million marks. As a secondary motion, the SPD also proposed an inheritance tax that envisaged a tax of 48% for inheritances over 2 million marks for relatives by marriage of the third degree and beyond and for nonrelated heirs (Reichstag, S.B., 5. Anlageband, vol. 223, Aktenstück 360, 3976).

109. Hilferding later criticized this position as overly simplistic. He pointed to possible undesirable economic effects from direct taxes (Hilferding 1912, qtd. in Hennicke 1929, 122).

110. One thing that is striking in Bernstein's speech is the argument—untypical for German Social Democrats—that inheritance taxation served to redistribute wealth. Since Bernstein spent many years in exile in England, he might have adopted this line of argumentation from the British discourse.

111. On the position of the German Conservatives in the finance reform see Hauptverein der Deutsch-Konservativen 1909. However, the observation that inheritances are family property is also found in other parties as a normative point of reference, though with a different accent. In that regard, the conception of familial property forms the structuring premise of the controversy. For example, the Social Democrat Bernstein (Reichstag, S.B., 9 May 1906, 3053) based his argument on the changing family structure, as a result of which relationships with more distant relatives hardly existed any more, which rendered bequests to collateral relatives problematic precisely from the perspective of family property and justified levying a high tax on them.

112. See also the account of this argumentation in the commission report (Reichstag, S.B., 5. Anlageband, vol. 223, Aktenstück No. 360).

113. For example, agricultural land was assessed not according to its market value, but at twenty-five times the value of its yield, which was a lower formula. Moreover, the tax for rural real estate was reduced by one-fourth across the board, and the tax could be deferred for up to ten years. If the land was passed on by inheritance once again within five years, that succession would be tax exempt. If it was passed on within ten years, the law called for a reduction of the inheritance tax by 50%.

114. In the first tax bracket, which comprised parents, siblings, and nephews and nieces, the law as enacted provided for an inheritance tax of 4% up to an amount of 20,000 marks. The rate rose by four steps, in accordance with greater kinship distance from the testator, to a total of 10%. Tax progressivity led, independent of the tax bracket, to a tax of between 10% and 25% for inheritances over one million marks. An exemption of 10,000 marks was granted to relatives in the first tax bracket. Three thousand marks could be inherited tax free by individuals who had been in an employment relationship with the testator. For all other heirs there was an exemption of 500 marks. Inheritances of charitable organizations were taxed at a flat rate of 5%. As in the Prussian law of 1873, the inheritances of children and spouses were not taxed. In addition, the territorial rulers were also exempt from the inheritance tax (Schanz 1906, 201f.).

115. The federal states were entitled to one-third of the tax revenue, a share that was to be reduced to one-fourth in 1909. In 1913, another reduction of the state portion to 20% of the inheritance tax revenue was enacted.

116. According to calculations by the Reich Office of Statistics, the inheritance tax ratio stood at around 6.4% of the wealth bequeathed, and it stayed within these

parameters until 1915. The calculation was based on yearly taxable inheritances of around 800 million marks. The total value of all inheritances, however, was estimated at around 4 billion marks (Schanz 1906, 198), which means that about 80% of the value of bequests was not subject to taxation. This is largely explained by the exemption for spouses and children. Calculated against the total amount of inherited wealth, the inheritance tax quotient was merely a little over 1%.

117. At this time there was a convergence between the state and the parties of the Left, insofar as both advocated an expansion of tax revenues, though from different motivations. See also Steinmo 1993, 22.

118. As revealed by the report of the Reichstag Commission (Reichstag, S.B., Anlagen, vol. 256, Aktenstück 1446), support for the estate tax bill was also weak on the level of the federal states. The ministers of finance of the states of Prussia, Saxony, and Württemberg defended the bill merely on the grounds that the Reich needed to boost its revenue, though they clearly demonstrated that they were in fact opposed to levying a tax on the inheritances of descendants and spouses.

119. Thus, the value of agricultural land was to be reckoned at twenty times the yield (instead of twenty-five times), and of this amount, only 75% would be subject to the estate tax; moreover, the tax could be paid in installments.

120. This provision was rejected by the Inheritance Law Commission in 1896, as a result of which the BGB established an unlimited kinship succession. See chapter 2. In the 1970s, Helmut Coing (1982, 258) revived this suggestion in an expert opinion he wrote for the Forty-Ninth Conference of Jurists. Coing attributed the incorporation of an unlimited right of kinship inheritance into the BGB to the interests of the aristocracy (257).

121. The debt burden in Germany reached 75 billion marks in 1919. Immediately before the outbreak of the war, it still stood below 3 billion. The Reich's running financial need was estimated at 17.5 billion marks, compared to 2.4 billion before the war. This was juxtaposed to less then 6 billion marks in tax revenue (van der Borght 1920, 137).

122. The rates were in fact even higher, namely up to 5% for estates over 2 million marks, with an exemption of 20,000 marks.

123. For a detailed discussion of the positions of the parties on the inheritance tax reform of 1919 see Hennicke 1929, 30ff., 50ff., 76ff., 100ff., 129ff.

124. The exceptions concerned marriages with an age difference of more than twenty years between the spouses, and marriages that had not lasted for at least five years.

125. On this see also Wischermann (2003, 51ff.). Compared to France, however, the motive of population policy played a much smaller role in Germany.

126. Initially, however, the exemptions for spouses were tied to the presence of joint offspring.

127. In the least favorable bracket, which affects only a small number of inheritances, though, the rates have fluctuated between 50% and 80%, and 14% to 20%.

128. The waning interest is especially apparent in the journal *Finanzarchiv*: up until the 1920s, it had regularly published essays on the topic of the inheritance tax; after 1945, it published only two (Tait 1966; Timm 1984).

129. See also Busch 2002, 18ff.

130. Rüstow (1949, 72–73) also saw the connection between inheritance law and family ideology: "Since we have been living for thousands of years under the

rule of a fundamentally unlimited feudal-plutocratic inheritance law, the traditional structure and ideology of the family has come to be confused with this form of inheritance law. A fundamental change of inheritance law in the direction envisaged here would thus necessarily entail changes in the structure and ideology of the family. I am convinced that these changes would for the most part be salutary for the family, that they would liberate it from the oftentimes crushing dominance of the interests of material ownership, without, however, depriving it of its indispensable economic foundation, and that they would substantially enhance the vitality and relevance of the sense of family."

131. The largely noncontroversial inheritance tax reform of 1951 revolved mostly around the question of tax relief for agricultural enterprises, with the goal of preventing a further fragmentation of land. Questions of distribution were hardly touched at all (*Stenographische Berichte*, vol. 5, Sessions 104, 118, 121, 138, and 139).

132. The previous top tax rate of 15% in the first tax bracket for inheritances over 10 million marks was raised to 35%, though this rate kicked in only for inheritances over 100 million marks.

133. One piece of electoral propaganda that became widely known was a poster by the Social Democratic graphic artist Klaus Staeck, who added these words to the picture of a villa: "German workers! The SPD wants to take away your villas in the Ticino."

134. If one assumes that the amount of wealth gained from inheritances and receipts from income are correlated (Szydlik 1999), the German inheritance tax has a degressive effect on overall taxation—in contrast to the United States.

135. In the legal discourse, Kahrs (1996, 156) maintained that a "stronger accentuation of the inheritance tax with respect to distribution policy" was appropriate.

136. See, for example, Ritter 1994.

137. In France, inheritance taxes are to this day part of what are called transaction taxes.

138. However, movable property was taxed at a lower rate than real estate, which expresses the reduced importance of movable property in the largely agrarian society of the late eighteenth century (Dupeyron 1913, 75). According to the law of 1790, bequests of landed property were taxed at 0.25% if left to the testator's children, at 1% if left to the surviving spouse, and at 4% if left to nonrelated heirs. For a listing of inheritance tax rates in France during the nineteenth century see Schanz 1901, 134.

139. Whereas the law of 1798 put the tax rate for nonrelated heirs at 5%, in 1850 it rose to 11.25%. For heirs in the direct line the tax rate remained 1% from 1798 to 1901; for spouses it has been 3% since 1816. The originally three inheritance tax brackets were gradually increased to eight in the reforms of 1816, 1832, and 1850, which means that France institutionalized the most differentiated system of kinship classification for the taxation of inheritances.

140. De facto, the taxation of inheritances in France before 1901 was degressive, because in addition to the inheritance tax, a stamp tax had to be paid, which was—relatively speaking—greater for small inheritances than for large ones.

141. One example of the parliamentary debates on this issue is the bill on the tax deductibility of debts introduced by the delegate André Folliet in 1871, in which he proposed to compensate for the loss of tax revenue through an income tax. The commission report drawn up by de Marcère as the submitting member supported

the deductibility of debts, though as compensation it proposed raising the inheritance tax rates. The report was not deliberated by parliament, however. The following quote from the commission report expresses the confused political situation very well: "If the objection is raised that the current tax inequity is merely shifted, in the sense that one refuses to include contractually recognized as well as not adequately documented debts in the calculation, we would respond that we have at least taken a large step in the direction of tax proportionality; and that, even though we must give up the hope of having achieved an absolutely final result because of the justified fear of fraud, we will at least have gotten closer to the desired goal" (Annales de l'Assemblée Nationale, Annexe, 25 April 1872, 15).

142. See the commission report of 1894, in which the bills previously initiated are listed (Assemblée Nationale, 24 July 1894, Annexe No. 885).

143. The provision stated that if the beneficiary is under the age of twenty, he or she must pay 70% of the inheritance tax, the owner 30%. As the age of the beneficiary rises, the ratio shifts in his or her favor by 10% per decade.

144. Assemblée Nationale, c.r., 4 July 1894, Annexe No. 885, 625.

145. On this see the bill of 1894.

146. Although Proudhon is best known for his statement "property is theft," it does not reveal that he regarded ownership of the means of production with which the farmer or the artisan worked as indispensable for the preservation of liberty.

147. A number of years ago, Ackerman and Alstott (1999) made a very similar proposal in the United States.

148. Assemblée Nationale, c.r., 3 July 1848, 321.

149. Assemblée Nationale, c.r., 1 September 1848, 670ff.

150. See also the discussion further below.

151. See also Zeldin 1979, 276ff.

152. By highlighting the right of inheritance, however, Durkheim did so within an area of reform that otherwise received little attention in France. In the Third Republic, reform efforts grounded in the principle of meritocracy were focused much more on the area of education, a subject that Durkheim also dealt with.

153. That is also true of Charles Gide (1891), who did advocate a progressive income tax, but not an inheritance tax. References to the literature can be found below.

154. Stanley Hoffmann (1960, 7–8) explains these attitudes as arising from the specifics of the French class struggles: "The bourgeoisie triumphed through a battle, and the battle explains both the continuation of industrial development as an element of bourgeois drive and the energy with which the bourgeoisie defended itself against any push from the new lower class, the proletariat. The aristocracy had offered a long and heated resistance; hence both the bitter equalitarian suspiciousness which pervaded French society and the deep impact which aristocratic values nevertheless made on bourgeois and even workers attitudes. Neither social reaction nor social revolution became the imperative that shaped French society."

155. Napoleon's legislations already brought back the system of indirect taxation. The income tax introduced during the Revolution was abolished again in the Restoration of 1816.

156. On the different nature of the state in France, Germany, and United States see Badie and Birnbaum 1983.

157. For a chart of the tax rates see, for example, West 1908 [1893], 25.

158. The differentiation of tax rates reflects once again the organization of blood relationships, which was discussed in chapter 3 with respect to the statutory right of inheritance.

159. On the gift tax see Bouzoraa 1994; Fischenich 1929, 60; and West 1908 [1893], 27.

160. The tax rate for inheritances over 50 million francs was now between 5% and 20.5% (*Finanzarchiv* 20 [1903], 858, no author given).

161. To be sure, the introduction of an estate tax after the English model was already discussed in France before the war, for example by Finance Minister Joseph Caillaux, who made this proposal in 1909 (Shultz 1926, 39; Dupeyron 1913, 96), and in 1914 by Charles Dumont (Worms 1917, 201). However, only the financial crisis triggered by the war produced the political majority for an estate tax.

162. The connection between inheritance taxation and the declining birthrate that was asserted in France was also noted in Germany and put forth by opponents of estate taxation (see Hennicke 1929, 17).

163. Children who had died after their sixteenth birthday were also counted. This provision was clearly aimed at families whose sons had been killed in the war.

164. French inheritance and estate taxes were calculated according to the principle of graduation (*par tranche*). The amount of tax is calculated separately for the various levels of progression and added up at the end. As an example, take an inheritance of 50,000 francs: first the tax for the first 2,000 francs is calculated, then the tax for the next level of progression (2,001 to 10,000 francs), and than for the third level (10,001–50,000). The effect is that the progression leads overall to a smaller tax burden. In adjusting the tax for the number of children, adoptive children and recognized illegitimate children were included. In addition, children of the testator who had been killed in war were also counted. An estate between 100,000 and 250,000 francs with three children present had to pay an estate tax of 1.25%, but if no children were present, the tax rose to 10%. The spread increased for estates over 50 million francs to a range of 3% to 24% (Graeff 1925, 25).

165. The demands were put forth by the representatives Bon and Brizon, for example: Assemblée Nationale, c.r., 21 December 1917, 3539 and 3542.

166. Incidentally, the Socialist proposal had also picked up the motive of population policy.

167. The law now introduced an element of special consideration for the number of children also with respect to the succession tax: if the testator had more than four children, 10% could be subtracted from the assets for each child for the assessment of the inheritance tax, though only up to a maximum of 15,000 francs per child (Fischenich 1929, 54). Parallel to this, the law of June 1921 also increased the rates of the estate tax. The estate of a childless testator now had to pay an estate tax of up to 39%. Even if there were three children, tax rates could go as high as 7.5% (previously 3%).

168. The law of 1921 also introduced a new classification of the surviving spouse, who was now placed into the second tax bracket alongside grandchildren. However, this meant that the tax rates were still higher than for the children of the testator, a fact that continues to reflect the notion that descendants assumed a more important position in the family system than the spouse.

169. The establishment of such maximum thresholds, which render the nominal inheritance tax rates purely fictive, is also interesting because it amounts effectively to a scaling back of progression and leads to a stronger proportional taxation,

which corresponds precisely to the skepticism against progressive taxes in the French tax debate that I have described. Remnants are still visible today in the French inheritance tax system, which taxes collateral relatives proportionally.

170. However, since 1981 the spouse is completely exempt from the estate tax in the United States.

CHAPTER 6: CONCLUSION

1. Economic institutionalism examines existing institutions in terms of their effect on economic efficiency. The new economic institutionalism emerged in a direct link with the study of property rights (Coase 1988 [1937]). In contemporary sociology, economic institutionalism is seen particularly in the theory of the firm and in economic history (North 1990; Williamson 1975 and 1985). Much less well known is the "law and economics" approach. It assumes that legal arrangements create a certain incentive structure for actors that influences their choices and therefore has consequences for economic productivity (Mercuro and Medema 1997, 22). In its normative orientation, the approach contains a strong theory about the development of the law by arguing that the latter can be understood as a development toward economically efficient incentive structures.

2. The efficiency concept of economic institutionalism is borrowed from welfare theory. A legal arrangement is characterized as efficient when the welfare gain of one party predominates over the loss of the other party (Kaldor-Hicks efficiency). Hence, it concerns maximizing social welfare. The problem of individual losses is solved by the possibility of compensation from the gain of the better-off party. Questions of distributive justice are not dealt with or are considered secondarily. Within the law-and-economics approach, four directions can be distinguished: What is examined is (a) whether the actual development of law follows the logic of efficiency; (b) how legal institutions must be shaped to generate efficient action; (c) what economic consequences legal provisions will have; and (d) which legal provisions will be implemented (Mercuro and Medema 1997, 23; Friedman 1987, 144ff.).

3. However, a critique of the law-and-economics approach does not necessarily follow from this observation. Only some of the authors writing in this tradition assert the efficient development of law as an empirical observation. The normative position, that law *should* be shaped according to criteria of efficiency, remains untouched by the observation that this is often not the case.

4. Douglass North (1990), in particular, has included the possibility of inefficient institutional structures in the new economic institutionalism based on the effects of rent seeking.

5. On the other hand, the present study paid virtually no attention to the role of the media and political lobbyists.

6. Tracing the perception of functional consequences of inheritance law back to interests and culturally based perspectives does not deny their objective effect. Legal rules have objective consequences, but these become relevant to action only in their interpretation through the actors involved in shaping law. If the causal effect of a legal institution and its meaning cannot be determined unambiguously, then existing legal structures cannot be explained—at least not exhaustively—by changes in functional demands. Instead, the attribution of functions itself becomes one of the facts to be reconstructed in terms of action theory. This reconstruction takes place through the analysis of discursive structures.

7. Of course, the very heavily emphasized aspect of cognitive frameworks in the sociological theory of institutions can also lead to deterministic models. This problem has been clearly understood since the early 1990s (Powell 1991; Beckert 1999b).

8. For this argument, see Lassalle 1880 [1861], 1:391.

APPENDIX

1. The method I have used is based on the analysis of parliamentary debates over electoral reform in Prussia carried out by Jörg Rössel (2000).

Ackerman, Bruce, and Anne Alstott. 1999. *The Stakeholder Society.* New Haven: Yale University Press.

Adams, Willi Paul. 1971. "Das Gleichheitspostulat in der amerikanischen Revolution." *Historische Zeitschrift* 212:59–99.

Aghion, Philippe, Eve Caroli, and Cecilia García-Peñalosa. 1999. "Inequality and Economic Growth: The Perspective of the New Growth Theories." *Journal of Economic Literature* 37:1615–60.

Ahrens, Heinrich. 1871. *Naturrecht, oder Philosophie des Rechts und des Staates.* 6th ed. Vienna: C. Gerold's Sohn.

Aker, J. Brooke. 1998. *Pennsylvania Probate, Estates and Fiduciaries Code Annotated.* Philadelphia: George T. Bisel.

Aldrich, Nelson W. 1996. *Old Money: The Mythology of America's Upper Class.* 2nd ed. New York: Vintage.

Allix, Edgard. 1927. *Traité élémentaire de science des finances et de législation financiére Française.* 5th ed. Paris: Librairie Arthur Rousseau.

Al-Omar, Salah Najib. 1959. *L'impôt sur les successions en Suisse et en France.* Lausanne: Imprimerie Henri Jaunin.

Alston, J. Lee, and Morton Owen Schapiro. 1984. "Inheritance Laws Across Colonies: Causes and Consequences." *Journal of Economic History* 44:277–87.

Alstott, Anne L. 1996. "The Uneasy Liberal Case against Income and Wealth Transfer Taxation: A Response to Professor McCaffery." *Tax Law Review* 51: 363–417.

Anderson, Margaret L. 2000. *Practicing Democracy: Elections and Political Culture in Imperial Germany.* Princeton: Princeton University Press.

Ardant, Gabriel. 1965. *Théorie sociologique de l'impôt.* Paris: S.E.V.P.E.N.

Aron, Gustave. 1901. "Etude sur les lois successorales de la révolution depuis 1791." *Revue historique du droit français et étranger,* ser. 3, 25:444–89.

Arrondel, Luc, and Anne Laferrére. 1994. "La transmission des grandes fortunes." *Économie et Statistique* 273:41–52.

Arrondel, Luc, André Masson, and Pierre Pestieau. 1997. "Bequest and Inheritance: Empirical Issues and France-U.S. Comparison." Pp. 89–125 in Guido Erreygers and Toon Vandevelde, eds., *Is Inheritance Legitimate?* Berlin: Springer.

Attias-Donfut, Claudine, ed. 1995. *Les solidarités entre générations.* Paris: Edition Nathan.

———. 2000. "Rapports de générations: Transfers intrafamiliaux et dynamique macrosociale." *Revue Française de Sociologie* 41:643–84.

Avery, Dianne, and Alfred S. Konefsky. 1992. "The Daughters of Job: Property Rights and Women's Lives in Mid-Nineteenth-Century Massachusetts." *Law and History Review* 10:323–56.

Bach, Stefan, and Bernd Bartholmai. 2002. *Perspektiven der Vermögensbesteuerung in Deutschland.* Endbericht eines Forschungsprojektes im Auftrag der Hans-Böckler-Stiftung. Berlin: Deutsches Institut für Wirtschaftsforschung.

Badie, Bertrand, and Pierre Birnbaum. 1983. *The Sociology of the State.* Chicago: University of Chicago Press.

Bailyn, Bernard. 1971. "Politics and Social Structure in Virginia." Pp. 135–59 in Stanley N. Katz, ed., *Colonial America*. Boston: Little, Brown.

Baltzell, E. Digby. 1964. *The Protestant Establishment: Aristocracy and Caste in America*. New York: Random House.

Baron, Julius. 1876. "Über Erbschaftssteuern." *Jahrbücher für Nationalökonomie* 26:275–95.

Bartels, Larry M. 2005. "Homer Gets a Tax Cut: Inequality and Public Policy in the American Mind." *Perspectives on Politics* 3:15–31.

Basedow, Jürgen, Klaus Dopffel, and Hein Kötz, eds. 2000. *Die Rechtsstellung gleichgeschlechtlicher Lebensgemeinschaften*. Tübingen: Mohr Siebeck.

Baudrillart, Henri. 1857. "De L'héritage et des lois de succession." *Journal des Économistes* 13:8–27.

———. 1883. *Philosophie de l'économie politique: Des rapports de l'économie politique et de la morale*. 2nd ed. Paris: Guillaumin.

Baumann, Anke. 1996. "Gesetzliche Erbfolge und Möglichkeiten testamentarischer Erbeinsetzung im französischen Code Civil." Dissertation, University of Münster.

Bayer, Bernhard. 1999. *Sukzession und Freiheit: Historische Voraussetzungen der rechtstheoretischen und rechtsphilosophischen Auseinandersetzungen um das Institut der Familienfideikommisse im 18. und 19. Jahrhundert*. Berlin: Duncker & Humblot.

Becker, Gary, and Nigel Tomes. 1979. "An Equilibrium Theory of the Distribution of Income and Intergenerational Mobility." *Journal of Political Economy* 87:1153–89.

Beckert, Jens. 1996. "What Is Sociological About Economic Sociology? Uncertainty and the Embeddedness of Economic Action." *Theory and Society* 25:803–40.

———. 1999a. "Erbschaft und Leistungsprinzip: Dilemmata liberalen Denkens." *Kursbuch* 135:41–63.

———. 1999b. "Agency, Entrepreneurs, and Institutional Change. The Role of Strategic Choice and Institutionalized Practices in Organizations." *Organization Studies* 20:777–99.

———. 2002. *Beyond the Market: The Social Foundations of Economic Efficiency*. Princeton: Princeton University Press.

———. 2003. "Economic Sociology and Embeddedness: How Shall We Conceptualize Economic Action?" *Journal of Economic Issues* 37:769–87.

Bedau, Klaus-Dietrich. 1998. "Auswertung von Statistiken über die Vermögensverteilung in Deutschland." *Beiträge zur Strukturforschung*. No. 173. Berlin: Deutsches Institut für Wirtschaftsforschung.

Begemann, Egbert. 1912. *Die Finanzreformversuche im Deutschen Reiche von 1867 bis zur Gegenwart*. Göttingen: Vandenhoeck & Ruprecht.

Bellamy, Charles. 1884. *The Way Out: Suggestions for Social Reform*. New York: G. P. Putnam's Sons.

Bennett, William J. 2001. *The Broken Hearth: Reversing the Moral Collapse of the American Family*. New York: Doubleday.

Bentham, Jeremy. 1864. *Theory of Legislation*. London: Trübner.

Berding, Helmut. 1973. *Napoleonische Herrschafts- und Gesellschaftspolitik im Königreich Westfalen, 1807–1813*. Göttingen: Vandenhoeck & Ruprecht.

Bergius, Carl Julius. 1865. *Grundsätze der Finanzwissenschaft*. Berlin: J. Guttentag.

Bernheim, Douglas B., Andrei Shleifer, and Lawrence H. Summers. 1985. "The Strategic Bequest Motive." *Journal of Political Economy* 93:1045–76.

Bernstein, Eduard. 1905. "Vorwort." Pp. I–XIV in Eugenio Rignano, *Los von der Erbschaft*. Berlin: Modernes Verlagsbureau Curt Wigand.

———. 1906. *Die neuen Reichssteuern: Wie sie wurden und was sie bedeuten*. Berlin: Buchhandlung Vorwärts.

Biernacki, Richard. 1995. *The Fabrication of Labor: Germany and Britain, 1640–1914*. Berkeley and Los Angeles: University of California Press.

Blackstone, William. 2001 [1771]. *Commentaries on the Laws of England*. 4 vols. London: Cavendish.

Bloch, Charles. 1972. *Die dritte französische Republik*. Stuttgart: K. F. Koehler.

Bluntschli, Johann Caspar. 1856. *Deutsches Privatrecht*. Munich: Literarisch-artistische Anstalt.

———. 1879. Das Erbrecht und die Reform des Erbrechts. *Aufsätze über Recht und Staat. Gesammelte kleine Schriften* 1: 233–59. Nördlingen: C.H. Beck'sche Buchhandlung.

Blyth, Mark. 2002. *Great Transformations: Economic Ideas and Institutional Change in the Twentieth Century*. Cambridge: Cambridge University Press.

Boissonade, Gustave. 1873. *Histoire de la réserve héréditaire et de son influence morale et économique*. Paris: Librairie de Guillaumin.

———. 1874. *Histoire des droits de l'époux survivant*. Paris: Ernest Thorin.

Boltanski, Luc, and Laurent Thévenot. 1991. *De la justification: Les économies de la grandeur*. Paris: Gallimard.

Bonnet, Victor. 1879. *Le question des impôts*. Paris: E. Plon.

Bookstaver, David R. 1982. "The Pennsylvania Death Tax." *Rutgers Law Review* 34:719–27.

Bös, Dieter, and Gunter Kayser. 1996. *Der Generationenwechsel in mittelständischen Betrieben*. IfM-Materialien No. 120. Bonn: Institut für Mittelstandsforschung.

Botsch, Elisabeth. 1992. *Eigentum in der französischen Revolution: Gesellschaftliche Konflikte und Wandel des sozialen Bewusstseins*. Munich: R. Oldenbourg.

Bouglé, Célestin, and Élie Halévy, eds. 1924 [1829]. *Doctrine de Saint-Simon: Exposition*. Paris: Marcel Rivière.

Bourdieu, Pierre. 1983. "Ökonomisches Kapital, kulturelles Kapital, soziales Kapital." Pp. 183–98 in Reinhard Kreckel, ed., *Soziale Ungleichheiten*. Göttingen: Schwartz.

Bourgeois, Léon. 1902 [1896]. *Solidarité*. Paris: Librairie Armand Colin.

Bouzoraa, M.-A. 1994. "France: Inheritance and Gift Tax." Special issue, "Comparative Study of Inheritance and Gift Taxes." *European Taxation* 34:358–63.

Brater, Karl. 1848. *Die Reform des Erbrechts zu Gunsten der Nothleidenden*. Munich: Self-published.

Brentano, Lujo. 1899. *Erbrechtspolitik: Alte und neue Feudalität*. Stuttgart: Verlag der J. G. Cotta'schen Buchhandlung.

Breuer, Franz. 2000. "Vorgänger und Nachfolger: Weitergabe von/in Betrieben und Organisationen als sozialwissenschaftliches Phänomen." *Gruppendynamik und Organisationsberatung* 4:451–83.

Brewer, Holly. 1997. "Entailing Aristocracy in Colonial Virginia: Ancient Feudal Restraints and Revolutionary Reform." *William and Mary Quarterly* 54:307–46.

Brittain, John. 1978. *Inheritance and the Inequality of Material Wealth*. Washington, DC: Brookings Institution.

Brocher, Charles. 1868. *Étude historique et philosophique sur la légitime et les réserves en matière de succession héréditaire*. Paris: Ernest Thorin.

Brown, Robert E., and B. Katherine Brown. 1964. *Virginia, 1705–1786: Democracy or Aristocracy*. East Lansing: Michigan State University Press.

Brownlee, W. Elliot. 2004. *Federal Taxation in America: A Short History*. 2nd ed. Cambridge: Cambridge University Press.

Brownson, Orestes. 1978a [1840]. "The Laboring Classes." Pp. 5–24 in *The Laboring Classes*. Delmar: Scholars' Facsimiles Reprints.

———. 1978b [1840]. "Defence of The Article on The Laboring Classes." Pp. 26–137 in *The Laboring Classes*. Delmar: Scholars' Facsimiles Reprints.

Bruns, Carl Georg. 1882. "Über Testierfreiheit und Pflichtteil." Pp. 139–91 in *Kleinere Schriften*, vol. 2. Weimar: Hermann Böhlau.

Buret, Eugène. 1840. *De la misère des classes laborieuses en Angleterre et en France*. Vol. 2. Paris: Chez Paulin.

Busch, Oliver. 2002. "Leistungsprinzip und Erbschaft: Eine politökonomische Analyse der deutschen Erbschaftsteuer." Graduate thesis, University of Frankfurt am Main.

Büttner, Thiess, Wolffram Scheffler, and Christoph Spengel. 2004. *Erbschaftssteuerbelastung in Deutschland, den Staaten der EU und anderen wichtigen Staaten bei unbeschränkter Steuerpflicht: Endbericht*. Mannheim: Zentrum für Europäische Wirtschaftsforschung.

Cahn, Edmond N. 1940. "Federal Regulation of Inheritance." *Pennsylvania Law Review* 88:297–314.

Callet, Pierre. 1962. "La bataille de l'impôt sur le revenue: Fiscalité moderne et réactions bourgeoises (1906–1917)." *Cahiers d'Histoire* 7:465–92.

Canal, Marcel. 1921. *Le régime fiscal des successions et la loi du 25 Juin 1920*. Lyon: Imprimeries Réunies.

Carnegie, Andrew. 1992 [1889]. "The Gospel of Wealth." Pp. 129–54 in Joseph Frazier Wall, ed., *The Andrew Carnegie Reader*. Pittsburgh: University of Pittsburgh Press.

Caron, François. 1991. *Frankreich im Zeitalter des Imperialismus 1851–1918*. Stuttgart: Deutsche Verlagsanstalt.

Carrier, James. 1991. "Gifts, Commodities, and Social Relations: A Maussian View of Exchange." *Sociological Forum* 6:119–36.

Chester, Ronald. 1982. *Inheritance, Wealth, and Society*. Bloomington: Indiana University Press.

Christmann, Walter. 1939. *Die Theorie der Erbschaftssteuer und ihre finanzpolitische Problematik*. Düsseldorf: G. H. Nolte.

Chused, Richard H. 1983. "Married Women's Property Law: 1800–1850." *Georgetown Journal of Law* 71:1359–1425.

Clignet, Remi. 1992. *Death, Deeds, and Descendents*. New York: De Gruyter.

———. 1995. "Efficiency, Reciprocity, and Ascriptive Equality: The Three Major Strategies Governing the Selection of Heirs in America." *Social Science Quarterly* 76:274–93.

Coase, Ronald. 1988 [1937]. *The Firm, the Market and the Law*. Chicago: University of Chicago Press.

Coing, Helmut. 1982. "Empfiehlt es sich, das gesetzliche Erbrecht und Pflichtteilsrecht neu zu regeln? Gutachten für den 49. Deutschen Juristentag." Pp. 227–87 in *Gesammelte Aufsätze zu Rechtsgeschichte, Rechtsphilosophie und Zivilrecht 1947–1975*. Frankfurt am Main: Vittorio Klostermann.

Commons, John R., and Florence J. Harriman. 1916. "Report of the Commissioners John R. Commons and Florence J. Harriman." Pp. 171–252 in United States Senate, ed., *Industrial Relations: Final Report and Testimony Submitted to Congress by the Commission on Industrial Relations*. Washington, DC: Government Printing Office.

Conrad, Hermann. 1954. *Deutsche Rechtsgeschichte*. Vol. 1. Karlsruhe: C. F. Müller.

Conrad, Johannes. 1888. "Agrarstatistische Untersuchungen." *Jahrbücher für Nationalökonomie und Statistik* 50:121–70.

Courcelle-Seneuil, Jean-Gustave. 1865. "Du droit de tester et de ses limites." *Journal des Économistes* 46:321–45.

Coutot, Maurice. 1925. *L'aggravation des impôts sur les successions*. Meulan: Imprimerie Auguste Réty.

Cunliffe, John. 1997. "The Liberal Case for a Socialist Property Regime: The Contribution of François Huet." *History of Political Thought* 18:707–29.

Cunliffe, John, and Guido Erreygers. 2000. "Collins and Huet: Two Examples of a French-Belgian Tradition of 'Basic Entitlements.'" Pp. 785–96 in Pierre Dockès et al., *Les traditions économiques françaises 1848–1939*. Paris: CNRS Éditions.

Dahl, Robert. 1985. *A Preface to Economic Democracy*. Berkeley and Los Angeles: University of California Press.

Dahlinger, Charles W. 1918. "The Dawn of the Women's Movement." *Western Pennsylvania Historical Magazine* 1:68–84.

Dainow, Joseph. 1940. "Forced Heirship in French Law." *Louisiana Law Review* 2:669–92.

Dann, Otto. 1975. "Gleichheit." Pp. 997–1046 in Otto Brunner, Werner Conze, and Reinhart Koselleck, eds., *Geschichtliche Grundbegriffe: Historisches Lexikon zur politisch-sozialen Sprache in Deutschland*. Stuttgart: Klett-Cotta.

Darrow, Margaret H. 1989. *Revolution in the House: Family, Class, and Inheritance in Southern France, 1775–1825*. Princeton: Princeton University Press.

Davies, James B. 1982. "The Relative Impact of Inheritance and Other Factors on Economic Inequality." *Quarterly Journal of Economics* 97:471–498.

Davies, James B., Susanna Sandstrom, Anthony Shorrocks, and Edward N. Wolff. 2006. *The World Distribution of Household Wealth*. Unpublished manuscript, University of Western Ontario.

Davis, Kingsley. 1939. "Illegitimacy and Social Structure." *American Journal of Sociology* 45:215–33.

Dawson, John P. 1980. *Gifts and Promises: Continental and American Law Compared*. New Haven: Yale University Press.

Déhon, Léon Gustave. 1898. *Catéchisme social*. Paris: Bloud.

Déprez, Ghislain. 2002. *Les mutations à titre gratuit*. http://www.minefi.gouv.fr/notes_bleues/nbb/nbb241/241_mtg.htm.

Desan, Suzanne. 1997. "'War between Brothers and Sisters': Inheritance Law and Gender Politics in Revolutionary France." *French Historical Studies* 20:597–634.

———. 1999. "Reconstituting the Social after the Terror: Family, Property and the Law of Popular Politics." *Past and Present* 164:81–121.

DiMaggio, Paul. 1994. "Culture and Economy." Pp. 27–54 in Neil Smelser and Richard Swedberg, eds. *Handbook of Economic Sociology*. Princeton: Princeton University Press.

Dippel, Horst. 1976. "Amerikanische und europäische Revolutionsideale bei Thomas Paine." *Amerikastudien* 21:203–15.

Ditz, Toby L. 1986. *Property and Kinship: Inheritance in Early Connecticut, 1750–1820.* Princeton: Princeton University Press.

Dobbin, Frank. 1994. *Forging Industrial Policy.* Cambridge: Cambridge University Press.

Donaldson, John E. 1993. "The Future of Transfer Taxation: Repeal, Restructuring and Refinement, or Replacement." *Washington and Lee Law Review* 50:539–64.

Dupeyron, André. 1913. *L'impôt sur les successions.* Bordeaux: Imprimerie de l'université.

Dupuit, Jules. 1865. "De la liberté de tester." *Journal des Économistes* 46:194–202.

Durkheim, Émile. 1984 [1893]. *The Division of Labor in Society.* New York: Macmillan.

———. 1992 [1957]. *Professional Ethics and Civic Morals.* New York: Routledge.

———. 1995 [1912]. *The Elementary Forms of Religious Life.* New York: Free Press.

Eckert, Jörn. 1992. *Der Kampf um die Familienfideikommisse in Deutschland.* Frankfurt am Main: Peter Lang.

Eisenach, Eldon J. 1994. *The Lost Promise of Progressivism.* Lawrence: University Press of Kansas.

Eisenstadt, Shmuel. 2000. "Multiple Modernities." *Daedalus* 129:1–30.

Eisenstein, Louis. 1956. "The Rise and Decline of the Estate Tax." *Tax Law Review* 11:223–59.

Eller, Martha Britton. 2001. "Charitable Bequests: Evidence from Federal Estate Tax Returns." *SOI Bulletin* 20:174–90.

Ely, Richard T. 1888. *Taxation in American States and Cities.* New York: Thomas Y. Crowell.

———. 1891. "The Inheritance of Property." *North American Review* 153:54–66.

Enfantin, Prosper. 1970 [1832]. *Économie politique et politique.* New York: Burt Franklin.

Erreygers, Guido. 1997. "Views on Inheritance in the History of Economic Thought." Pp. 16–53 in Guido Erreygers and Toon Vandervelde, eds., *Is Inheritance Legitimate? Ethical and Economic Aspects of Wealth Transfer.* Berlin: Springer.

Eschenbach, A. 1891. *Erbrechtsreform und Erbschaftssteuer.* Berlin: Carl Heymanns.

Evans, Sara M. 1989. *Born for Liberty: A History of Women in America.* New York: Free Press.

Farber, Bernard. 1973. *Family and Kinship in Modern Society.* Glenview, IL: Scott, Foresman.

Faure, Henri. 1922. "La taxe successorale instituée par la loi du 31 décembre 1917, modifiée par la loi du 25 juin 1920." Dissertation, Université de Rennes.

Fehrenbach, Elisabeth. 1974. *Traditionale Gesellschaft und revolutionäres Recht: Die Einführung des Code Napoléon in den Rheinbundstaaten.* Göttingen: Vandenhoeck & Ruprecht.

Felix, Ludwig. 1903. *Entwicklungsgeschichte des Eigenthums unter culturgeschichtlichem und wirthschaftlichem Gesichtspunkte.* Pt. 4, second half. Leipzig: Duncker & Humblot.

Fénolhac, Gabriel. 1919. *L'évolution de l'impôt progressif en matière de taxes successorales et les sanctions de cet impôt.* Paris: Librairie Arthur Rousseau.

Ferid, Murad, and Hans Jürgen Sonnenberger. 1987. *Das französische Zivilrecht.* Vol. 3. Heidelberg: Recht und Wirtschaft.

Fichte, Johann Gottlieb. 1979 [1800]. *Der geschloßne Handelsstaat.* Hamburg: Felix Meiner.

———. 2000 [1796]. *Foundations of Natural Right: According to the Principles of the Wissenschaftslehre.* Ed. Frederick Neuhouser. Cambridge: Cambridge University Press.

Fischenich, Heinrich. 1929. "Die Erbschaftsbesteuerung in England, Frankreich und Deutschland." Dissertation, University of Cologne.

Fisher, Irving. 1919. "Economists in Public Service: Annual Address of the President." *American Economic Review, Papers and Proceedings* 9:5–21.

Fitzhugh, George. 1967 [1854]. *Sociology for the South, or the Failure of Free Society.* New York: Burt Franklin.

Frank, Rainer. 1999. "Familie als Abstammungsgemeinschaft? Unterschiede im französischen und deutschen Rechtsbewusstsein." Pp. 199–215 in Joseph Jurt, Gerd Krumeich, and Thomas Würtenberger, eds., *Wandel von Recht und Rechtsbewusstsein in Frankreich und Deutschland.* Berlin: Berlin Verlag Arno Spitz.

Freund, Ernst. 1919. *Illegitimacy Laws in the United States.* Washington, DC: Government Printing Office.

Fried, Albert. 1999. *FDR and His Enemies.* New York: St. Martin's Press.

Friedman, David. 1987. "Law and Economics." Pp. 144–47 in *The New Palgrave: A Dictionary of Economics,* vol. 3. London: Macmillan.

Friedman, Lawrence M. 1966. "The Law of the Living, the Law of the Dead. Property, Succession, and Society." *Wisconsin Law Review* 1:340–78.

———. 1985. *History of American Law.* 2nd ed. New York: Simon and Schuster.

———. 1999. "Tod, Eigentum und Familie: Die Vereinigten Staaten im 19. und 20. Jahrhundert." Pp. 45–62 in Hannes Siegrist and David Sugerman, eds., *Eigentum im internationalen Vergleich.* Göttingen: Vandenhoeck & Ruprecht.

Friedman, Milton, and Rose Friedman. 1980. *Chancen, die ich meine.* Berlin: Ullstein.

Fuchs, Maximilian. 2002. "Empfiehlt es sich, die rechtliche Ordnung finanzieller Solidarität zwischen Verwandten im Unterhalts-, Pflichtteils-, Sozialhilfe- und Sozialversicherungsrecht neu zu gestalten?" *Juristenzeitung* 57:785–98.

Gale, William G., and Joel Slemrod. 2001. "Overview." Pp. 1–64 in William G. Gale, James R. Hinnes, and Joel Slemrod, eds., *Rethinking Estate and Gift Taxation.* Washington, DC: Brookings Institution Press.

Gallo, Eileen, and Jon Gallo. 2001. *Silver Spoon Kids.* Chicago: Contemporary Books.

Gallup. 1997. *Global Study of Family Values.* Princeton, NJ: Gallup Organization.

Gamson, William. 1988. "Political Discourse and Collective Action." *International Social Movement Research* 1:219–44.

Gans, Eduard. 1824–35. *Das Erbrecht in weltgeschichtlicher Entwicklung—Eine Abhandlung der Universalrechtsgeschichte.* 4 vols. Berlin: Maurer.

Gates, William H., Jr., and Chuck Collins. 2003. *Wealth and Our Commonwealth: Why America Should Tax Accumulated Fortunes.* Boston: Beacon Press.

Geffken, Heinrich. 1881. "Erbrecht und Erbschaftssteuer." *Jahrbuch für Gesetzgebung, Verwaltung und Volkswirthschaft im Deutschen Reich* 5:189–207.

Gephart, Werner. 1993. *Gesellschaftstheorie und Recht: Das Recht im soziologischen Diskurs der Moderne.* Frankfurt am Main: Suhrkamp.

Gerber, Carl Friedrich Wilhelm von. 1857. "Beiträge zur Lehre vom deutschen Familienfideikommiß." *Jahrbücher für die Dogmatik des heutigen römischen und deutschen Privatrechts* 1:53–100.

Gerhards, Jürgen, and Dieter Rucht. 1992. "Mesomobilization: Organizing and Framing in Two Protest Campaigns in West Germany." *American Journal of Sociology* 98:555–95.

Gide, Charles. 1891. *Principes d'économie politique*. 3rd ed. Paris: L. Larose et Forcel.

Gierke, Otto von. 1873. *Das deutsche Genossenschaftsrecht*. Vol. 2. Berlin: Weichmann.

———. 1889. *Der Entwurf des bürgerlichen Gesetzbuchs und das deutsche Recht*. Leipzig: Duncker & Humblot.

———. 1892. "Familienfideikommiß." *Handwörterbuch der Staatswissenschaften* 3:104–16.

———. 1948 [1889]. *Die soziale Aufgabe des Privatrechts*. Frankfurt am Main: Vittorio Klostermann.

Giesey, Ralph E. 1977. "Rules of Inheritance and Strategies of Mobility in Prerevolutionary France." *American Historical Review* 82:271–89.

Goody, Jack, Joan Thirsk, and Edward P. Thompson. 1976. *Family and Inheritance*. Cambridge: Cambridge University Press.

Gotman, Anne. 1988. *Hériter*. Paris: Presses Universitaires de France.

Graeff, Friedrich. 1925. "Die Fortbildung der Erbschaftssteuer in Deutschland, England, Frankreich und Belgien seit dem Weltkriege." Dissertation, Friedrich-Wilhelms-Universität zu Berlin.

Graetz, Michael J. 1983. "To Praise the Estate Tax, Not to Bury It." *Yale Law Journal* 93:259–86.

Graetz, Michael J., and Ian Shapiro. 2005. *Death by a Thousand Cuts: The Fight over Taxing Inherited Wealth*. Princeton: Princeton University Press.

Gülich, Christian. 1989. "'Organisation' der Wirtschaft: Von Durkheims Berufsgruppen zu Bouglés Solidarismus." *Zeitschrift für Soziologie* 18:220–29.

Habermas, Jürgen. 1987. *The Theory of Communicative Action*. 2 vols. Boston: Beacon Press.

Hall, Peter, and Rosemary Taylor. 1996. "Political Science and the Three New Institutionalisms." *Political Studies* 44:952–73.

Hanisch, Ernst. 1978. "Der 'vormoderne' Antikapitalismus der Politischen Romantik." Pp. 132–46 in Richard Brinkmann, ed., *Romantik in Deutschland*. Stuttgart: J. B. Metzlersche Verlagsbuchhandlung.

Hansen, Klaus P. 1992. *Die Mentalität des Erwerbs: Erfolgsphilosophien amerikanischer Unternehmer*. Frankfurt am Main: Campus.

Harbury, Colin D. 1962. "Inheritance and the Distribution of Personal Wealth in Britain." *Economic Journal* 72:845–68.

Harbury, Colin D., and David M.W.N. Hitchens. 1979. *Inheritance and Wealth Inequality in Britain*. London: Allen and Unwin.

Hartz, Louis. 1955. *The Liberal Tradition in America: An Interpretation of American Political Thought since the Revolution*. New York: Harcourt.

Haslett, David. 1986. "Is Inheritance Justified?" *Philosophy and Public Affairs* 15:122–55.

Haupt, Heinz-Gerhard. 1989. *Sozialgeschichte Frankreichs seit 1789*. Frankfurt am Main: Suhrkamp.

Hauptverband der Deutsch-Konservativen, ed. 1909. *Die konservative Partei und die Reichsfinanzreform 1909*. Berlin: Hauptverband der Deutsch-Konservativen.

Hauser, Karen A. 1997. "Inheritance Rights for Extramarital Children: New Science Plus Old Intermediate Scrutiny Add Up to the Need for Change." *University of Cincinnati Law Review* 65:891–962.

Hauser, Richard, and Holger Stein. 2001. *Die Vermögensverteilung im vereinigten Deutschland*. Frankfurt am Main: Campus.

Havens, John J., and Paul G. Schervish. 1999. *Millionaires and the Millennium: New Estimates of the Forthcoming Wealth Transfer and the Prospects for a Golden Age of Philanthropy*. Report of the Boston College Social Welfare Research Institute. Boston: Boston College.

———. 2003. "Why the $41 Trillion Wealth Transfer Estimate Is Still Valid: A Review of Challenges and Questions." *Journal of Gift Planning* 7:11–15, 47–50.

Hayek, Friedrich A. von. 1960. *The Constitution of Liberty*. Chicago: University of Chicago Press.

Hazareesingh, Sudhir. 1994. *Political Traditions in Modern France*. Oxford: Oxford University Press.

Hedemann, Justus Wilhelm. 1910. *Die Fortschritte des Zivilrechts im 19. Jahrhundert*. Vol. 1. Cologne: Carl Heymanns.

———. 1930. *Die Fortschritte des Zivilrechts im 19. Jahrhundert*. Vol. 2, pt. 1. Cologne: Carl Heymanns.

Hegel, Georg Friedrich. 1991 [1821]. *Elements of the Philosophy of Right*. Ed. Allen W. Wood. Cambridge: Cambridge University Press.

Heideking, Jürgen. 1999. *Geschichte der USA*. Tübingen: A. Franke.

Hennicke, Ilse. 1929. "Die Rolle der Erbschaftssteuer in der Steuerpolitik der großen politischen Parteien." Inaugural dissertation, University of Heidelberg.

Heß, Klaus. 1990. *Junker und bürgerliche Großgrundbesitzer im Kaiserreich*. Stuttgart: Franz Steiner.

Hilgard, Theodor. 1847. *Zwölf Paragraphen über Pauperismus und die Mittel, ihn zu steuern*. Heidelberg: Julius Groos.

Hoffmann, Albrecht R. 1907. *Das Reichserbschaftssteuergesetz vom 3.6.1906*. Leipzig: Roßberg'sche Verlagsbuchhandlung.

Hoffmann, Johann Gottfried. 1840. *Die Lehre von den Steuern*. Berlin: Verlag der Nicolaischen Buchhandlung.

Hoffmann, Stanley. 1960. "Paradoxes of the French Political Community." Pp. 1–117 in Stanley Hoffmann et al., *In Search of France*. Cambridge: Harvard University Press.

Holtfrerich, Carl-Ludwig. 1991. *Wirtschaft der USA*. Munich: Oldenbourg.

Holthöfer, Ernst. 1982. "Frankreich." Pp. 863–997 in Helmut Coing, ed., *Handbuch der Quellen und Literatur der neueren europäischen Privatrechtsgeschichte*, vol. 3, pt. 1. Munich: C. H. Beck.

———. 1987. "Fortschritte in der Erbrechtsgesetzgebung seit der französischen Revolution." Pp. 121–75 in Heinz Mohnhaupt, ed., *Zur Geschichte des Familien- und Erbrechts*. Frankfurt am Main: Vittorio Klostermann.

Holtz-Eakin, Douglas. 1996. "The Uneasy Empirical Case for Abolishing the Estate Tax." *Tax Law Review* 51:495–515.

Holtz-Eakin, Douglas, David Joulfaian, and Harvey S. Rosen. 1993. "The Carnegie Conjecture: Some Empirical Evidence." *Quarterly Journal of Economics* 108: 414–435.

Hoover, Glenn. 1927. "The Economic Effects of Inheritance Taxes." *American Economic Review* 17:38–49.

Horwitz, Morton J. 1973. "The Transformation in the Conception of Property in American Law, 1780–1860." *University of Chicago Law Review* 40:248–90.

———. 1977. *The Transformation of American Law, 1780–1860.* Cambridge: Harvard University Press.

———. 1992. *The Transformation of American Law, 1870–1960.* New York: Oxford University Press.

Hudson, David M. 1983. "Tax Policy and the Federal Taxation of the Transfer of Wealth." *Willamette Law Review* 19:1–60.

Huet, François. 1853. *Le règne social du christianisme.* Paris: Firmin Didot.

Hughes, Jonathan R. T. 1976. *Social Control in the Colonial Economy.* Charlottesville: University Press of Virginia.

Humboldt, Wilhelm Freiherr von. 1993 [1792]. *The Limits of State Action.* Ed. J. W. Burrow. Indianapolis: Liberty Fund.

Hurd, Michael, and James Smith. 2002. "Expected Bequests and Their Distribution." NBER Working Paper Series 9142. Cambridge, MA: NBER.

Husbands, Clement M. 1878. *Law of Married Women in Pennsylvania.* Philadelphia: T. and J. W. Johnson.

Huston, James. L. 1993. "The American Revolutionaries, the Political Economy of Aristocracy, and the American Concept of the Distribution of Wealth, 1765–1900." *American Historical Review* 98:1079–1105.

———. 1998. *Securing the Fruits of Labor: The American Concept of Wealth Distribution, 1765–1900.* Baton Rouge: Louisiana State University Press.

Hütte, Rüdiger. 1988. *Der Gemeinschaftsgedanke in den Erbrechtsreformen des Dritten Reichs.* Frankfurt am Main: Peter Lang.

Ihering, Rudolf von. 1877. *Der Zweck im Recht.* Vol. 1. Leipzig: Breitkopf & Härtel.

Infratest Dimap. 2002. *DeutschlandTREND Oktober 2002.* http://www.infratest-dimap.de/politik/deutschlandtrend/dt0210/dt0210home.html.

Internal Revenue Service. 2001. *Estate Tax Returns Filed in 1999: Gross Estate by Type of Property, Deductions, Taxable Estate, Estate Tax and Tax Credits, by Size of Gross Estate.* Statistics of Income. Unpublished data, revised. http://www.irs.gov/tax_stats/soi/est_etr.html.

Jakob, Ludwig Heinrich von. 1837. *Die Staatsfinanzwissenschaft.* 2nd ed. Halle: C. A. Schwetschke.

Jefferson, Thomas. 1959 [1829]. *Autobiography.* New York: Capricorn.

Joas, Hans. 2000. *The Genesis of Values.* Chicago: University of Chicago Press.

———. 2004. *Braucht der Mensch Religion? Über Erfahrungen der Selbsttranszendenz?* Freiburg: Herder Verlag.

Johnson, Barry W., and Martha Britton Eller. 1998. "Federal Taxation on Inheritance and Wealth Transfers." Pp. 61–90 in Robert K. Miller and Stephen J. McNamee, eds., *Inheritance and Wealth in America.* New York: Plenum Press.

Johnson, Barry W., and Jacob M. Mikow. 1999. "Federal Estate Tax Returns, 1995–1997." *SOI Bulletin* 19:69–89.

Jones, Jo Ann, et al. 1985. "Nonmarital Childbearing: Divergent Legal and Social Concerns." *Population and Development Review* 11:677–93.

Jostock, Paul, and Albert Ander. 1960. "Konzentration der Einkommen und Vermögen." Pp. 179–235 in Helmut Arndt, ed., *Die Konzentration der Wirtschaft.* Berlin: Duncker & Humblot.

Joulfaian, David. 2000. "Estate Taxes and Charitable Bequests by the Wealthy." NBER Working Paper Series 7663. Cambridge: NBER.

Jürges, Hendrik. 2001. "Do Germans Save to Leave an Estate? An Examination of the Bequest Motive." *Scandinavian Journal of Economics* 103:391–414.

Kaelble, Hartmut. 1991. *Nachbarn am Rhein: Entfremdung und Annäherung der französischen und deutschen Gesellschaft seit 1880*. Munich: C. H. Beck.

Kahrs, Werner. 1996. "Einheitswertsteuern in den Zeiten des Steuerchaos." *Kritische Justiz* 29:128–63.

Kant, Immanuel. 1965. *The Metaphysical Elements of Justice: Part I of The Metaphysics of Morals*. Indianapolis: Bobbs-Merrill.

Katz, Stanley N. 1976. "Thomas Jefferson and the Right to Property in Revolutionary America." *Journal of Law and Economics* 19:467–87.

———. 1977. "Republicanism and the Law of Inheritance in the American Revolutionary Era." *Michigan Law Review* 76:1–29.

Kaufmann, Franz-Xaver. 2001. *Der deutsche Sozialstaat im internationalen Vergleich*. Baden-Baden: Nomos.

Kautsky, Karl. 1988 [1899]. *The Agrarian Question*. 2 vols. London: Zwan Publications.

Keim, C. Ray. 1968 [1926]. "Primogeniture and Entail in Colonial Virginia." *William and Mary Quarterly*, 3rd ser. 25:545–86.

Keister, Lisa A. 2000. *Wealth in America: Trends in Wealth Inequality*. Cambridge: Cambridge University Press.

Kennickell, Arthur B. 2000. "An Examination of Changes in Distribution of Wealth from 1989 to 1998: Evidence from the Survey of Consumer Finances." Working Paper No. 307. Washington, DC: Federal Reserve Board.

Kent, James. 1971 [1826–30]. *Commentaries on American Law*. 4 vols. New York: DaCapo.

Kessler, Denis, and André Masson. 1988. *Modelling the Accumulation and Distribution of Wealth*. Oxford: Clarendon Press.

Ketteler, Wilhelm Emmanuel. 1977 [1872]. "Die Centrums-Fraction auf dem ersten Deutschen Reichstage." Pp. 65–165 in *Schriften, Aufsätze und Reden 1871–1877*. Ed. Erwin Iserloh and Christoph Stoll. Mainz: v. Hase & Koehler.

Kim, Sung Bok. 1978. *Landlord and Tenant in Colonial New York: Manorial Society, 1664–1775*. Chapel Hill: University of North Carolina Press.

King, Willford I. 1915. *The Wealth and Income of the People of the United States*. New York: Macmillan.

Kisker, Klaus Peter. 1964. *Die Erbschaftssteuer als Mittel der Vermögensredistribution*. Berlin: Duncker & Humblot.

Klippel, Diethelm. 1984. "Familie versus Eigentum: Die naturrechtlich-rechtsphilosophischen Begründungen von Testierfreiheit und Familienerbrecht im 18. und 19. Jahrhundert." *Zeitschrift der Savigny-Stiftung für Rechtsgeschichte* 101:117–68.

———. 1987. "Sozialgeschichte und Rechtsgeschichte: Recht und Rechtsgeschichte in der historischen Familienforschung." Pp. 267–80 in Heinz Mohnhaupt, ed., *Geschichte des Familien- und Erbrechts*. Frankfurt am Main: Vittorio Klostermann.

Knight, Jack. 1992. *Institutions and Social Conflict*. Cambridge: Cambridge University Press.

Kohli, Martin. 1994. "Commentary: Rural Families as a Model for Intergenerational Transmission." Pp. 66–78 in Vern L. Bengston, Warner Schaie, and Linda Burton, eds., *Adult Intergenerational Relations*. Berlin: Springer.

———. 1997. "Zwischen den Generationen: Entfernungen, Beziehungen, Leistungen." Berlin: Unpublished manuscript.

———. 1999. "Private and Public Transfers between Generations: Linking the Family and the State." *European Societies* 1:81–104.

Koselleck, Reinhart. 1989. *Preußen zwischen Reform und Revolution*. Munich: DTV/Klett-Cotta.

Kosmann, Marianne. 1998. *Wie Frauen erben: Geschlechterverhältnis im Erbprozeß*. Opladen: Leske und Budrich.

Kotlikoff, Laurence J. 1988. "Intergenerational Transfers and Saving." *Journal of Economic Perspectives* 2:41–58.

Krause, Harry. 1967. "Equal Protection for the Illegitimate Child." *Michigan Law Review* 65:477–506.

Lamont, Michèle, and Laurent Thévenot. 2000. "Introduction: Toward a Renewed Comparative Cultural Sociology." Pp. 1–22 in Michèle Lamont and Laurent Thévenot, eds., *Rethinking Comparative Cultural Sociology: Repertoires of Evaluation in France and the United States*. Cambridge: Cambridge University Press.

Landau, Peter. 1997. "Die Testierfreiheit in der Geschichte des Deutschen Rechts im späten Mittelalter und in der frühen Neuzeit." *Zeitschrift der Savigny-Stiftung für Rechtsgeschichte. Germanistische Abteilung* 114:56–72.

Langbein, Ulrike. 2003. "Erbstücke: Zur individuellen Aneignung materieller Kultur." Pp. 233–62 in Frank Lettke, ed., *Erben und Vererben: Gestaltung und Regulation von Generationenbeziehungen*. Constance: Universitätsverlag Konstanz.

Lassalle, Ferdinand. 1880 [1861]. *Das System der erworbenen Rechte*. Vol. 1: *Das Wesen des römischen und germanischen Erbrechts in historisch-philosophischer Entwickelung*. 2nd ed. Leipzig: Brockhaus.

Lauterbach, Wolfgang, and Kurt Lüscher. 1996. "Erben und die Verbundenheit der Lebensläufe von Familienmitgliedern." *Kölner Zeitschrift für Soziologie und Sozialpsychologie* 48:66–95.

Le Play, Frédéric. 1855. *Les ouvriers européens*. Paris: Imprimerie impériale.

———. 1864. *La réforme sociale en France*. 2 vols. Paris: Henri Plon.

Legoyt, A. 1857. "De la loi des successions en France." *Journal des Économistes* 14:351–69.

Lehmann, Daniel, and Oliver Treptow. 2006. "Zusammensetzung und Diskrepanz der Schenkungs- und Erbschaftssteuer 2002." Universität Mannheim, Zentrum für Unternehmensnachfolge. Unpublished manuscript.

Leipold, Dieter. 1997. "Einführung." Pp. 8–22 in Kurt Rebmann, Franz J. Säcker, and Roland Rixecker, eds., *Münchener Kommentar zum Bürgerlichen Gesetzbuch*, vol. 9: *Erbrecht*. Munich: C. H. Beck.

———. 2000. *Erbrecht*. 13th ed. Tübingen: Mohr Siebeck.

Leroy-Beaulieu, Paul. 1901. "L'état d'esprit parlementaire et l'impôt progressif sur les successions." *L'économiste français* 29:261–63.

Leslie, Melanie B. 1996. "The Myth of Testamentary Freedom." *Arizona Law Review* 38:35–290.

Lettke, Frank, ed. 2003. *Erben und Vererben: Gestaltung und Regulation von Generationenbeziehungen*. Constance: Universitätsverlag Konstanz.

Leveneur, Laurent, and Sabine Leveneur. 1999. *Leçons de droit civil. Successions—Libéralités*. Paris: Montchrestien.

Levy, Michael B. 1983. "Liberal Equality and Inherited Wealth." *Political Theory* 11:545–64.

Lewis, William. 1868. *Das Recht des Familienfideikommisses.* Berlin: Weidmann.

Liebknecht, Wilhelm. 1876. *Zur Grund- und Bodenfrage.* Leipzig: Genossenschaftsbuchdruckerei.

Limbach, Jutta. 1988. "Die Entwicklung des Familienrechts seit 1949." Pp. 11–35 in Rosemarie Nave-Herz, ed., *Wandel und Kontinuität der Familie in der Bundesrepublik Deutschland.* Stuttgart: Enke.

Lingenthal, Karl Salomo Zachariä von. 1835. *Abhandlungen aus dem Gebiethe der Staatswirtschaftslehre.* Heidelberg: Osswald.

Lingenthal, Karl Salomo Zachariä von, and Carl Crome. 1894–95. *Handbuch des französischen Civilrechts.* 4 vols. Freiburg: Ernst Mohr.

Löhle, Annette. 2001. *Verfassungsrechtliche Gestaltungsspielräume und -grenzen bei der Besteuerung von Erbschaften und Schenkungen.* Tübingen: Köhler Druck.

Lübtow, Ulrich von. 1982. *Erbrecht.* Berlin: Duncker & Humblot.

Lüscher, Kurt. 2002. "Facetten des Erbens—eine soziologische Annäherung." *Evangelischer Pressedienst* 33:50–55.

Lüth, Erik. 2001. *Private Intergenerational Transfers and Population Aging: The German Case.* Heidelberg: Physica-Verlag.

Manly, Basil M. 1916. "Final Report of the Commission on Industrial Relations." Pp. 17–167 in United States Senate, ed., *Industrial Relations: Final Report and Testimony Submitted to Congress by the Commission on Industrial Relations.* Washington, DC: Government Printing Office.

Marais, Jean-Luc. 1999. *Histoire du don en France de 1800 à 1939: Dons et legs charitables, pieux et philanthropiques.* Rennes: Presses Universitaires de Rennes.

Martiny, Dieter. 2002. *Empfiehlt es sich, die rechtliche Ordnung finanzieller Solidarität zwischen Verwandten in den Bereichen des Unterhaltsrechts, des Pflichtteilsrechts, des Sozialhilferechts und des Sozialversicherungsrechts neu zu gestalten? Unterhalts- und erbrechtliches Teilgutachten. Gutachten A für den 64. Deutschen Juristentag.* Munich: C. H. Beck.

Märtz, Thomas. 1990. *Interessengruppen und Gruppeninteressen in der Demokratie: zur Theorie des Rent-Seeking.* Frankfurt am Main: Peter Lang.

Marx, Karl. 1869. "Speech on the Right of Inheritance." *The General Council of the First International, 1868–1870.* Moscow. http://www.marx.org/history/international/iwma/documents/1869/inheritance-speech.htm.

———. 1970 [1843]. *Critique of Hegel's "Philosophy of Right."* Ed. Joseph O'Malley. Cambridge: Cambridge University Press.

Marx, Karl, and Friedrich Engels. 1970 [1848]. *Manifest der kommunistischen Partei.* Frankfurt am Main: Marxistische Taschenbücher.

Masson, André, and Pierre Pestieau. 1991. "Tests des modèles d'héritage: un inventaire critique." *Économie et Prévision* 100–101:73–92.

———. 1997. "Bequests Motives and Models of Inheritance: A Survey of the Literature." Pp. 54–88 in Guido Erreygers and Toon Vandervelde, eds., *Is Inheritance Legitimate? Ethical and Economic Aspects of Wealth Transfer.* Berlin: Springer.

May, Raphael Ernst. 1909. "Zum Kampf um die Nachlasssteuer." *Finanzarchiv* 26:228–47.

Mayer, Valentin. 1871. *Das Eigenthum nach den verschiedenen Weltanschauungen.* Freiburg im Breisgau: Trömer.

McCaffery, Edward J. 1994. "The Uneasy Case for Wealth Transfer Taxation." *Yale Law Journal* 104:283–365.

McMurray, Orin K. 1919. "Liberty of Testation and Some Modern Limitations Thereon." *Illinois Law Review* 14:96–123.

Medzeg, Gisela, and Dieter Nohlen. 1969. "Frankreich." Pp. 441–554 in Dolf Sternberger and Bernhard Vogel, eds., *Die Wahl der Parlamente und anderer Staatsorgane*, vol. 1. Berlin: Walter de Gruyter.

Mellon, Andrew W. 1924. *Taxation: The People's Business.* London: Macmillan.

Menger, Anton. 1927 [1890]. *Das bürgerliche Recht und die besitzlosen Volksklassen.* Tübingen: Verlag der H. Laupp'schen Buchhandlung.

Mercuro, Nicholas, and Steven G. Medema. 1997. *Economics and the Law.* Princeton: Princeton University Press.

Merk, Walther. 1934. *Das Eigentum im Wandel der Zeiten.* Langensalza: Hermann Beyer & Söhne.

Mertens, Hans-Georg. 1970. *Die Entstehung der Vorschriften des BGB über die gesetzliche Erbfolge und das Pflichtteilsrecht.* Berlin: Walter de Gruyter.

Meynen, Erich D. 1912. *Die Erbschaftssteuer im internationalen Rechte.* Berlin: Juristische Verlagsbuchhandlung Dr. jur. Frensdorf.

Miaskowski, August von. 1882a. *Das Erbrecht und die Grundeigenthumsverteilung im Deutschen Reiche.* Schriften des Vereins für Socialpolitik 20. Leipzig: Duncker & Humblot.

———. 1882b. "Grundeigenthumsvertheilung und Erbrechtsreform in Deutschland." Pp. 6–56 in *Verhandlungen der am 9. und 10. Oktober 1882 in Frankfurt a.M. abgehaltenen Generalversammlung des Vereins für Socialpolitik.* Schriften des Vereins für Socialpolitik 21. Leipzig: Duncker & Humblot.

Michaux, Hubert Ernest. 1885. *L'impôt.* Paris: Callamelaine.

Mill, John Stuart. 1968 [1848]. *Principles of Political Economy.* Fairfield, NJ: Augustus M. Kelley.

Mirabeau, Honoré-Gabriel Riquetti. 2003 [1791]. "Rede über die Gleichheit der Teilung bei Erbfolge in direkter Linie." Pp. 11–22 in Frank Lettke, ed., *Erben und Vererben: Gestaltung und Regulation von Generationenbeziehungen.* Constance: UVK.

Mixon, Eleanor. 2000. "Deadbeat Dads: Undeserving of the Right to Inherit from Their Illegitimate Children and Undeserving of Equal Protection." *Georgia Law Review* 34:1771–1800.

Modigliani, Franco. 1988. "The Role of Intergenerational Transfers and Life Cycle Saving in the Accumulation of Wealth." *Journal of Economic Perspectives* 2: 15–40.

Modigliani, Franco, and Richard Brumberg. 1954. "Utility Analysis and the Consumption Function: An Interpretation of Cross-Section Data." Pp. 388–436 in Kenneth K. Kurihara, ed., *Post-Keynesian Economics.* New Brunswick: Rutgers University Press.

Moniteur-Documents. 1961. *L'impôt sur les successions.* Paris.

Montesquieu, Charles-Louis. 1899 [1748]. *The Spirit of Laws.* 2 vols. New York: Colonial Press.

Montgomery, John R. 1916. "The Inheritance Tax and the Constitution." *Illinois Law Review* 10:633–44.

Morris, Richard B. 1927. "Primogeniture and Entailed Estates in America." *Columbia Law Review* 27:24–51.

Müller, Adam Heinrich. 1922 [1809]. *Die Elemente der Staatskunst.* 2 vols. Jena: Gustav Fischer.

Müller, Ernst Wilhelm. 1983. "Sozialethnologie." Pp. 145–79 in Hans Fischer, ed., *Ethnologie: Eine Einführung*. Berlin: Dietrich Reimer.

Murphy, Liam, and Thomas Nagel. 2002. *The Myth of Ownership: Taxes and Justice*. Oxford: Oxford University Press.

Myers, Gustavus. 1969 [1939]. *The Ending of Hereditary American Fortunes*. New York: Augustus M. Kelley.

Nearing, Scott. 1915. *Income*. New York: Macmillan.

Nedelsky, Jennifer. 1990. *Private Property and the Limits of American Constitutionalism*. Chicago: University of Chicago Press.

Nicolau, Émile-Georges. 1922. *Le prélèvement sur les successions en France*. Paris: Jouve.

Nipperdey, Thomas. 1983. *Deutsche Geschichte, 1800–1866: Bürgerwelt und starker Staat*. Munich: C. H. Beck.

———. 1990. *Deutsche Geschichte, 1866–1918: Machtstaat vor der Demokratie*. Munich: C. H. Beck.

Noël, Octave. 1884. *Étude sur la gestion financière en France depuis 1789*. Paris: Guillaumin.

———. 1902. *Le socialisme et la question sociale*. Paris: A. Pendone.

Nolte, Ernst, 1965. *Three Faces of Fascism: Action Française, Italian Fascism, National Socialism*. London: Weidenfeld and Nicolson.

North, Douglass. 1990. *Institutions, Institutional Change and Economic Performance*. Cambridge: Cambridge University Press.

Nozick, Robert. 1974. *Anarchy, State, and Utopia*. Oxford: Basil Blackwell.

———. 1989. *The Examined Life: Philosophical Meditations*. New York: Simon and Schuster.

Nussbaum, Arthur. 1937. "Liberty of Testation." *American Bar Association Journal* 23:183–86.

Oberdieck, Joachim. 1934. *Die bisherigen Auswirkungen der preußischen Gesetzgebung zur Auflösung der Fideikommisse*. Grimma: F. Bode.

OECD Factbook. 2006. *Economic, Environmental and Social Statistics*. Paris: Organisation for Economic Co-operation and Development.

Offe, Claus. 1996. "Designing Institutions in East European Transitions." Pp. 199–226 in Robert E. Goodin, ed., *The Theory of Institutional Design*. Cambridge: Cambridge University Press.

Orth, John V. 1992. "After the Revolution: 'Reform' of the Law of Inheritance." *Law and History Review* 10:33–44.

Parieu, Félix Esquiroux. 1852. "Successions." Pp. 670–78 in Charles Coquelin and Gilbert-Urbain Guillaumin, eds., *Dictionnaire de l'économie politique*, vol. 2. Paris.

Parsons, Talcott. 1954. "The Kinship System of the Contemporary United States." Pp. 177–96 in *Essays in Sociological Theory*. Glencoe: Free Press.

Paul, Randolph E. 1954. *Taxation in the United States*. Boston: Little, Brown.

Pessen, Edward. 1971. "The Egalitarian Myth and the American Social Reality: Wealth, Mobility, and Equality in the 'Era of the Common Man.'" *American Historical Review* 76:989–1034.

Peterson, Merrill D., ed. 1966. *Democracy: Liberty, and Property. The State Constitutional Conventions of the 1820's*. Indianapolis: Bobbs-Merrill.

Pfizer, Paul Achatius. 1842. *Gedanken über Recht, Staat und Kirche*. Stuttgart: Hallberger'sche Verlagsbuchhandlung.

Phillips, Kevin. 2002. *Wealth and Democracy: A Political History of the American Rich.* New York: Broadway Books.

Phillips, Percy W. 1937. "Social Control through Taxation of Estates and Trusts." *Cornell Law Review* 23:113–116.

Piketty, Thomas. 2001. *Les hauts revenus en France aux XXe siècle: Inégalités et redistributions 1901–1908.* Paris: Grasset.

Piketty, Thomas, and Emmanuel Saez. 2001. "Income Inequality in the United States 1913–1998." NBER Working Paper 8467. Cambridge, MA: NBER.

Powell, Walter W. 1991. Expanding the Scope of Institutional Analysis. Pp. 183–203 in Walter W. Powell and Paul J. DiMaggio, eds., *The New Institutionalism in Organizational Theory.* Chicago: University of Chicago Press.

Powell Walter W., and Paul J. DiMaggio, eds. 1991. *The New Institutionalism in Organizational Theory.* Chicago: University of Chicago Press.

Proudhon, Pierre-Joseph. 1995 [1860]. *Théorie de l'impôt.* Paris: Éditions L'Harmattan.

Puhle, Hans-Jürgen. 1967. *Agrarische Interessenpolitik und preußischer Konservatismus.* Hannover: Verlag für Literatur und Zeitgeschehen.

Puynode, Gustave du. 1859. "Des diverses lois successorales envisagées sous le rapport économique." *Journal des Économistes,* 2nd ser. 24:19–48.

Quebe, Jutta. 1993. "Die Erbrechtsgarantie: Inhalt und Schranken." Dissertation, Universität Bielefeld.

Randall, Henry S. 1858. *The Life of Thomas Jefferson.* Vol. 1. New York: Derby and Jackson.

Ratner, Sidney. 1967. *American Taxation: Its History as a Social Force in Democracy.* New York: W. W. Norton.

Rau, Karl Heinrich. 1997 [1832]. *Lehrbuch der politischen Ökonomie.* Hildesheim: Olms-Weidmann.

Rawls, John. 1971. *A Theory of Justice.* Cambridge: Harvard University Press.

Read, Harlan E. 1918. *The Abolition of Inheritance.* New York: Macmillan.

Renaut, Marie-Hélène. 1997. "Le droit de l'enfant adultérin de l'époque romaine à aujourd'hui: Ou l'histoire d'un exclu accédant à la vie juridique." *Revue Historique* 602:369–408.

Renner, Karl. 1965 [1929]. *Die Rechtsinstitute des Privatrechts und ihre soziale Funktion: Ein Beitrag zur Kritik des bürgerlichen Rechts.* Tübingen: Mohr.

Respondek, Erwin. 1918. *Steuer- und Anleihepolitik in Frankreich während des Krieges.* Berlin: Julius Springer.

Rheinstein, Max. 1971. "Rechte der Vereinigten Staaten von Amerika (Leitsätze)." Pp. 9–14 in Ernst von Caemmerer, ed., *Schriftenreihe Arbeiten zur Rechtsvergleichung,* vol. 50: *Das Erbrecht von Familienangehörigen.* Frankfurt am Main: Alfred Metzner.

Ricardo, David. 1977 [1817]. *Principles of Political Economy and Taxation.* London: Everyman's Library.

Rieg, Alfred. 1971. "Französisches Recht." Pp. 79–94 in Ernst von Caemmerer, ed., *Schriftenreihe Arbeiten zur Rechtsvergleichung,* vol. 50: *Das Erbrecht von Familienangehörigen.* Frankfurt am Main: Alfred Metzner.

Riehl, Wilhelm Heinrich. 1889 [1855]. *Die Naturgeschichte des deutschen Volkes als Grundlage einer deutschen Social-Politik,* vol. 3: *Die Familie.* 10th ed. Stuttgart: Verlag der J. G. Cotta'schen Buchhandlung.

Rignano, Eugenio. 1901. *Di un socialismo in accordo colla dottrina economica liberale*. Turin: Bocca.

———. 1904. *Un socialisme en harmonie avec la doctrine économique libérale*. Paris: Giard & Brière.

———. 1905. *Das Los von der Erbschaft*. Berlin: Modernes Verlagsbureau Curt Wigand.

———. 1924. *The Social Significance of the Inheritance Tax*. New York: Knopf.

Ritter, Gerhard A. 1996. *Arbeiter, Arbeiterbewegung und soziale Ideen in Deutschland*. Munich: C. H. Beck.

Ritter, Wolfgang. 1994. "Gedanken zur Erbschaftssteuer." *Betriebsberater* 33:2285–91.

Robbins, Horace H., and Francis Deak. 1930. "The Familial Property Rights of Illegitimate Children: A Comparative Study." *Columbia Law Review* 30:308–29.

Röder, Karl David August. 1860 [1846]. *Grundzüge des Naturrechts oder der Rechtsfilosofie*. 2nd ed. Leipzig: C. F. Winter.

Roosevelt, Theodore. 1909. Message to the Senate and House of Representatives, March 12, 1906. P. VII in House of Representatives, *Papers Relating to the Foreign Relations of the United States*, pt. 1. Washington, DC: Government Printing Office.

Röpke, Wilhelm. 1948. *Die Gesellschaftskrisis der Gegenwart*. 5th ed. Erlenbach: Rentsch.

Roscher, Wilhelm. 1886. *System der Finanzwissenschaft*. 2nd ed. Stuttgart: Verlag der J. G. Cotta'schen Buchhandlung.

Rössel, Jörg. 2000. *Soziale Mobilisierung und Demokratie: Die preußischen Wahlrechtskonflikte 1900 bis 1918*. Wiesbaden: Deutscher Universitäts-Verlag.

Rosenfeld, Jeffrey. 1979. *The Legacy of Aging: Inheritance and Disinheritance in Social Perspective*. Norwood, NJ: Ablex.

———. 1982. "Disinheritage and Will Contests." *Marriage and Family Review* 5:75–86.

Rousseau, Jean-Jacques. 1978 [1762]. *On the Social Contract, with Geneva Manuscript and Political Economy*. Ed. Roger D. Masters. New York: St. Martin's Press.

Rüstow, Alexander. 1949. *Zwischen Kapitalismus und Kommunismus*. Godesberg: Küpper.

Ryan, John A. 1920. *A Living Wage*. New York: Macmillan.

Sagnac, Philippe. 1898. *La législation civile dans la révolution française*. Paris: Hachette et cie.

Samter, Adolf. 1879. *Das Eigenthum in seiner sozialen Bedeutung*. Jena: Gustav Fischer.

Schäffle, Albert. 1895. *Die Steuern*. Leipzig: C. L. Hirschfeld.

Schanz, Georg. 1900–1901. "Studien zur Geschichte und Theorie der Erbschaftssteuer." *Finanzarchiv* 17:1–62 and 18:53–195.

———. 1901. "Die Reform der französischen Erbschaftssteuer durch das Budgetgesetz vom 26. Februar 1901." *Finanzarchiv* 18: 727–40.

———. 1906. "Die Reichsfinanzreform von 1906." *Finanzarchiv* 23: 179–229.

Scheel, Hans von. 1877a. *Erbschaftssteuern und Erbschaftsreform*. Jena: Friedr. Mauke.

———. 1877b. *Eigenthum und Erbrecht*. Berlin: Carl Habel.

———. 1877c. "Volkswirthschaftliche Bemerkungen zur Reform des Erbrechts." *Annalen des Deutschen Reiches*, 97–108.

Schimmer, Ralf. 1996. "Wider die Legende von der unüberbrückbaren Distanz." Pp. 265–98 in Reinhard Penz and Holger Wilkop, eds., *Zeit der Institutionen—Thorstein Veblens evolutorische Ökonomik*. Marburg: Metropolis.

Schliepkorte, Jörg. 1989. *Entwicklungen des Erbrechts zwischen 1933 und 1953*. Bochum: Studienverlag Dr. N. Brockmeyer.

Schmale, Wolfgang. 2000. *Geschichte Frankreichs*. Stuttgart: Eugen Ulmer.

Schmoller, Gustav. 1882. "Einige Bemerkungen über die zunehmende Verschuldung des deutschen Grundbesitzes und die Möglichkeit, ihr entgegen zu wirken." *Landwirthschaftliche Jahrbücher* 11:613–29.

Schnerb, Robert. 1973. *Deux siècles de fiscalité française XIXe–XXe siècle*. Paris: Mouton Éditeur.

Schoelkens, Joseph. 1900. *Das Erbrecht und die Bodenverteilung in Frankreich vor und nach der Revolution*. Munich: Self-published.

Schröder, Rainer. 1981. *Abschaffung oder Reform des Erbrechts: Die Begründung einer Entscheidung des BGB-Gesetzgebers im Kontext sozialer, ökonomischer und philosophischer Zeitströmungen*. Ebelsbach: Rolf Gremer.

———. 1987. "Der Funktionsverlust des bürgerlichen Erbrechts." Pp. 281–94 in Heinz Mohnhaupt, ed., *Zur Geschichte des Familien- und Erbrechts*. Frankfurt am Main: Vittorio Klostermann.

Schultheis, Franz. 1999. *Familien und Politik: Formen wohlfahrtsstaatlicher Regulierung von Familie im deutsch-französischen Gesellschaftsvergleich*. Constance: Universitätsverlag Konstanz.

Schultz, David A. 1992. *Property, Power, and American Democracy*. New Brunswick, NJ: Transaction Publishers.

Schumpeter, Joseph. 1928. "Erbschaftssteuer." *Der deutsche Volkswirt* 4:110–14.

Schunck, Peter. 1994. *Geschichte Frankreichs*. Munich: Piper.

Schwab, Dieter. 1975. "Eigentum." Pp. 65–115 in Otto Brunner, Werner Conze, and Reinhart Koselleck, eds., *Geschichtliche Grundbegriffe: Historisches Lexikon zur politisch-sozialen Sprache in Deutschland*. Stuttgart: Klett-Cotta.

Schwägler, Georg. 1970. *Soziologie der Familie*. Tübingen: Mohr.

Seligman, Edwin R. A. 1894. *Progressive Taxation in Theory and Practice*. Baltimore: American Economic Association.

———. 1925 [1895]. *Essays in Taxation*. 10th ed. New York: Mcmillan.

Sering, Max. 1904. "Noch einige Bemerkungen zum vorläufigen Entwurf eines preußischen Gesetzes über Familienfideikommisse." *Schmollers Jahrbuch* 28: 61–75.

Sering, Max, and Constantin von Dietze. 1930. *Die Vererbung des ländlichen Grundbesitzes in der Nachkriegszeit*. Munich: Duncker & Humblot.

Shammas, Carole. 1987. "English Inheritance Law and Its Transfer to the Colonies." *American Journal of Legal Theory* 31:145–63.

Shammas, Carole, Marylynn Salmon, and Michael Dahlin. 1987. *Inheritance in America from Colonial Times to the Present*. New Brunswick: Rutgers University Press.

Shultz, William J. 1926. *The Taxation of Inheritance*. Boston: Houghton Mifflin.

Sieweck, Jörg. 2000. *Erbschaften: Marktstudie der BBE Unternehmensberatung*. Stuttgart: BBE Unternehmensberatung.

Simes, Lewis M. 1955. *Public Policy and the Dead Hand.* Ann Arbor: University of Michigan Law School.

Simmel, Georg. 1992 [1908]. *Soziologie: Untersuchungen über die Formen der Vergesellschaftung.* Frankfurt am Main: Suhrkamp.

Skidmore, Thomas. 1829. *The Rights of Man to Property.* New York: Alexander Ming.

Smith, Adam. 1978 [1776]. *The Wealth of Nations.* Chicago: University of Chicago Press.

Smith, James Morton, ed. 1995. *The Republic of Letters: The Correspondence between Thomas Jefferson and James Madison, 1776–1826.* Vol. 1. New York: Norton.

Snow, David A., and Robert D. Benford. 1988. "Ideology, Frame Resonance, and Participant Mobilization." *International Social Movement Research* 1:97–217.

Solinger, Rickie. 1992. *Wake Up Little Susie: Single Pregnancy and Race before Row v. Wade.* New York: Routledge.

Söllner, Alfred. 1976. "Zur Rechtsgeschichte des Familienfideikommisses." Pp. 657–69 in Dieter Medicus and Hans Hermann Seiler, eds., *Festschrift für Max Kaser.* Munich: C. H. Beck.

Spengler, Joseph L. 1979 [1938]. *France Faces Depopulation.* Durham, NC: Duke University Press.

Spilerman, Seymour. 2000. "Wealth and Stratification Processes." *Annual Review of Sociology* 26:497–524.

Spillman, Lyn. 1995. "Culture, Social Structures, and Discursive Fields." *Current Perspectives in Social Theory* 15:129–54.

Stahl, Friedrich Julius. 1845. *Die Philosophie des Rechts. Rechts- und Staatslehre.* Pt. 1, vol. 2.1. Heidelberg: Mohr.

Statistisches Reichsamt. 1930. "Die deutsche Erbschaftsbesteuerung vor und nach dem Kriege." *Statistik des deutschen Reichs.* Vol. 376. Berlin: Reimar Hobbing.

Stein, Lorenz von. 1888 [1870]. *Handbuch der Verwaltungslehre.* Pt. 3, *Die Verwaltung und das gesellschaftliche Leben.* 3rd ed. Stuttgart: Verlag der J. G. Cotta'schen Buchhandlung.

———. 1959 [1850]. *Geschichte der sozialen Bewegung in Frankreich von 1789 bis auf unsere Tage.* Vol. 1. Hildesheim: Georg Olms.

Steinberg, Marc W. 1998. "Tilting the Frame: Considerations on Collective Action Framing from a Discursive Turn." *Theory and Society* 27:845–72.

———. 1999. "The Talk and Back Talk of Collective Action: A Dialogic Analysis of Repertoires of Discourse among Nineteenth-Century English Cotton Spinners." *American Journal of Sociology* 105:736–80.

Steiner, Philippe. 2004. "Quand l'agent économique meurt. . . . Choix individuel, affection familiale et solidarité sociale." Paris. Unpublished manuscript.

Steinmo, Sven. 1993. *Taxation and Democracy: Swedish, British and American Approaches to Financing the Modern State.* New Haven: Yale University Press.

Stichling, Gottfried Theodor. 1850. "Ueber die Anforderungen des Staats an die Hinterlassenschaften seiner Bürger, mit besonderer Rücksicht auf die Geschichte des Steuerwesens in Deutschland." *Zeitschrift für die gesamten Staatswissenschaften* 6:504–25.

Stiglitz, Joseph E. 1978. "Notes on Estate Taxes, Redistribution, and the Concept of Balanced Growth Path Incidence." *Journal of Political Economy* 86:137–50.

———. 2000. *Economics of the Public Sector.* 3rd ed. New York: W. W. Norton.

Stourm, René. 1912. *Systèmes généraux d'impôts.* Paris: Librairie Félix Alcan.

Strunck, Wolfgang. 1935. *Der Gedanke der Erbrechtsreform seit dem 18. Jahrhundert.* Leipzig: Risse.

Surkis, Judith. 2002. "Universalism, Heterosexuality, and Recent Debates on the Family in France." Cambridge, MA. Unpublished manuscript.

Sussman, Marvin B., Judith N. Cates, and David T. Smith. 1970. *The Family and Inheritance.* New York: Russell Sage Foundation.

Svarez, Carl Gottlieb. 1960 [1790–91]. *Vorträge über Recht und Staat.* Cologne: Westdeutscher Verlag.

Swidler, Ann. 1986. "Culture in Action: Symbols and Strategies." *American Sociological Review* 51:273–86.

Szydlik, Marc. 1999. "Erben in der Bundesrepublik Deutschland. Zum Verhältnis von familialer Solidarität und sozialer Ungleichheit." *Kölner Zeitschrift für Soziologie und Sozialpsychologie* 51:80–104.

———. 2000. *Lebenslange Solidarität? Generationenbeziehungen zwischen erwachsenen Kindern und Eltern.* Opladen: Leske und Budrich.

T.G. 1849. "Primogeniture and Entail." *United States Magazine and Democratic Review* 24:17–27.

Tait, Allan A. 1966. "A Comment on Rates of Taxation Varied According to Consanguinity." *Finanzarchiv* 25:263–67.

Thelen, Kathleen, and Sven Steinmo. 1992. "Historical Institutionalism in Comparative Politics." Pp. 1–32 in Sven Steinmo, Kathleen Thelen, and Frank Longstreth, eds., *Structuring Politics: Historical Institutionalism in Comparative Analysis.* Cambridge: Cambridge University Press.

Thomas, Edward. 1886. "About Wills and Testaments." *Forum* 1:361–69.

Thompson, James Matthew, ed. 1934. *Napoleon Self-Revealed, in Three Hundred Selected Letters.* Boston: Houghton Mifflin.

Thurow, Lester. 1975. *Generating Inequality: Mechanisms of Distribution in the U.S. Economy.* New York: Basic Books.

Timm, Herbert. 1984. "Entwicklungslinien in Theorie und Praxis der Erbschaftsbesteuerung während der letzten hundert Jahre." *Finanzarchiv,* new ser., 42: 553–76.

Tocqueville, Alexis de. 1980 [1835]. *Democracy in America.* 2 vols. New York: Knopf.

Tolles, Frederick B. 1954. "The American Revolution Considered as a Social Movement: A Re-Evaluation." *American Historical Review* 60:1–12.

Troll, Max, Dieter Gebel, and Marc Jülicher. 1999. *Erbschaftssteuer- und Schenkungssteuergesetz. Kommentar.* Munich: Franz Vahlen.

Tschäppeler, Hans-Peter. 1983. *Die Testierfreiheit zwischen Freiheit des Erblassers und Gleichheit der Nachkommen.* Zurich: Schultheiss Polygraphischer Verlag.

Tulard, Jean. 1989. *Frankreich im Zeitalter der Revolutionen 1789–1851.* Stuttgart: Deutsche Verlags-Anstalt.

Tullock, Gordon. 1971. "Inheritance Justified." *Journal of Law and Economics* 14:465–74.

Turner, Frederick Jackson. 1976 [1920]. *The Frontier in American History.* Huntington: Robert E. Krieger.

Umpfenbach, Karl. 1874. *Des Volkes Erbe.* Berlin: Weidmann.

Van der Borght, Richard. "Die Reichssteuergesetze von 1919." *Finanzarchiv* 37:136–215.

Veblen, Thorstein. 1979 [1899]. *The Theory of the Leisure Class*. New York: Penguin.

Villequez, François F. 1863. "Sur les substitutions prohibées." *Revue historique de droit français et étranger* 9:97–121 and 189–214.

Villey, Michel. 1974. "Das Römische Recht in Hegels Rechtsphilosophie." Pp. 131–51 in Manfred Riedel, ed., *Materialien zu Hegels Rechtsphilosophie*, vol. 2. Frankfurt am Main: Suhrkamp.

Wacker, Gerd. 1997. *Der Erbrechtsausschuß der Akademie für Deutsches Recht und dessen Entwurf eines Erbgesetzes*. Frankfurt am Main: Peter Lang.

Wagner, Adolph. 1872. *Rede über die soziale Frage*. Berlin: Wiegandt und Grieben.

———. 1879. *Allgemeine oder theoretische Volkswirthschaftslehre*. Pt. 1. 2nd ed. Leipzig: C. F. Winter'sche Verlagsbuchhandlung.

———. 1880. *Finanzwissenschaft*. Pt. 2. Leipzig: C. F. Winter'sche Verlagsbuchhandlung.

———. 1894. *Grundlegung der politischen Ökonomie*. Pt. 2: *Volkswirthschaft und Recht, besonders Vermögensrecht*. 3rd ed. Leipzig: C. F. Winter'sche Verlagsbuchhandlung.

Wagner, Richard E. 1977. *Inheritance and the State*. Washington, DC: American Enterprise Institute.

Weber, Marianne. 1907. *Ehefrau und Mutter in der Rechtsentwicklung*. Tübingen: Mohr.

Weber, Max. 1904. "Agrarstatistische und sozialpolitische Betrachtungen zur Fideikommißfrage in Preußen." *Archiv für Sozialwissenschaft und Sozialpolitik* 19:503–74.

———. 1978 [1922]. *Economy and Society*. 2 vols. Berkeley and Los Angeles: University of California Press.

———. 2002 [1920]. *The Protestant Ethic and the Spirit of Capitalism*. Los Angeles: Roxbury.

Wedgwood, Josiah. 1928. "The Influence of Inheritance on the Distribution of Wealth." *Economic Journal* 38:38–55.

Wegmann, Franz. 1969. "Die Begründung des Erbrechts im 19. Jahrhundert." Dissertation, University of Münster.

Wehler, Hansulrich. 1980. *Das deutsche Kaiserreich 1871–1918*. 4th ed. Göttingen: Vandenhoeck & Ruprecht.

———. 1995a. "Modernisierungstheorie und Geschichte." Pp. 13–59 in *Die Gegenwart als Geschichte*. Munich: C. H. Beck.

———. 1995b. *Deutsche Gesellschaftsgeschichte, 1849–1914*. Vol. 3. Munich: C. H. Beck.

Weicher, John C. 1996. *The Distribution of Wealth: Increasing Inequality?* Washington, DC: AEI Press.

Weil, Gordon L. 1973. *The Long Shot: George McGovern Runs for President*. New York: W. W. Norton.

Weitling, Wilhelm. 1955 [1842]. *Garantien der Harmonie und Freiheit*. Berlin: Akademie Verlag.

———. 1968 [1843]. "Das Evangelium des armen Sünders." Pp. 322–60 in Thilo Ramm, ed., *Der Frühsozialismus: Ausgewählte Quellentexte*. Stuttgart: A. Kröner.

Welker, Karl. 1982. "Hegelianischer Freiheitsbegriff und Geschichtsschreibung im Vormärz: Testierfreiheit bei Hegel und Gans." Pp. 65–81 in Gerhard Dilcher and Rudolf Hopke, eds., *Grundrechte im 19. Jahrhundert*. Frankfurt am Main: Peter Lang.

West, Max. 1908 [1893]. *The Inheritance Tax*. 2nd ed. New York: Columbia University Press.

Willenbacher, Barbara. 2003. "Individualism and Traditionalism in Inheritance Law in Germany, France, England, and the United States." *Journal of Family History* 28:208–25.

Williamson, Oliver. 1975. *Markets and Hierarchies*. New York: Free Press.

———. 1985. *The Economic Institutions of Capitalism*. New York: Free Press.

Wilson, Graham K. 1990. *Interest Groups*. Oxford: Basil Blackwell.

Wischermann, Clemens. 1994. "Die Erbschaftssteuer im Kaiserreich und in der Weimarer Republik. Finanzprinzip und Familienprinzip." Pp. 171–96 in Eckart Schremmer, ed., *Steuern, Abgaben und Dienste vom Mittelalter bis zur Gegenwart*. Stuttgart: Franz Steiner.

———. 2003. "'Mein Erbe ist das Vaterland.' Sozialreform und Staatserbrecht im Kaiserreich und in der Weimarer Republik." Pp. 31–57 in Frank Lettke, ed., *Erben und Vererben: Gestaltung und Regulation von Generationenbeziehungen*. Constance: UVK.

Wisman, Jon D., and Larry Sawers. 1973. "Wealth Taxation for the United States." *Journal of Economic Issues* 7:417–36.

Witt, Peter-Christian. 1970. *Die Finanzpolitik des Deutschen Reiches von 1903–1913*. Lübeck: Matthiesen.

Wolff, Edward N. 2002. *Top Heavy: A Study of the Increasing Inequality of Wealth in America*. 2nd ed. New York: New Press.

Worms, René. 1917. *Natalité et régime successoral*. Paris: Librairie Payot.

Wuthnow, Robert. 1987. *Meaning and Moral Order: Explorations in Cultural Analysis*. Berkeley and Los Angeles: University of California Press.

———. 1989. *Communities of Discourse: Ideology and Social Structure in the Reformation, the Enlightenment, and European Socialism*. Cambridge: Harvard University Press.

Wypyski, Eugene M. 1976. *The Law of Inheritance in All Fifty States*. 3rd ed. New York: Oceana Publications.

Zeldin, Theodore. 1973. *France, 1848–1945*. Vol. 1. Oxford: Clarendon Press.

———. 1979. *France, 1848–1945: Politics and Anger*. Oxford: Oxford University Press.

Zingo, Martha T., and Kevin E. Early. 1994. *Nameless Persons: Legal Discrimination against Non-Marital Children in the United States*. Westport, CT: Praeger.

Zürn, F. 1892. *Handbuch des preußischen Erbrechts*. Berlin: Carl Heymanns.

GOVERNMENT DOCUMENTS

Annales de L'Assemblée Nationale. Compte-endu in extenso des seances. Paris. 1871–76.

Annales de la Chambre des Députés (Nouvelle série). Débats parlementaires and Documents parlementaires. 1881–1936.

Archives parlementaires de 1787 à 1860. Recueil complet des débats législatif et politiques des Chambres françaises. Series 1 and 2.

Congressional Record. Containing the Proceedings and Debates of the Congress. Washington, DC: Government Printing Office. 1895–2002.

Journal of the House of Representatives of the Commonwealth of Pennsylvania. Harrisburg. 1810–60.

Journal officiel de la République Française. Débats parlementaires. Assemblée Nationale. Compte rendu intégral des séances. 1958–2002.

Stenographische Berichte über die Verhandlungen des Preußischen Herrenhauses 1867–1915.

Stenographische Berichte und Drucksachen über die Verhandlungen der Zweiten Kammer des Preußischen Hauses der Abgeordneten 1849–1918.

Stenographische Berichte und Drucksachen über die Verhandlungen des deutschen Reichstages 1891–1933.

United States House of Representatives. Committee on Ways and Means. 1976. *Background Materials on Federal Estate and Gift Taxation.* Washington, DC: Government Printing Office.

United States Senate. 1909. *Inheritance-Tax Laws.* 61st Congress, 1st Session, Document No. 114. Washington, DC: Government Printing Office.

United States Treasury Department. 1969. *Tax Reform Studies and Proposals.* Washington, DC.

Verhandlungen des Deutschen Bundestages. Stenographische Berichte. 1949–2002.

Wigard, Franz, ed. 1848. *Stenographischer Bericht über die Verhandlungen der deutschen constituierenden Nationalversammlung zu Frankfurt am Main.* 6 vols. Leipzig: Breitkopf und Härtel und B. G. Teubner.